Safeguarding Children Living with Trauma and Family Violence

Best Practice in Working with Children Series
Edited by Brigid Daniel, Professor of Social Work, Department of Applied Social Science, University of Stirling

The titles in the *Best Practice in Working with Children* series are written for the multi-agency professionals working to promote children's welfare and protect them from harm. Each book in the series draws on current research into what works best for children, providing practical, realistic suggestions as to how practitioners in social work, health and education can work together to promote the resilience and safety of the children in their care. **Brigid Daniel** is Professor of Social Work in the Department of Applied Social Science at the University of Stirling. She is co-author of several textbooks and practice resources on child care and protection. She was a member of the multi-disciplinary team that carried out a national ministerial review of child protection practice in Scotland.

also in the series

Safeguarding Children and Schools
Edited by Mary Baginsky
Foreword by Brigid Daniel
ISBN: 978 1 84310 514 5

Child Neglect
Practice Issues for Health and Social Care
Edited by Julie Taylor and Brigid Daniel
Foreword by Olive Stevenson
ISBN: 978 1 84310 160 4

Safeguarding Children in Primary Health Care
Edited by Julie Taylor and Markus Themessl-Huber
Foreword by Brigid Daniel
ISBN: 978 1 84310 652 4

Safeguarding Children Living with Trauma and Family Violence

Evidence-Based Assessment, Analysis and Planning Interventions

Arnon Bentovim, Antony Cox,
Liza Bingley Miller and Stephen Pizzey

Foreword by Brigid Daniel

Jessica Kingsley Publishers
London and Philadelphia

Crown copyright material is reproduced with the permission of the controller of
HSMO and the Queen's Printer in Scotland

First published in 2009
by Jessica Kingsley Publishers
116 Pentonville Road
London N1 9JB, UK
and
400 Market Street, Suite 400
Philadelphia, PA 19106, USA

www.jkp.com

Library of Congress Cataloging in Publication Data
Safeguarding children living with trauma and family violence : evidence-based assessment,
analysis and planning interventions / Arnon Bentovim ... [et al.] ; foreword by Brigid Daniel.
    p. cm. -- (Best practice in working with children)
    Includes bibliographical references and index.
    ISBN 978-1-84310-938-9 (pb : alk. paper) 1. Children and violence. 2. Family
violence--Psychological aspects. 3. Children--Services for. 4. Social work with children. I.
Bentovim, Arnon.
    HQ784.V55S23 2009
    362.76'20973--dc22
                                2008051578

British Library Cataloguing in Publication Data
A CIP catalogue record for this book is available from the British Library

ISBN 978 1 84310 938 9

Printed and bound in Great Britain by
Athenaeum Press, Gateshead, Tyne and Wear

Contents

List of Tables

List of Figures

Foreword

This latest book in our series exemplifies our aim to offer support for 'Best Practice in Working with Children'. Based on contemporary research evidence and rooted in a consistent theoretical framework the book offers systematic and detailed guidance on how to help traumatized children.

As a result of significant policy development, and associated training, professionals who encounter children now have greater awareness of the symptoms and indications of abuse and neglect. Teachers, doctors, nurses, psychologists, adult mental health workers, substance misuse workers and others are now much more sensitive to signs of unmet childhood developmental needs. They are also much clearer about the need for a timely response to prevent significant harm to ongoing development and the key role they can play in ensuring that the professional network is mobilized. However, increased awareness is of no benefit unless it leads to children getting the help that is needed.

All too often our systems stall or run into the sand once the initial process of identification of abuse or neglect is completed. Once the priority of immediate safety is addressed children and their parents can often feel as if they are left adrift with little support. But it is at this point that the right kind of professional support can make the crucial difference for the trajectory of a child's ongoing development. Certainly, many abused and neglected children can be supported effectively by non-abusing parents, carers, wider family and friends. But, equally, there are many children whose lives in the short, and longer, term will be transformed by sensitive and appropriate therapeutic support, tailored to their needs.

The book addresses trauma and its impact upon children. Trauma is often associated with individual events or disasters and their aftermath and the book provides a detailed and sophisticated analysis of trauma and helps to explain the impact of traumatic incidents of physical or sexual abuse. But the book takes the subject much further by exploring the impact of more chronic circumstances. This detailed attention to the 'climate' of care is timely and essential. There is now an accumulation of evidence about the devastating impact of growing up under enduringly stressful conditions.

Recent policy developments have also stressed the importance of comprehensive assessment and planning. Practitioners often struggle with making sense of all the information that can be collated from a range of sources. And, again, there is no point to assessment activity if it does not lead to a purposeful plan for intervention. Using detailed worked examples, this book takes the Department of Health triangle as the starting point and augments it with dynamic new concepts to assist with assessment and analysis. Crucially, there is detail about how to consider the interaction of factors across different domains and how to analyse the implications for intervention.

For decades our systems have been preoccupied with investigation; this book takes us beyond investigation and re-asserts the importance of offering children considered and effective therapeutic support.

Brigid Daniel,
University of Stirling

Introduction

This book focuses on working with children and families living in a climate of trauma and family violence. This includes families where there may be recurrent patterns of violence between adults; verbal, sexual or physical violence involving children; extensive abuse of one or more children, or multiple forms of maltreatment at various phases of development, causing physical, sexual and emotional harm and impairment of health and development.

The core task for professionals where a child or young person has experienced significant harm is to assist them and their families or carers in their journey to recovery. The book is intended as a guide for all social work, health and educational professionals involved in the identification, assessment and intervention with children and families caught in such destructive cycles. The evidence-based assessment tools and planning approaches described are relevant throughout this process and can be used in assessments by a range of professionals, including those involved in court proceedings, whose duty it is to represent and articulate the interests and views of the child.

In 1999 the UK government commissioned overview reports of serious case reviews (usually where a child has died) in England on a biennial basis to draw out the key findings. Rose and Barnes (2008) studied serious case reviews during the period 2001–2003 and highlighted the need to give careful attention to the processes of analysis of information, decision-making and planning (Rose and Barnes 2008).

Brandon *et al.* (2008) studied serious case reviews during the period 2003–2005 and recommended that:

> Information and evidence should be collected, and systematic observation assessed within the context of an ecological framework based on clearly understood developmental and psychosocial theories including the relationship and developmental histories and processes that have shaped parents' families and children.
>
> The ecological developmental framework should also provide a conceptual structure and language for presenting a case formulation that should

include (i) a clear case summary and synthesis of the knowledge brought together by the assessment, (ii) a description of the problem/concern, (iii) a hypothesis about the nature, origins and cause of the need/problem/concern, and (iv) a plan of the proposed decisions and/or interventions. It needs to be emphasised that the *Assessment Framework* provides an ecological developmental structure which, if used well, should ensure that both practitioners and managers work together in a clear, co-ordinated and collaborative way. (Brandon *et al.* 2008, p.67)

This book aims to address the issues raised in the above serious case reviews using the Framework for the Assessment of Children in Need and their Families (*Assessment Framework*) (Department of Health, Department for Education and Employment and Home Office 2000) as the conceptual map for gathering, categorizing and analysing the available material and planning how to intervene effectively.

For the professionals involved in cases where there are safeguarding concerns, the journey is one of discovery. The journey starts at the point of first referral, through assessing a child's needs and whether and how they are being met and, in some cases, the discovery of possible significant harm or likelihood of harm to a child. The safety of the child needs to be ensured and during the unfolding assessment the professionals must learn about and explore the processes, which may be contributing to the harm or likelihood of harm to the child. This includes understanding the links between the child and their developmental needs, the parenting or care they are receiving and the family and environmental factors impacting on both. The next step in the journey is to plan with all concerned how best to intervene to help the child begin to recover and to support those caring for them or otherwise involved in their lives.

This journey for the professionals and others involved with the child and family is one of increasing complexity with each step and requires a staged approach to assessment, planning and intervention which supports evidence-based, interdisciplinary and child-focused work with children and their families. The book focuses less on the immediate steps to protect a child and more on approaches to the understanding, assessment and planning that is needed to ensure the future safety, health and development of the child.

The authors aim to tell the story of the journey by giving an overview which describes the broader picture and some of the recent research on trauma and family violence (Chapter 1), introducing a model for analysing what is going on for the child and family (Chapter 2) and introducing assessment tools to help launch the journey (Chapter 3). A case history which starts with a boy who is late for school, and appears anxious and neglected, is used to track through the process of assessment at the earlier stages of initial and core assessment (Chapter 4) and then at a safeguarding level, when the nature of the family's difficulties and strengths become clearer through the use of a structure to describe the level of strengths and difficulties where children are living with trauma and family violence (Chapter 5).

The journey moves on to exploring how to assess those families where there are major difficulties, including predicting whether change is feasible and alternative ways of intervening (Chapter 6). An exploration of ways of preventing and intervening in trauma and family violence follows (Chapter 7), and the journey is completed with a case example of a complex family situation which involved a network of professionals and where the court was involved (Chapter 8). Different 'lenses' are used with the same family throughout the book, along with other case examples, to help provide a 'guide' to the various stages involved in working with children and families where there are safeguarding concerns. The book provides a structure, language and process for assessment, analysis, intervention and measuring outcomes and can be used as a handbook to support evidence-based practice and effective inter-professional and inter-agency work.

Chapter One

Growing Up in a Climate of Trauma and Violence

Frameworks for Understanding Family Violence

Arnon Bentovim

Introduction

A constant theme in the media is a concern about children's welfare living in a 'climate of violence'. In 2006 headlines reported a UNICEF study that one million children in the UK are affected by exposure to domestic violence (UNICEF 2006). This study of violence against children underlined the international problem of children exposed to violence as victims of warfare, of starvation and conflict, being unwanted, living in the streets, working as sex workers – a negation of what we consider to be the meaning and purpose of childhood.

This book focuses on the theme of children exposed to trauma and family violence. When trauma and family violence are referred to, this indicates that rather than living in a family where parents have reasonable capacities to meet their children's needs, and provide adequate care, affection, safety, stimulation, guidance and boundaries and stability:

- There may be *extensive recurrent patterns of violence between adults*, family members, partners or extended family members. Such violence can take the form of physical, emotional or sexual violence, and is often associated with living in a context of environmental stress.

- The *family atmosphere may be characterized by a high level of violence*, verbal, physical, emotional or sexual involving the children. Parental capacities may be affected by physical or mental ill-health factors, or extensive drug or alcohol abuse. Children's care may be disrupted and compromised as a result of abusive relationships between the parents and extended family.

- There may be *extensive abuse of one or more children within the family*. This abuse may be physical, sexual or emotional or may involve significant neglect of children's needs affecting their physical, emotional, educational and social development, causing harm and evoking traumatic responses. Children may experience multiple forms of abuse and maltreatment, at various phases of development, or suffer extensive forms of one type of abuse. This may be by a parent or by an individual with authority over the child, which can include older siblings or other family members.

Aims of the book

This book seeks to explore the impact for children of living in such a context of trauma and family violence and the implications for assessment, planning and intervention for professionals working with the children and young people and their families.

This book aims:

1. To *examine current literature* on children who are living in a climate of trauma and family violence, to raise awareness of the cumulative nature of traumatic and stressful events which occur in such children and families and their impact over the lifespan, and to understand factors which result in harmful effects and those which protect.

2. To examine how the *UK Framework for the Assessment of Children in Need and their Families* (Department of Health *et al.* 2000) (the *Assessment Framework*) can be effectively applied using the evidence-based approaches to assessment which we have introduced. This includes a *model for the analysis* of children's developmental needs, parenting capacity and family functioning and other family and environmental factors based on the *Assessment Framework*.

3. To *operationalize the Assessment Framework* itself in a way which further develops its use as an effective tool to describe strengths and difficulties in children's health and development and functioning, parenting and family and environmental factors.

4. To present a *model of assessment, analysis, planning interventions and measuring outcomes* using the *Assessment Framework* for use in the safeguarding context and to introduce a process for assessing the harmful effects of adverse experiences and protective factors in all three domains on children and their welfare.

5. To present an *analysis of the potential for successful intervention,* and whether the child's needs can be met by the abusive and/or the non-abusing parent or other family members. A 12-step approach will be described, which assesses the level of harm, strengths and difficulties in parenting, including harmful parenting, the parents' capacity to take relevant responsibility and the impact of family and environmental factors, as well as identifying the interventions required by the child, and the prospect for change within the child's timeframe.

6. To explore the *principles and phases of intervention required in the safeguarding context* to target children's developmental needs, parenting capacity and relevant family and environmental factors.

Children in need and children who have experienced harm

Although this book is particularly concerned with assessments and planning interventions where a child has experienced or is likely to experience harm as a result of being exposed to the varying forms of family violence, the approaches described are appropriate for all the children with developmental needs who require additional intervention.

What children actually experience when there is abuse, whether emotional, physical or sexual, can vary considerably. Research findings demonstrate that outcomes are determined not only by direct experiences of abuse, threats of abuse or witnessing violence, but also by pre-existing developmental needs, pre-existing and subsequent parenting, and pre-existing and subsequent family and environmental factors. It is a combination of these pre-existing processes and those that are set in train by abusive experiences which lead to changes in a child's pattern of health and development. Protective processes may mean that the child is healthy despite experiences of abuse. Where adverse processes predominate, outcomes can range from impairments in limited areas of development, for example, educational progress, to transformation of the child's development so that they develop antisocial or withdrawn patterns of relating to others.

A perspective from the USA

When considering the needs of children living with trauma and family violence, both risk and protective factors need to be taken into account. Harris, Lieberman and Marans (2007) in an article reflecting a perspective from the USA comment that:

> each year, exposure to violent trauma takes its toll on the development of children. When their trauma goes unaddressed, children are at greater risk of school failure; anxiety and depression and other post-traumatic disorders;

alcohol and drug abuse, and, later in life, engaging in violence similar to that to which they were originally exposed. The majority of severely and chronically traumatised children and youth are typically seen as 'troubled children' in the education system, or emerge in the child protective, law enforcement, substance abuse treatment and criminal justice system where the root of their problems – exposure to violence and abuse is typically not identified or addressed. (Harris *et al.* 2007, p.393)

These authors are indicating that where children in the USA are exposed to high levels of extensive and recurrent patterns of violence, these experiences can have a cumulative traumatic effect which results in children presenting significant difficulties in many contexts. Studies by Finkelhor, Ormrod and Turner (2007), which will be referred to in some detail later, indicate that a significant number of children in the USA experience a number of violent events both within the home and in their social context. These have a strikingly negative effect on their mental health and on the development of antisocial behaviour. Also of considerable relevance are the studies of factors which can protect against such outcomes.

A UK perspective on violence and abuse involving children

In the UK, there remain concerns about children and families living on the margin and in poverty. Despite an understandable public focus on violence sustained in the community, such as concerns about knife crime, the main source of violence and abuse against children is located in the family context. Consistent observations indicate that there are substantially more children affected by violence and abuse in the home than those identified by the relevant services. Family violence is associated with silence and secrecy so that identification often occurs by chance through the concerned neighbour hearing shouting and hitting, the alert Accident and Emergency doctor who realizes that a child's injuries do not match the explanation given, the teacher who is concerned about a sudden withdrawal, anger or sexualized behaviour in a child or young person's presentation, the paediatrician who is concerned with the child's frequent presentation with unusual medical symptoms.

One of the key concerns at the end of the twentieth century was to identify children at risk of harm and to take action to protect them. Following a series of research approaches in the field of family violence, neglect and abuse during the 1990s, it became clear that a narrow focus on abuse resulted in protection, but tended not to impact on the complex processes of family life which gave rise to abusive action. For the child, often little was done to reduce the persistent negative emotional and behavioural effects, even if basic protection was being offered. For the family, it tended to mean that problems in parenting and the other relevant aspects of family life impacting on parenting or the child were not clearly identified and acted upon, in terms of offering support, until the situation had become serious.

When tragedies are revealed, such as Maria Colwell in 1973 (Field-Fisher 1974) or Victoria Climbié in 2000 (Laming 2003), or in the recent case of Baby P, there is not only horror that parents or family members can cause such severe harm but also a condemnation of professionals who are perceived as failing to protect, failing to be aware of warning signs or to communicate and having over-reacted or under-reacted in their response.

Such tragic events have been instrumental in numerous reviews of professional practice and the introduction of systems change. The most recent changes, set in motion by the Laming Report, include recommendations for extensive restructuring and reorganization in professional practice introduced in *Every Child Matters* (Department for Education and Skills 2004b), including bringing together professionals in education, health and social work, establishing Local Safeguarding Children Boards with a more extensive remit for the protection of children in the community.

The Assessment Framework and the Common Assessment Framework

The *Framework for the Assessment of Children in Need and their Families* (Department of Health *et al.* 2000) (the *Assessment Framework*) used in the UK was introduced as part of the process of enlarging the field of vision of professionals concerned with children in need of services, as well as in need of protection. This ecosystemic framework was intended to help professionals consider the child's functioning and needs, the capacity of parents to provide for those needs, the way their needs were being met (or not) and the role of family and environmental factors on the child or the parenting capacity of their carers. The approach was intended to extend professional practice from a narrow focus on 'risk assessment' and protection to a broader holistic consideration of the child and their family and the context in which they lived, to raise the standard of professional understanding of needs and to focus interventions more effectively.

A *Common Assessment Framework* was also introduced (Department for Education and Skills 2004a) for a wider range of professionals to assist in developing a shared language and understanding of children's needs in context. The aim was to achieve the five outcomes which were considered key to securing well-being in childhood and later life, being healthy, staying safe, enjoying and achieving, making a positive contribution, and achieving economic well-being (Rose, Gray and McAuley 2006).

The *Assessment Framework* – which informs this book – is a conceptual framework which maps three domains of information – *child developmental needs* (including children's current functioning), *parenting capacity* and *family and environmental factors* – which can contribute to effective assessment and intervention. Chapter 2 describes a model of assessment, analysis and planning interventions using the *Assessment Framework*. In the safeguarding context, an understanding of these factors provides a basis for analysing the processes that precede and are associated with exposure to violence, and can determine whether the impact of such experiences have or are likely to lead to traumatic effects.

Inter-agency guidance Working Together

The statutory inquiry into the death of Victoria Climbié (Laming 2003) and the first joint chief inspectors' report on *Safeguarding Children* (Department of Health 2002) highlighted the lack of priority status given to safeguarding children.

Working Together to Safeguard Children: A Guide to Inter-agency Working to Safeguard and Promote the Welfare of Children (HM Government 2006) forms part of the UK government's response to these findings. The focus in *Working Together* is on shared responsibility and the need for effective joint working between agencies and professionals that have different roles and expertise required if children are to be protected from harm and their welfare promoted. The roles, responsibilities and duties of the different personnel and organizations working directly or indirectly with children and young people are outlined and guidance is provided on the involvement of the relevant services, the responsibilities of the Local Safeguarding Children Boards, training and the development of inter-agency working and on the management of individual cases involving children and families. Local Safeguarding Children Boards were identified as having a key role in ensuring effective inter-agency and inter-professional working.

The context in Scotland, Wales and Ireland

The legislative context differs in Scotland (Scottish Executive 2000, 2002, 2004; Scottish Government 2008; Scottish Office 1997, 1998; Stafford and Vincent 2008) and Ireland (Department of Education and Science 2001; Department of Health and Children 1999, 2002). The *Guide to Getting it Right for Every Child* approach in Scotland (Scottish Government 2008) and assessment tools and practice guidance in Ireland such as the *Framework for the Assessment of Vulnerable Children and their Families* (Buckley, Howarth and Whelan 2006) provide guidance for professionals working with children and families in a comparable way to the *Assessment Framework* and the *Common Assessment Framework* within the overarching policy of *Every Child Matters* (Department for Education and Skills 2004b) in England and *Children and Young People: Rights to Action* (Welsh Assembly 2004) in Wales. While the principles and practice presented in this book may need some adaptation to these differing legislative and policy contexts, they should nevertheless be of direct relevance to professionals in Scotland, Wales and Ireland.

The development of evidence-based approaches to assessment

To assist professionals in carrying out the complex task of applying the *Assessment Framework*, the authors, with others, were commissioned by the government to develop and test a number of evidence-based approaches to assess all aspects of functioning, with associated training programmes (Bentovim and Bingley Miller 2001; Cox and Walker 2002a, 2002b; Department of Health, Cox and Bentovim 2000), some of which have been updated (Pizzey *et al.* 2009), and a team of accredited trainers. The assessment tools and the model of analysis and planning involved are described in greater detail in Chapters 2 and 3.

The assessment tools are recommended by the UK Department for Children, Schools and Families (DCSF) in a range of government guidance and procedures relating to children's services and the development of an *Integrated Children's System* (Department of Health 2000b). A training organization (Child and Family Training) has been established to train and support professionals in the use of these evidence-based approaches when undertaking the task of carrying out effective initial and core assessments. The aim of such assessments is to describe and evaluate the complex situations which characterize children living in a context of trauma and family violence and to plan and carry out effective child-centred and outcome-focused interventions.

Evidence-based approaches to assessment and intervention provide an approach which can enrich and systematize everyday practice, and in turn help to ensure that children's needs are adequately safeguarded and that tragedies are prevented.

Aims of Chapter 1

This chapter aims to explore some of the recent research literature related to children and families who are living in a climate of trauma and family violence and includes sections on the following:

- Definitions of harm.
- Prevalence.
- The impact of family violence on children and young people growing up: a review of recent research.
- Theoretical frameworks for understanding trauma and family violence.

- Children living with trauma and family violence – developmental issues: a review of recent research.

- Factors affecting the capacity to parent: a review of recent research.

- The characteristics of families when violence occurs.

- The impact on the future parenting of children and young people growing up in a climate of trauma and family violence.

- The J family – a case study illustrating key themes from the review of research.

Other case examples are provided at various points to illustrate the research and key themes presented.

Definitions of harm

The general principle is to consider harm in the safeguarding context as the effect of being exposed to violence, neglect and abuse:

> a compilation of significant events, both acute and longstanding, which interact with the child's ongoing development and interrupt, alter or impair physical development and significantly psychological development. Being the victim of violence and abuse or neglect is likely to have a profound effect on a child's view of themselves as a person, their emotional lives and their attachments, and on their future lives. (Bentovim 1998 p.98; HM Government 2006 p.36)

Current definitions of specific forms of harm through abuse in *Working Together* (HM Government 2006) are included in Box 1.1.

Box 1.1 Forms of harm

- *Neglect* refers to the failure of a parent to provide for the development of the child – where the parent is in a position to do so – including areas such as health, education and emotional development, nutrition, shelter and safe living conditions. There is a distinction made between neglect from the circumstances of poverty and neglect occurring when reasonable resources are available to the family or caregiver.
- *Physical abuse* is defined as those acts of commission or omission by a caregiver which cause actual physical harm, or have the potential for harm. Physical abuse also includes the Induction of Illness States through the administration of medication or noxious substances.

- *Sexual abuse* is defined as those acts where a caregiver uses a child for sexual gratification. Acts range from exposure and witnessing sexual activities – non-contact abuse, to forms of contact abuse, genital touching, mutual masturbation, attempts or actual intercourse. The essential issue is the child or young person not having the knowledge or maturation to be able to consent.
- *Emotional abuse* includes the failure of a caregiver to provide an appropriate and supportive environment including acts that have an adverse affect on the emotional health and development of a child. This includes inappropriate restriction, denigration, ridicule, threats and intimidation, discrimination or other non-physical forms of hostile treatment. Involvement in activities such as prostitution, antisocial activities. Exposure to domestic violence or marital conflict, drug addiction or mental illness may also represent forms of emotional abuse depending on the nature of the child's role, i.e. failure to protect from or active involvement in the process of conflict, addiction or mental health difficulties.

The legal definition of harm

The legislative framework in England and Wales when considering the welfare and protection of children is set out in the Children Act 1989. When legal intervention is being considered under the Children Act 1989, the key issue is the notion of the threshold which would justify intervention in family life. This requires the establishment of criteria which indicate the need for the court to intervene, and for the state to share care with parents and make decisions which ensure protection of the child, facilitate their recovery, and help them meeting their potential for future development. Local authority children and young people's services are responsible for initiating actions to protect the child and to ensure their needs will be met. The court has to make a judgment that significant harm to the child has occurred, or is likely to occur.

The Children Act 1989 Section 31(9) (as amended) in England and Wales provides the following definitions:

- 'Harm' means ill treatment, or the impairment of health or development, including for example impairment suffered from seeing or hearing the ill treatment of another.
- 'Development' means physical, intellectual, emotional, social or behavioural development.
- 'Health' means physical or mental health.
- 'Ill treatment' includes sexual abuse and forms of ill treatment which are not physical – including emotional abuse.

It will be noted that there needs to be the establishment of a *specific form of harm, ill treatment, impairment of health or development,* including mental health.

There is also a requirement to establish whether the harm is significant or not. This involves comparing the health and development of the child with what might be reasonably expected of a child from a similar context, to ensure that social context does not 'stigmatize' the child. The court needs to be helped in its decision-making by being presented with a full assessment of the way the children's needs have been met, the capacity of their parents or carers to meet those needs, and the impact of the family and social context. Using evidence-based approaches and Standardized Assessment Tools, and the research-based information on norms and validation which they provide, helps to confirm the impact on the child and compare the level of parenting and associated factors with other children and families and confirm the impact on the child.

Section 120 of the Adoption and Children Act 2002 updated the definition of 'harm' in the Children Act 1989 Section 31(9). The addition is 'including for example impairment suffered from seeing or hearing the ill-treatment of another' and has the effect of strengthening the case for significant harm through domestic violence, or the abuse of another in the household.

Prevalence

A survey conducted by the National Society for the Prevention of Cruelty to Children (NSPCC) (Cawson *et al.* 2000) established a prevalence of the number of children who were abused or neglected over their childhood in the UK, i.e. the number of young people exposed to violence, abuse and neglect. This was a national randomized survey of young adults who it was assumed would be likely to recall their childhood with reasonable accuracy. The study used a sophisticated approach to interviewing to establish the findings described in Box 1.2. It is important to note that the prevalence reported in the study is based on adult self-report and the findings indicate that the number of young people who recall harmful life events is far greater than the number who reported them at the time.

Box 1.2 Prevalence of harmful experiences

- *Serious physical abuse and violence,* causing physical injury, or leading to physical effects occurs in *7 per cent* of children and young people's lives.
- *A serious absence of physical care acts* which carry a high risk of injury or long-term harmful effects occur in *6 per cent* of children and young people's lives.

- *Serious absence of supervision* – being allowed to stay out overnight without adult supervision under the age of 10, or without parents knowing their whereabouts under the age of 14 occurred in *5 per cent* of children and young people.
- *Serious emotional maltreatment* and control, domination and humiliation, terrorising, withdrawing affection occurred in *6 per cent* of children and young people.
- *Sexual abuse aged 12* and under occurred in *16 per cent* of children and young people. This included contact and non-contact, *11 per cent* of children and young people described experiencing *unwanted contact.*

(Cawson et al. 2000)

The impact of family violence on children and young people growing up: a review of recent research

In 1962 Henry Kempe described the Battered Children's Syndrome (Kempe *et al.* 1962). This initiated 50 years of a growing awareness of the traumatic impact on the lives of children and young people of being exposed to a range of abusive experiences. There has been increasing awareness of different forms of abuse and of the effects of abuse and trauma on children, young people and adults, extending to the impact on future parenting and adult mental health functioning. Extensive follow-up studies from childhood into adult life constructed by researchers such as Widom (1989), the groundbreaking longitudinal studies in New Zealand (Fergusson and Lynskey 1997; Fergusson, Boden and Horwood 2006) and, in the UK, the follow-up of families growing up in a context of adversity (Bifulco *et al* 2004; Brown 2002) have illustrated the pathways which:

- make it more likely that children and young people will experience abuse, violence and adversity

- distinguish which children are likely to be affected, and which protected

- influence the likely impact on their future lives.

Some effects of different forms of harm

CHILDREN WHO HAVE BEEN PHYSICALLY AND EMOTIONALLY ABUSED AND NEGLECTED

Being subject to severe forms of physical abuse, neglect and emotional abuse can have a directly harmful effect, depending on the age and stage of development of the child (Bentovim 2006a). Assessing the impact or likely impact on children and their development of harmful forms of parenting or care will be explored in greater depth in Chapter 6. Children in the first years of life are uniquely vulnerable to shaking injuries and forms of physical violence which would have far less of an impact on an older child. Children's general development in the most vulnerable phases of growth may be seriously affected by a failure to feed or provide adequate nutrition. This can be associated with withholding nourishment as form of 'induced illness' (Gray and Bentovim 1996) or associated with failure in parenting capacity (Iwaniec, Herbert and Sluckin 2002). Severe neglect and failure to thrive can, of course, result in death. Severe emotional abuse, humiliation and negation of a child or young person can have a profoundly harmful impact on a child's emotional functioning.

The harmful effects of physical abuse on health and development

Physical abuse usually occurs in a context of an abusive atmosphere within the home. High levels of punitiveness, unexpected pain and hurt, the misuses of power and authority involved in physical abuse also have major effects on the behavioural pattern of the child. Physically abused infants demonstrate high levels of negative feelings and little positive. Such feeling states persist; children are rated as overactive, distractible and aggressive.

There is a connection between the sense of powerlessness, resulting from invasion of the body, vulnerability, absence of protection and a repeated fear and helplessness. This can result in fear, anxiety and an inability to control events, along with learning difficulties, despair, depression and low sense of efficacy seen as 'frozen watchfulness'. This sense of helplessness may lead to the development of a need to control and dominate, to aggressive, abusive patterns, or the development of 'a shell' to ward off feelings about the other person.

Within the school, patterns of behaviour may include attention seeking, extremely provocative behaviour to adults and bullying. Children are perceived as difficult to manage, less socially mature, rejected by peers, deficient in social skills, more liable to be responsible for antisocial behaviour.

The harmful effects of emotional abuse

Emotional abuse may also be associated with emotional neglect and may take many forms. It can take the form of a lack of care of physical needs, a failure to provide consistent love and nurture, and also overt hostility and rejection. The long-term consequences on social, emotional and cognitive and behavioural development may be far-reaching and profound if the child is habitually subject to verbal harassment, or if a child is disparaged, criticised, threatened and ridiculed. The inversion of love by substituting rejection and withdrawal for affection, verbal and non-verbal is the epitome of emotional abuse and neglect.

Emotional or psychological abuse has been defined as the destruction of the child's competence to be able to function in social situations. Being denied appropriate contact with peers within or outside school, being forced to take on a particular role in relation to parents, can therefore be seen as having a major destructive effect on the child's competence to function in social contexts. Qualitative dimensions have been described, including persistent, negative inaccurate attributions; emotional unavailability, unresponsiveness or neglect; failure to recognize individuality and boundary; inconsistent expectation and mis-socializations (Prior and Glaser 2006).

Children can be inducted into parental caretaking roles, and may not be encouraged to be involved in appropriate play, relationships with peers, and development of a true self. The extreme of the parental role occurs when there is incestuous abuse and the use of the child as a sexual partner whether by father or mother, inducting the male or female child into a parental or partner role inappropriately.

In marital breakdown one parent may use a child as partner against the other parent, and the attachment relationships are disrupted. There is a potential for the creation of a rejecting, resentful relationship. Blaming and fault-finding may undermine what may have been a good enough relationship. Accusations of abuse by the other parent can further undermine the potential for developing a secure attachment with parents, despite separations. Marital violence and exposure to violence can have a similar effect as being physically abused.

When parents have a psychiatric illness, a major concern is the adult's involvement of the child in their psychotic process, such as a shared delusionary state or paranoid beliefs, as well as the accompanying neglect. Adaptation to parental lifestyles may also cause significant harm, e.g. where children become part of their parents' drug culture, prostitution or other antisocial activities, and become confused in terms of socialization into the appropriate moral views of what are appropriate societal values. The boundary between a lifestyle and sharing family beliefs versus being persuaded to use drugs, become prostituted, or involved in direct antisocial acts, may be a fine one, and depends on a comprehensive assessment of the child and family.

Harmful effects of physical neglect

Physical neglect comprises both a lack of both physical caretaking and supervision, and a failure to fulfil the developmental needs of the child in terms of cognitive stimulation. Severe neglect is associated with major retardation of cognitive functioning and growth, poor hygiene, withdrawal and in extreme states a pseudo-autistic state, all of which can rapidly reverse in alternative care. These states are associated with the sense of parental hopelessness and helplessness, or poor quality institutional care. Professionals, like parents, may feel helpless and overwhelmed by large families living in very poor conditions, with very little social support. Neglect can result in serious problems in every dimension of a child's development needs and yet it can be challenging for professionals to predict the outlook for the child if appropriate and timely intervention is delayed. In 2008 an analysis of serious case reviews (Brandon *et al.* 2008) notes the risks associated with professionals adopting a '*start again syndrome*' without taking into account of past history and the impact of living with domestic violence, parental mental ill-health and parental substance misuse and emphasizes the crucial role of the careful collection of information and evidence and dynamic analysis using an ecological developmental framework.

The harmful effects of illness induction

In recent years there has been major concern about children who are actually induced into illness states by the administration of medications (non-accidental poisoning) or are perceived and described as having symptoms which require investigation, particularly fits and faints: 'Munchausen Syndrome by Proxy'.

Smothering in which a pillow or similar object is used to cause mechanical obstruction to the child's airways presents in infancy, either as an alleged apnoeic attack, or, in the most serious cases, an apparent cot death or Sudden Infant Death Syndrome (SIDS). There may be a substantially increased risk to siblings of the victim. Being in hospital, caring for a sick child, gives 'care by proxy' to the parent. Parents often have a history of prolonged contact with health agencies, 'seeking support' through illness states.

Unnecessary medical investigations may cause unnecessary pain and risk, and inappropriate treatments can have dangerous side-effects. For a child to see itself as having a major handicapping condition or disability or take on an invalid role where there is a normal potential for health is also a cause of significant harm.

Children who have been sexually abused

There have been extensive studies of children who have been sexually abused (Fergusson and Mullen 1999), including the description of a sequence of 99 children referred to Great Ormond Street Children's Hospital (Monck *et al.* 1996). There is general agreement that the impact of sexual abuse on a child depends on a number of factors including the severity of abuse, the presence of other forms of abuse, the age and developmental stage of the child and the context of care and support which preceded and followed the identification of abuse (Ramchandani and Jones 2003).

A variety of different mental health effects have also been described, including affective symptoms, self-harming behaviour, bulimia and anorexia. A specific effect of sexual abuse is to enhance the sexualization of the child so that a young child may respond with intense masturbatory behaviour. There may be confusion of boundaries between themselves and others resulting in the initiation of sexualized behaviour with other young children and adults. Older children may respond in a similar fashion, adolescents may be frozen or promiscuous, and there may be widespread impact on emotional and behavioural functioning. The development of more seriously sexually abusive behaviour has been referred to above.

There is a complex interactive effect between 'direct' effects and 'traumatic' pathways. To be subject to abuse – sexual, physical or emotional – is to be at risk of sustaining a traumatic impact because of the overwhelming nature of the event in the child's life, and the difficulty in being able to process and come to terms with experiences which may intensely shock the child, cause distress and evoke frozen responses. Traumatic responses may in turn evoke a variety of processes which organize behaviour and affect mood.

The Great Ormond Street research (Monck et al. 1996) found that it was not the extensiveness of sexual abuse which predicted the degree of anxiety or depressive symptomatology suffered by the child, but other factors, such as whether the children were believed and whether they had an appropriate degree of emotional support from a carer, particularly their mothers. There was a group of older girls who were not believed by their mothers and so were doubly abused, having been not only sexually abused, but also emotionally rejected. This combination of factors again triggered a cumulative process which resulted in them having high levels of suicidal ideation, depressed affect and considerable anxieties.

Extensive research on adult females who were sexually abused in childhood (Mullen et al. 1996) demonstrated that long-term harmful effects were more likely to take place if as young people they had been living in contexts of poor care and/or had suffered physical abuse, emotional abuse and neglect, in addition to having been sexually abused. Negative long-term processes included the triggering of bulimic, self-harming, addictive and depressive responses, and the risk of developing unstable personality functioning.

Adult females, who had been sexually abused but who lived in contexts of better care and had not been severely physically or emotionally abused or neglected, had a different outcome. They were able to function more adequately. However, if penetrative sexual abuse had been suffered, there were some longer term negative effects. This is an important finding because it indicates that there may be a need for specific therapeutic work focused on particular experiences of abuse, which may not be processed by the normal protective processes of good quality emotional support and positive parenting. Fergusson, Boden and Horwood's (2008) follow-up of individuals who had been sexually or physically abused in childhood to adult life confirmed the risk of mental health effects in those exposed to sexual abuse which included attempted nor completed sexual penetration. The risk was increase 2.5 compared to those who were not abused.

Factors which mediate the impact of abuse on health and development

The specific impact of abuse on the child is influenced considerably by a range of factors including the age and stage of development of the child, the care they have received preceding a phase of severe physical, emotional abuse or neglect, the nature and intensity of the abuse itself and the availability of alternative care and support. This can be observed in large sibship groups, where, for example, there has been a phase of significant neglect and poor care. There can be a differential effect on each of the children, despite them all experiencing a uniform level of abuse. This is illustrated in the J family case example in Box 1.3.

Box 1.3 Case example: the J family

The J family were a family of five children, the oldest being a boy aged 16 with learning difficulties, the next a girl aged 14, then a boy aged 11, and two young children aged four and three years old. Their mother had a long childhood history of sexual and emotional abuse. In her early adult life she had severe mental health difficulties associated with heavy alcohol and drug use and self-harm.

She achieved a significant period of stability during her early twenties through a partnership with a somewhat older individual. The early childhood of the three older children was therefore generally more satisfactory, although there had been concerns about the oldest child, who was diagnosed with a significant learning difficulty. However, help had been sought for him appropriately. There were no general concerns about the development of the three older children.

Some two years before it was realized there was evidence of serious neglect of the children's care, there had been a breakdown in the couple's relationship with allegations of severe marital violence. The mother then cared for the children alone. The two younger children were between 18 months and 2½ years at the time, i.e. early in their development, and the older children were already in primary and secondary school. The mother then experienced a period of considerable instability; there were concerns about heavy drinking, depressive symptoms and fluctuation in her capacity to care. She had episodes of self-harming, suicidal attempts and hospitalization and there was a significant degree of disruption to the children's lives. There was evidence of considerable neglect of their care; the home was in a very poor state, and the children were showing evidence of neglect. However, each of the children responded in a different way to what was the uniformly very significant change and deterioration in the care provided for them.

The oldest of the children, the 16-year-old boy with learning difficulties, became extremely anxious and fearful and his social skills regressed to a significant degree. He was particularly anxious about his mother. The next child, the 14-year-old girl, also showed a significant pattern of regression, failing to eat, being withdrawn in school, and scarcely speaking to teachers or other children in class (a form of 'selective mutism') and demonstrating 'pervasive refusal' (Lask *et al.* 1991). The next boy, the 11-year-old, youngest of the three older siblings, took on a 'parentified' role caring for his mother and siblings. He seemed to be most resilient and was attempting to support his mother and both his older brother and sister, and the two younger children, although he too was anxious. The two younger children were showing significant developmental failure. The four-year-old child was emotionally extremely distressed, while the three-year-old was failing to acquire speech and language, had significant difficulties with self-care skills, and was showing general developmental failure.

This case example illustrates the fact that, although specific forms of abuse can have specific effects, e.g. the impact of neglect and poor care on the younger children, and young people, it is the cumulative impact of stressful events in their lives which has a negative effect. The specific phase of development of each of the children and young people at the time, their history of previous care, their role in the family, their unique responses and the interacting processes between these elements all influence the outcome in terms of evidence of harm to health and development, or a more resilient response to adversity.

Cumulative effects of adverse experiences and family violence on children's health and development: research findings

A key theme emerging from research findings is the cumulative effect of adverse experiences and violence on children and young people's health and development, and the way these impacts on their functioning in adult life (Edwards *et al.* 2003). This has been accompanied by a concern to identify the factors which ameliorate and help children and young people to develop resilience and find a route to well-being and satisfactory functioning as adults, despite exposure to and experience of adversity and violence (Cicchetti *et al.* 1993; Rutter 2007). Some of the key findings from relevant research are now considered using sexual abuse as an example.

RESEARCH STUDY INTO THE ORIGINS OF SEXUALLY ABUSIVE BEHAVIOUR IN ADOLESCENT BOYS

Research investigating the origins of sexually abusive behaviour in studies conducted at Great Ormond Street Children's Hospital and the Institute of Child

Health (Bentovim 2002; Salter *et al.* 2003; Skuse *et al.* 1998) looked at these issues of risk and resilience. The aim of the research was to examine the common assumption that boys who had been sexually abused themselves were at significant risk of perpetrating sexually abusive behaviour at a later stage of their development. Specific evidence was sought about the 'risk' and pathways to abusive behaviour, and the 'resilience' factors which protected against re-enactment of abuse they had experienced with others.

THE RESEARCH APPROACH

Cross-sectional studies compared adolescent boys who had been sexually abused, and had later abused others, with those who were of a similar age and developmental stage who had also been victimized but who showed no evidence of perpetration of sexual abuse. A longitudinal study followed boys referred to Great Ormond Street Children's Hospital into adult life, and examined police and social work records to see how many of these individuals had been responsible for abusive behaviour. A proportion of the young men were also directly interviewed.

SOME FINDINGS FROM THE RESEARCH

What became evident was that, although having been sexually abused was a risk factor associated with subsequent sexually harmful behaviour, it was exposure to a set of interlinked, highly stressful, abusive life experiences not balanced by sufficient protective factors which resulted in a negative outcome. Children and young people who had been sexually abused as well as subject to physical abuse, witnessed physical violence, and lived in a climate of emotional abuse, rejection and neglect, were most at risk of abusing others sexually and physically. It was the cumulative process of exposure to these factors which resulted in the development of externalizing abusive symptoms and the trans-formation of the child's patterns of behaviour in an antisocial direction. There was also evidence of higher rates of interpersonal violence.

Table 1.1 demonstrates the association between adverse experiences in the family and increased chances of a boy who has been sexually abused going on to behave abusively himself. It will be noted that experiencing physical violence in addition to being sexually abused, increased the likelihood of abusing sexually 18 times. Witnessing violence between parents, being emotionally rejected, or experiencing family breakdown increased the likelihood 7–8 times.

Table 1.1 The impact of factors related to living in a climate of violence and the likelihood of development of abusive behaviour

Significant factors	Likelihood of developing abusive behaviour (odds ratio)
Experiencing intrafamilial violence: recurrent acts of physical abuse	18 times more likely
Witnessing family violence: recurrent exposure to marital violence or sibling abuse	8.1 times more likely
Rejection by family: rejection, emotional abuse or neglect	7.5 times more likely
Discontinuity of care: marital breakdown in care, children's home, foster care	7.2 times more likely

These children and young people were assessed in fine clinical detail using a variety of approaches, including psychodynamic interviews, questionnaires and scales, and the Adolescent Attachment Interview (Main and Goldwyn 1984). These assessments demonstrated that these were young people who were not only showing dangerous offending patterns of behaviour, but also experiencing intense post-traumatic experiences, such as flashbacks and nightmares, as a result of their harmful experiences. A case from the research group is described in more detail later.

THEORETICAL FRAMEWORK FOR UNDERSTANDING THE DEVELOPMENT OF SEXUALLY ABUSIVE BEHAVIOUR USED IN THE STUDIES

The researchers adopted a psychodynamic theory, illustrated in Figure 1.1, which generated hypotheses that, for such young people, exposure to abusive experiences in infancy gives rise to a sense of powerlessness and, in turn, aggressive fantasies. In middle childhood, such fantasies may be sexualized through being exposed either directly to sexual abuse, or witnessing a family member being sexually abused. Aggressive fantasies become sexualized and with adolescent development there is an explosion of aggressive and sexualized behaviour. The young person's thinking about relationships become organized by traumatic experiences.

FINDINGS FROM A LONGITUDINAL RESEARCH STUDY

Longitudinal research following up boys referred for having been sexually abused in early life looked at their adult functioning. This gave the opportunity to assess whether there were other resilient pathways followed by young

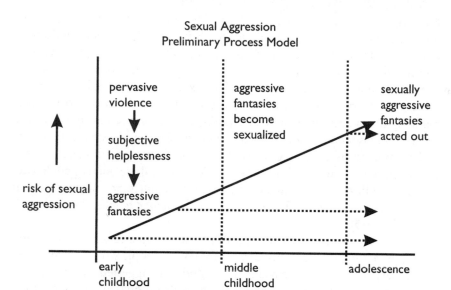

Figure 1.1: Theoretical model for understanding processes involved in developing sexually abusive behaviour

people as a result of having the benefit of protective factors during the intervening years.

A number of factors were assessed, including whether there had been a positive relationship with one parent, whether there was evidence that the young person had a reasonable friendships network, had had a period of satisfactory alternative care, or had received appropriate therapeutic help. Such factors were found to be helpful in developing a more resilient response, reducing the potential to behave abusively.

Overall there was a lower incidence of abusive behaviour than expected in what was considered to be a high risk group of young people who themselves had been sexually abused, and had been subject to significant stressful life events. However, when there were an overwhelming number of risk factors, despite adequate protection, there was a negative outcome, with the development of abusive behaviour. At interview, some adults with a high profile of risks had admitted to behaving abusively even if they had not been reported by their victims.

FINDINGS FROM TWO OTHER RESEARCH STUDIES

Edwards, Dunn and Bentovim (2007) considered boys referred to a residential unit as a result of pervasive sexually abusive behaviour against peers and adults, both males and females. The findings revealed that young people who were referred for residential treatment as a result of highly dangerous behaviour had been exposed to the most extreme set of life experiences and the lowest level of protective factors. They had the greatest needs and were the most at risk of perpetrating abusive action themselves requiring careful supervision and extensive therapeutic resources. They required a multimodal, multisystemic approach, which included 're-parenting' as well as focused therapeutic help, to work effectively with their complex needs. A follow-up of these young people after treatment indicated that there could be a positive outcome and these young people could live an abuse-free life, and could be helped to meet their potential (Edwards 2005).

Vizard, Hickey and McCrory (2007) followed up a series of 280 young people presenting to a specialized clinic for young people who were responsible for sexually abusive behaviour. Their findings suggested that the young people who showed the most serious long-term effects on their personality and emotional functioning:

- tended to have behaved in a sexually abusive fashion at an early age under the age of 11 years
- showed the most negative behavioural patterns during their adolescence, and had been subject to the most significant level of adversity
- had parents with significant mental health difficulties whose parenting was inconsistent, and where there was lack of supervision and poor boundaries.

These observations paint a powerful picture of the cumulative effect of negative life experiences on children and young people's health and development. The follow-up research also indicates, however, that there are a significant group of young people who are responsible for sexually abusive behaviour who have a more satisfactory outcome. In common with the Great Ormond Street research, their findings suggest that this group of boys:

- tend to start abusing others at a later stage of development
- do not show extensive adolescent conduct difficulties
- have more satisfactory parenting and supervision.

These findings related to risk, protection and resilience demonstrate the complexity of the relationships, and point to the importance of an assessment process that can give weight to all aspects of the child or young person's health and development and functioning. It is essential to establish the way needs have been met during development and the role of parenting, family and environmental processes if effective interventions are to be identified and implemented.

The impact of multiple adverse factors on children and young people's health and development

THE IMPACT OF SOCIAL ADVERSITY AND INDIVIDUAL AND FAMILY FACTORS

Beck and Shaw (2005) followed a group of boys who were growing up in an environment with uniformly high levels of social adversity. The research was questioning whether living in such a social context resulted in a negative effects, or whether individual and family factors were also playing a role and whether these could have both harmful and/or protective effects.

Research approach

Beck and Shaw (2005) assessed a range of factors which included the following:

- Perinatal complications, e.g. prematurity, injury, precipitate births, traumatic births which were assumed to result in a risk of impaired brain function.

- Observation and assessment of the emotional climate of parenting, including the use of the *HOME Inventory* (Caldwell and Bradley 2003), which describes the environment of care provided for a child.

- An index of family adversity was constructed, based on family size, criminality in the area, dangerousness in the neighbourhood and the presence of stressful life events in the family.

- The level of parenting, daily hassles and conflict within the family's mode of relating was also assessed.

Findings from the research

It might be expected that living in a context of significant social adversity would have a uniformly negative effect on the lives of young people growing up in such a context. In fact, it was found that it was the cumulative effect of negative factors which resulted in the transformation of the young people's, particularly boys', personality towards showing high levels of conduct disorder or antisocial patterns of behaviour. The findings from the research also questioned, however, whether other factors modified or enhanced the impact of living in a generally high-risk community. Despite living in a context of social adversity, if only one of these other adverse factors, e.g. factors associated with impaired brain functioning, the emotional climate of parenting, the level of parenting, daily hassles and conflict were present, the young person's development was not likely to demonstrate high levels of conduct or antisocial behaviours.

This is an important study because it indicates how vital it is to look at all three domains of the UK *Assessment Framework for Children in Need and their Families* – *children's developmental needs* and functioning, *parenting capacity* and the care provided for them and *family and environmental factors*, including the family climate and environmental adversity – critically to understand the impact on children and young people's health and development. Assumptions should not be made that difficulties in one dimension or domain will cause problems, without understanding the total context of care.

POLYVICTIMIZATION OR MULTIPLE MALTREATMENT

Finkelhor *et al.* (2007) have focused in their research in the child protection field on sexual abuse and its effects, physical abuse, emotional abuse and neglect. They were concerned to assess whether in reality children and young people have far more diverse and extensive experiences of abuse, both within the family and indirectly in the community, than reported.

Research approach

A national representative sample of children was interviewed about their experiences of victimization. They use a well-validated questionnaire (Finkelhor *et al.* 2005) which asks about areas such as sexual abuse, physical assault, being stolen from, peer or sibling victimization, and witnessing or indirect victimization. Children between 2 and 17 years old were interviewed either directly or, in the case of younger children, through parents.

Findings from the research

There was a spectrum of victimization described: 15 per cent of children suffered low rates of victimization, 78 per cent moderate, and 7 per cent were described as 'polyvictims'. This group of children and young people had suffered more than seven types of victimization in the previous year, both inside and outside the family. These young people were more likely to experience sexual violence, to have witnessed abuse of a sibling or parent, or suffered physical abuse themselves. They were also observed to be angry and aggressive in their style of relating, which in turn meant that they were vulnerable to being revictimized. They did, however, describe protection by siblings who were supportive, or by a friendship network. This polyvictimized group were noted to have higher rates of clinical symptoms, depression and anxiety, and the family contexts in which they grew up were characterized by interpersonal violence, disruption and environmental adversity. Experiencing sexual violence had a particularly negative effect, making that specific group of children particularly vulnerable to revictimization.

LINKS BETWEEN BEING VICTIMIZED AND OFFENDING OR CONDUCT DISORDER

Finkelhor and his colleagues (Cuevas *et al.* 2007) also researched the important question of whether these young people, as well as being subject to victimization, were also responsible for offending or conduct disorder themselves.

Findings from the research

The research identified a typology of three distinct types of victimized young people who had developed delinquent or antisocial behaviour:

- They were young people who showed high levels of bullying behaviour and who had also been victimized. They were predominantly boys and had high rates of antisocial delinquent behaviour, high rates of victimization, polyvictimization experiences and high levels of environmental adversity. They showed considerable levels of anger.

- They were young people who were responsible for damage to property, thefts and breaking into cars. They had lower rates of victimization, lower levels of anger and depression, and showed less abusive behaviour within their family.

- They were young people who had a history of having been sexually maltreated and they also went on to commit delinquent acts. They were predominantly girls and they showed high levels of mental health symptoms, particularly depression, anger, minor delinquent acts, and significant substance abuse. They experienced a higher percentage of abuse within the family.

The point where a transformation to interpersonal violence and bullying behaviour by the young people themselves developed was around the age of 14 years – a peak age for young people who show conduct disorders in the community. Interestingly, there were around half the sample who showed mild evidence of delinquency with or without victimization.

This research demonstrates the diversity of processes that young people experience when they are growing up, and indicates that there are a small group of young people who have extensive experiences of victimization who are vulnerable to responding by developing antisocial and abusive behaviour themselves. There are also many young people who are exposed to lesser levels of victimization and where protective factors both within the family, social network and community protect against some of the ill-effects. They have less serious conduct problems.

THE IMPACT OF CUMULATIVE FORMS OF MALTREATMENT ON PHYSICAL AND MENTAL ILL-HEALTH

Research on maltreatment and hospitalization

The theme of the impact of exposure to cumulative or multiple forms of maltreatment is demonstrated in a number of different approaches. Boxer and Terranova (2008) explored the subject by assessing the maltreatment experiences of young people hospitalized for mental health concerns. They noted that as in other studies already referred to, that sexual abuse had a particularly negative effect. They also observed that multiple maltreatment was associated with higher levels of mental health difficulties.

Research on negative childhood events as predictors of adult physical and mental health

The Adverse Childhood Experiences (ACE) research (Felitti et al. 1998) studied over 13,000 enrolees in the Kaeser Permanente Health Insurance Plans in the USA. Negative childhood events emerged as the most significant predictors of adult illness – physical and mental (Felitti et al. 1988). Nine categories of traumatic family childhood events included psychological, physical and sexual abuse; violence against the mother; living as a child with a household member who abused substances, was suicidal or mentally ill, or was ever imprisoned; absence of one or both parents; physical or emotional neglect.

The results confirmed that the more events to which the individual was exposed, the more likely it was that there would be a negative outcome for them. Exposure to such factors made it more likely that males would be perpetrators of violence and that females would be victims.

This research, however, while confirming the negative effect of multiple adversities through a large-scale study, does not provide pointers as to what creates the more resilient group of individuals who have been shown to develop more adequate coping mechanisms despite a significant degree of adversity. These mechanisms have been explored by Vranceanu, Hobfoll and Johnson (2007), who gathered a group of women who had experienced what they described as 'child multi-type maltreatment' – those individuals who had been subject to multiple abuses, physical, sexual and emotional, and exposure to violence. They noted the influence of the degree of social support as a protective factor, and post-traumatic stress disorder as a risk.

CUMULATIVE TRAUMA AND THE DEVELOPMENT OF RESILIENCE

The thrust of the studies we have reviewed have stressed the cumulative nature of adversity and the resulting negative effects. To make assessments which are meaningful in practice, it is also necessary to understand and identify strengths and protective factors which foster resilience. We have noted that significant adversity over a number of domains and dimensions of the UK *Assessment Framework for Children in Need and their Families* has a negative effect on health and development and that protective factors can be overwhelmed.

The development of resilience

Research on the development of resilience contributes to an understanding of the processes which can prevent the development of negative outcomes, e.g. Egeland, Carlson and Sroufe (1993), McGloin and Widom (2001) and Cohen and Mannarino (1987). It can be postulated that evidence of resilience is present when an individual who has been subject to significant stressful experiences shows reasonable achievement in education, emotional health, resists substance abuse and avoids antisocial behaviour.

Research on protective and vulnerability factors

Banyard and Williams (2007) describe a complex analysis of the factors which operated over a lengthy 23 years' follow-up of a group of sexually abused children. They describe the risks associated with experiencing further abusive experiences as against the protective factors which resulted in the development of a satisfactory role as a parent, partner or worker. Their work showed that achieving a satisfactory sense of community and belonging helped with the development of resilience and described the importance of 'turning points' when significant unexpected change can occur.

General protective factors have also been described by DuMont, Widom and Czaja (2007). These included factors such as intelligence, health and attractiveness, female gender, being the first born or youngest in a large family with limited resources, having a reasonable period of time before another sibling is born, receiving support outside the family from pre-school and school professionals as well as support from the extended family, community and health services.

In another study it has been shown that the availability of therapeutic work at key points (Egeland, Borquet and Chung 2002a), being identified with a parent who evokes positive responses and certain temperamental factors, such as having a low threshold for stress responses, are all factors which may influence the development of a secure attachment with one parent or extended family member.

Vulnerability factors make it more likely that a particular child is likely to be rejected, or receive poorest care in terms of resources, show opposite characteristics. These include lower levels of intelligence, prematurity, disability, twin births, being factors identified with a parent where feelings are negative and the lack of external family or community support (Browne *et al.* 2002b).

Theoretical frameworks for understanding trauma and family violence

It is helpful to consider models which attempt to explain the extensive research findings about trauma and violence and the associated factors. There is no one satisfactory model and there tends to be an overlap between models. Some of the key theoretical models include the following.

Cycles of family violence

The concept of the intergenerational transmission of violence is focused upon understanding the balance of risk and protective factors associated with the experiences of the parents and children, including the risk factors associated with the experiences of parents re-enacted with their children. It is suggested that a balance of risk and protective factors can help towards negative outcomes being neutralized. Kaufman and Zigler's (1989) research made comparisons between individuals who showed high levels of victimization or victimizer behaviour. In their study, such individuals retrospectively described a high level of early experiences of abuse and adversity. However, studies following up children and young people who have experienced adversity, such as the Great Ormond Street research on the outcome of boys who had been sexually abused, have indicated a lower than expected incidence of later victimization or victimizer behaviour. This model highlights that the pathways from experiences of abuse and adversity to adult functioning are a complex process and that there are intervening factors which influence a positive or negative outcome.

Shaffer, Huston and Egeland (2008) have showed that to fully understand lifetime experiences of maltreatment requires bringing together information both prospectively and retrospectively. This approach again confirms the impact of multiple incidents of abuse on functioning in adult life, and can advance our knowledge on factors which maintain or break the cycle of family violence.

Psychopathological explanations

These explanations link the inability of some adults to control violent impulses and those showing a pervasive sense of discontent, anger and irritability with attitudes which arise from childhood experiences of abuse and privation.

Social interactional explanation

This focuses on the interactional processes between parent and child within their specific familial context and in the context of larger social structures, to explain why some parents abuse their children and how children are affected who are growing up in a climate of violence, abuse and neglect. It is suggested that abusers hold stable, global, negative attributions about children and partners whom they subsequently victimize and who, in turn, are then predisposed to developing later distress, grievance and anger.

Cumulative models

Cumulative models demonstrate the interaction of a number of different areas of vulnerability and stress – biological, genetic and environmental – which give rise to violent interactions between family members. Such factors are additive and mutually reinforce and influence each other, creating a systemic effect. The risk of abuse is seen to be increased when there are a higher number of stress factors present which overwhelm protective capacities. The impact of 'poly-victimization' or 'multiple maltreatment' on children's and young people's development in turn affects the capacity of parents to provide adequate care, and the risk of abuse and family violence persists.

Sociocultural models: ecological explanations

This theoretical framework stresses the view that human behaviour should be studied in context. It is argued that social and economic privation can transform predisposed high-risk individuals into abusers and the consequent violence is seen as an attempt to control stressful events. Parents may be socialized into abusive practices and interactions as a result of cultural, community and family influences, harsh punishment in childhood with patriarchal societal views being seen as normative. Unemployment and limited occupational opportunities are seen as stressors that can provoke abusive action.

This model has been developed into the ecosystemic model which provides the structure for the *Assessment Framework*. This model attempts to delineate the areas of vulnerability and stress including biological, genetic and environmental factors in children's development, the impact of the parenting they receive and the way in which parents' capacities to meet the needs of children are influenced by the characteristics of their children and family and environmental factors. Such factors mutually reinforce and influence each other. The *Assessment Framework* is explored in more detail in later chapters.

Children living with trauma and family violence – developmental issues: a review of recent research

The processes by which abuse and family violence can impact on children's health and development has been the subject of much thought and research. Some of this will now be reviewed. The description of these processes and their possible consequences bring useful hypotheses about what may be going on and how a particular child may have been affected. However, the research discussed above emphasizes that the outcomes of abuse and family violence, and what underlies those outcomes, can be very varied. In the individual case it will always be vital to examine the evidence carefully and not jump to conclusions.

The pre-birth stage and the young child

EARLY INFLUENCES ON THE CHILD'S HEALTH AND DEVELOPMENT

The child's developmental needs commence in-utero from the moment of conception. Ensuring an adequate physical environment of care requires the parent to have adequate nutrition and appropriate health care to promote the welfare of the growing foetus. There needs to be protection from influences such as alcohol and drugs, which can cross the placental barrier and harm the growing foetus, causing a range of abnormalities and developmental problems and increased vulnerability of the foetus.

The psychobiological impact of harm on children's development has been of growing interest. Glaser (2000) reviewed neurobiological research on the impact of growing up in a context of adversity and abuse. She argues that the available research confirms that the brain is the 'mirror of development'. Environmental experiences come to 'organize' brain responses. This means that at a later date, for children who are more vulnerable due to in-utero experiences, even if a child is protected from violence, he or she may continue to respond with a state of arousal, i.e. reflecting preparation for a fight or flight response even when it is not necessary.

Intense stress responses associated with maltreatment can lead to progressive impairment of brain functions which register experiences. As a result, there may be a failure of integration and a failure to learn from experience so that the child has problems in forming a coherent picture of the world and relationships between themselves and others. Overwhelming fear and anxiety may become associated with experiences of violence and abuse. Arousal, fight-flight responses may be re-evoked when there are reminders of contexts where violence has occurred. The traumatic responses of re-enactment, avoidance and arousal – the key elements of post-traumatic responses can result in the disorganization of attachments. When moods and emotions cannot be regulated and a child's capacities to relate to others are damaged and they are vulnerable to further stressful events, genetic factors can act either as a source of further vulnerability or as protective factors which are brought into play by the presence of stressful experiences (Rutter, Moffitt and Caspi 2006).

THE ROLE OF ATTUNED CARING

Closely allied to neurobiological functioning, and the regulation of emotion, is the role of the mother and other significant carers providing the growing infant with the capacity to manage his or her emotional states. Fonagy *et al.* (2002) have described the way in which the regulation of the child's affects emerges from the nature of the parent–infant relationship. To optimize the infant's capacity to manage his or her emotions, it is essential that the infant has the experience of an attuned, responsive parent who can engage themselves in a detailed process of interaction with them. Fonagy (2008, in Sharp and Fonagy 2008) describes the process of mirroring. Using a variety of other work (Bion 1962b; Gergely and Watson 1996, 1999; Sroufe 1988; Winnicott 1956), they have suggested that if there is a failure of attunement, a failure of containment, a failure of managing the infant's unintegrated affect due to an inaccurate mirroring in the caregiver's expression, then 'the infant internalizes a mismatched or amplified parental mental state as a part of the self' (Fonagy 2008, in Sharp and Fonagy 2008).

It is suggested that these contained self-states create disorganization within the self, and are associated with disorganized attachment states (see Box 1.4).

Box 1.4 Case example: Christine A

An example of the process of failed mirroring was observed in Christine A, a six-month-old baby being cared for by her 18-year-old mother, Emma. The mother herself had grown up in a context of significant adversity, exposed to violence between her parents and her father's severe alcoholism. She had developed severe conduct problems herself, and in her early teenage period had drunk very heavily as a coping strategy. She was involved in highly volatile relationships and had a deep sense of insecurity and considerable difficulty in trusting. She was devoted to her baby, Christine, and worked extremely hard to care for her. However, it was observed that her care was 'relentless'; she found it hard to allow Christine to have appropriate periods of rest. She enjoyed aspects of Christine's care, playing, caring for her and bathing her, but observations indicated that Christine was anxious, aroused and distressed during these activities. She avoided making eye contact with her mother. Her mother showed evidence of mirroring, responding when Christine made sounds, but also would make sudden tickling responses unrelated to Christine's responses. Despite attempts to help her observe and fit into Christine's rhythm, she was unable to do so. Christine was becoming overwhelmed with her mother's failure to mirror appropriately: there was a

> failure of attunement, Christine had difficulty sleeping, her feeding was increasingly tense, she was distressed and developed an aversive, disorganized response when her mother separated from her and then returned.

THE DEVELOPMENT OF ATTACHMENTS AND THE CAPACITY TO MENTALIZE

During the early years, a key to ensuring that developmental potential unfolds satisfactorily and the child's developmental needs are met is the formation of two centrally significant structures – the development of attachments and the capacity to mentalize.

The development of attachments

Development attachments refers to the capacity to relate to particular individuals in a focused way to create a context of security. The original concept of attachment as described by Bowlby (1959, 1969) has now been seen to have a more extensive role in the organization of biological development and the development of relationships, based on the nature of attachment.

The capacity to mentalize

Mentalization is a term which bridges biological and psychological factors and is defined as a mental process which provides a capacity to reflect on the thoughts and feelings of others, and to have an awareness of one's own and other's intentions, desires and thoughts. (Fonagy *et al.* 2002).

The presence of the capacity to develop satisfactory attachments and to mentalize – underpins social and emotional development and enables the child to make relationships in social contexts.

The impact of maltreatment on attachments and mentalization

It is always important to consider the range of possible factors and processes other than maltreatment which may result in attunement and attachment problems. However, there is evidence that children who are exposed to the adversity of maltreatment can develop highly insecure, disorganized patterns of attachment (Cicchetti and Toth 1995). In such situations the abnormal relationship between the maltreated child and the abusive parental figure deprives the child of an attuned mutual engagement which focuses around the internal states of the child. Instead of the child developing a sense of confidence in the world and an expectation that any fear experienced will be brief and that support will be provided, they are likely to have a sense of fear and anxiety. The child may therefore fail to develop a capacity to cope with, understand and manage their own emotions or to understand the emotional states of others. This can lead to the sort of disorganized attachment responses – clinging, rejecting and avoidant responses – characteristic of children who have been subject to extensive abusive experiences. Together with other negative aspects of parenting, such as failure of care, stimulation, boundaries, stability, this may undermine the child's development in terms of educational, identity, family and social relationships. 'Internal representations of relationships are distorted' and maintain a sense of insecurity and fear (Jones 2008).

The child's capacity to understand the relationships between oneself and the other in a coherent fashion – the development of mentalization – may become disrupted by experiencing intense emotions in contexts of intimacy such as in family relationships. Instead of the child viewing relationships with confidence, closeness evokes fear in the child and perceived rejection evokes anger. This can result in a disruption of the development of child's sense of self and other and the 'shadows associated with experiences of family violence are projected onto relationships even when they are neutral and positive in intention' (Bentovim 1992, 1995 p.82).

Fonagy, Gergely and Target. (2007) assert that limitations in the skills required in negotiating social interactions with peers and friends acts like a sensory deficit. Other researchers show that abused children in common with children who have social communicational disorders fail to develop symbolic or dyadic play (Alessandri 1991) or to show an empathic response to the distress in other children (Howes and Espinosa 1985). Maltreated children show highly emotionally dysregulated behaviour (Maughan and Cicchetti 2002) and may not understand universal facial expressions conveying emotion (Fonagy et al. 2007). There is a delay in the development of their understanding different emotional states, a tendency to show dissociative responses and a disruption of the child's sense of themselves and their understanding of relationships with parental figures (Macfie, Cicchetti and Toth 2001).

This is the sort of pattern which persists for those adults who are not able to develop effective interpersonal skills. Children who suffer abuse in the early years tend to respond with dissociative responses which persist to adult life (Carlson 1998). These may be associated with a failure of empathy and a risk that they may act abusively. Relationships may be 'organized' by the responses to abusive experiences, and rather than resolution and processing of experiences there is persistence and re-enactment (Bentovim 1995).

The development of attachment trauma

It can therefore be conceptualized that growing up in a climate of violence, being subject to abusive action, witnessing violence and experiencing high levels of adversity can have a major impact on all dimensions of the health and development of a child and a young person. These children and young people may have a lifespan impact of traumatic and stressful experiences. Fonagy (2006) has described the response as 'attachment trauma'. In relation to emotionally charged issues, the child or young person is unable to imagine what other people might be thinking or feeling, or to understand their own experiences. Disorganized attachments can persist and the phenomenon of children clinging to abusive parents or showing avoidance of potentially protective and supportive carers may be observed. Closeness and clinging to the abusive parent appears to evoke a physiological response in the child which minimizes their capacity to think or to mentalize and to understand the need for safety.

Lack of awareness of the relationship between internal and external reality

Fonagy (2006) identifies other features affecting traumatized children and young people, including having a lack of flexibility in their thought patterns and finding it difficult to distinguish between what is thought and felt and what is actually occurring in reality. Even with events and experiences which are not taking place, children can have a feeling of certainty that what they are experiencing and thinking is actually happening. This may be a product of the intensity of flashbacks or re-experiencing of traumatic events leading to the confusion of internal and external reality.

A feeling of being separated from reality

Traumatic experiences can result in children and young people feeling separated from their current contexts and literally reliving the traumatic experiences. Responses associated with post-traumatic stress maintain the sense of separation from external reality. These include arousal, re-enactment and dissociation or avoidance.

- *Arousal* is the state of fright and flight which occurs biologically as a result of being exposed to traumatic events; it has the function of preparation to protect oneself against perceived adversaries and experience. However, with children who have been traumatized, it is a response which is maintained long after the event itself and affects relationships with carers and other children through triggering of arousal through reminders.

- *Re-enactment* is the replaying of traumatic events through flashbacks, play or actions that are either spontaneous or triggered by reminders such as people or places associated with traumatic experiences. This is a further factor leading to a separation from reality.

- *Dissociation or avoidance* is an associated response which involves a separation from reality and a feeling of blankness, emptiness and a dissociated state. This is a coping mechanism which has been described as literally 'a hole in the mind'. There may also be the development of a dissociated form of reality which is sometimes described as a false-self or pretend mode that also becomes a form of coping strategy.

These experiences can come to organize reality and, in children or young people, uncoordinated states are experienced as here-and-now realities and identified with abusive actions and an abused sense of self (Bentovim 1992, 1995).

Re-traumatizing responses

The phenomenon of re-traumatization can often be noted when children have contact with parents who have previously traumatized them through abuse and neglect. Contact with abusive parents can re-evoke memories of abuse and the phenomenon of re-traumatization can be widely observed in maltreated children, although it is not always recognized as such by professionals. Neutral contacts or discussion of traumatic events can also trigger wide-reaching reactions in the child or young person and need to be understood in the context of their past traumatic experiences.

Re-traumatization shows through as the process of activation and deactivation of the disorganized attachment system occurs. This may be associated with the breakdown of dissociation or avoidance responses which may be observed in the form of a series of clinging and/or avoidance responses which reflect the re-enactment of unintegrated traumatic memories.

Identification with the aggressor

In some cases, traumatized children and young people may appear to adopt the behaviours of their abuser and this may be linked to a range of factors including the child or young person being unable to integrate abusive experiences, disorganization of their attachments, reinforcement and/or encouragement of perverse responses by the abuser. This is one form of trying to survive the trauma of being abused and can be seen as 'taking the perspective of the malevolent other' (Fonagy 2006 p.103) or identification with the aggressor. This is a form of accommodation to the other with the construction of an 'alien being within the self-representation' (Fonagy 2006p.105) which may be projected on to others or the self, leading to self-harm or aggressive attack (see Box 1.5).

Box 1.5 Case example: Catherine B

Catherine B, aged five, was a child who had been abused sexually by her father, Alan B, throughout her childhood through a pattern of her father grooming her, intensifying and sexualizing his relationship with her and excluding Catherine's mother, Joanne B, who was forced to participate in sexual activities perhaps as a way of silencing her through being complicit.

Once the abusive situation was recognized, Catherine was placed in a foster home. Catherine was clearly markedly distressed by the move, which involved separation from both her parents. This showed itself in the extreme avoidance and dissociated state which Catherine demonstrated, consistent with the nature of the trauma she had experienced. She would isolate herself, sitting facing the wall. She was unable to relate to her carers or other children. The nursery school she attended prior to her placement reported that she had been a quiet child who had never mixed well with other children.

In addition to her strikingly frozen, rigid, avoidant, controlled behaviour, she would also respond to any frustration with extreme arousal, screaming temper tantrums which could go on for a significant period, over half an hour on occasions, panic, flight-fight responses. As part of her rigid pattern of behaviour regimentation, frozenness, absolute self-control, she was also highly restricted in her choice of objects. She would play with one puzzle, one toy for a whole day, not shift once she was launched on her activity. She would only allow herself to eat one particular foodstuff at a time.

Over the initial months Catherine demonstrated a good deal of re-enacting sexual play, dolls being pushed against each other, dolls being licked, dolls being made to sit on the heads of other dolls, associated with sexualized behaviour which had been observed since early in the placement. This included frequent and intense masturbation, which would take place when she was sitting in the bath, sitting on round toys or rocking. She would pose, standing with legs apart, putting on lipstick, rubbing her arms and legs. She would sit on the foster carer's lap without clothes, rubbing against her knee. In the early stages of the placement, she made provocative, sexualized responses to the foster father. Catherine was recreating the sexualized responses organized by her father, and accommodated to by the mother, also identification with the 'malevolent' abusive action from her father – confusion of internal and external reality.

Catherine's foster carers gradually dealt with these extreme situations, she had fewer extreme emotional outbursts. She started to feel safe, particularly with her foster mother, seeking 'normal' cuddles and reassurance from her. She was able to talk to her, held her hand when she was out and built up a significant focused attachment to her. Her foster carer worked with her to try to help her develop much more choice in her play. She also discouraged Catherine's sexualized activities, which gradually lessened in intensity so that there was less masturbation, rocking on objects or provocative sexualized posing. In summary, there was the gradual emergence of a more bouncy, happy, responsive child.

Catherine talked about missing her father, but not her mother – a traumatic attachment – describing dreams of being cuddled by her father.

Catherine's mother was able gradually to acknowledge the abusive nature of family life organized by the father, and responded to by herself. The father maintained his stance that he was not responsible for Catherine's responses.

Following a lengthy period, contact was initiated with Catherine's mother. There was an immediate return of Catherine's regressed behaviour, including sexualized responses and intense masturbation. She shut down emotionally, isolated herself, wanting to watch television, not playing, and again showing outbursts of anger. She began to wet herself at home and at school. After the second session she was weeping; she looked forward to seeing her mother, but then would show regressed behaviour with periods of low, distressed mood. This may have been an example of a re-traumatization response, provoked by seeing her mother again, triggering memories of the sexualized acts, combined with the triggering of sadness and loss feelings seeing her mother after an interval.

Describing the abusive experiences of the child and his or her behaviour in different contexts can help to develop hypotheses about the factors and processes in place and to predict the possible impact of traumatic events on the child's development and functioning. It is always important to consider other relevant factors and process which may be influencing a child's behaviour and therefore the possible outcomes. The information on Catherine's experiences of abuse gives rise to hypotheses about relevant factors and processes in play and indicates that impact on her development may be extensive as shown in Box 1.6 (with some additional indicators which may be relevant for other children).

Box 1.6 Case example: Catherine B's developmental needs

Health

Catherine's health needs are not met as a result of extensive exposure to sexual abuse. Other children may show evidence of neglect and failure to thrive; injury or induction of health states associated with unsatisfactory care or a failure of protection.

Education

Catherine's cognitive development, language development, understanding and play may be affected as a result of lack of stimulation or as a result of frozenness, withdrawal, intense anxiety. She may have difficulties in focusing and concentration may be associated with arousal patterns associated with neurobiological dysfunctioning. Children may fail to benefit from pre-school or subsequent educational opportunities.

Emotional and behavioural development

Catherine demonstrated disorganized attachment patterns at times which may result in a pattern of indiscriminate sociability, failure to develop selective attachments, over-responsiveness or clinging to unfamiliar strangers and initiating sexualized contexts may also occur. Avoidant attachment responses may result in a failure to respond in social interactions. Behaviour may be affected by a degree of frozen watchfulness, panic, or through hyperarousal, explosive outbursts, intense sexualization, associated with difficulties regulating emotional states.

Identity

Catherine was not nurtured to perceive herself as having a separate identity. Her sense of separateness may be significantly undermined by the confusion of being perceived as a sexual object by her father, and her mother being organized to reinforce this pattern. Her identity is likely therefore be strikingly different from other children in her social contexts. Catherine may perceive herself to be different and stigmatized. She may feel the abuse is her responsibility and become identified with the role of the sexual individual, despite her age and developmental stage.

Family and social relationships

Catherine's capacity for understanding her role in relation to others has been very seriously undermined by the disruption of relationships with her parents, her father's seriously abusive behaviour and the failure of her mother to protect her. Catherine may have considerable difficulties understanding or responding to the feelings of others. She is likely to experience a confusion of her role, including having had to act as a 'partner figure' for her father. There is confusion between herself at an emotional adult or child level impairing her capacity to develop family and social relationships, as observed when she was placed in the foster family. Her relationships in school may be affected by intense sexualization, frozen avoidance or fight/flight responses.

Social presentation

This becomes confused by her inappropriate sexualized role. Catherine responds to strangers identified with her father in an inappropriately sexualized way and she has an intense preoccupation with sexual thoughts and feelings which puts her at risk of rejection and negative perceptions.

Self-care skills

Self-care skills may be affected as a result of Catherine's failure to develop an appropriate sense of independence, or awareness of a need to protect herself in contexts outside the family, putting her at risk of re-abuse.

It is striking to note the general improvement in a context of good care, where Catherine's needs are met more appropriately, inappropriate responses are not reinforced and alternative appropriate responses are rewarded. Her potential to function more satisfactorily in all dimensions is demonstrated through her positive responses to a positive foster care environment.

Some developmental issues for children at a later stage

When children become older and if they experience an increasing diversity of abusive episodes, this usually reflects an extensive failure to meet their developmental needs, with significant negative effects on their functioning. The case example in Box 1.7 describes some of the factors and processes which may be involved.

Box 1.7 Case example: Frank C

Frank was a 13-year-old who was studied as part of the research on the origins of sexually abusive behaviour (Skuse *et al.* 1998). He was referred as a result of his sexually abusive actions perpetrated against his five-year-old half-sister, Susie, including having attempted to penetrate her. He was living in foster care at the time of referral. His early life was disrupted, his mother having left his father as a result of violence. Frank and his sister remained in his father's care. Frank's father abused him physically and sexually. He was also neglected and forced to be sexually active with his sister. When he was seven years of age his mother was able to persuade the court that he was being harmed in his father's care, as a result of having bruising. He and his sister moved to live with his mother, her new partner and their newborn baby. As he approached adolescence, he behaved abusively towards his young half-sister.

Reviewing Frank's needs in terms of the way a young person moving into early adolescence may be affected by living in a context of trauma and family violence, hypotheses about possible processes in play and potential outcomes for his future development may include those described in Box 1.8.

Box 1.8 Case example: Frank C's developmental needs

Health

Frank's health is likely to be affected as a result of the cumulative impact of poor early attention to his health and care needs, exposure to violence and experiences of physical and sexual abuse. A period of later more satisfactory care may protect against negative effects, or there may be persistent difficulties in the area of mental health.

Education

Frank's educational functioning is likely to have been affected by the significant disruption in his early years, lack of consistent stimulation, poor encouragement to attend school as well as the impact of abusive experiences on his cognitive capacity. The fact that his needs were more appropriately met during the later years and early adolescence, encouragement, regular school attendance, a climate of more positive care may result in improved functioning, or there may be persistent difficulties with concentration, oppositional behaviour and learning difficulties.

Emotional and behavioural development

Frank's emotional and behavioural development may show positive functioning as a result of the positive emotional care provided by his mother, or there may be persistent difficulties with regulating his emotional state as a result of exposure to, and experiences of disruption, physical and sexual abuse. At the point of assessment when he was placed with a foster carer, he clung to his foster carer and was highly anxious when meeting new individuals. Exploration of his account of relationships with his parents indicated that he was basically dismissive in his attachments, having little language for relationships. He denied having any early memories and appeared dissociated in respect of early abusive experiences.

Frank indicated significant difficulties managing his emotional states. He described his thoughts as being filled with 'psychopathic fantasies', extremely aggressive thoughts, such as wanting to set his father on fire. He described his shame at experiencing intense arousal, having seen his sister unclothed, and overwhelming impulses to behave abusively to her. Frank justified the abuse of his sister, overcoming his internal resistance, by telling himself that her having displayed her genitals was an invitation to be sexual. Frank also described intense flashbacks of being beaten up by his father and memories of sexual activities with his sister. He also described intense feelings of fear and helplessness. He was terrified that he would be responsible for a terrible act of aggression and was fearful of his potential to harm others.

Identity

Identity functioning depends on the quality of care and the identification with parents and other key individuals in the young person's life. Although there were a number of individuals in Frank's life including a supportive stepfather and his mother who 'rescued' him, Frank found it difficult to see himself in any other perspective than his father's. He felt frightened of becoming like his father. He felt the 'shadow' of his father and was anxious about the way he felt preoccupied by aggressive fantasies and impulses to harm, which he associated with being like his father's. He was fearful of being hurt, always expecting the worst, clinging to his foster carer. He seemed to show confusion in his identity, both as a victim, and also as an abuser.

Family and social relationships

Frank tended to relate to others in a suspicious, distant, unconfiding way in his family and social relationships. He seemed to fear being exploited, used and abused in the way he had been by his father. He felt closer to his mother and her new family, grateful for having been rescued from his father's care. He found himself feeling resentful; jealous of his younger sister and the care she was given. This may have been one of the 'justifications' for abusive action.

Frank's social skills were limited, his preoccupation with anger, explosive fantasies and intense traumatic memories appeared to interfere with his capacity to relate to his peers or to protect himself in educational contexts and in the community. He tended to isolate himself; he was rejected and unpopular, with a risk of putting himself in danger of bullying and attack.

Social presentation

Social presentation may be associated with the quality of care, and the way the young person thinks of themselves. Although Frank's mother attempted to reverse the poor standard of care and the rejection by his father, Frank had very little interest or pride in his appearance. He presented himself as poorly cared for despite the support and positive care provided by his mother and subsequently by his foster family.

Self-care skills

Frank's self-care skills were limited and he showed little interest in taking responsibility for his own self-care. The context of fostering provided a secure base where he was able to make some progress with learning how to develop more skills in self-care.

Developmental issues in later adolescence towards adult functioning

In later adolescence, moving towards early adulthood, young people who have grown up with an extensive set of abusive experiences, perpetuated through childhood to adolescence, risk developing antisocial or unstable personality functioning. In mental health terms, in serious cases, this may involve the young person developing a personality disorder. Such disorders can be conceptualized as pervasive patterns of failures of both emotional regulation, attachment behaviours and in functioning of the self in relationships. In children who have been abused and traumatized, early evidence of such disorders may be seen in adolescence, and there is significant impact on all dimensions of developmental needs.

YOUNG PEOPLE SHOWING ANTISOCIAL PERSONALITY FUNCTIONING

Young people showing antisocial personality functioning may have some of the following significant difficulties.

Health

Health functioning may be affected as a result of failure to address health needs associated with disruptions of care, neglect, physical and sexual violence, inside and external to the family. Young people may be directly involved in antisocial acts inside and outside the family, putting their own health and the health of others at risk

Education

Education may be disrupted through failure of school attendance, attentional difficulties, and volatile, aggressive relationships with other young people and with educational staff.

Emotional and behavioural development

Emotional and behavioural development may be affected as a result of a continuation of intense arousal patterns, poorly regulated emotion, explosive outbursts and/or a frightening style of relating. These young people may have dismissive or controlling attachment styles and a blaming, angry style of relating to others and a risk of aggression and sexual responses towards younger children and their peers or to adults.

Identity

The young person's sense of identity may be strongly connected to an abusive parent who is idealized and perceived in a positive light despite also being a frightening figure.

Family and social relationships

Family and social relationships may be affected by family disruption. First, a young person exposed to domestic violence, physical abuse and disruptive care may adopt an abusive, aggressive, bullying, controlling role towards younger siblings in the absence of a father as a result of marital breakdown. Second, there may be a pattern of 'identification with the abuser' reflected by the young person displaying physically or sexually abusive behaviour inside or outside the family. Third, educational difficulties may be reinforced by poor relationships between family and school.

Social presentation

There may be identification with an aggressive role which is presented through dress, style of relating, involvement in peer violence, truanting and criminal activities.

Self-care skills

Self-care skills may be ignored or rejected through the adoption of an antisocial, violent role model.

YOUNG PEOPLE WITH UNSTABLE PERSONALITY FUNCTIONING

Young people who are showing evidence of developing unstable personality functioning also may have extensive difficulties in all dimensions of their functioning and development.

Health

The young person may have had extensive experiences of non-accidental and accidental injuries, exposure to sexual abuse, and/or unsatisfactory disrupted care.

Education

Education may have been disrupted because of poor support by the family, or learning may have been affected by the development of significant emotional and behavioural difficulties disrupting approaches to learning, or school.

Emotional and behavioural development

Emotional and behavioural difficulties characterized by considerable dysfunctional processes may be evident. First, significant disorganization of attachments can result in a pattern of unstable and intense interpersonal relationships developing. The young person may cling to individuals who are potentially abusive and switch from positive to extreme negative emotional responses, within the family or externally.

Second, emotional states may be poorly regulated; there may be a marked reactivity of mood lasting for a few hours or some days. Some young people attempt to manage their mood through the extensive use of alcohol, or by drugs such as cannabis which is perceived as having a mood regulating effect, although there are associated risks of reinforcing the instability cycle of risky drug use continuing.

Third, traumatic symptoms related to early abusive experiences may persist alternating with dissociative symptoms; there is a risk of switching into states of altered identity, associated, chronic traumatic responses. Such states 'encapsulate' unintegrated experiences triggered by reminders or flashbacks of early abuse.

Fourth, there is a risk of substance abuse, binge eating, promiscuous sexual behaviour, vomiting bulimic symptoms, recurrent suicidal behaviour, self-harming.

Finally, inappropriate, intense anger may be triggered by the intense shifts of emotional states with resulting involvement in extreme volatile relationships, mutual violence, physical harm.

Identity

Identity issues and functioning of the self and self-perception may show significant difficulties in functioning. There may be an unstable sense of self, a pervasive sense of emptiness, emotional loneliness which can lead impulsivity of a potentially self-damaging nature. This includes intense seeking of sexual partners as with the young person described in Box 1.9.

Box 1.9 Case example: Beth D

Beth D was 16 years old, referred because of early pregnancy. She had an early history of sexual abuse, neglect and disrupted care in her first five years. There were breakdowns of foster care, with a period of stable care from the ages of 12 to 16. She could not settle into vocational training, and dealt with her sense of 'emptiness' by a determination to become pregnant. She was 'organized' by a network of paedophilic, dangerous individuals, idealizing each until the level of abusive responses reached a level when the relationship became intolerable, when she moved on to other members of the network. Her functioning was characterized by a 'pretend' state in which she asserted she was in love with each individual and that she had known them significantly longer than the reality. She downplayed and dismissed the concerns expressed about their histories of criminal abusive activities, abandoning her foster family, who had been devoted to caring for her despite the challenges of her behaviour. She described an overwhelming feeling of emptiness, terror and fears of abandonment which she tried to hold at bay by maintaining the clinging responses. She put herself at considerable risk. She had persistent traumatic imagery associated with her early abuse, and continuing difficulties in managing her mood, never being able to predict how she would feel on any one day.

Looking at Beth's traumatic and abusive past history and the factors and processes currently operating, some of the key areas of her current and future development which are likely to be affected are described in Box 1.10.

Box 1.10 Case example: Beth D's developmental needs

Family and social relationships

Beth's family and social relationships are affected to a significant degree as a result of the extreme changing nature of her emotional states and her pattern of the rapid making and breaking of relationships as a result of being part of an unstable family network. This is reflected in her relationships within her original family, in her foster families and each new partnership being disrupted. The risk of being involved with other young people who are functioning in an unstable fashion through patterns of excess alcohol and drug use becomes a maintaining factor.

Social presentation

Beth's social presentation is likely to be affected by her impulsive responses which have a role as part of the coping responses. This leads to her presenting with inappropriately sexual responses and a pattern of significant avoidance of social relationships and self-isolation, alternating with intense seeking of relationships.

Self-care skills

Beth's self-care skills may be very significantly affected by the impulsive drive to find new relationships. She may become involved in drug or alcohol misuse. This and her significant changes of mood or angry responses have put her into highly risky situations including association with individuals who present with high risk in the community or within family networks and the risk of unplanned pregnancy.

Factors affecting the capacity to parent: a review of recent research

In the safeguarding context, when there are concerns about harm sustained by children, assessment of parenting capacities is a key task. It is also important to investigate some of the major family and environmental factors which may be influencing parents' capacity to care for their child. Some of the research relating to problems which may be affecting parenting capacity are now reviewed.

Mental health problems of parents, alcohol and drug abuse or involvement in domestic violence

The research of Cleaver, Unell and Aldgate (1999) examines the links between child maltreatment and problems and difficulties experienced by parents such as mental ill-health, alcohol and drug abuse or involvement in domestic violence. The studies examined the risk of harm to children and looked at the prevalence of mental health difficulties, alcohol and substance misuse and domestic violence at different stages of the process of assessment of harm. Four stages were examined:

1. Where a referral had been made through a report by a neighbour, a school, general practitioner or child health professional resulting in the calling of a strategy meeting.

2. When the nature of the report and the initial strategy meeting indicated that a fuller social work assessment, i.e. a core assessment was required, because there were legitimate concerns about a child being harmed and difficulties with parenting capacities.

3. When the concerns were at a sufficient level to warrant a child protection conference bringing together professionals and information from various sources, i.e. significant concerns about harm and parenting capacities.

4. When the level of concern was such that it was felt that protective action needed to be taken through the courts, i.e. the presence of significant harm.

Table 1.2 Relationship between the rate of recorded parental problems and the level of social work intervention (Cleaver et al. 1999)

Parental problems	Referral stage	First enquiry	Child protection conference	Care proceedings
Mental illness	13%	20%	25%	42%
Alcohol or drug abuse	20%	25%	25–60%	70%
Domestic violence	27%	40%	35–55%	51%

At each stage the presence of key family and environmental factors which might have affected the parents' capacity to care for their children was assessed. Table 1.2 indicates that at each stage there was an increasing level of concern about the presence of parental mental illness, alcohol or drug abuse, or the presence of domestic violence. When full care proceedings were required, it will be noted the rate of parental mental illness was 42 per cent, alcohol or drug abuse 70 per cent, and domestic violence 51 per cent. When such factors coexisted, there was increasing concern about the need to take protective action. These key family and environmental factors can have direct impact on the capacity to parent or indirect effects through the impact on other factors, e.g income, social isolation and emotional and physical availability. They can also have a direct impact on the child and their developmental needs.

The impact of different forms of parental pathology

Cleaver et al. (1999) also looked at the way different forms of parental pathology affected parenting capacity. Their findings indicated the following:

- *Parents with mental illness* were at risk of their emotions being blunted, their children were sometimes neglected, and the parents may have been responsible for bizarre or violent actions. Parents with unstable personality functioning were particularly prone to extensive difficulties in their parenting capacity, and the intensity of their emotional responses to children in the family in turn had a profound impact on children's emotional functioning.

- *Parents who misused alcohol and drugs* showed a varied risk effect on parenting depending on the type of drug used, the amount used, how the substance was administered, the mental state evoked and factors relating to individual personal tolerance.

- *Domestic violence:* parenting was affected by physical assaults and psychological abuse. This impacted on the parents' caregiving capacity, and also generated intense fear in the victimized parent and children. A climate of fear, intimidation and secrecy affected all family members, including about the risks associated with revealing the reality of domestic violence to people outside the family. The impact of being exposed to domestic violence has a very similar impact to being physically abused for a child or young person.

General observations on the impact of parenting by parents affected by mental health, substance abuse or domestic violence

In addition, parents affected by these factors were observed in some circumstances (Cleaver *et al.* 1999):

- to have difficulties organising their lives – leading to inconsistent and ineffective parenting
- to experience loss of consciousness, or contact with reality, putting the physical safety and emotional welfare of children at risk
- to have loss of emotional control or violent and irrational behaviour which frightens children, and leads to negative emotional effects
- to be divorced from reality leading to neglect of their own and their children's physical needs
- for their children to have insecure attachments resulting from parents' insensitivity, unresponsiveness, anger and criticism
- for their children to need others to provide care to minimize the impact of such events.

The following social consequences were identified in some situations:

- Family income dropped or was used to satisfy parental needs; essential needs of children were sacrificed.
- There was a risk of family members being drawn into criminal activities or being organized by parents' beliefs for children – a form of emotional abuse.
- Standards of hygiene and basic care were neglected.
- Separation disrupted children's lives.
- Families were alienated, networks were disrupted. Problems were sometimes hidden from potentially supportive network, and social lives were focused around parents' needs.

- Marital or partnership breakdown occurred and there were intergenerational effects.

Risk factors and protective factors at different stages of development

Cleaver *et al.* (1999) have reviewed the impact of these factors alongside protective factors on children's welfare and responses at different stages of development.

Table 1.3 looks at the stages of development, identifying which factors lead to increased risk and which factors can be protective.

The developmental stages examined are:

- Pre-birth and infancy.

- The first two years of life: 0–2 years.

- Toddler stage: 3–4 years.

- School years: 5–9 years.

- Older school years: 10 years and above.

The impact of mental health, drug and alcohol abuse and domestic violence on parenting: specific effects

Although exposure to parental mental illness, alcohol and drug abuse and domestic violence cause general stress and impacts on children and young people's health and development, there are some specific effects which need to be considered. One example is the extent to which children born to parents with mental illness carry a genetic loading and predisposition to becoming mentally ill themselves.

THE IMPACT OF MENTAL ILLNESS ON PARENTING

In 2006 research by Rutter *et al.* (2006) indicated that exposure to high levels of stress and adversity may make it more likely that children born with a genetic predisposition, e.g. a close relative suffers from schizophrenia, are at risk of developing symptoms at an early age. This implies that when assessing children living in families where a parent has a mental illness, it is essential to assess the quality of family life and support, as children may be uniquely sensitive to stress and adversity.

This observation is underlined by the research of Wynne *et al* (2006a, 2006b), who followed the fate of children of schizophrenic parents who had been adopted to families who did not have a psychotic family member. They showed that if the child was adopted into a family which was well-functioning, there was a low likelihood of that child developing a psychotic illness themselves. However, if the child had been adopted into a family which itself had

Table 1.3 Risk and developmental factors for children with parents with psychiatric problems, substance abuse and domestic violence (Cleaver *et al.* 1999)

Stage	Risk factors	Protective factors
Pre-birth and infancy	• Foetal damage – drugs, alcohol • Physical violence • Spontaneous abortions • Premature birth	• Adequate nutrition, food • Antenatal care • Avoidance of drug use • Safe residence
0–2 years	• Neurological damage • Parental withdrawal • Neglect, impoverished environment • Rejection, irritability • Insecure, disorganized attachments	• Presence of an alternative supplementary caring adult • Integrating primary health, mental health and social services plan • Use of Sure Start, family centres, family support
3–4 years	• Continuing hidden neglect, violence and inconsistency • Delayed cognitive development • Post-traumatic stress responses • Inappropriate modelling	• Supplementary care • Integrated care plan • Enhanced income supports physical standards • Respite accommodation • Consistent pre-school provision
5–9 years	• Children may be at risk of physical injury, and show symptoms of extreme anxiety and fear • Academic attainment is negatively affected, behaviour problematic • Boys are more sensitive, girls are affected if difficulties long term • Attachments disorganized, fear of hostility expressed • Unexpected separations cause distress, embarrassment and shame over parents' behaviour • Children take on responsibility for themselves and siblings	• Children can understand drug and alcohol use as a form of illness • An alternative, consistent, caring adult responsive to needs, or supportive older sibling when both parents are affected • Regular school attendance, supportive, sensitive teachers • Supportive friendships and social support • Learning specific coping strategies • Physical or psychological separation from stressful situations
10 years and above	• Coping with puberty alone • Fear of hurt and injury • Emotional and conduct disorder • Bullying behaviour • Education suffers • Reject families • Emotional loneliness • Vulnerability to abuse • Inappropriate responsibility taken	• Supplementary care • Integrated care plan • Practical domestic help • School attendance, trusted adult, a champion • Basic education on sex, puberty, contraception • Information, recognition of caring role, balanced with own needs • Mutual friendships • Coping strategies to separate self and parent

high levels of family difficulties, then it was more likely that the child would develop a psychotic illness. Being exposed to adversity had a significantly negative effect in bringing forward the child's genetic vulnerability. Sluzki (2007) has described the reciprocal relationship between mental processes, biological factors, the social or relational milieu and genetic constraints.

The case examples in Boxes 1.11 and 1.12 illustrate the complexity of genetic vulnerability and environmental stress.

Box 1.11 Case example: Ruth E

Ruth E, a girl of 16 years, was seen in a secure unit as a result of extreme self-harming and violent actions. Her uncle, her father's brother, had a severe paranoid schizophrenic illness and she was exposed to his paranoid attacks against her mother over the first ten years of her life. In early adolescence she showed extreme anxiety and suspiciousness, and later showed far more extensive disturbance, including the development of hallucinations. It was difficult initially to make a distinction between her genetic vulnerability and her traumatic response to the life situation and it is likely both were playing a part.

Box 1.12 Case example: Daniel F

A similar situation was seen in Daniel F, a boy of 14 living with his mother, who had prevented him attending school as a result of her paranoid beliefs. He was at home for a six-month period. Because of the mother's illness there was no stable base to their lives. When placed in foster care he began to develop rigid behavioural patterns. He was suspicious in his responses, which were disorganized and loud, and he was preoccupied with sexual thoughts. A diagnosis of a psychotic illness was made. This appeared to be the product of genetic predisposition and high levels of environmental stress including the model of his mother's illness and the poverty and failure of her day-to-day care.

THE IMPACT OF DRUG AND ALCOHOL ABUSE ON PARENTING

Drug and alcohol abuse plays a complex role in terms of their impact on parenting, depending on the type of drug used, the amount used, and frequency. With alcohol misuse, it depends, along with other factors, on whether there is binge drinking with patterns of sobriety alternating with serious drunkenness, or continuous alcohol use. Two clinical cases illustrate the situation where risk predominates, and where protective factors can operate (see Boxes 1.13 and 1.14).

Box 1.13 Case example: Joanne G and Jamie G

The mother was caring for Joanne, a ten-year-old girl, and Jamie, a five-year-old boy, on her own, having managed to separate herself from her extremely violent partner. Her mode of coping with the impact of violence on herself was to use alcohol in ever-increasing amounts, to such an extent she became addicted. As a result of alcohol misuse, the care of her children became poor, she found it increasingly difficult to get the children to school, or to provide for their basic care. She increasingly used the ten-year-old girl as a companion, keeping her up very late. The children's attendance at school became progressively worse, and the children were rejected and bullied because of their unkempt appearance and clothing.

There was no alternative to reception of the children into care as the mother rejected services from the community Drug and Alcohol Service. She denied the level of alcohol abuse, and found it difficult to find alternatives to deal with her extensive traumatic symptoms related to severe domestic violence. She became extremely depressed, there were high levels of conflict between the ten-year-old and herself, and it was very difficult to see any possibility of returning the children to her care.

Box 1.14 Case example: Luke H and Duane H

A mother caring for Luke, a ten-year-old boy, and Duane, a five-year-old boy, separated from her partner who had been violent to her. Her response was to become heavily addicted to street heroin and she struggled to substitute heroin with methadone using the support of the Drug and Alcohol Service. Following a crisis which occurred with the death of the maternal grandmother, the point was reached where it was felt the two children needed to be taken into care for their protection because of the extreme negative effects of their mother's abusing street heroin as well as methadone.

However, with support from the community Drug and Alcohol Service, the children's mother was able to stabilize her drug use, although the ten-year-old did take on some parental supportive tasks in terms of caring for the five-year-old. She gradually was able to use community resources to improve the quality of her parenting and her care, and despite her continuing methadone use. There was a prospect of her being able to diminish methadone and use psychotherapeutic services to address the basic issues associated with experiences in her family of origin and subsequent domestic violence which were key factors in leading her to use heroin as a form of self-medication.

DOMESTIC VIOLENCE AND ITS IMPACT ON PARENTING AND ON CHILDREN'S HEALTH AND DEVELOPMENT

A key observation in considering the impact of domestic violence is the overlap between domestic violence and physical abuse. The presence of domestic violence provides an intense climate of trauma and family violence, and can have far-reaching effects on parents, children and young people growing up in this context. A key concern is whether a parent responsible for perpetrating violence against a partner, will also perpetrate violence against a child – a significant risk (Kelly 1994). In addition, exposure to the climate of anger, identifying with a parent who may be hurt, confusion in terms of gender role are all factors which have been noted to have a particular effect in contexts of domestic violence. The risk of severe forms of intimate partner violence resulting in homicide of adult partners and children results in overwhelming trauma and bereavement for surviving children (Jones 2008). There are concerns about children and young people growing up in such a climate, being caught in a cycle of externalizing behaviour, interpersonal violence in adolescence, early pregnancies, and re-enacting the patterns of violence to which they have been exposed (Moffitt and Caspi 1998).

The genetic contribution has been demonstrated by Caspi *et al.* (2002) in the Dunedin longitudinal study. This showed that genetic factors associated with the production of neurotransmitter hormones which modulate mood could predispose or protect some children from responding with antisocial behaviour patterns despite being exposed to high levels of family stress.

Other family and environmental factors which can influence parenting capacity

Research indicates a number of other family and environmental factors which can influence parenting capacity, and affect the child's needs directly. As noted in looking at underlying factors associated with difficulties in parenting, the history of the parents and individual family members has a significant impact on the child, and on the parent and their capacity to provide adequate care. Other environmental factors can help or hinder the child's functioning.

The characteristics of families when violence occurs

RISKS AND PROTECTIVE FACTORS ASSOCIATED WITH THE
CHARACTERISTICS OF THE FAMILY AS A SOCIAL STRUCTURE

The notion of risk factors associated with abusive parenting implies that there is contrast between families which protect and those where there are risks. Taking a sociological perspective, Straus and Gelles (1987) conceptualized the family as a social structure which was prone to conflict and violence as a result of the inherent contradictions of family life. They argue that the fact of often opposing values of men and women, adults and children meant there was always a likelihood of conflict occurring. They postulate that it was not a question of whether there was violence in the family or not, but whether the particular factors which predisposed to violence were operating, or whether there were more protective, benign responses. These factors included the following:

- *The time families spent together* provides opportunity for support and nurturance, but could also mean that there is more opportunity for conflict. Factors such as poor environmental conditions, low income, property, unemployment are all factors which mitigate against positive use of time spent together.

- *A wide range of activities and interests* can foster talents and strengths, but can also result in the disproportionate expression of negative or aversive behaviour when there are opposing wishes and activities. Intensity of involvement provides emotional fulfilment and close emotional connectedness, but can also result in mutual antagonism, high levels of criticism, threats and shouting.

- *Rights to influence* can be an influence for good, giving children appropriate directions and guidance. However, if there are extremes of authoritarian parenting insensitive to children's needs, opposition and continuing conflict results.

- *Age and sex differences* can provide a test-bed for understanding and tolerance, but can also lead to major conflict between generations, families and sexes. Ascribed roles, i.e. differentiation between males and females, can provide strength and identity, but there can also be distorted beliefs about rights to punish and demand compliance. Involuntary membership implies commitment and care, but means that there is a demand to maintain loyalty and there is no escape.

- *Families coping with stress* can provide resources and resilience to provide a sense of mastery, but can also lead to breakdown and disorganization.

- *Family members' knowledge of social biography* can lead not only to tolerance, care and understanding, but also to criticism and hurt on the basis of knowledge and information.

TRAUMA-ORGANIZED FAMILY SYSTEMS

Characteristic of all forms of family violence, abuse and adversity are the negative interlocking aspects of the relationship between child, parent and family within a social context. Associated with a climate of violence is a negative, emotionally abusive attitude by the victimizer towards the child or partner – a prerequisite to any form of abuse, physical, sexual or emotional. As noted this can be seen as a 'trauma-organized system' (Bentovim 1992, 1995) or set of relationships, sometimes described as 'relationship trauma' (Sheinberg and True 2008).

This model originates in the work of Straus and Gelles (1987) on abusive families who observed the process of interlocking emotional responses by which individuals with complementary difficulties come together and the resulting reciprocal nature of abusive interaction in family life. Parents may have had a belief that similar experiences can assist in the development of understanding and empathy but unfortunately the likelihood is that each partner comes to represent the focus of fear, panic and distress in the context of intimacy and such responses come to organize the reality of relationships. Relationships in such situations are 'organized' by traumatic events – and these can be described as trauma-organized systems (Bentovim 1992, 1995). They come to dominate family life, and because of family characteristics of secrecy, loyalty and exclusiveness, patterns of trauma and family violence may be maintained over many years without discovery. There are self-reinforcing cycles between family members – involving 'here and now' interaction between parents and children as well as cycles over time linked to the unresolved nature of events in parents, and family member's history which continue to impact on parenting capacity and the way children's needs are met.

In families where there is violence or abuse, there is often an absence of a protective individual or, alternatively, potential protectors are neutralized and unavailable. The perpetrator feels overwhelmed by impulses towards actions of a physically, sexually or emotionally abusive nature, which are felt to be beyond control. The cause is attributed to the victim, who in line with individual, family and cultural expectations is construed as responsible for the victimizer's feelings and intentions. Actions on the victim's part to avoid abuse are interpreted as further cause to provoke more violent action, or as a justification for further sexual or emotional abuse. The victim comes to internalize and is organized by the justifications, and an intergenerational recursive pattern is established.

A process of silencing by the victimizer and disassociation by the victim spreads to incorporate both the victim and victimizer and those who could potentially protect. This may lead to the maintenance of a context of secrecy and silence and the delayed recognition of severe abusive patterns. There is a tendency for the victim when identified to deny and minimize experiences, or to blame themselves. The perpetrator may in turn deny allegations and/or attribute any account given by the victim to the professional interviewing the child. Potential protective parents may side with the perpetrator or share in blaming the victim.

As a result of the repeated nature of violent actions, traumatic stressful effects come to organize the reality and the perceptions of those participating. This includes potential protectors, and professionals who become involved in the family situation. There is a pressure not to see, not to hear or not to speak, so that identification becomes problematic and complex.

SOCIAL ADVERSITY

Risk factors which need to be assessed and addressed include living in poverty, overcrowding, poor, substandard housing, unemployment, large family size, isolation in the community from wider family and poor community resources, especially when there is limited primary care (Bergner, Delgado and Graybill 1994; Finkelhor 1980).

The impact on the future parenting of children and young people growing up in a climate of trauma and family violence

Examining the impact and development of interpersonal violence introduces the theme of the effect of early experiences living with trauma and family violence on the child or young person's later capacity to parent. It has been recognized for many years that parents who behave abusively have often been abused themselves, so that there is an intergenerational influence. However, given the concern to understand both risk and protective factors, we need to understand what promotes harmful parenting and what is protective, which in turn can result in more resilient functioning and therefore more satisfactory parenting and care for the next generation.

Risk and protective factors in relation to future parenting of children who have grown up in a climate of trauma and family violence in childhood

LONGITUDINAL ISLE OF WIGHT COMMUNITY STUDY

To explore this process Collishaw *et al.* (2007) followed up the Isle of Wight Community Study to adult life. They assessed the rate of abuse suffered by those individuals in childhood, and through longitudinal research, looked at whether there were particular risk factors, or protective factors resulting in more resilient functioning with the likelihood of more satisfactory parenting. While they confirmed that childhood adversity is a potent factor in causing mental health difficulties, there were personality strengths that protected individuals, and resulted in more satisfactory parenting. Developing competencies to make and maintain supportive interpersonal relationships was the most significant protective factor.

ADULT AND PARENTS' ATTACHMENT STYLE

In their study of women growing up in adversity, and the impact on their mental health and parenting capacities, Bifulco and Moran (1998) noted the importance of adults' or parents' attachment style – a key aspect of which is the ability to make and maintain relationships – in pathways from childhood to adult functioning. Bifulco and Moran (1998) observed that the pathway to poor parenting tended to involve parents who had insecure attachments and who showed a higher degree of clinging, avoidance, fear or anger in their general approach to relationships, together with significant adversity in marital or partner relationships, including domestic violence. This resulted in incompetent, neglectful parenting, which in turn had a negative effect on children's mental health showing higher levels of depression or anxiety.

'MULTIPLICATIVE' IMPACT OF COMBINATIONS OF FACTORS ON FUTURE PARENTING

Another study dramatically demonstrated the 'multiplicative' or escalating level of effects on parenting for individuals who were abused in childhood (Dixon, Browne and Hamilton-Giachritsis 2005a; Dixon, Hamilton-Giachritsis and Browne 2005b). This was a community study which followed up first-time parents to assess the risk of child abuse when parents had themselves been abused in childhood. They found that having been abused in childhood led to a four times higher risk of abuse occurring against the child. If the parent was under 21, had been treated for mental health problems or had a partner with violent tendencies, there was a 14-fold increase in the risk of abusive action. Risk increased further when a mother had negative unrealistic expectations of the child, was insensitive towards the infant and when there was a negative response and a lack of development of a specific attachment preference by the infant. Abusive action was then 17 times more likely.

The J family: a case study illustrating key themes from the review of research

Parents with a history of adversity who have grown up in a climate of violence may be drawn together, perhaps with beliefs about 'rescue' or 'fit'. This can create a complex family organization and the effects on parenting can lead to significant difficulties for care of the children. This is demonstrated in the case example of the J family (Box 1.15). This is a complex case which nevertheless illustrates many of the key themes drawn out in the literature review.

Box 1.15 Case example: the J family

The J family consisted of Jim and Mary J, the two parents and their four children, who were referred as a result of the increasingly aggressive truanting behaviour of Harry and Damien, the 13- and 16-year-old boys, and the increasing anxiety of Rosie and Charmaine, the 10- and 12-year-old girls. There were complaints by the girls of bullying and sexual harassment, they felt unsafe; there were incidents of self-harming and eating disorders. An assessment which followed the approach of the *Assessment Framework* provided the following information.

Children's developmental needs

HEALTH

There were concerns about the health of all the children as a result of phases of poor care of the children and the home. Bullying of the girls by the boys led to physical and sexual harm.

EDUCATION

The education of the boys had become increasingly concerning as they moved towards adolescence. Their behaviour was increasingly oppositional in school and they had poor concentration. They were truanting and had been excluded from school because of fighting and swearing. The girls attended school more regularly; they were compliant and tried to work. Both received a good deal of support from the educational system, but not from their parents.

EMOTIONAL AND BEHAVIOURAL DEVELOPMENT

The boys' emotional and behavioural development had become increasingly aggressive, challenging, oppositional, stealing, joining gangs, rejecting rules. Both girls were prone to depressed affect and both had begun to self-harm and starve themselves. Both described traumatic imagery associated with exposure to domestic violence. Father was described by both girls as the object of fear and also of warmth. They avoided emotional contact with their mother, and did not confide in her. Attachments were disorganized, with clinging behaviour, alternating with avoidance and confusion.

IDENTITY

The boys identified with their father's angry, controlling style; they indicated that they felt nurtured and reinforced by his affection. The girls identified with their mother's withdrawn, anxious, fearful style. The interaction between the siblings maintained these marked gender differences, and their need to have a more balanced view of themselves was not met.

FAMILY AND SOCIAL RELATIONSHIPS

Family and social relationships were confused. The boys were involved in intense squabbling and competitiveness, with each other and with the girls. The girls were more supportive of each other and more compliant and sociable with the wider family. The boys were defiant and oppositional.

SOCIAL PRESENTATION

The boys presented as over-confident, forceful and aggressive in their style of presentation. This was reflected by their involvement with gangs in the community, identifying with the notion of being 'hard'. The girls had poor social presentation skills. They presented with far more diffidence, and were anxious about themselves and unfriendly in their approach towards others.

SELF-CARE SKILLS

The boys' approach to basic care put themselves and others at considerable risk through association with antisocial elements in the community. The girls were vulnerable to the bullying and sexually aggressive style of the boys and they felt powerless and unprotected.

Parenting capacity

Jim and Mary J had difficulties in all dimensions of their parenting capacity.

BASIC CARE

The basic care they provided was poor. There were difficulties in providing adequate basic care and parental differences and arguments led to failures of adequate care of children and the home.

ENSURING SAFETY

Parents were in conflict with each other, with authorities, and with the neighbourhood and social context. There was a sense of a lack of safety. The father Jim's angry mood and threatening, bullying style created a dangerous atmosphere. He dismissed the girls' complaints about the boys' bullying abusive behaviour, while Mary, the children's mother, remained unresponsive and emotionally withdrawn.

EMOTIONAL WARMTH

Emotional warmth was provided by the father, in contrast with his angry, bullying style. The mother's responses were far more withheld and unresponsive. Parents were inconsistent in their involvement or understanding of difficulties experienced by the children.

STIMULATION

Jim and Mary provided limited stimulation for the children. There was poor preparation and support for the children attending school: the girls were more responsive to school, whereas the boys were truanting.

GUIDANCE AND BOUNDARIES

The guidance and boundaries set by the parents were inconsistent. The control exercised was both oppressive and over-controlling, and sometimes absent altogether. The parents' expectations of the children were inappropriate. Boundaries over the boys' truanting patterns as they moved towards adolescence were not managed.

STABILITY

Some stability was provided through the parents remaining together, but the inconsistent nature of their relationship provided a pervasive feeling of instability.

Family and environmental factors

There was a range of family and environmental factors influencing Jim and Mary's capacity to parent their children and impacting on the children directly.

FAMILY HISTORY

Both parents grew up in a climate of violence, being hit by belts and witnessing violence perpetrated against maternal figures. Jim had been taken into care because of his significant antisocial behaviour in adolescence. He attributed this to his father's extensive punitiveness, reinforced by physical punishment to a degree, which he deemed to be unnecessary given his perception of his father's authority. He described himself as becoming increasingly rebellious as he was growing up, getting into criminal activities and battles with authority from an early age.

Mary described her exposure to an extensive set of cumulative, stressful and abusive experiences, including sexual abuse perpetrated by her father, her mother's punitive and neglectful care, and her exposure to disruption of care. She described her own traumatic response, including the development of an eating disorder. She too was resentful of her mother's abandoning her to her abusive father and her mother's failure of protection.

FAMILY AND INDIVIDUAL FUNCTIONING

There was a degree of stability in the household; however, the parents had been exposed to an unstable family environment in their own childhood and exposed to violence and abuse, and this continued to impact on their lives.

In terms of individual functioning, Jim had an externalizing, explosive, angry, aggrieved style of relating to others. This was associated with the use of anger to control and phases linked with alcohol and possibly drug use.

His externalizing style also allowed him to be more outgoing and adolescent in his style of relating to others, including the children.

Mary was anxious and dissociated. She was withdrawn and distant from others, including the children. She had an intense, enmeshed, dependent relationship with Jim and recent attempts to assert herself had resulted in extensive arguments and episodes of violence.

WIDER FAMILY

The wider family had attempted to be supportive without success.

HOUSING

The family's housing has been poorly maintained.

INCOME AND EMPLOYMENT

Work for both Jim and Mary had been unpredictable and they had not applied for available welfare benefits. The family income was therefore inconsistent and resources were poorly managed.

FAMILY'S SOCIAL INTEGRATION

The family was isolated and found it difficult to integrate into their local community. The family had experienced some discrimination, with the family being labelled by neighbours as a 'problem family'.

COMMUNITY RESOURCES

Jim in particular had been in a significant degree of conflict with community agencies. Attempts had been made to support the family with very limited success.

Analysis of processes and factors operating in the J family

The dynamics of the parents' relationship and their responses to their own pattern of abusive care had had a serious impact on the nature of the relationships between the parents and children and the quality of parenting the children had experienced. These patterns were complementary and self-reinforcing and were maintained through responses to traumatic and stressful events and experiences organizing relationship patterns. There was a gender divide between 'perpetrator' and 'victim' modes, associated with insecure attachment styles.

Through these processes each parent had developed an opposing personality style, which influenced, shaped and maintained the response of the other, and provided models for the children and organized their differing modes of development. The children's responses mirrored their parents' mode of relating, reinforced by the parenting they were receiving and the cumulative impact of traumatic and stressful events. As a result the intergenerational cycle of abusive events had been perpetuated rather than broken. Although there were protective factors – the stability of the family, and a capacity for warmth on the father's part – there was a predominance of risk factors.

> Despite these pervasive patterns there was hope that the children, later being cared for separately, might be able to benefit from the care and therapeutic work they were receiving, and that the parents might be able to begin to contemplate what changes they needed to make and whether they could accept help to reach turning points in their own lives.

Conclusion

In looking at the J family the implications of some of the research findings are illustrated and the complexity of practice becomes clear.

Subsequent chapters describe in detail the process of making evidence-based assessments, analysis and planning interventions and measuring outcomes using the *Assessment Framework* when children have been living with trauma and family violence.

Chapter Two

Assessing Children's Needs

A Model of Assessment, Analysis, Planning Interventions and Identifying and Measuring Outcomes for the Child

Antony Cox, Liza Bingley Miller
and Stephen Pizzey

Introduction

This chapter presents a model of assessment, analysis, planning and measuring outcomes for children and families based on the *Assessment Framework* triangle.

The model was developed in response to the findings from research on the use of the *Assessment Framework* (Cleaver and Walker 2004) and from experience of training staff in the use of the Standardized Assessment Tools. The picture is one of information-gathering that was often conscientious and skilled but not necessarily systematic or evidence based. The process of analysing information was more challenging. There was a tendency to come to premature conclusions about the nature of the presented problems, the factors underlying them, and the action thought appropriate. Without a sufficient understanding and analysis of the child's needs, their family and their wider context, planning cannot be appropriate and effective.

A systematic approach to assessment, analysis and the planning of intervention is likely to result in a fuller identification of strengths and difficulties in children and their environment, and a better understanding of underlying processes. This in turn leads to better focused intervention, a more efficient use of resources and better outcomes for children.

Contents of the chapter

There are seven steps to the model and these are discussed in detail in the chapter:

1. Consider the safety of the child, the referral, and the aims of the assessment.

2. Gather additional information.

3. Categorize available information and organize it within the *Assessment Framework* triangle: what is known and not yet known.

4. Analyse the processes influencing the child's health and development.

5. Predict the likely outlook for the child.

6. Plan interventions.

7. Identify outcomes and measures which would indicate whether interventions are successful.

Step 1: Consider the referral, the safety of the child, and the aims of the assessment

In a safeguarding context, the first consideration on receiving a new referral where there are concerns about maltreatment is to assess whether steps need to be taken to ensure the child's immediate safety, i.e. removal from family or carers, removal of abusive adult from the household, or removal to different family members. This initial assessment of whether the child is suffering or likely to suffer significant harm is not a straightforward process and requires consideration of the immediate threats to the welfare of the child, the factors affecting the child's safety and the risk of harm continuing or escalating if no action is taken. Ongoing consideration of whether the child is suffering or likely to suffer significant harm is important throughout the assessment process. The assessment of the risk of harm is considered in detail in Chapter 6.

Once the professional is assured of the child's safety the next step is to review the referral and establish the *focus* and the *aims* of the assessment. The overall aims will always be to:

*   develop an understanding of the nature and level of a child's needs

*   gain an understanding of the factors affecting the child and their needs, including the parenting they receive and other family and environmental factors

*   develop partnerships with family members and others, including relevant professionals

*   prepare for intervention if necessary.

How extensive or deep the exploration should be is judged by viewing the nature of the referral and any available information against the range of information outlined in the *Assessment Framework* triangle. The domains and dimensions are a guide to the range of areas where further information may be relevant. It should be remembered that in all dimensions history should be considered as well as current status, as this can also inform hypotheses about processes relevant to the child's development. How deep the exploration should be must be guided by timing as well as the need to know. Some information may be available only when trusting relationships have been formed.

Questions that arise include whether it is essential to have a thorough assessment of the child's developmental status or vital to have a full appraisal of the family? Are there environmental factors which need to be better understood?The information-gathering procedure provides a basis for evaluating how and whether a working relationship can be established with the family: what is their capacity to cooperate in action to foster their child's development? This is a particularly crucial issue where there has been, or is likely to be, severe abuse. This aspect will be addressed more fully in Chapter 7.

Step 2: Gather additional information

The information-gathering approach should be systematic to ensure that the data obtained is adequate in its scope and well evidenced, and that time is used effectively. Sources of information need to be considered. They include family members, members of the community where relevant and professionals or agencies who have been involved with the family. Thought should be given also to the combination of family members that might be seen and in what contexts. It is important to remember that what will be learnt will be influenced by the combination and the context. For example, different information will be obtained from seeing a child alone, from interviewing them with a parent, or observing them in their own home as opposed to school.The approaches used to gather information should be considered. They range from reviewing existing files and requests for reports from professionals or agencies previously involved or already engaged in work with the family, to interviewing, observation, use of Standardized Assessment Tools and referral for specialist assessment.The *Standardized Assessment Tools* were commissioned by the Government to assist professionals working with children and families are all potentially valuable for information-gathering and making evidence-based assessments.

These tools, the approaches underpinning their use, the skills involved in using them in practice and the information they can provide are more fully described in Chapter 3 (see p. 106) but in summary, they are as follows:

- The *Family Pack of Questionnaires and Scales* (Department of Health, Cox and Bentovim 2000) helps a worker to look at a range of aspects of a child's developmental needs, parenting and factors relating to individual well-being and family life.

- The *HOME Inventory* (Cox 2008; Cox and Walker 2002a) provides an assessment of the child's day-to-day experience, parenting and the context of care provided for the child.

- The *Family Assessment* (Bentovim and Bingley Miller 2001) enables workers to assess family functioning and family relationships, including parenting, and the impact of family history.

- *In My Shoes* (Calam *et al.* 2000) is a computer-assisted interview approach to help professionals communicate with children and vulnerable adults about their experiences, relationships and feelings in the various settings in which they spend their life.

- An additional tool, the *Attachment Style Interview* (Bifulco *et al.* 2002a, 2002b) developed by the Lifespan Research Group at Royal Holloway University of London, helps to assess the quality of the marriage or partnership between two adults, their support systems, their attitudes towards support and their overall attachment style.

Step 3: Categorize available information and organize it within the *Assessment Framework* triangle: what is known and not yet known

Once information has been gathered, the next step is to categorize that information to ascertain what is known, identify crucial information that is not yet known and needs to be known, and to prepare for analysis. The *Assessment Framework* triangle provides the basis for collecting together and then analysing the available information on a child's developmental needs and the factors affecting them. The information obtained is categorized according to the three domains: child's developmental needs (CDN), parenting capacity (PC) and family and environmental factors (F&EF) and the dimensions within each domain (Figure 2.1).

At this stage there should be no attempt to explore how the different factors or items are affecting each other. Although the assessor is beginning to form ideas or hypotheses about what is going on with the child, their parents and in the family and other factors which may be relevant, these hypotheses need to be put on hold until all the information has been categorized. If links are made too early, false assumptions can be made about a child's level of functioning and needs, the nature and reasons for any difficulties and strengths in parents' and carers' capacity to care, and the family and environmental factors affecting the child and/or their carers. In a safeguarding context, this can lead in turn to misplaced planning for the changes thought appropriate to ensure the

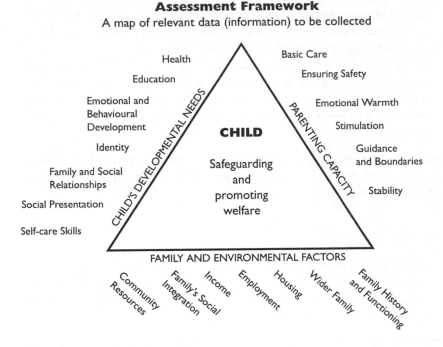

Figure 2.1: The Assessment Framework (Department of Health et al. 2000)

child's safety and welfare. Interventions are then less likely to be targeted in an appropriate and effective way.

Categorizing information under domains and dimensions of the Assessment Framework triangle

In categorizing the information there should be a clear distinction as to which domain is appropriate, otherwise hypotheses about processes involving the child and their family may be mistaken.

The descriptions in the *Assessment Framework* for each domain and dimension, along with key questions to be considered at this stage are as follows:

Child's developmental needs

Assessment of what is happening to a child require that each aspect of a child's developmental progress is examined, in the context of the child's age and stage of development. Account must be taken of any particular vulnerability, such as a learning disability or a physically impairing condition, and the impact they may have on progress in any of the developmental dimensions. Consideration should also be given to the social and environmentally disabling factors that have an impact on the child's development, such as limited access for those who have a disability and other forms of discrimination. Children who have been maltreated may suffer impairments to their development as a result of injuries sustained and / or the impact of the trauma caused by their abuse. There must be a clear understanding of what a particular child is capable of achieving successfully at each stage of development, in order to ensure that he or she has the opportunity to achieve his or her full potential. (Assessment Framework, p.18:2.3)

How is the child functioning in each of the dimensions in terms of their development and well-being? How are they doing? Where is the child *at* in terms of their developmental needs?

Parenting capacity

Critically important to a child's health and development is the ability of parents and caregivers to ensure that the child's developmental needs are being appropriately and adequately responded to, and to adapt to his or her changing needs over time. (Assessment Framework, p.120:2.9)

What is the nature of the parenting that the child is receiving? What are the parents or carers *doing* in terms of the care they provide for their child(ren) on each dimension of parenting capacity?

Family and environmental factors

The care and upbringing of children does not take place in a vacuum. All family members are influenced both positively and negatively by the wider family, the neighbourhood and social networks in which they live. The history of the child's family and of the individual family members may have a significant impact on the child and parents. A range of environmental factors can either help or hinder a family's functioning. (Assessment Framework, p.22:2.13)

What are the family and environmental factors which may be *influencing* parenting or *impacting directly* on the child's development?

Child's developmental needs: dimensions

What strengths or difficulties does the child have in each dimension?

HEALTH

Health includes growth and development as well as physical and mental well-being. The impact of genetic factors as well as of any impairment should be considered. Involves receiving appropriate health care when ill, an adequate and nutritious diet, exercise, immunizations where appropriate and developmental checks, dental and optical care and, for older children, appropriate advice and information on issues that have an impact on health, including sex education and substance misuse. (Assessment Framework, p.19)

Is the child healthy? What health problems do they have? What are they? Have they experienced any in the past?

EDUCATION

Education covers all areas of a child's cognitive development which begins from birth. Includes opportunities for play and interaction with other children, access to books, the development of skills and interests and the need to experience success and achievement. Involves an adult interested in educational activities, progress and achievements, who takes account of the child's starting point and any special educational needs. (Assessment Framework, p.19)

Has the baby started making any sounds? Has the toddler started to speak? Is the child participating and learning at nursery or mothers' and toddlers' group? How are they doing at school? Are they achieving educationally at the level expected for their age and stage of development, or do they have educational difficulties? What are they?

EMOTIONAL AND BEHAVIOURAL DEVELOPMENT

Emotional and behavioural development concerns the appropriateness of response demonstrated in feelings and actions by a child, initially to parents and caregivers and, as the child grows older, to others beyond the family. Includes the nature and quality of early attachments, characteristic of temperament, adaptation to change, response to stress and degree of appropriate self-control. (Assessment Framework, p.19)

Is the child's level of emotional and behavioural development as expected for their age? Are they showing emotional or behavioural difficulties? What form do these take, e.g. depression, aggressive behaviour or problems in social communication?

IDENTITY

Identity concerns the child's growing sense of self as a separate and valued person. Includes the child's view of self and abilities, self-image and self-esteem and having a positive sense of individuality. Race, religion, age, gender, sexuality and disability may all contribute to this. Feelings of belonging and acceptance by family, peer group and wider society, including other cultural groups. (Assessment Framework, p.19)

What is known about the child's sense of self-esteem and self-worth? How do they express their own thoughts, feelings and wishes? What sense do they have of themselves as a person?

FAMILY AND SOCIAL RELATIONSHIPS

Family and social relationships concern the development of empathy and the capacity to place self in someone else's shoes. Includes a stable and affectionate relationship with parents or caregivers, good relationships with siblings, increasing importance of age-appropriate friendships with peers and other significant persons in the child's life and response of family to these relationships. (Assessment Framework, p.19)

What evidence is there about the quality of the child's relationships with other family members? Do they have any difficulties relating to their peers and others in their social network? What are they?

SOCIAL PRESENTATION

Social presentation concerns the child's growing understanding of the way in which appearance, behaviour and any impairment are perceived by the outside world and the impression being created. Includes appropriateness of dress for age, gender, culture and religion; cleanliness and hygiene; and availability from parents or caregivers about presentation in different settings. (Assessment Framework, p.19)

How does the child present themselves in different social situations? Is that appropriate to their age and stage of development? Is their dress in keeping with the settings in which they live?

SELF-CARE SKILLS

Self-care skills concern the acquisition by a child of practical, emotional and communication competencies required for increasing independence. Includes early practical skills of dressing and feeding, opportunities to gain confidence and practical skills to undertake activities away from the family and independent living skills as older children. Includes encouragement to acquire problem-solving approaches. Special attention should be given to the impact of a child's impairment and other vulnerabilities, and on social circumstances affecting the development of self-care skills. (Assessment Framework, p.19)

In what way does the child care for themselves? For example, washing, dressing, personal hygiene, travelling, or managing issues such as drug and alcohol use? Are they able to care for themselves at a level appropriate for their age and stage of development? Do they take inappropriate responsibility for self-care skills? Are they more self-sufficient than is appropriate at their stage of development?

For all these dimensions there will be the relevant *history* to consider.

Parenting capacity: dimensions

What are the parents doing or not doing that may be relevant to the child's development?

BASIC CARE

Basic care involves providing for the child's physical needs, and appropriate medical and dental care. Includes the provision of food, drink, warmth and shelter, clean and appropriate clothing and adequate personal hygiene. (Assessment Framework, p.21)

How are the parents providing food, warmth, clothing and shelter for the child? When there is a need for medical and other assistance, what do they do?

ENSURING SAFETY

Ensuring safety involves ensuring a child is adequately protected from harm or danger. Includes protection from significant harm or danger, and contact with unsafe adults or other children and from self-harm. Recognition of hazards and danger both in the home and elsewhere. (Assessment Framework, p.21)

How do they attempt to make sure the child is safe? What about when the child is not at home? What happens if there is domestic violence? What protection do they provide from contact with individuals who may pose a risk to them?

EMOTIONAL WARMTH

Emotional warmth includes ensuring that the child's emotional needs are met and giving the child a feeling of being especially valued and a positive sense of his or her own racial and cultural identity. Includes ensuring the child's requirements for secure, stable and affectionate relationships with significant adults, with appropriate sensitivity and responsiveness to the child's needs. Appropriate physical contact, comfort and cuddling sufficient to demonstrate warm regard, praise and encouragement. (Assessment Framework, p.21)

What warmth and affection do the parents show towards the child? How do they respond when the child is distressed? What encouragement, praise and reassurance do they give in response to the child's emotional needs?

STIMULATION

Stimulation relates to the need to promote a child's learning and intellectual develop-ment through encouragement, cognitive stimulation and providing social opportuni-ties. Includes facilitating the child's cognitive development and potential through interaction, communication, talking and responding to the child's language and ques-tions, encouraging and joining the child's play, and promoting educational opportu-nities. Enabling the child to experience success and ensuring school attendance or equivalent opportunity. Facilitating child to meet the challenges of life. (Assessment Framework, p.21)

How do the parents talk with the child? Is this in a way likely to promote their development of language? What social and learning opportunities do they provide inside and outside the home? What help do they give with reading and homework? How do they encourage their child's learning and development of social skills?

GUIDANCE AND BOUNDARIES

Guidance and boundaries include enabling the child to regulate their own emotions and behaviour. The key parental tasks are demonstrating and modelling appropriate behaviour and control of emotions and interactions with others, and guidance, which involves setting boundaries, so that the child is able to develop a internal model of moral values and conscience, and social behaviour appropriate for the society within which they will grow up. The aim is to enable the child to grow up into an autono-mous adult, holding their own values, and able to demonstrate appropriate behaviour with others rather than having to be dependent on rules outside themselves. This includes not over-protecting children from exploratory and learning experiences, and also includes social problem-solving, anger management, consideration for others, and effective discipline and shaping of behaviour. (Assessment Framework, p.21)

How do the parents manage the child's behaviour? What guidance do they provide and how? How do the parents set boundaries for the child? What rewards and sanctions do they use?

STABILITY

Stability involves providing a sufficiently stable family environment to enable a child to develop and maintain a secure attachment to the primary caregiver(s) in order to ensure optimal development. Includes ensuring secure attachments are not disrupted, providing consistency of emotional warmth over time and responding in a similar manner to the same behaviour. Parental responses change and develop according to the child's developmental progress. In addition, ensuring children keep in contact with important family members and significant others. (Assessment Framework, p.21)

What steps do the parents take to maintain a stable home and family life for the children? In what ways do they promote the development of secure attachments in the child? How do they help them cope with any moves, separations or losses? Again it is important to understand the course of parenting throughout the child's life.

Family and environmental factors: dimensions

Are there factors that may be promoting or adversely affecting the child's development directly, or by influencing parenting?

FAMILY HISTORY AND FUNCTIONING

Family history includes both genetic and psychosocial factors. Family functioning is influenced by who is living in the household and how they are related to the child; significant changes in family or household composition; history of childhood experiences of parents; chronology of significant life events and their meaning to family members; nature of family functioning, including sibling relationships and its impact on the child; parental strengths and difficulties, including those of an absent parent; the relationship between separated parents. (Assessment Framework, p.23)

What is the nature of relationships within the family? How does the family function as a unit? In what joint activities do they engage? Is there any conflict or domestic violence? Has a parent a mental health problem or difficulties with substance or alcohol misuse? What was it? Is it still an issue? What changes in family composition have there been in the child's life? How have family relationships changed? What is the nature of the links between previous partners and children now? What significant events, relationships or circumstances from the past has each family member experienced? Which of those is still affecting them now and how? Are there specific behaviours or interactions between family members that may reflect the impact of family history on current individual and family functioning? What are they?

WIDER FAMILY

Who are considered to be members of the wider family by the child and parents? Includes related and non-related persons and absent wider family. What is their role and importance to child and parents and in precisely what way? (Assessment Frame-work, p.23)

Who are the members of the wider family? Which of those people is particularly significant to the child or family? What contact do the child and family have with them? How do members of the wider family support the child or family?

HOUSING

Does accommodation have basic amenities and facilities appropriate to the age and development of the child and other resident members? Is the housing accessible and suitable to the needs of disabled family members? Includes the interior and exterior of the accommodation and immediate surroundings. Basic amenities include water, heating, sanitation, cooking facilities, sleeping arrangements and cleanliness, hygiene and safety and their impact on the child's upbringing. (Assessment Frame-work, p.23)

What is the nature, size and location of the family's accommodation? Does the available space reach the standard required by the housing regulations? What specific housing needs of the family are provided for, e.g. adaptations, access, and number of rooms? What is the nature of the neighbourhood in which the child is living?

EMPLOYMENT

Who is working in the household, their pattern of work and any changes? What impact does this have on the child? How is work or absence of work viewed by family members? How does it affect their relationship with the child? Includes children's experience of work and its impact on them. (Assessment Framework, p.23)

How are the adults in the family employed? What is the nature of their work? What are the hours, conditions, locations etc. of their work? How does this affect family activities and interaction? If the adults are not in employment, how does this affect the family?

INCOME

Income available over a sustained period of time. Is the family in receipt of all its benefit entitlements? Is there a sufficiency of income to meet the family's needs? In what way are resources available to the family used? Are there financial difficulties which affect the child? (Assessment Framework, p.23)

What level of income does the family have? How do they manage financially on that income? Is the family in debt? What welfare benefits and allowances are they receiving? What are they eligible for?

FAMILY'S SOCIAL INTEGRATION

> *Exploration of the wider context of the local neighbourhood and community and its impact on the child and parents. Includes the degree of the family's integration or isolation, their peer groups, friendship and social networks and the importance attached to them. (Assessment Framework, p.23)*

What links do the family have with their local neighbourhood and wider community? What friends and neighbours can they talk to and access support from? How is the family involved in local social, leisure, sporting or other activities, groups and organizations?

COMMUNITY RESOURCES

> *Describes all facilities and services in a neighbourhood, including universal services of primary health care, day care and schools, places of worship, transport, shops and leisure activities. Includes availability, accessibility and standard of resources and impact on family, including members with disabilities. (Assessment Framework, p.23)*

What relevant resources and services are available for the family members in the local community? What relevant specialist services and provision is there? How accessible are they? How do the family use the services and support that might benefit them? If not, what are the barriers to their accessing them?

History

When gathering and categorizing information, it is essential to collect information about past history relating to factors being considered in each dimension and domain. This enables the assessor to understand current issues and concerns better when analysing the information collected.

Monitoring information known and not yet known

Throughout the information- and data-gathering stage, it is vital to monitor what dimensions mapped on the *Assessment Framework* triangle have been covered in detail and those where knowledge is lacking. There will always be aspects that are not fully understood. Once the available information has been mapped into the *Assessment Framework* triangle, it may become obvious whether crucial information is missing, e.g. how a child is doing at school; whether a parent protects their child from witnessing domestic violence; whether there are wider family members who might be able to offer support. In some areas historical data may be missing. Consideration needs to be given to what is not yet known as it could be significant and therefore warrant further enquiry.

Being clear about what is not yet known guides what should be explored further. It may be clear that without this information it will be hard to assess whether the child's needs are being met and whether there is any risk to their safety, health and development. Ideally, such information will be gathered and mapped before moving on to detailed analysis.

Step 4: Analyse the processes influencing the child's health and development

The fourth step is to hypothesize processes which may be affecting the child's development. The core questions in the analysis using the *Assessment Framework* triangle are:

- What needs of the child are being met – *and how?*

- What needs of the child are not being met – *and why?*

The aim is to raise hypotheses or theories about how the factors on the dimensions in the three domains are impacting on each other both *within* and *across* the domains of the *Assessment Framework* triangle. For example:

- How are the child's strengths and difficulties impacting on each other?

- How are parenting strengths and difficulties affecting each other?

- How are family and environmental factors affecting each other?

- How is the parenting that is provided for the child affecting the child's health and development, both in terms of resilience and protective factors and vulnerability and risk factor?

- How are family and environmental factors impacting on parenting and/or on the child directly?

Checks need to be made as to whether there is evidence to confirm or refute the hypotheses, which should be revised as new information emerges.

Concepts which help with analysis and planning: factors and processes

In developing hypotheses about why some children's needs are met and some are not, it is helpful to distinguish *processes* (the *pattern of influences*) and their *strength* or *weight*, i.e. their impact, as shown in Box 2.1.

Box 2.1 Principles underlying analysis: processes and impact

In analysing the information collected, it is necessary to consider:
- Processes – the pattern of influences
- Impact – the weight or effect of factors and processes

Factors are each individual item identified in each dimension for which there is evidence. Processes refer to the ways in which individual factors relate to others in the same or different dimensions and domains – the pattern of influences.

Weight or effect refers to the amount of impact of the various factors and processes on other factors or dimensions or other processes. Which are the factors or processes having the greatest effect on child development? What are the severest problems or the greatest strengths? For example, low income can result in less ability to take children out and provide a range of experiences, which could have a negative impact on the child's education. If the child attends a good school, its positive impact on their education could compensate and reduce the negative impact of low income. Here a negative pattern of influences is countered by a positive pattern which reduces the impact of the negative process.

DISTINGUISHING BETWEEN PROCESSES

Processes – the pattern of influences – should be explored before considering their impact. Distinctions need to be made between:

- processes which may have brought something about

- processes which may be keeping something going

- processes which can help to predict what might happen in the future.

Distinguishing between the processes which may have brought about difficulties or strengths and those that may be maintaining them is important because they are often different. The understanding that this brings will affect what interventions are chosen.

For example, a child breaks his leg and misses school for three weeks. Although fit to return, the child remains at home; his mother, who is suffering from depression, has enjoyed his company during the day and does not encourage his return to school. What brought about school absence was the broken leg, but what kept the boy off school was his mother's desire for him to remain at home.

In trying to understand how these different processes are affecting a child's developmental needs, it is useful to distinguish between linear and circular processes (see Box 2.2).

Box 2.2 Principles underlying analysis: linear and circular processes

Processes that take account of past, present or future may be linear or circular

Linear processes:
- How did the child get here?
- Where might the child be going?

Circular processess:
- Sustain what may be satisfactory or unsatisfactory

LINEAR PROCESSES

A linear process is when two factors are thought to be directly linked so that alterations in one lead to changes in the other. This is when one factor (A) influences another (B), but the second factor does not influence the first, i.e. B does not affect A. Linear processes may be chains: A affects B, B affects C and so on. This type of process can be relevant to:

- where factors relating to the child (and family) brought things about
- where they are now
- where they might be going.

For example, delayed language development (CDN – health) (A) predicts that a child will have difficulty learning to read (CDN – education) (B), which may lead to future behavioural problems (CDN – emotional and behavioural development)(C).

CIRCULAR PROCESSES

Circular processes can serve to sustain a strength or a difficulty. The identification of circular processes affects choice of intervention. Circular processes are recurrent so that one factor (A) affects (B), which in turn affects A. Several factors may be involved so that A affects B which affects C which influences A.For example, a child has difficulty with learning to read (CDN – education) (A). The child worries about not reading well (CDN – emotional and behavioural development) (B). This leads to poor concentration (CDN – emotional and behavioural development) (C) which in turn leads to difficulty learning to read (A).A check is needed as to whether there are other processes, which help to maintain the identified strength or difficulty.

In the example given above further exploration might reveal that the child who has difficulty learning to read (CDN – education) (A) worries about it (CDN – emotional and behavioural development) (B) and as a result does not sleep well (CDN – health) (C). They are tired when they get to school (health) (D). Tiredness combined with anxiety about reading further impacts on concentration (emotional and behavioural development) (E). They find reading even harder (A). This is a circular process within the child's developmental needs domain, which serves to maintain the child's reading problem.This analysis of the circular processes that are at work helps to give an idea of what actions might help the child's difficulty and therefore how to intervene.Linear and circular processes may operate *within or across* domains: see Box 2.3.

As an example of a linear process occurring across all domains, the family has enough income (F&EF – income) to buy books (PC – stimulation), thus the child has the opportunity to read and develop (CDN – education).As an example of circular processes occurring across all domains, and expanding the example of the child with difficulty in reading, a child who is not reading well (CDN – Education) worries about it (CDN – emotional and behavioural development) and doesn't sleep well (CDN – health). He is tired at school (CDN – health) and cannot concentrate to do his reading well (CDN – emotional and

---

Box 2.3 Principles underlying analysis: how linear and circular processes operate

Linear or circular processes:

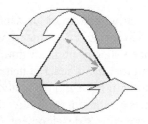

- within domains
- Within or between dimensions

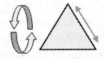

- Across domains

behavioural development and education). His teacher is concerned about his reading difficulties and writes to his parents (F&EF – community resources). His mother is angry and reprimands the child (PC – emotional warmth and guidance and boundaries). She tells his father, who threatens him with sanctions (F&EF – family functioning; PC – guidance and boundaries and emotional warmth). The parental actions feed into the negative cycle, increasing the child's anxiety and difficulties in sleeping and concentrating. Circular processes help to highlight situations where the factors that brought things about may not be what are keeping them going. It is necessary to understand that the trigger for a problem (or indeed a strength) may have stopped being relevant and that another process has taken over. This may have important implications for how to intervene.

Expanding an earlier example, a boy who has broken his leg has time off school (CDN – health; F&EF – community resources). He finds the relief he experiences from not being bullied makes him reluctant and anxious about going back to school (CDN – emotional and behavioural). His mother wishes to protect him from unhappiness at school and therefore lets him stay off school long after his leg has healed (PC – guidance and boundaries and emotional warmth). The longer the time off school, the more anxious the boy is about going back, and the more difficult it is for his mother to support him in returning. Thus a circular process has taken over from the original health problem and is sustaining the boy's absence from school.

ANALYSING LINEAR AND CIRCULAR PROCESSES AND PLANNING

The analysis of the linear and circular processes at work can generate ideas about what interventions may help with a child's need. It may be more effective to support a process that is building on a strength than attempt to alleviate one that is causing a difficulty.

Although one process may appear particularly relevant, it is vital to consider any others that could be influential. Evidence may run counter to what may be intuitively considered the relevant process. For example, a mother's depression may not impair her parenting. On the other hand, relief of maternal depression may not improve a poor relationship with her child. In analysing information gathered during an assessment, what is paramount is whether there is impairment or likelihood of impairment of the child's development. This means holding in mind that difficulties or impairments in parenting or broader family and environment factors may or may not be producing impairments in the child's development or in parenting capacity. It is easy to assume factors are linked, but it is essential always to have evidence as this will affect hypotheses about processes and intervention and expected outcomes. Wrong assumptions about the links will lead to interventions being incorrectly targeted and therefore unlikely to achieve the hoped for outcome. The task of the assessor is to collect sufficient information and analyse it carefully to establish which factors are impacting on the child and in what way. The understanding developed about the links between the child and their family and wider environment will affect plans for intervention and expected outcomes.

Exploring the impact of factors and processes

Once the processes (i.e. pattern of influences or factors) have been analysed, it is useful to look at the severity of any negative process and/or the weight of any positive process (Box 2.4). In other words:

- What processes seem to be having the biggest effect on the child's development or on processes that affect it?

- Which are the greatest protective processes, which might help mitigate against any difficulties?

Box 2.4 Principles underlying analysis: impact

- Severity of difficulty: *the weight of negative processes*
      or
- Magnitude of strength: *the weight of positive processes*

This approach helps to accurately identify strengths on which it may be possible to build and pinpoint areas of vulnerability or risk factors which need action.

ASSESSING THE DEGREE OF SEVERITY OF DIFFICULTIES AND THE MAGNITUDE OF STRENGTHS

The two key elements are severity of difficulty and magnitude of strengths. *Severity of difficulty* is the magnitude or weight of a negative factor or process within or across domains. A factor may look significant but its impact on a child's health and development may or may not be great, e.g. severe poverty. *Magnitude of strengths* is the magnitude or weight of a positive factor or process within or across in any particular dimension (Angold *et al.* 1995). Analysing the impact of positive or negative factors and processes provides a fuller assessment of risk and protective factors. This helps to prioritize where interventions may be needed most urgently and where strengths can be most readily enhanced. There are six aspects of factors and processes that help to gauge their impact, i.e. severity of difficulties or magnitude of strengths. These are:

- intrusiveness

- pervasiveness

- modifiability
- frequency
- duration
- unusualness.

Intrusiveness refers to the extent (or depth) to which a behaviour, emotion, experience, etc. interferes with or contributes to family activity such as family conversation or a child's developmental needs, such as learning, sleep or physical activity. For example, to what extent does a parent's behaviour distract a child who is concentrating, or on the other hand to what extent does a parent's participation extend the child's play? *Pervasiveness* refers to the range (or breadth) of people, situations and activities on which a strength or difficulty has an impact. For example, the greater the number aspects of child development, people or situations that are affected, the greater the concern or benefit. For example, poor concentration at both school and home is a more severe problem than that present in only school or home. *Modifiability* refers to the extent to which other actions, experiences or situations alter or change a factor. For example, a parent is calm and caring despite marital discord; a child's temper tantrums occur only with their mother; a child can distract themselves from anxious or depressing thoughts. *Frequency* refers to the frequency of occurrence of behaviours, experiences and events. How often factors or processes occur is relevant to their effect on child's developmental needs, parenting capacity and family and environmental factors. The more frequent a factor or process, the greater its impact. For example, rows between parents that occur daily as opposed to those occurring monthly. Joint family activity occurring weekly as opposed to yearly. *Duration:* in general, the longer the duration of the strength or the difficulty, the more weight that factor carries, i.e. the more benefit in terms of a strength and the more impairment in terms of difficulty. For example, recurrent stealing over a two-year period versus a one-off episode. A good relationship between a child and teacher that has persisted for a year versus a couple of weeks. *Unusualness:* there are some factors which are exceptional and should be seen as major factors in their own right, even though they may not be frequent, of long duration or pervasive. This is because some behaviours or thought processes that are unusual may indicate a severe need even if there is only a single episode. For example, suicide attempt, a fixed delusion, fire-setting, a non-accidental injury in a young child or running away from home. Some child behaviour or ways of thinking may be normal at one age but unusual at another age, for example, enuresis. Some 'usual' behaviours, emotions or thoughts are common and normal when at low intensity, low frequency or short duration, e.g. depression and anxiety but become more significant at higher levels of frequency or duration.

PARENTAL ACTIONS AND FAMILY AND ENVIRONMENTAL FACTORS

Evaluation of impact can relate also to parents' actions and/or family and environmental factors. For example, parental intrusion may not be pervasive, but involving only one dimension of parenting or one dimension of child need. Or a parent may express anxiety only when the child is ill or may be approving only when the child is engaged in sport. In these contexts, the extent of the parent's involvement – their *intrusiveness* – will affect the degree of influence, i.e. impact. Frequency and duration are also relevant, for example, an isolated or infrequent derogatory remark, occurring only at home, will have less effect than such comments that occur several times a day, not only at home but also in front of peers, teachers and shopkeepers.

Among unusual parenting factors, an episode of physical or sexual abuse may also be 'severe'. Unusual events are more likely to have enduring impact either by their nature or because of other processes that are set in train. Ultimately the greater the effect or impact a factor has on child development, the more severe or beneficial it is. For example, if a child's anxiety has been persistent for six months, and present in all situations in the day, keeping them awake at night and adversely affecting their relationships with family and peers, it is severe. It is intrusive, pervasive across situations, activities and people, not modifiable, frequent and of long duration.

Contributing to the assessment of risk of significant harm

The analysis of the degree of severity of the negative factors in the child's developmental needs and in the parenting capacity and family and environmental factors domains helps to accurately assess the level of risk of harm to a child, and identify the nature of the steps or interventions which may be required to safeguard that child's welfare.

Analysis of the magnitude of positive factors operating in and across all three domains points to protective factors and sources of resilience which should be supported in planning interventions.

Severe negative factors in the parenting or family and environmental domains may signify the likelihood of impairment in development even where none is detectable at the time of assessment. In exploring the degree of severity of negative factors, it is usually the case that

- the more dimensions of domains that show difficulty
- the more frequently those difficulties are manifest
- the longer they have existed
- the less modifiable they are
- the more they intrude upon or adversely affect child development
- then the greater the severity of the problem to be addressed.

Step 5: Predict the likely outlook for the child

The next step is to predict the likely outlook for the child in the light of the analysis of the factors and processes affecting their development. Before planning interventions, it is important to consider what a child's future would be if needs that are being met continue to be met, and needs that are not being met continue to be unmet. The question here is what is likely to happen for a child and family if nothing changes in the current situation. What are likely to be the consequences for the child if there is no intervention?

Both the short-term and long-term consequences need to be considered. Short-term factors relate to how a child is functioning now and in the immediate future, but there may be also important long-term effects for a child if nothing changes in their circumstances. Analysis of the likely shorter and longer-term effects may affect the level of concern and any plans to intervene. At this stage hypotheses are developed predicting the future. Without trying to predict the likely outcome for a child, serious implications of the current situation may be missed. When drawing out the potential implications for a child if things continue as they are, however, it is always important to ask what evidence there is to support the predictions. Neglect is an example where longer term consequences of a poor level of care may not always be recognized.

Predicting the short-term and long-term outlook for the child relates just as much to strengths as it does to difficulties. Having at least some needs met both over the short term and the long term is likely to protect a child against the impact of any difficulties they are likely to encounter. Protective factors in the parenting a child receives and the benefits that come from positive family and environmental factors help children to develop resilience. So it is important to take account of strengths in all domains and dimensions which can be built on, and not just focus on areas of difficulty and risk of harm.

So the questions at this stage are:

1. What are the consequences for the child if each particular need continues to be met:

   (a) in the short term?

   (b) in the long term?

2. What are the consequences for the child if each particular need continues to be unmet:

   (a) in the short term?

   (b) in the long term?

Where possible, predictions should be based on research. For example, that delayed language development predicts difficulties in learning to read; that living with persistently discordant relationships between parents of caregivers reduces the chances of forming satisfactory partner relationship in adult life; that living with a parent who recurrently engages in criminal activity increases the chances that the child will also do so; that in the context of several negative factors, having a good, available and enduring relationship with an adult reduces the likelihood of mental health and relationship difficulties in adult life (Cleaver *et al.* 1999).

Step 6: Plan interventions

The sixth step is planning interventions based on the analysis of the information that has been gathered. The following questions need to be considered:

1. What are the options for interventions which might help support strengths and/or help meet the unmet needs?

2. Which met or unmet child need is each intervention targeted towards?

3. What resources are available?

4. Which agency or professional and approach is the family most likely to cooperate with?

5. Which intervention is likely to produce the most immediate benefit and which might take time?

6. What should be the sequence of interventions and why?

7. Given the severity of the child's needs and the capacity of the family to cooperate, what is the likelihood of achieving sufficient change within the child's timeframe?

These questions are useful in building targeted, focused and realistic plans for intervention.

Options

It is vital to consider options for interventions which might help support strengths as well as those which might help meet the unmet needs.

Target of each intervention

When interventions are being planned, it is essential to be clear as to which met or unmet needs each intervention is targeted towards. This is necessary if interventions are to be effectively monitored.

Available resources

Plans need to be based on the resources actually available in the area and grounded in practical reality. The focus is therefore on what is available and not on what the assessor thinks should be available in the area they work. Existing strengths, for example good relationships or positive activities, should be used and developed.

Cooperation of family

The next question is which of the available resources and approaches are the family most likely to cooperate with or engage with? There is little point in suggesting interventions which the family might struggle to understand or would have little motivation to engage with. If family members have a good relationship with a particular professional, for example, a parent with a health visitor or a child with a particular teacher, this may point to particular interventions or facilitate their implementation.

Immediate and longer term benefits

Some interventions are likely to produce immediate benefits whereas others might take time. For example, practical assistance might have an immediate benefit, while family therapy is likely to take time.

Sequence of interventions

It is also important to consider what sequence of interventions will meet the child and family's needs best. All too often families are given a raft of interventions to engage in. This may reduce their effectiveness. It is a better use of resources and more manageable for the family to limit the number of interventions and deliver them in a sequence which makes sense to the child, family and worker. It may be that some interventions need to be prioritized over others. Experience shows that a success in one intervention is likely to have benefits in other areas.

Timeframe of child

In planning interventions, given the severity of the child's needs and the capacity of the family to cooperate, it is important to consider the likelihood of achieving sufficient change within the child's timeframe and adjust plans accordingly.

Step 7: Identify outcomes and measures which would indicate whether interventions are successful

The seventh step is to identify how it will be known:

- if there has been an improvement in the child's health and development, i.e. whether the unmet child need(s) have been met

- whether that improvement is related to what has been done, i.e. the intervention(s). For example, was the intended intervention implemented and was it implemented at the frequency intended and with the appropriate skill? Has the process or factor at which the intervention is targeted been changed in the desired direction?

Aims in identifying outcomes

The aims in identifying outcomes for a child are to enable measurement of change following intervention. The outcomes must relate to the analysis of the child's developmental needs the contribution of the parenting they are receiving to meet their needs (or not) and the impact of family and environmental factors on both parenting and the child's needs directly. Identifying outcomes requires the following assessments.

ASSESSMENT OF THE CHILD'S DEVELOPMENTAL PROGRESS WITH RESPECT TO A SPECIFIC STARTING POINT

This assessment can be an initial or core assessment, or the commencement of a given intervention. In particular the goal is to explore which dimensions have improved in their developmental trajectory, which are unchanged and which have fallen back. Key outcomes relate to aspects of child development.

At the starting point or commencement of a focused intervention, an assessment will have identified dimensions of the child's development that need to be enhanced. Intervention may have addressed some of these directly, rather than by attempting to influence factors affecting parenting.

For example, a remedial reading scheme may have been instituted for a child with reading difficulties. Outcome assessment aims to check whether the child has progressed on the relevant dimension. If there has been no progress the process will need to be examined.

ASSESSMENT OF CHANGES IN THE FACTORS OR DIMENSIONS OF PARENTING OR IN THE FAMILY AND ENVIRONMENT WITH RESPECT TO THE STARTING POINT

At initial assessment hypotheses will have been made about processes that are thought to be affecting the child's development in either a positive or a negative way. Interventions may have aimed to work on these processes.

Assessment of processes seek to determine whether changes in those processes relate to child development outcomes or factors thought crucial to the child's progress.

It is not just a matter of assessing factors; processes need to be explored also. This must be done systematically in the light of original hypotheses. In the reading example above, progress might be related to frequency. Frequency of remedial sessions could be monitored. In another example, it may have been hypothesized that a mother's unresponsive parenting was due to her depression. The mother's mental state could be monitored and matched with her responsivity towards her child.

ASSESSMENT OF THE EFFECTIVENESS OF ANY INTERVENTIONS

Interventions may aim to work directly on a child need or by addressing relevant factors and processes. In either event an intervention does itself initiate a process. For example, the reading scheme referred to above will have characteristics that influence its effectiveness such as method, e.g. emphasis on phonics, and frequency. The skill of the person implementing the approach can vary. The characteristics of the child will also determine outcome. Some will respond to one approach, others to another. In the preceding example, the depressed mother may have received treatment. Was it effective?

UNDERSTANDING THE CHILD'S PROGRESS AND MODIFYING
INTERVENTIONS

Overall, the aim is to understand the child's progress or lack of it and why, so that interventions can be modified appropriately. This is summarized in Box 2.5.

Box 2.5 Outcomes

The key outcome is the child's developmental progress

The aims are to assess:
- whether the child has progressed and in which dimensions
- how improvements or deteriorations have come about.

Considerations when identifying outcomes

BASELINE ASSESSMENTS AND FOLLOW-UP MEASURES

The assessment of outcomes of intervention necessitates the capacity to measure change over time in:

- the child's development
- the factors and processes thought to influence the child's development.

To assess change there must have been a baseline assessment and follow-up measures so that any changes over the time of the intervention can be identified.

HYPOTHESES ABOUT THE IMPACT OF INTERVENTIONS

It is necessary that there are hypotheses about processes at baseline, or it will not be possible to assess the effectiveness of interventions because the appropriate measures will not have been employed at baseline. The analysis of information gathered during the assessment will have led to hypotheses about what factors and processes are contributing to the child's needs being met or unmet. The interventions need to be based on those hypotheses (see Box 2.6).

Box 2.6 Selecting Measures

To select appropriate measures at baseline there need to be Hypotheses about what the Interventions will do.

NB If change is shown that supports the hypotheses is does not guarantee that it is the Interventions that have brought about the change.

The hypotheses about the processes which are affecting a child and their family should also inform understanding of what the various interventions are predicted to achieve and how they will accomplish this. It is always important to remember that if change is shown which supports the hypotheses it does not necessarily guarantee that it is the interventions that have brought about the change. For example, it may be hypothesized that a mother's excessive alcohol use is linked to poor basic care (PC – basic care) and that changes in her use of alcohol will bring about improvements in hygiene and the diet provided for the child (PC – basic care) and hence improvements in the child's health (CDN – health) and school attendance (CDN – emotional and behavioural). This may prove to be the case. When drinking less the mother becomes more organized and is able to get the child ready for school (PC – basic care and guidance and boundaries). On the other hand, the child's attendance at school may have improved but rather than being attributable to the mother's reduced drinking it may be attributable to other factors such as increased involvement of the grandmother or support from a teacher (F&EF – wider family or community resources) thus increasing his or her motivation to attend school by themselves.

VALIDITY, RELIABILITY AND NORMS OF BASELINE AND FOLLOW-UP MEASURES

Validity

Baseline and follow-up measures need to be valid, i.e. measure what they are intended to measure. This means the assessor knows that the factor they wish to be assessed is addressed by the measure being used.

For example, the *Adult Wellbeing Scale* (Snaith *et al.* 1978) measures aspects of adult well-being and not something else. In using the *Adult Wellbeing Scale*, the assessor can be assured they will obtain a measure of the level of a parent's depression, anxiety and/or inwardly directed and outwardly direct irritability. They will not get ratings of how that parent cares for their child, just as a school register measures attendance at school but not achievement while in school.

Reliability

The measures also need to be reliable (i.e. replicable over time, and give the same results when used by different assessors). This means that the 'measure' returns similar results over at least short time periods, and that trained assessors under comparable circumstances obtain similar scores when used with the same individual or family; for example, when the *Adult Wellbeing* Scale is used by different assessors or the school register by different teachers.

Norms

Standardized measures often provide population norms and scores that can help understand the significance of any change. Population norms means the range of scores obtained in research with a large general population. Norms are the spread of scores found for a defined population of respondents. Thus, it is possible to state what percentage of the population score at different points on the possible range of scores. For example, with the *Strengths and Difficulties Questionnaire* (SDQ: Goodman 1997; Goodman, Meltzer and Bailey 1998) it is possible to predict what percentage of the population (within the relevant age range) would be expected to get the score that a particular child has obtained. In the case of the SDQ the level of scores has also been validated against intensive assessments, so it is possible to predict the likelihood of a substantive problem. This gives an indication about the likely level of strengths and difficulties being presented by that child in terms of their emotional and behavioural development and well-being.

STANDARDIZED AND CASE-SPECIFIC MEASURES

For baseline measures to be replicated at a follow-up, they need to be standardized or operationally defined. It is then possible to assess whether change has taken place between the time of original (baseline) assessment and once the interventions have been implemented.

Standardized measures

Standardized measures are those assessment tools which have operationally defined items which are then scored, e.g. the *Family Pack of Questionnaires and Scales* and the *HOME Inventory*. With questionnaires the range of answers is specified and the respondent just ticks the appropriate response for them. The responses are then summed up and scored according to the scoring instructions for that questionnaire or scale. The resultant score gives a guide as to the presence or absence of a particular factor or problem. With the *HOME Inventory* or the *Attachment Style Interview*, both of which have semi-structured interviews to guide the collection of information, the ratings for scoring the information gathered in the interviews is defined by glossaries. Assessors need to be trained to rate using the glossaries to achieve reliability in their ratings.

Case-specific measures

Case-specific measures can also be used provided they are operationally defined so that they can be replicated over time or used in a comparable fashion by different assessors. To be operationally defined they need to have agreed criteria for counts or ratings. Ratings must be guided by markers for each point on the scale. Otherwise there can be no certainty that baseline and follow-up assessments are comparable. Ratings of behaviour over a period of time, such as a school day, may be unreliable. It may be easier to achieve reliable results by methods that count defined behaviours such as a bed-wetting chart, counting the number of days a child is excluded from school, counting the number of days a child has taken medication for hyperactivity or scoring the number of times a child is 'on task' at fixed times during the day.

There has to be agreement about what measure might indicate that change had taken place. For example, if a child's unhappiness was hypothesized to be linked to parental rows, and couple work had been instituted, how could improvements in the parents' relationship be measured? Possibilities include:

- frequency or number of times parents confided with each other in last month

- frequency or number of parental rows in last month

- joint parental activity in last month.

Criteria would be needed for the outcomes measured, i.e. confiding, rows and joint activity. For example, rows could be defined in terms of raised voices and subsequent tense atmosphere for at least an hour. To assess the child's mood, a possibility would be that the caregiver and/or teacher rates the child's predominant mood each day: happy, neutral, miserable. Then count the days per week for each state over a two-week period at baseline and follow-up. The *Adolescent Wellbeing Scale* (Birleson 1980) might be simpler, but for a younger child it is a less good indicator, because of young children's more rapid shifts of mood. The caregiver and teacher could fill out an SDQ (Goodman 1997; Goodman *et al.* 1998 before and after a period of intervention but, particularly for a younger child this might not reflect the child's predominant state over that period.

The tailor-made rating suggestion would have a more comprehensive cover but even with rating guidance relies on imprecise impressions. It could be better to choose a specific time of day to asses the child's mood – for example, when they come home from school. The caregiver could be asked to chart the child's mood at that point on each day. Criteria would be needed. The caregiver can be asked how they know the child was happy or unhappy. They might say that the child smiles and spontaneously chats about what has happened to them at school, when they are happy; is silent, does not respond to invitations to talk and is unsmiling when they are unhappy. The number of days a week when either of these states was so would be recorded by the caregiver, with intermediate mood being scored as neutral. This is more precise than the rating of daily mood but covers less of the child's life. It could however be a good indicator of the child's state over more than the moment of arriving home from school. In another example, a child might be frequently on report for 'bad' behaviour at school. Number of days on report over a two-week period could be used at baseline and at follow-up because it is readily defined by whether or not there is an entry in the relevant register. Although the measure is relatively crude and superficial, it could have value as representing the extent to which an undesirable process is present. Ideally any intervention would need to be based on hypotheses about the nature of the 'bad' behaviour and the reasons for it. Observation of defined behaviours in class could be used. If the behaviour was poor concentration leading to the child repeatedly getting up from their chair during a lesson, then number of times 'out of chair' in a specific lesson could be used as a measure closer to the actual problem.

However it is only by having an hypothesis about why the child's concentration is poor that intervention can be assessed. For example, if the poor concentration is thought to reflect, for example, an Attention Deficit Hyperactivity Disorder (ADHD) medication could be instituted and any changes noted using school report or times out of chair. If the cause is considered to be due to the child's limited ability, this could be checked and their curriculum modified.

Conclusion

These examples are intended to draw attention to the way that measures may reflect a child's developmental need, and/or the relevant processes, more or less closely. Examination of the various factors involved in these processes leads to a better understanding and assessment of whether interventions are working. Measures can employ a variety of modes such as questionnaire, interview and observation, and may be conducted with any relevant person, child, teacher or caregiver, and in several different settings. The issue for outcome is that the measure, person and setting must be the same at follow-up as at baseline. Children's behaviour may vary according to situation so that outcomes need to be assessed in all appropriate contexts.

Chapter Three

Collecting Information

Evidence-Based Approaches to Assessment

Antony Cox, Liza Bingley Miller
and Stephen Pizzey

Gathering information is the first step in any assessment. Assessments benefit from a systematic approach to understanding a child's needs and how far they are being met. Chapter 2 looked at the value of the *Assessment Framework* (Department of Health *et al.* 2000) as a map of the information which needs to be gathered in order to understand a child's world, and at concepts and principles that underpin information-gathering, analysis and evaluation of outcomes. This chapter considers in more depth the value of *Standardized Assessment Tools* in information-gathering.

It has been seen that good assessment requires a systematic approach planned to ensure the safety of the child, and engagement of the children and other family members. This requires sensitivity to the family's context and circumstances, for example their ethnicity, cultural and religious affiliation, housing, work, schooling and neighbourhood.

So, how can children and families be effectively involved in the assessment process? Can *Standardized Assessment Tools* support a systematic approach that also involves children and families in the assessment process? Do they help to provide evidence both for families themselves and for others and professionals?

This chapter explores:

- The *Standardized Assessment Tools* and associated training packs.

- What are the principles underpinning the use of the assessment tools?

- Why use *Standardized Assessment Tools?*

- What are *Standardized Assessment Tools?*

- Benefits of using *Standardized Assessment Tools.*

- Limitations to using *Standardized Assessment Tools.*

- Training requirements.

- The contribution of the *Standardized Assessment Tools* to assessments using the *Assessment Framework.*

The Standardized Assessment Tools and associated training packs

The Department of Health commissioned the selection of a range of *Standardized Assessment Tools* for professionals working with children in need and their families to help them to make evidence-based assessments relevant to the *Assessment Framework.* Because most of the tools had been developed in a research context, the Department of Health also commissioned the preparation of user guides and associated training packs and courses. The authors of the training pack trained a group of accredited trainers to deliver the training, to enable practitioners to use the tools effectively in practice. The Department for Children, Schools and Families recommends use of these tools in a wide range of assessments involving children and families. Subsequently the authors developed a model of assessment, analysis, planning interventions and identifying and measuring outcomes set out in Chapter 2.

In brief, the assessment tools are: The *HOME Inventory* (Caldwell and Bradley 2003; Cox 2008) which provides an assessment of the quality of parenting and the home environment experienced by the child. The *Family Pack of Questionnaires and Scales* (Department of Health, Cox and Bentovim 2000) which covers a range of individual and family factors affecting both children and adults.

The *Family Assessment* (Bentovim and Bingley Miller 2001) enables practitioners to make an assessment of key aspects of family life and relationships and the impact of family history on the current way in which the family functions.

In My Shoes (Calam *et al.* 2000a, 200b, 2005; Cooper 2006; Cousins 2006; Glasgow 2004; Watson, Calam and Jimmieson 2002) is a computer-assisted interview for helping professionals communicate more effectively with children and vulnerable adults, particularly those with disabilities or learning difficulties. It addresses their experiences, thoughts, feelings and wishes in the various contexts in which they live.

The *Attachment Style Interview* (Bifulco *et al.* 2002a, 2002b) developed by the Lifespan Research Group, Royal Holloway University of London, helps to assess the quality of a couple's marital or partner relationship, their other close relationships, their use of support and their attitudes towards using support. It also provides an assessment of the individual attachment styles of the adult(s) concerned.

What are the principles underpinning the use of the assessment tools?

The principles identified as central to making assessments using the *Assessment Framework* also governed the development of the user guides and training packs for these *Standardized Assessment Tools*. These principles are laid out in the *Assessment Framework* (pp.10–16) and are summarized below. They contribute to well-grounded, evidence-based and fair assessments and should be at the heart of any assessment work with children and families.

Ensuring assessments are child centred

The principal focus should always be the child's health and development. The concerns of the adults in the family are directly relevant, and should be considered in relation to the child's development, but the child's perspective, their understanding and feelings must always be taken into account.

Assessments are rooted in child development

It is critical that workers have a sound understanding of children's development and the factors which influence it. This includes what to expect at different ages and stages, and how a disabled child's development may vary according to the nature of their impairments. Developmental milestones should not be rigidly applied but workers should have knowledge of what to expect at different ages and stages of children's development, so they can identify when further assessment may be required.

Ensuring assessments are ecological in their approach

The child and their needs should be understood within the context of his or her family and wider environment. For example, the impact of supportive grandparents or friendship groups should be taken into account. The difficulties presented by living in a context of economic disadvantage, poor housing, racial discrimination or being a member of a marginalized group have to be understood.

Ensuring equality of opportunity

Ensuring equality of opportunity emphasizes that all children should have the opportunity to achieve their optimal development, and access to appropriate services to achieve that end. This means professionals working sensitively and knowledgeably with diversity of needs, culture, spiritual, religious and social contexts. For example, where English is not a parent's first language, interpretation may be necessary during assessment. Particular effort is required to ensure that children with disabilities understand and participate fully in their assessment.

Working with children and families in partnership

The aim should be to work in partnership with families wherever possible, not as an end itself, but in order to safeguard children and promote their welfare. This means using assessment approaches which are congenial to children and parents, which they can influence, and which help them express their concerns and demonstrate their strengths.

Building on strengths and identifying difficulties

Building on strengths as well as identifying difficulties emphasizes the importance of seeking out strengths, resilience and potential resources in children and families on which to build, as well as making an accurate assessment of areas of difficulty, vulnerability and risk.

Coordinating an inter-agency approach to assessment and provision of services

Children in need, including those who are in need of safeguarding, often have a range of professionals and agencies involved with them and their families. A coordinated and consistent approach is required with a common language. This is facilitated by a balanced, evidence-based approach to assessment.

Ensuring assesssment is a continuing process, not a single event

Understanding what is happening to a vulnerable child requires gathering information from a variety of sources and making sense of it with the family and with other professionals. This has several aspects:

- establishing good working relationships with the child and family
- developing a deeper understanding through multiple approaches to the assessment task
- setting up joint or parallel assessments with other agencies as appropriate
- analysing the findings from these various assessments

- determining what interventions are most likely to be effective for what needs

- identifying outcomes against which the success of the interventions can be tested.

Assessment is therefore an iterative or developing process that should have a number of components and be repeated over time, depending on the child's needs and the outcome of any interventions.

Ensuring assessment fits the purpose

Assessment always needs to fit the purpose it is intended for and should not be over-intrusive, repeated or continued unnecessarily or conducted without any clear purpose or outcome. Using *Standardized Assessment Tools* can help to maintain a clear focus for assessment and provide both qualitative information and quantitative measures of different aspects of children and families' lives. They can be used for baseline assessment at the start of any interventions, monitoring the impact of interventions, and the assessment of change over time.

Providing actions and services in parallel with assessment

It is an important principle that the process of assessment should be therapeutic in its impact on the child and family, rather than detrimental. They should not be left in a worse place than they were prior to the assessment. Assessment can itself have therapeutic value if, for example, it helps the family gain greater understanding of the difficulties they are experiencing and recognize the strengths and resources they have available. This itself may lead to change.

In the safeguarding context there may be an immediate need to take steps to protect a child or provide services. Whenever necessary, actions and services should be provided in parallel with the assessment process, according to the needs of the child, rather than waiting for the completion of the assessment.

Grounding assessment in evidence-based knowledge

Standardized Assessment Tools are evidence based. Their use can add strength to systematic assessment, and promote analysis of processes which leads to well-focused intervention. Continued systematic recording gives an evidence base for monitoring progress in a way that informs each new stage of work.

Why use Standardized Assessment Tools?

It has been seen that assessment aims to

- develop an understanding of the nature and level of a child's needs
- gain an understanding of the factors affecting the child and their needs, including the parenting they receive and other family and environmental factors
- develop partnerships
- prepare for intervention if necessary.

Different assessment approaches access different information. *Standardized Assessment Tools* extend the range of approaches available to the assessor. Their standardized format gives structure to the process, and their use deepens understanding of a child's predicament. Using *Standardized Assessment Tools* brings additional benefits to the assessment both in terms of the quality of the information gathered and the way they help engage children and families. Their use helps to ensure wide coverage of relevant information, including identification of strengths as well as difficulties.

What are Standardized Assessment Tools?

The selected *Standardized Assessment Tools* (the *Family Pack of Questionnaires and Scales*, the *HOME Inventory* and *Family Assessment*, *In My Shoes* and the *Attachment Style Interview*) have all been developed and tested within a research context. The way they are used has been adapted for use in practice.

Standardized Assessment Tools have a range of formats, including questionnaires, scales, semi-structured interviews and observation.

Questionnaires and scales

Questionnaires and scales have lists of items with fixed wording to which a person is invited to respond. For each item the respondent is given a fixed range of options to tick, for example, in the *Adolescent Wellbeing Scale* (Birleson 1980), the person responding looks at each item, such as 'I feel sad' and ticks one of four options: 'never', 'hardly ever', 'sometimes', 'all of the time'. The responses are collated and summed. The resulting score gives guidance about the presence or absence of the factors which that questionnaire or scale is designed to assess, for example, depression in adolescents in the *Adolescent Well-Being Scale*, emotional and behavioural difficulties in children and young people in the *Strengths and Difficulties Questionnaire* (Goodman 1997; Goodman *et al.* 1998).

The development of each questionnaire involved trying out many items relevant to the characteristic or problem to be assessed. The items selected were those which most effectively measured the extent to which the difficulty in question was present or absent.

Family Pack of Questionnaires and Scales

Relevant references to the selected questionnaires and scales are to be found in the *Family Pack of Questionnaires and Scales* (Department of Health, Cox and Bentovim 2000).

This process of development ensures that the questionnaires and scales are both valid and reliable so that they:

- address the areas which are the focus of that particular questionnaire or scale (validity)

- effectively distinguish differences between respondents

- can be scored to give a measure of the feature being assessed, e.g. alcohol use: *Alcohol Scale* (Piccinelli *et al.* 1997); the degree to which daily hassles presented by parenting impact on a caregiver: *Parenting Daily Hassles Scale* (Crnic and Booth 1991; Crnic and Greenberg 1990)

- give a similar score for the same respondent over time if the relevant problem has not changed

- are reliable between raters, i.e. obtain the same score when concurrently scored by different raters or administered by different assessors to the same respondent within a short period of time.

Questionnaires and scales can therefore be relied upon to give useful guidance about the presence or absence of particular factors, such as depression, anxiety and irritability (*Adult Wellbeing Scale*: Snaith *et al.* 1978) or emotional and behavioural strengths and difficulties in children (*Strengths and Difficulties Questionnaire*: Goodman 1997; Goodman *et al.* 1998). Because questionnaires and scales are statistically valid for populations rather than individuals, they cannot guarantee to give a correct assessment for a given individual person on a particular occasion. Any findings must always be considered in the light of a wider assessment.

Using questionnaires and scales in practice

The crucial difference when using questionnaires and scales in practice, rather than research, is to ensure that the meaning underpinning the 'ticks' placed by the respondent on the questionnaire or scale in question are understood. Administration is therefore always followed by discussion of specific responses.

This gives the opportunity to explore the relevant area building on what the respondent has done and clarifies the significance for the child, young person or adult concerned of what they have ticked.

For example, if a young person completing the *Adolescent Well-Being Scale* responds 'most of the time' to the item 'I feel so sad I can hardly bear it' (rather than 'never', 'hardly ever' or 'some of the time'), a practitioner needs to understand more about what the young person is currently experiencing.

If a parent reports a high level of intensity of 'hassle' on one of the 20 daily parenting hassles for those caring for young children (e.g. trouble at mealtimes, arguments and bad behaviour going to the shops), the practitioner asks more about that experience and the pressures and concerns contributing to the level of stress.

Semi-structured interviews and observation

The three selected assessment tools that use a combination of semi-structured interviewing and observation – the *HOME Inventory*, the *Family Assessment* and the *Attachment Style Interview* – are more similar to usual day-to-day practice. The aim is to provide a substantive assessment of parenting and other factors affecting child development. In these assessment tools, the goals of the assessment, i.e. what is to be measured, are carefully defined, but the way in which the information is gathered is more flexible than with the questionnaires and scales. The practitioner meets with the caregiver, caregiver and child or the whole family and questions and observes until they have sufficient information to be able to score the relevant items, guided by a glossary which defines each item. The items or factors being assessed depend on the focus of the assessment tools being used.

The HOME Inventory

The *HOME Inventory* assesses the quality of parenting and the home environment provided for a child. The focus is on the day-to-day experiences of a child that influence their development.

Each *HOME Inventory* consists of a number of items grouped together into subscales which assess relevant aspects of parenting and the child's home context. The inventories were constructed on the basis of research used to generate scorable items reflecting that experience. These were tested in large samples for the strength of their association with relevant aspects of child development, parenting, the home environment and family activities. Items were organized statistically into subscales concerned with different types of child experience, e.g. 'learning materials', parental 'responsivity', 'acceptance' and 'modelling'. When the scales were tested in large samples they were found to be strongly associated with the cognitive, social, emotional and behavioural development of children.

Inventories have been developed for four different age groups between birth and 14 years of age. There are also inventories for children with disabilities and those that are in day care settings. The areas of parenting and the home environment covered for each of the age groups for which there is a *HOME Inventory* are shown in Table 3.1.

Table 3.1 Contents of the *HOME Inventory* subscales

0–3 subscale	3–6 subscale	6–10 subscale	Early adolescent subscale
Responsivity	Learning materials	Responsivity	Physical environment
Acceptance	Language stimulation	Encouragement of maturity	Learning materials
Organization	Physical environment	Emotional climate	Modelling
Learning materials	Responsivity	Learning materials and opportunities	Fostering self-sufficiency
Involvement	Academic stimulation	Enrichment	Regulatory activities
Variety	Modelling	Family companionship	Family companionship
	Variety	Family integration	Acceptance
	Acceptance	Physical environment	

The *HOME Inventory* is scored on the basis of an hour-long home visit with the main carer and child of concern. The task of the assessor is to gather the information needed to score the items in the relevant inventory through questioning and observation, and then add up each subscale. Each item is carefully defined in a glossary to promote consistency in the assessors' rating. The assessor derives a total for each subscale on the basis of scores for individual items, and calculates an overall score by adding subscale scores. Once completed, the *HOME Inventory* provides the assessor with a reliable and validated profile of scores reflecting strengths and difficulties in the areas of parenting and the quality of the home environment addressed.

The interviewing approach used in the HOME Inventory

The *HOME Inventory* was originally developed as a research tool in the USA (Caldwell and Bradley 2001). In the UK version a semi-structured interview schedule has been developed to assist practitioners in the UK to gather the relevant information. The focus of the interview is on a specific day for the child and carer. Unless it is very atypical the previous day is explored in detail to get a full picture of the child's experiences. The aim is to obtain detailed descriptions of events and behaviours by appropriate questioning. This helps to establish what has actually happened as opposed to the caregiver's opinions about what has happened or what 'usually' happens. For use in practice exploration of the child's experience extends beyond the home to other contexts that impact on their development including school and out-of-school activities. The interview schedule provides a series of key questions which take the assessor through the various stages of the child's day. Examples are collected with follow-up questioning about the sequence of behaviours and interactions surrounding any particular event or incidents. Prompts and follow-up questions are provided to facilitate exploration of important areas and to ground the information collected in examples. Details are collected about the frequency, duration and intensity of any difficulties or areas of strength identified. If appropriate, the assessor then seeks information about frequency and duration in the last week, month, six months etc. The questions in the interview schedules are for guidance. It is not expected that they are followed rigidly. Practitioners are encouraged to go beyond the prompts until they can score the items. Once a professional is familiar with the approach the interview schedule can be put to one side and a more flexible style can be used.

The careful exploration of the child's experience of being cared for in the home and other locations they encounter (e.g. school and out-of-school activities) on a particular day, grounded in concrete examples, helps the carer and child to recall actual events. This in turn enables the assessor to gain a more evidence-based assessment derived from reports of what actually happened, added to by observations of the interaction between the carer and child and the home environment itself.

Attachment Style Interview

The *Attachment Style Interview* (ASI) is similarly constructed, with a semi-structured interview designed to help the researcher or practitioner collect sufficient information to be able to score a range of items derived from research. The ASI takes an hour to complete. The practitioner uses the ASI with an adult to explore and assess their partner (if relevant) and other close relationships, quality of other support and attitudes about closeness or distance and overall adult attachment style. This includes areas which can be difficult to explore such as the levels of trust and confiding in a marital or partner relationship, negative aspects of that relationship, any conflicts or violence, as well as attitudes towards seeking and using support.

The *Attachment Style Interview* makes an assessment of:

• quality of marriage or partnership

- quality of close supportive others
- ability to make and maintain supportive relationships and use of support
- secure, avoidant and ambivalent attitudes to attachment
- overall attachment style and strengths and impairments in relating.

The interviewer takes the interviewee systematically through their close relationships and asks for grounded examples of behaviour or sequences of interaction that have taken place recently. The follow-up questioning establishes frequency, duration and intensity. The aim is to gather specific factual descriptions which provide the basis for an evidence-based assessment rather than the more opinion-based descriptions which can form part of such assessments. The interview is audio-recorded to allow the assessor to play back the interview and code and score the information gathered. A manual is provided with benchmark descriptions for all the scored items to increase the reliability of ratings made. As with the other assessment tools, the systematic interviewing approach used in the ASI means the assessor gains a wealth of evidence-based qualitative information about the person's close relationships and their use of support as well as many other aspects of their life.

The Family Assessment

The *Family Assessment* is based on a model of family life and relationships derived from research, clinical practice and the literature on working with families. The model identifies three key areas which it is useful to assess when trying to understand a child's family context:

- family character
- family organization
- family history.

Family character concerns family communication – talking, listening and participation of family members, the emotional life of the family – how feelings are expressed and responded to, family alliances – the nature of different relationships within the family, and family identity – how issues of identity are dealt with by the family.

Family organization involves the everyday tasks undertaken by families. There are two main areas:

- family adaptability – roles and responsibilities and adapting to family life, making decisions and problem-solving, managing and resolving conflicts, and managing relationships with the wider family and the community

- parenting – promoting the development of the children, the nature of attachments between the children and their parents, guidance, care and management of the children.

Family history is the third area explored, looking at the impact of family history – past significant events, circumstances and relationships – on the way family members relate to each other and the manner in which they carry out family tasks.

The model of family life and relationships or family functioning which is used in the *Family Assessment* is illustrated in the Figure 3.1.

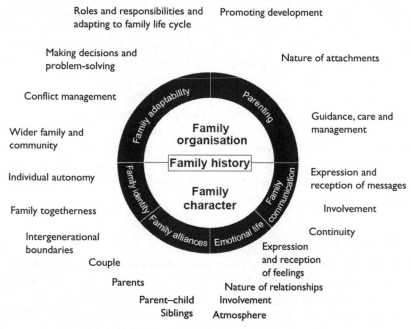

Figure 3.1: The Family Assessment model of family functioning

The model is systemic and interactional in that it particularly focuses on the impact of the different components on each other. So the way family members communicate with each other (family communication) and manage feelings (emotional life) will have an impact on how effectively the family is able to make decisions (making decisions and problem-solving) and manage conflicts (managing and resolving conflicts). Family history affects the way all areas are approached by the family because of past significant events, circumstances, relationships and patterns of relating which adult family members bring to the current family. Positive earlier experiences can increase the resilience of family members and act as protective factors in the face of current difficulties. Past unresolved losses or traumatic experiences or past insecure attachments can all represent sources of vulnerability and risk and impact negatively on the way the current family functions.

The approach uses semi-structured interviews and family tasks for the assessor to gather the relevant information. The assessor is encouraged to collect information about each area of family functioning and family history, and obtain illustrative examples.

A manual provides anchor descriptions for each element of interaction and features that might be observed for families with 'reasonable strengths', 'moderate strengths and difficulties' and 'considerable difficulties' for each element. These were derived from specific research during the development of this *Standardized Assessment Tool* (Kinston, Loader and Miller 1987). This enables the assessor to make both qualitative and quantitative (i.e. score) assessment for each area. A continuum of strength and difficulty (called a *Family Competence Scale*) for each element allows the assessor to make a numerical rating for each element being assessed.

As with the *HOME Inventory* and the ASI, the *Family Assessment* provides a profile of strengths and difficulties in a range of areas. In this case the main focus is family life and relationships and the impact of family history. Again, the use of semi-structured interviews – and in this case also family tasks – provides a wealth of qualitative information which goes far beyond what is scored formally. This helps the assessor to understand the child and family and provides evidence for the assessment.

In My Shoes interview

In My Shoes is a computer-assisted interview which aims to help children, young people and vulnerable adults communicate with a professional about their experiences and feelings in the various settings in which they live. The computer program presents images combined into a carefully structured series of modules designed to help communication about the different settings in which the child lives, the people in those settings and their experiences with those people. The settings could be, for example, their birth, foster or adoptive family, school, leisure activities or contact sessions. The program also includes a module designed to help children show what physical or emotional pain or sensations they have experienced, including abuse.

The approach involves a three-way interaction between child, computer and interviewer. The child is encouraged to be an active participant in using the programme. Manipulation of the images and the use of a range of other tools such as speech and thought bubbles, sculpting figures, writing text messages in boxes and a drawing tool, engage children, giving them a greater degree of control and participation in the interview process.

A results file, generated for every interview, records each choice and input made on the computer and can be printed out, along with the pictures completed during the interview (e.g. of a child's house and family members, or the text messages written by the child). The sequence of modules provides a structured framework which contributes to a systematic approach. *In My Shoes* can be used as a therapeutic tool as well for assessment. Unlike the other *Standardized Assessment Tools* described, *In My Shoes* does not lead to a measure or rating, but it can give information on many aspects of a child's development and experiences, for example their emotional literacy and understanding of different aspects of their world.

Because *In My Shoes* is based on the use of pictures or icons to represent the different aspects of the child's life being explored (e.g. the child themselves, emotions, settings, people in those settings, pain or hurt experienced), it can be particularly helpful for children who are young, those with disabilities and those with difficulties in communication or concentration. It also helps where children or vulnerable adults find it hard to talk face to face or who have language problems. The approach opens up discussion with a child about key experiences and gives them a 'voice' in an exceptional way. The results file is useful for sharing with the child or young person, with other professionals and family members and for forensic purposes.

Benefits of using Standardized Assessment Tools

Because of the way *Standardized Assessment Tools* were developed and tested, they bring a number of benefits to making evidence-based assessments, which include the following.

Consistency

The standardized structure and content of the *Standardized Assessment Tools* and the systematic way they are designed to be administered provides consistency across assessments made by different workers.

Reliability and validity

The sound research background of the *Standardized Assessment Tools* helps to ensure the scores derived from using them have both reliability and validity when administered by professionals trained in their use. This means that different assessors using the same *Standardized Assessment Tool* with a child and/or family will arrive at a similar score (inter-rater reliability), and that the score will also be consistent for assessments made at different points in time (reliability across time) if the characteristic being measured has not changed. Validity means that trained practitioners using the *Standardized Assessment Tools* can also be confident that they are assessing the factors the particular *Standardized Assessment Tool* concerned is focused upon (rather than something else). For example, the *Adult Wellbeing Scale* does address whether a person may be experiencing anxiety, depression or irritability rather than other aspects of that adult's experience.

Norms

The large number of respondents involved in the development of most of the *Standardized Assessment Tools*, and their validation against other measures, enables the assessor to determine not only where their subject's score falls within the general population, but also areas of strength or difficulty.

In the context of practice, it is essential to explore what underpins such scores further to discover their meaning for a specific child or family. With questionnaires and scales, follow-up questioning is necessary. As with all approaches to assessment, none of the *Standardized Assessment Tools* should be used in isolation and all *Standardized Assessment Tools* findings should always be checked against other information and assessments.

Structuring the assessment process

The use of *Standardized Assessment Tools* helps to structure the assessment process by providing a systematic framework for exploring a particular area. This helps the worker to focus on key areas and to cover the range and depth of information necessary to make a sound assessment.

Giving a voice to children and other family members

The various approaches involved in the use of *Standardized Assessment Tools* often give a 'voice' to children and other family members who might otherwise find it hard to contribute to the assessment process. There can be a range of reasons for their not being involved or participating fully in the assessment. Sometimes particular family members feel disempowered because of their place in the family, for example, young children or family members who have experienced violence or abuse. Some may find direct face-to-face communication difficult or have a disability or speech and language problem. Using *Standardized Assessment Tools* may help. Some people find it easier to communicate via a questionnaire than they can in a face-to-face conversation. The triangle created by the worker, the person concerned and their completed questionnaire can establish a more appropriate space for discussion of responses and their significance. Families involved together in a 'family task', from the *Family Assessment*, may be able to be more 'themselves' than when being interviewed as a family group.

Young children are often more able to take part in a 'family task' than they can in a family interview involving questions and answers and discussion.

Identifying strengths as well as difficulties

The use of *Standardized Assessment Tools* helps workers to identify strengths as well as difficulties. It is all too easy, in a problem-focused referral system and service, to miss the areas of strengths and resilience presented by families. The systematic exploration of the full range of experience and behaviours surrounding a specific area helps the worker to avoid focusing only on areas of difficulty and risk. They can help discussion to extend beyond parental preoccupations. Identifying strengths can help to engage families and build a better rapport between the worker and family members. They can also point towards interventions which build on existing strengths as well as tackling difficulties and problems.

Additional data and information

Standardized Assessment Tools not only give guidance about strengths and difficulties in the areas being assessed, but also provide a great deal of additional data gathered through observation and reporting by the child and family. A semi-structured interview approach, for example, may mean workers ask about aspects of a family's life or experience they would not usually ask about (e.g. how family members communicate, decision-making or problem-solving in the *Family Assessment*). Discussion of the meaning of a particular answer in a questionnaire may lead to new information or better understanding of a person's experience, for example, why a past event in the *Recent Life Events Questionnaire*, (Brugha 1985) is still affecting someone and in what ways. A focus on what has actually happened for a child on a specific day using the *HOME Inventory* can reveal much about family relationships.

Assessment of change

Standardized Assessment Tools provide a systematic, reliable and valid assessment of a specific area, therefore they are ideally suited to assist with the assessment of change over time. They can therefore help monitor the effectiveness of an intervention or support package and identify whether targets have been achieved. If two different workers administer the same *Standardized Assessment Tool* at different points – i.e. at the beginning and end of a piece of work with a family – then greater reliability can be placed on the evaluation of the nature and degree of any changes that have taken place. Thus one worker could administer a *Standardized Assessment Tool* at the start of an assessment and another worker could use it at the end of a six-month period to monitor change.

Limitations to using Standardized Assessment Tools

There are limitations to using *Standardized Assessment Tools* that need to be taken into account when planning an assessment, for example focus, validity and multiple sources of information.

Focus

Each *Standardized Assessment Tool* is designed to assess specific areas of individual or family functioning or experience and, while additional information is likely to be gathered from their use, they cannot be relied on to provide all the information needed for an assessment. It is important to check what is not known or understood and use a range of sources and approaches to gain a full appraisal of the child and the factors affecting their well-being and development.

Validity

The statistical validity derived from the development of the *Standardized Assessment Tools* as research tools does give greater weight to findings resulting from their use. However, the validity is statistical and what is statistically valid in a large research population may not apply in an individual case in a particular context. A professional using a *Standardized Assessment Tool* must always check whether the information obtained matches up with and makes sense in the light of other information known about the child and family. If it does not, further exploration will be needed.

Multiple sources of information

The basic principle that good assessments should build on different sources of information (e.g. child, family, school, wider family, health visitor and other professionals), use different approaches and occur on different occasions is equally true for *Standardized Assessment Tools*. It may be crucial to know, for example, that children's behaviour varies when they are with different people (e.g. with each parent during contact) or in different contexts (e.g. at school or at home). Varied methods of assessment on different occasions and the perspectives of different assessors or professionals, add depth and weight to assessments.

Professional judgements therefore need to be based on an integration of information from a whole range of sources and perspectives.

Training requirements

Skills in interviewing children and families

There are specific skills for interviewing and observing children and families and for scoring each *Standardized Assessment Tool*, so training is required to use them effectively. The training programmes to teach professionals to use the *Standardized Assessment Tools* presented in this book have several key components – the first being the interview approaches and specific interviewing methods associated with using each *Standardized Assessment Tool*. These skills help a worker to explore a specific area in a systematic, structured way using both observation and careful exploration of examples. These approaches are central to enabling an assessor to test hypotheses about what is going on with the child and family and provide evidence for the emerging assessment.

Workers are trained to use a range of questioning approaches to help children and other family members talk more easily about their experiences and take a more active part in the assessment process.

Assessment skills using Standardized Assessment Tools

Training is also required to learn how to use the *Standardized Assessment Tool* to gather reliable and evidence-based information in a systematic way that is consistent with the guidance associated with the tools. Assessors need to score each *Standardized Assessment Tool* reliably, know how to interpret the scores which are obtained, and to place those findings in the context of the wider assessment.

Having gathered information efficiently, the next step (which was outlined in Chapter 2) is to categorize and analyse that information and plan outcome-focused interventions based on that analysis. Training professionals in the use of a model of analysis and outcome-focused planning using the *Assessment Framework* triangle as the basis for the analysis and planning forms the third component of a number of the training programmes linked to each *Standardized Assessment Tool*.

The contribution of the Standardized Assessment Tools to assessments using the *Assessment Framework*

How can these standardized tools and evidence-based approaches be used in assessment? What information do the *Standardized Assessment Tools* help to gather about the child's developmental needs, parenting capacity, and family and environmental factors? The charts in the Appendix (see p.325) lay out some of the factors which may emerge in each of the dimensions when using the different tools. Assessors will also explore the impact of different factors on each other following the administration of the questionnaires and scales and during the HOME, Family Assessment and Attachment Style Interview. Some examples are given.

Chapter Four

Gathering Information, Analysis and Planning Interventions

A Case Example – The Ward Family

Stephen Pizzey, Liza Bingley Miller
and Antony Cox

This chapter uses a case example, the Ward family, to demonstrate the application of the principles of *assessment, analysis, planning interventions and measuring outcomes* set out in Chapter 2 and the use of some of the *Standardized Assessment Tools* described in Chapter 3 to gather information.

Ward family structure

Mrs Moira Ward is in her early thirties and is the mother of Laura, aged 14 years, and Michael, who is eight years old. Laura and Michael's father is Bill Ward, who they have not seen for six years. Over 15 months ago Moira Ward's previous partner, Gary Wills, left the family after three years. He had been much loved by all the family and his departure caused them considerable distress. The family structure is illustrated in Figure 4.1.

Ian Ross is Moira Ward's partner, and he has been living with the family for the past year. He is in his late thirties. Ian Ross has a son of Michael's age, called Alan, who lives with his own mother. Ian Ross does not currently see his son.

Step 1: Consider the referral, the safety of the child, and the aims of the assessment

Michael's school has referred him to children's services because of its concern about a marked change in his behaviour and appearance over the last year. He has become increasingly anxious, distracted and unable to concentrate. He is

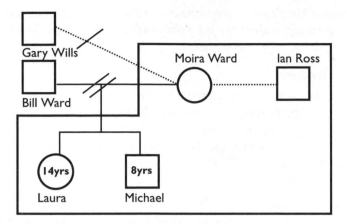

Figure 4.1: Ward family structure

persistently late and has a neglected appearance, having previously always been smartly turned out. He often appears to be hungry. His performance at school has deteriorated. Michael has talked about his mother's new partner shouting at him and sometimes hitting him if he does not do what he is told. No evidence of marks or injury has been noted.

Michael's presentation at school contrasts quite significantly with how he appeared a year ago. Then he seemed quite a happy child who had a reasonable circle of friends and who was generally performing at an average level at school. His circle of friends has reduced and he is sometimes seen to be on his own at playtime. His teacher has noted that he often complains of headaches or stomach-aches, seems worried, comes to her for more attention than he used to and is generally less confident.

Laura, his sister, has been truanting from school and Moira Ward was asked to go into school for a meeting but unusually did not attend.

The referral information did not raise a concern about the need for immediate protection, notwithstanding that there was reference to Michael reporting he had been hit on occasions by Ian Ross. Michael's reported deterioration appears to have occurred during the time that Ian Ross has lived in the home and after Moira Ward's separation from Gary Wills. It was decided in the first instance to meet Michael after school with his mother and Ian Ross to get a picture of his experience in their care.

Step 2: Gather additional information

An assessment using the *HOME Inventory* was carried out with Michael and his mother during the first meeting. Ian Ross could not attend because of work commitments. He arrived towards the end of the meeting and completed some questionnaires and scales from the *Family Pack of Questionnaires and Scales.*

HOME Inventory

The *HOME Inventory* provides an assessment of the quality of parenting and the home environment provided for the child. The procedure for administering the *HOME Inventory* in the UK is to take the child and main carer(s) through a specific day, usually the previous day or previous weekday, using a semi-structured interview approach.

UK INTERVIEWING APPROACH

Interview schedules, structured in terms of a specific day, have been developed for use in training and practice (Cox 2008; Cox and Walker 2002a). When the interviewer takes the parent or carer and child or young person through the specific chosen day, the interviewer asks for a detailed description of what actually happened that day and follows this up by enquiring about the frequency and duration of similar incidents in the last week, month etc. If something important has not happened in the day in question (for example, seeing friends, setting boundaries), the interviewer then asks about the last time the particular factor occurred. Flexible questioning is encouraged to ensure coverage of the items in the inventory, which are scored on the basis of what is observed and reported. Structuring and conducting the interview this way helps to get a grounded evidence-based picture of the child's experience of parenting and their life at home. The interview takes about an hour.

HOME INVENTORY INTERVIEW WITH MOIRA WARD AND MICHAEL

At the outset of the interview Moira Ward said she was more concerned about Laura. She said, 'Laura's the one giving me all the trouble'.

The interviewer asked how long the family had been in their current house and Moira Ward said she had lived in the house for about 15 months, following a move because she 'didn't want any reminders of Gary'. She said Ian Ross had moved in about a year ago. Michael said, 'February 19th'. The interviewer noted that Michael had a good memory and Moira Ward replied with a smile, 'You're my little brain box aren't you?'

It was explained that school had expressed concern about Michael and that a helpful way to understand the situation was to go through a school day. It was agreed to discuss the previous day. The interviewer asked Moira what happened right at the start of the day. Moira Ward said Ian Ross got up but that she had not heard him. Michael said he heard Ian Ross 'having a go at Laura in the bathroom' at 7.00a.m. He said, 'They are always arguing him and Laura'.

Michael woke Moira Ward who 'had been a bit tired recently and had overslept' (all week). Laura had already left for school.

Moira was then asked what had happened about Michael's breakfast yesterday. Michael got his own breakfast. Moira Ward thought that being nearly nine years old he ought to be able to do this. Michael had a bun for breakfast, which surprised Moira Ward. He said there was no cereal and that on a number of occasions he had 'told' his mother to get some in the shopping. Moira Ward dressed while Michael had his breakfast.

Michael said he could not find any clothes. Moira Ward said she thought Michael was old enough to get his own clothes. This was Ian Ross's idea and she agreed with him. Moira Ward was not sure whether Michael had washed that morning. Moira Ward said she could not do everything and said to Michael, 'That's probably why I'm so tired running after you all the time'. She agreed that getting Michael ready was a bit of a 'hassle' and that Michael 'got under her skin' and 'it got to the point of shouting' because he is late for school and the teachers complain and try to give him detention. When asked how often this had happened that week, she said it had happened every day.

Michael was asked about what happened when he arrived at school, and he said he had to sign the late book. Moira Ward said it was not her fault he was late because 'he should get his stuff ready the night before'. She said, 'Michael, you're really gonna get it if you don't buck your ideas up'. She was asked what 'get it' meant and said he would get 'a really good telling off'. Michael said, 'Hits me'. Moira Ward clarified this saying that Ian Ross 'doesn't hit him hard' and that it was 'just a little smack on the back of the legs or something. Just disciplining him.' Moira Ward was asked how often this sort of thing happened. She replied 'a lot lately' and that the letters from school 'wind Ian up'. She said Ian Ross 'has a word with Michael' and 'We've got to knock it on the head now; we've got to discipline him'.

On being asked the last time it had happened, Michael said 'Monday'. Moira Ward explained that 'as Michael was always late for school, he was grounded and not allowed to go out'. Michael had then pulled funny faces. Ian Ross thought this was being cheeky so he gave him a 'clip'. Moira Ward said, 'He don't hurt him or nothing'. When asked what she had done at this point, Moira Ward said that she could not stand it any more and sat down and cried. She said she had felt much better after a good cry. Moira Ward was asked how often Ian Ross 'clipped' Michael. She said it 'happened quite a lot recently but not every day'. She thought it was about two or three times a week. The interviewer asked Moira Ward and Michael where Ian Ross 'clipped' Michael. Moira Ward said it was mainly on his legs although occasionally he gave Michael a 'clip' on the ear. While this discussion was taking place, Michael periodically interjected saying he was hungry, but his mother did not respond.

Michael was asked about his school day. He liked 'computing'. He had only played once or twice this week with his friend Jamie at playtime. He was not allowed to have any friends home. Moira Ward explained that this was because he was usually grounded and if he had friends home, 'he's not gonna learn a lesson'. On being asked how often different family members went out together, Moira Ward said she had 'not taken Michael out lately'. When shopping Laura did not like Michael hanging around because 'he plays up'. Ian Ross and Michael last went out together 'about two weeks ago' to play football. Ian Ross came back in 'a really bad mood because Michael was winding him up because he wasn't trying to play'. The family have few visitors. Moira Ward last saw a member of her family just before she moved to their present address.

Next the interviewer asked about Michael's homework. Moira Ward said she did not insist on homework being completed until shortly before Ian Ross was due home. Moira Ward was not sure whether Michael completed his homework. On being asked, she said that neither she nor Ian Ross gave Michael any help with his homework. She said Michael did not need this and that this was the job of teachers. Michael has few hobbies or interests. Michael was going to join a computer club but they could not afford the fees.

The interviewer asked when Ian Ross had got home from work, and what happened at that point. Moira Ward said he got home about 6.30p.m. and everyone sat down for dinner at 7.00p.m. She explained, 'Dinner's ready when Ian gets home'. On further enquiry, it emerged that Laura did not eat with the family. Moira Ward said Laura does not like eating with Ian Ross. Moira Ward was not sure whether Laura had eaten anything that night and said that Laura was 'fussy' about what she ate and 'concerned about her weight'. Ian Ross, Moira Ward and Michael had shepherd's pie and peas. She said Michael 'eats what he gets'. He prefers crisps to fruit.

Next the interviewer asked what had happened about getting Michael to bed. Moira Ward said she told Michael to get ready for bed at 9.00p.m. When she went upstairs at 9.30p.m., he had not had a bath and as it was late she told him to go straight to bed. She turned the light off in the hall. She said, 'Michael's got a problem with the hall light. He likes to keep it on but Ian thinks he's being a wimp'. Moira Ward said she felt a bit guilty turning the light off but felt that he was not going to learn unless she did it. Moira Ward said Michael just had to get used to having the light off. She said, 'You've got to be cruel to be kind'.

HOME INVENTORY: SCORING THE INFORMATION GATHERED DURING THE INTERVIEW

The *HOME Inventory* focuses on an exploration of the nature and variety of a child's day-to-day experiences, the quality of the child's home environment and the parenting capacity of the caregivers from a perspective that is as close as possible to that of the child. The *HOME Inventory* is based on a substantial body of research regarding factors, which are supportive of positive child development. The *HOME Inventory's research base, which is worldwide, has steadily expanded since the 1960s.*

There are a number of *HOME Inventories* for children aged 0–3, 3–6, 6–10 and 10–14. The Middle Childhood *HOME Inventory* (6–10) was used to assess Michael's experience of care with his mother and Ian Ross. The inventory comprises a number of subscales, which measure different aspects of a child's experience. They are:

- *Responsivity* – parental warmth and affection, approval and verbal interaction.

- *Encouragement of maturity* – the extent to which parents expect the child to demonstrate socially responsible behaviour and conform to family rules. Individual items reflect parental actions designed to foster the acquisition of these indicators of maturity.

- *Emotional climate* – punishment experienced by the child, parental emotional composure and response to child's negative feelings.

- *Learning materials and opportunities* – the availability of a range of materials to meet the child's developmental needs.

- *Enrichment* – the extent to which the parents consciously utilize family and community resources to enrich the development of the child in activities outside of the home.

- *Family companionship* – the extent the child is involved with the parents in activities providing companionship and mutual enjoyment.

- *Family integration* – the involvement of a 'father figure' in the child's life and a life history characterized by a consistent primary family group.

- *Physical environment* – aspects of the child's physical environment that may impact on their development – for example, health or concentration.

Each of the above subscales has a number of items, which are set out in the HOME Inventory Record Form. Each item is scored 'plus' or 'minus' according to its definition in the glossary. The total number of 'pluses' make up the subscale score. The sum of all the subscale scores provides a total overall score. The scores for each subscale are compared to the median score for the particular subscale, that is, the most commonly occurring score in the research on general population samples. Where actual scores are two or three points below the median, concerns are raised. Similarly where the total score is seven points below the median, a concern is raised about the child or young person's overall experience of care. The *HOME Inventory* scores have been found to discriminate better between 'good enough' care and low quality care for a child, than between 'good enough' and high quality care.

RESULTS OF THE HOME INVENTORY INTERVIEW

The *HOME Inventory* scores revealed significant concerns regarding Michael's overall experience of care in the family household. The total overall score was 19 points below the median score. In particular, concerns were raised in the following areas: *responsivity, encouragement of maturity, emotional climate, enrichment* and *family companionship*. Most of the subscales in which Michael's care was found to be inadequate were those involving parental actions and family events. Those subscales where there was less concern were those that included household objects and residential conditions, i.e. *learning material and opportunities, family integration* and *physical environment*.

The interview revealed that Ian Ross was hitting or 'clipping' Michael as often as two or three times a week, Moira Ward often got up late, Michael had to prepare his own breakfast from what he could find available and Michael was being required to sleep without the hall light on, causing him distress. Michael appeared to have few friends at school and few opportunities to sustain friendships as he appeared to be regularly 'grounded'.

Family Pack of Questionnaires and Scales

Some of the questionnaires and scales were chosen to use with Moira Ward and Michael. All the questionnaires and scales contained in the pack were selected because of their value in obtaining information relevant to assessing children and families. Most of the questionnaires and scales have been designed to be completed by respondents but can also be used as mental checklists for the assessor. Many questionnaires have been designed to screen for particular problems or needs. They have been standardized so that a score above a particular cut-off point indicates the strong probability of a significant problem of the type for which the questionnaire or scale is screening. This can be a useful guideline, but it must be remembered that scores above or below a particular cut-off do not guarantee the presence or absence of a significant problem in the individual case. Further discussion is necessary to clarify whether respondents are over-or under- representing their needs. In day-to-day practice, each of the questionnaires and scales provides a useful indicator as to the presence of strengths and difficulties and, equally importantly, can be used as a vehicle for opening up further for discussion between the worker and the respondent about relevant areas of individual and family life.

STRENGTHS AND DIFFICULTIES QUESTIONNAIRE

The *Strengths and Difficulties Questionnaire* (SDQ: Goodman 1997; Goodman *et al.* 1998) was used with Michael (see below). The SDQ focuses on children's emotional and behavioural strengths as well as difficulties. It incorporates five scales: *pro-social* (kind, cooperative and helpful behaviour), *hyperactivity, emotional problems conduct* (behavioural) *problems* and *peer problems*. There are versions of this scale to be completed by adult caregivers, teachers for children aged 3–16, and young people between the ages of 11 and 16.

The scores are grouped into four bands so that in the general population roughly 80 per cent of children score 'close to average', 10 per cent score 'slightly raised', 5 per cent score 'high' and 5 per cent score 'very high'. The exception is the scale for 'kind and helpful behaviour' with roughly 80 per cent scoring 'close to average', 10 per cent 'slightly low', 5 per cent 'low' and 5 per cent 'very low'.

The information provided by the respondents is used to predict how likely a child is to have emotional, behavioural or concentration problems severe enough to warrant a diagnosis. For each diagnostic grouping, there are three possible predictions: 'low risk', 'medium risk' and 'high risk'. In general, these predictions agree fairly well with what an expert would conclude after a detailed assessment of the child. Around 25–60 per cent of the children who are rated as 'high risk' do turn out to have the relevant diagnosis according to experts. So do around 10–15 per cent of 'medium risk' children but only about 1–4 per cent of 'low risk' children.

It should be stressed that these are questionnaires that are used for screening for the possibility of the presence of difficulties. Greater reliance can be placed on the results if they are supported by other assessments, which point to similar conclusions.

Results from Michael's Strengths and Difficulties Questionnaires

Moira Ward and Michael's class teacher completed the SDQ. The results varied in that the teacher rated Michael as having overall a high level of need whereas Moira Ward rated him as having a low level of need. The teacher has known Michael for a considerable time, raising the possibility that Moira Ward's reporting reflected her perception of Michael in the past rather than in his present circumstances. Alternatively Michael may present differently at school as compared to how he presents in the home. Michael was rated as having low pro-social needs, thus the outlook for intervention with him is better.

Michael was not rated by either his mother or his teacher as having any conduct problems but was seen as having significant emotional needs and peer problems. The picture that emerged was of Michael being rather isolated and being picked on and bullied by other children. He was noted to complain often of headaches, stomach-aches and sickness, and he appears unhappy, downhearted and tearful. He was rated as having 'some need' in the area of hyperactivity, being easily distracted and with concentration that tended to wander.

The interviews with Moira Ward and Michael's teacher corroborated this picture. Moira Ward could name only one friend, Jamie. Moira Ward said that on the previous night Michael squirmed and fidgeted when Ian came home, and was nervous and clingy when the hall light was turned off at bedtime. Michael's teacher said that in the last week he played only with Jamie, was bullied at least twice, and was seen standing near the dinner ladies at playtime.

Overall Michael was found to be at 'high risk' of having an emotional disorder, 'medium risk' of a hyperactivity or concentration disorder and low risk of a 'behavioural' disorder.

ADOLESCENT WELLBEING SCALE

The *Adolescent Well-Being Scale* screens for depression in young people between the ages of 11 and 16. It was originally validated for children as young as seven or eight although this younger group of children have been found to be less consistent in their reporting of their feelings.

Results from Michael's Adolescent Wellbeing Scale

Michael's completion of this scale revealed that he scored significantly above the cut-off point indicating the probability that he might be suffering from a depressive disorder. It was particularly noteworthy that 'most of the time' Michael felt he could not stick up for himself, and he felt very lonely and very bored. The subsequent interview with Michael on his own corroborated this picture. He said he 'felt lonely in the playground every day'. He could not stick up for himself in the playground on the previous day when he was called names and this happened all the time. He 'is bored all the time because he has no one to play with'. These findings reinforced the teacher's comments about his peer relationships reported earlier using the *Strengths and Difficulties Questionnaire*.

FAMILY ACTIVITY SCALE

The *Family Activity Scale* (Smith 1985) provides an opportunity to explore with carers the environment provided for their children, through joint activities and support for independent activities. The scale asks questions about activities that were undertaken with a child over the last year. Some of the questions refer to the previous three months.

Results from Family Activity Scale completed by Moira Ward and Michael Ward

Michael and his mother completed the *Family Activity Scale*. Michael had not had a friend visit in the last month, had not been out with the family in the last three months, nor had he seen family members. The overall impression was that

Michael's opportunities for social contact with others were quite restricted. The social worker asked Michael and Moira Ward what they thought the results would have been if the scale had been completed a year ago. They both indicated that he had been involved in more activities in the past.

HOME CONDITIONS SCALE

The *Home Conditions Scale* addresses various aspects of the home environment (for example, smell, state of surfaces in the house and the floors). Total scores have been found to correlate highly with indices of development in children.

Results of Home Conditions Scale for Ward family

The scale revealed a satisfactory level of household cleanliness in the home, notwithstanding that Michael's bedroom was dusty and appeared not to have been cleaned recently.

RECENT LIFE EVENTS QUESTIONNAIRE

The *Recent Life Events Questionnaire* focuses on recent life events and respondents are asked to indicate whether the event has occurred and, if so, whether it still affects them.

Results from Moira Ward's Recent Life Events Questionnaire

Moira Ward said the separation from Gary Wills still affected her. She said her family disapprove of her relationship with Ian Ross and that as a consequence she had not seen them for some time. Her recent house move had not been by choice. She felt she had to move because she found it difficult remaining in the same home that she had shared with Gary Wills.

Brief family meeting using part of the Family Assessment

A brief meeting was held with Moira Ward, Ian Ross, Michael and Laura. A module of the *Family Assessment* called *Mapping the current identified problem(s), concerns and difficulties* was used as a basis for the discussion. This module seeks to obtain a detailed description from family members of the current identified problem, which has resulted in the referral and to get the views or perspectives of different family members on the 'problem'. The impact of the problem on individual family members and on family life is explored as well as the attempted solutions, which have already been tried. The interviewer also gathers information about other current concerns or difficulties being experienced by different family members.

RESULTS OF BRIEF FAMILY MEETING WITH THE WARD FAMILY

Ian Ross and Moira Ward said their main concern was Laura's behaviour. They said she was giving them trouble by arguing with Ian Ross, spending increasing time out of the home and returning late without saying where she had been. Laura said the family had changed following the arrival of Ian Ross, who had altered how they did things in the family. She said this had affected Michael, who was not sleeping properly and was left to get himself ready for school because Moira Ward did not get up on time. Laura said she had to take Michael to the doctor one morning recently because their mother was still in bed. Moira Ward said she was tired of all the arguments. The couple were asked about discipline in the household and whether physical punishment was used. Ian Ross said he didn't use physical punishment preferring to use other techniques such as 'grounding'. Michael remained quiet throughout the discussion.

Ian Ross and Moira Ward were agreed that the main problem was the arguments between Ian Ross and Laura. They were asked about the last time this had happened. Laura said that last week Ian Ross came into her room without her permission at about 11.00p.m. She said he was aggressive in tone and he demanded that she tell him where she had been. Ian Ross said that Moira Ward had been worried about where Laura had been and with whom she had been associating. Laura replied that he tried to tell her what to do even though he was not her father. Michael was asked if he heard the argument. He nodded and said it had kept him awake.

Moira Ward gave her permission to the social worker to contact the family doctor about Michael. The doctor reported that Michael has generally enjoyed good health. He was last seen about a heavy cold, and unusually was brought to the surgery by his sister, Laura, rather than his mother.

Using further questionnaires and scales with the family

Further questionnaires and scales were administered with the family to gather further information relating to concerns raised in the brief family meeting.

RESULTS FROM LAURA'S STRENGTHS AND DIFFICULTIES
QUESTIONNAIRES

Moira Ward, Laura's teacher and Laura were asked to complete the SDQ in respect of Laura. The results vary in that Moira Ward rated Laura as having a 'very high' level of need in terms of behavioural difficulties. This was having a 'very high' impact on Laura's life. In contrast the teacher rated the level of concern in these same areas as 'slightly raised'. Laura rated herself as having a 'slightly raised' level of need in terms of behavioural difficulties, which were having a 'very high' impact on her life.

Moira Ward, Laura's teacher and Laura were interviewed. Moira Ward and Laura referred to regular arguments taking place between Ian Ross and Laura.

The teacher referred to Laura becoming involved in arguments with peers and not being as cooperative as she used to be. Laura reported that her concentration had suffered over the last year. Moira Ward reported that Laura had become disobedient and Laura referred to herself as being angry and unhappy.

Overall Laura was found to be at 'high risk' of having a 'behavioural' disorder and 'low risk' of an emotional disorder, hyperactivity or concentration disorder.

RESULTS FROM LAURA'S ADOLESCENT WELL-BEING SCALE

Laura's completion of the *Adolescent Well-Being Scale* revealed that she scored above the cut-off point, indicating the probability that she might be suffering from a depressive disorder. Laura's scoring of specific items on the scale revealed that Laura 'never' 'looked forward to things as much as she used to'. She 'sometimes' did not 'sleep well', had 'horrible dreams', 'thought life isn't worth living', felt 'lonely' and 'so sad she could hardly bear it'. The subsequent interview with Laura on her own revealed that the source of much of her unhappiness was the impact of Ian Ross's arrival in the home; she spoke of having less time with her mother, arguing constantly with Ian Ross, and feeling lonely and sad in the home.

Parenting Daily Hassles Scale

The *Parenting Daily Hassles Scale* (PDH) aims to assess the frequency and intensity or impact of 20 potential parenting 'daily' hassles experienced by adults caring for children. It has been used in a wide variety of studies concerning children and families – particularly families with young children. It has been found that parents (or caregivers) generally like filling it out, because it touches on many aspects of being a parent that are important to them. Although the scale is primarily aimed at parental stresses involved in raising younger children, the scale can be used with older children.

RESULTS FROM PARENTING DAILY HASSLES SCALE COMPLETED BY MOIRA WARD AND IAN ROSS

Moira Ward and Ian Ross completed the PDH, which revealed they were both experiencing a high level of intensity of challenging behaviour. Events such as mealtimes, requesting children to do things and being in public with the children were rated as 'high hassle' for Ian Ross. The couple had a discussion about the results. Ian Ross spoke about Moira Ward sometimes 'almost giving up' and allowing the children, particularly Laura, to walk all over her. Moira Ward was asked whether the children had presented such high levels of challenging behaviour when they were younger and she said that she thought this was not the case. Laura emerged as one of the principal causes of 'hassles' for both Ian Ross and Moira Ward.

Adult Wellbeing Scale

The *Adult Wellbeing Scale* looks at how an adult is feeling in terms of depression, anxiety, outward-directed irritability and inward-directed irritability. Inward-directed irritability can point to the possibility of self-harm and outward-directed irritability raises the possibility of angry actions towards a child or children. Respondents are given the choice of four answers to 18 questions, ranging from cheerfulness, to appetite and to angry responses. Scores are provided for each area of adult well-being and individual scores are rated as either being 'above the borderline', indicating the possibility of a problem, to 'borderline' and 'below borderline'

RESULTS FROM ADULT WELLBEING SCALES COMPLETED BY MOIRA WARD AND IAN ROSS

Ian Ross and Moira Ward each completed the *Adult Wellbeing Scale*. The results showed that Moira Ward was 'above the borderline' for depression and in the 'borderline area' for anxiety, outward-directed irritability and inward-directed irritability. Ian Ross was found to be 'below the borderline area' for everything except outward-directed irritability where he was in the 'borderline area'. It should be borne in mind that men are often found to under-report emotional matters in questionnaires. The results of the scale were discussed with Moira Ward and Ian Ross. Moira Ward felt she had been a bit 'down lately' but did not think she was depressed. She felt tense and wound up most of the time about Ian and Laura arguing and angry with herself a lot of the time because she's been oversleeping and not getting Michael to school on time. She experienced an uncomfortable feeling like butterflies every day when Ian Ross was due to return home and felt panicky when Ian Ross insisted on turning the light out when Michael went to bed.

Ian Ross was surprised he was in the 'borderline area' for outward-directed irritability. He said he was a man who 'liked to be able to keep control of himself' and 'liked things to be clear and straightforward'. He said he saw himself as sorting out the family's problems. Ian Ross said he felt tense or wound up when Laura argued with him and that could cause him to slam the door in frustration. He becomes angry when Michael fails to do his homework and snaps at Michael when he behaves like a 'wimp'. He feels irritated with Moira Ward when she 'gives in to Michael and Laura'.

Alcohol Use Questionnaire

Alcohol misuse is estimated to be present in about 6 per cent of primary carers, ranking it third in frequency behind major depression and generalized anxiety. Adults often underestimate their levels of drinking when reporting them to their doctor and others, but when completing questionnaires have been found to be more honest about their drinking habits. The primary benefit of this particular scale is that it opens up an opportunity for discussion about alcohol use.

RESULTS FROM ALCOHOL USE QUESTIONNAIRE COMPLETED BY MOIRA
WARD AND IAN ROSS

Moira Ward and Ian Ross completed the *Alcohol Use Questionnaire*. Ian Ross's completion of the questionnaire suggested a low level of regular consumption of alcohol. Moira Ward's completion of the questionnaire revealed past concerns expressed by others about her consumption of alcohol. She denied there were any current difficulties in this regard.

Step 3: Categorize available information and organize it within the *Assessment Framework* triangle: what is known and not yet known

The referral in this case example focused on Michael. As the interviews progressed, particularly when the family were interviewed together, it became apparent that there were concerns about Laura and that these appeared to be linked to the arrival of Ian Ross in the family home. It was recognized that further discussion with the family was required to make sense of this. At this stage a focus on Michael will be followed. Consideration of Laura's situation will be included in Chapter 5. The information gathered during the two interviews was then categorized into the relevant dimensions of each domain of the *Assessment Framework*.

Michael's development needs

HEALTH

Michael is reported to have generally enjoyed good physical health. More recently he is reported to be tired on arrival at school so may have suffered from lack of sleep. He has a consistent evening meal but he either goes without breakfast or has very little. He is reported to be hungry at school in the morning. Michael is reported to complain of headaches and stomach-aches at school.

EDUCATION

Michael's performance at school has deteriorated. Previously he had been performing at an average level and he is now underachieving. His school report emphasized his concentration was often poor and he had difficulty in settling to tasks.

EMOTIONAL AND BEHAVIOURAL DEVELOPMENT

The results of the *Adolescent Well-Being Scale* suggest he may be suffering from a depressive disorder and the results of the SDQ provided a diagnostic prediction that Michael is at high risk of having an emotional disorder. There is evidence from the SDQ that Michael is at medium risk of having hyperactivity or concentration disorder.

IDENTITY

The results of the *Adolescent Well-Being Scale* suggest Michael is suffering low self-esteem. He lacked confidence and did not appear to be experiencing much success or achievement.

FAMILY AND SOCIAL RELATIONSHIPS

Michael has little contact with his extended family, and no contact with his birth father or with his mother's former partner with whom he was said to have a positive relationship. He does not get out and see friends. He has a poor relationship with Ian Ross who is reported to hit him two or three times a week. He interacted with his mother when they were alone together but did not participate in a family meeting, remaining quiet throughout. The results of the SDQ regarding his pro-social behaviour suggest that he has developed social skills and has an ability to relate to others. He is lonely among his peers at school. The *Family Activity Scale* showed that he had not had a friend visit him in the last month. In the last year his number of friends at school has reduced.

SOCIAL PRESENTATION

Michael's physical appearance has changed over the last year. He used to be well turned out at school but now has a neglected appearance.

SELF-CARE SKILLS

Michael is not able to perform some of the self-care tasks expected of him by his mother and Ian Ross such as taking a bath, washing himself in the morning or getting his own breakfast and getting to school on time.

Moira Ward and Ian Ross's parenting capacity

BASIC CARE

Evidence from school and the *HOME Inventory* interview suggests that the standard of basic care provided for Michael and his sister has deteriorated. The provision of breakfast in the morning is variable. Moira Ward does not always ensure there are the basic supplies necessary for breakfast available, has been sleeping in and not been able to prepare breakfast for Michael. She has not been able to supervise his personal hygiene or ensure the availability of clean clothing. The couple have been able to ensure the provision of warmth and shelter for the children. They appear unable to ensure that Michael has adequate sleep at night.

ENSURING SAFETY

There is evidence that Michael has been hit or 'clipped' by Ian Ross two or three times a week recently. Moira Ward referred to Ian Ross occasionally giving Michael 'a clip on the ear' and she has not been able to prevent this happening. The results of the *emotional climate* subscale of the *HOME Inventory*, which is the amount of restriction and punishment experienced by the child, showed a raised level of concern.

EMOTIONAL WARMTH

While Moira Ward has demonstrated a capacity to provide emotional warmth in the past and to a limited degree in the present, there is evidence that this capacity has reduced. Ian Ross has more rigid approach to discipline and a stricter regime has been implemented by the couple. Michael is being required to 'grow up'. An example of this is Ian Ross's insistence, supported by Moira Ward, that the hall light is turned off at night when Michael goes to bed. Michael experienced more physical warmth with his mother when they were interviewed together than he did when the family including Ian Ross were interviewed. The score for the *responsivity* subscale of the *HOME Inventory* raised a concern regarding parental warmth and affection.

STIMULATION

The results of the *HOME Inventory* interview showed a lack of involvement on the part of Moira Ward and Ian Ross in any activities with Michael or, indeed, in supervising his homework, although there was an adequate supply of *learning materials* and *opportunities* as measured by the *HOME Inventory*. The subscale of *enrichment*, which is the extent to which Moira Ward and Ian Ross consciously utilize family and community resources to enrich the development of Michael in activities outside of the home, showed an elevated level of concern. Michael appears to be frequently grounded and has few opportunities for socializing with friends. He is not allowed to have friends in the home. Discussion of the *Family Activity Scale* revealed that Michael had been engaging in more activities a year ago than he does now.

GUIDANCE AND BOUNDARIES

The key parental tasks are demonstrating and modelling appropriate behaviour and control of emotions and interactions with others, and guidance, which involves setting boundaries, so that the child is able to develop an internal model of moral values and conscience in social behaviour appropriate for the society within which they will grow up. There is evidence from the *encouragement of maturity* subscale of the *HOME Inventory* of an elevated level of concern about Moira Ward and Ian Ross's capacity to help Michael in this area. They clearly expect Michael to get his own breakfast, attend to his own personal hygiene, tidy his room and so forth, but provide him with little support to help him do this. These expectations have changed substantially with the arrival of Ian Ross and are not consistent with what had been previously expected of him.

STABILITY

Michael has had at least three significant male father figures in his life. He had developed a positive relationship with Moira Ward's former partner, Gary Wills, which is in marked contrast to Ian Ross's relationship with him. Ian Ross is unyielding towards Michael and displayed little evident affection towards him. Moira Ward has always cared for her children and they have never lived separately from her.

Family and environmental factors

FAMILY HISTORY AND FAMILY FUNCTIONING

The results of the *Recent Life Events Questionnaire* show that Moira Ward continues to be affected by the separation well over a year ago from Gary Wills, her former partner. The interviews demonstrated that Ian Ross's views about parenting are very different from Moira Ward's. There is persistent discord between Ian Ross and Laura. Moira Ward says this is affecting her. The results of the *Adult Wellbeing Scale* show that Moira Ward is above the borderline for depression and that Ian Ross was at the top of the borderline area for outward-directed irritability. Moira Ward was also on the borderline for anxiety, outward-directed irritability and inward-directed irritability and may well be experiencing mental health difficulties at the moment. The results of the *Alcohol Use Questionnaire* do not raise concerns about current levels of drinking but do highlight there have been concerns in the past about Moira Ward's level of alcohol consumption.

WIDER FAMILY

The family do not have contact with members of the wider family. In respect of Moira Ward and her extended family, this appears to be because they disapprove of her relationship with Ian Ross. They have not seen her mother for over a year.

HOUSING

The family home is a rented council house, which is adequately maintained. The *Home Conditions Scale* did not reveal any concerns about domestic hygiene apart from a general lack of cleanliness in Michael's room.

EMPLOYMENT

Ian Ross is in full-time employment although the nature of it has not been established. This may require further investigation.

INCOME

There appears to be a satisfactory level of income coming into the home to meet the family's needs.

FAMILY'S SOCIAL INTEGRATION

The *HOME Inventory* interview and the *Family Activity Scale* revealed the family has little contact with neighbours and a relatively restricted social life.

COMMUNITY RESOURCES

The family do not use the library as they had a fine to pay. Michael attends the local school. Moira Ward used to visit school regularly for parents' evenings and generally maintained good contact but of late she has been noted not to respond to school letters. Teaching staff have been responsive to Michael's current situation both by writing to Moira Ward and making a referral to children's social care. The family is registered with a local general practitioner (GP).

Identifying gaps in information

Having concluded the process of categorizing the information by the dimensions and domains of the *Assessment Framework*, it is necessary to consider whether there are any gaps in information. With the Ward family, it is apparent that there are gaps in terms of an understanding of:

- the extent and impact of any physical abuse that may be taking place
- a lack of detail about how Moira Ward and Ian Ross parent the children
- the detailed nature of family relationships and family interaction
- the nature of the relationship between Ian Ross and Moira Ward
- the history of Laura and Michael's development

- Laura and Michael's early family and social relationships, particularly with Moira Ward's extended family

- family history (including Ian Ross and Moira Ward's respective childhood experiences)

- Laura and Michael's relationship (both past and present) with their father and Moira Ward's former partner, Gary Wills

- Ian Ross's work and family finances.

Of particular concerns are the reports from Michael, his mother and the school that he has reported being hit or 'clipped' by Ian Ross. Although denied by Ian Ross, this appears to be continuing. There has been no evidence of any bruising or other physical signs to date. It was decided that it was necessary to have a better understanding of the situation in the family before discussing the hitting or 'clipping' further with Michael or Laura on their own. Any disclosures from them could increase their vulnerability in the household, particularly in the absence of engaging with Ian Ross. Arrangements were made to carry out a further family interview using the *Family Assessment* and thereafter individual interviews with both the adults and Laura and Michael. The results will be described in Chapter 5.

In the meantime thought can be given to making sense of the information already gathered and categorized according to the *Assessment Framework*.

Step 4: Analyse the processes influencing the child's development and well-being

Michael's met and unmet needs

In order to hypothesize about the processes, which might be affecting Michael's development, Michael's met and unmet needs must be identified. It is not necessary to have an exhaustive list of met or unmet needs in order to begin to understand the processes that are in operation.

On the basis of what is known thus far, Michael's met needs include that he:

- gets to school (albeit late)

- has age-appropriate clothing (albeit that it is sometimes dirty)

- has a reasonable evening meal

- receives appropriate health care when ill

- has some cuddles and joint activity with his mother

- can clearly communicate and show affection to his mother

- is not notably disobedient

- has a reasonable sibling relationship with Laura.

Examples of his unmet needs are that he:

- is unhappy and unconfident to a significant degree
- is being hit
- gets up late
- gets to school without a proper breakfast
- gets to school late
- is tired in school
- is scared when the light is turned off at night
- has few friends
- struggles with his homework
- has few interests and hobbies
- cannot stick up for himself
- has dirty and smelly clothes
- does not have a happy relationship with Ian Ross.

Exploring factors and processes relating to Michael's met and unmet needs

SOME OF MICHAEL'S MET NEEDS

The exploration of processes and the weight or effect of the factors or processes is made easier by taking as the starting point a single met or unmet need. Michael last received appropriate health care when he was ill because Laura took him to the doctor. This is an example of a linear process. This action by Laura potentially benefited Michael's health but did not have a significant impact. It did not pervade other aspects of Michael's development and happened only once. Although a beneficial process, it is not one that is having a significant impact across the range of Michael's needs.

Michael has a regular evening meal. The process by which this is achieved is that Ian Ross expects to have an evening meal when he gets in from work and Moira Ward ensures this happens and Michael is expected to be at the evening meal. There is a circular process operating between Ian Ross and Moira Ward in which Ian Ross expects something and Moira Ward provides it and this serves to maintain an aspect of their relationship. One of the outcomes of this process is that Michael gets a reasonable evening meal. This has the benefit that Michael will not go to bed hungry but does not appear to have a significant impact on him getting to sleep, nor to have a generally beneficial impact on other aspects of his development, even though it happens each evening and has been going on for quite a long time. This is an example of another beneficial process which is meeting one aspect of Michael's needs but does not appear to extend very far beyond that particular need.

SOME OF MICHAEL'S UNMET NEEDS

Turning to unmet needs, the question that needs to be asked is why is a particular need unmet? An example of one of Michael's unmet needs is that he has few friends both in and out of school. A hypothesis for why this might be so is that he is 'grounded' and not allowed to have friends to visit. This is because the teacher writes letters home about him being late for school and Ian Ross's response, agreed to by Moira Ward, is to insist that he should not be allowed out. This means Michael has reduced opportunities to socialize or sustain friendships, which makes him less happy and contributes to his low level of self-esteem. School staff have reported that he is rather isolated and bullied by other children. The teachers, who have noted a contrast in his presentation from about a year ago, have become more concerned about him and raised their concerns in further correspondence to Moira Ward, leading to further altercations with Ian Ross over the situation and Michael being hit or 'clipped' by Ian Ross. Conflict between Michael's sister Laura and Ian Ross is generating a tense and unhappy family atmosphere. Michael's low mood is affecting his capacity to sustain friendships both in and out of school. Ian Ross's rows with Laura and restriction of Michael's visits to and from friends which are a result of rules he has established, supported by their mother, can be seen as having a pervasive effect on a range of aspects of Michael's development. Disciplinary action is happening often and has been going on for several months. There is little evidence that this pattern has been modified.

These processes can be summarised as follows: Michael's needs (CDN) interact with each other in a circular fashion, namely 'lack of friends' brings unhappiness, which in turn brings 'lack of friends'; but Michael's needs (CDN) are also influenced by factors in the parenting and family and environmental needs domains. The arguments in the family (F&E) are 'getting down' Moira Ward (F&E). She gets up late in the morning and so does not ensure that Michael is up, has an adequate breakfast and is off to school on time (PC), which contributes to his lateness at school, his often being hungry on arrival and having more difficulties in concentrating (CDN), causing the teacher to report the school's concerns to Moira Ward (F&E) leading to 'grounding' by Moira Ward and Ian Ross and being hit by Ian Ross (PC) leading to Michael's unhappiness and lack of friends (CDN).

The focus on one unmet need rapidly exposes processes that can be hypothesized to be generating and sustaining Michael's unmet needs in several developmental dimensions: health, education, emotional and behavioural development, family and social relationships and social presentation. The wide range of persistent impairments points to a high level of unmet need. The frequency, duration and pervasiveness of the processes involving family conflict, and the mental health of Moira and Michael indicate that they are having a severe impact.

Thus it can be seen that starting with one unmet need and analysing processes can generate hypotheses about what underlies impairments in the child's development. However it is important to remember and consider factors that have not been included in the formulation, which may point to other significant processes impacting on Michael's health and development. Possibilities include factors in Michael such as specific educational difficulties, other aspects of parenting such as the management of Michael's fear of the dark, lack of parental supervision, support of homework and involvement in joint activities, or family and environmental factors such as housing, neighbourhood, debt and family history, including the absence of contact with Michael's birth father and the impact of Moira Ward's separation from Gary Wills.

Step 5: Predict the likely outlook for the child

Likely consequences for Michael if his situation does not change

If nothing were to change in Michael's situation, what would be the likely consequences? If he continues to be unhappy and lack confidence, be scared when the light is turned out at night, have few friends, go to school without a proper breakfast, and arrive at school hungry, anxious and less able to concentrate, then in the short term he is likely to increasingly fall behind in school work and become increasingly isolated at school with a consequent impact upon his self-esteem and capacity to relate to others. In the long term, he is unlikely to make the most of his educational opportunities, may well begin to develop school attendance difficulties and have long-term problems in forming relationships as an adult as well as potential mental health problems. This rather poor outlook for Michael is accentuated if one also takes account of his other unmet needs, not least his unhappiness, which is contributed to by not only the factors discussed above but also the physical chastisement that he is presently suffering.

Step 6: Plan interventions

Interventions may be directed towards helping support strengths or helping meet unmet needs. Michael has quite an extensive number of unmet needs, which have been referred to above. Interventions will need to be targeted towards the particular processes currently taking place within the family.

A significant factor that was identified during the analysis of processes was that of the relationship between Moira Ward and Ian Ross and the impact it is having on a range of aspects of Michael's development. However, at this stage this has not been sufficiently explored and the planning of any interventions focusing on this factor must await the outcome of the further interviews using the *Family Assessment* described in Chapter 5.

A factor that was also having a significant impact was Moira Ward not being able to get up in the morning, which was attributed to possible depression and interventions could be directed towards this. It was recognized that the possible link with depression was an untested hypothesis at this stage and that further exploration was required as there may be other relevant factors and processes involved.

Interventions at this stage could be directed more specifically towards the unmet need itself rather than necessarily the factors hypothesized to be causing it. Interventions could be directed at ensuring Michael had a breakfast, ensuring he left the home on time and in trying to support him at school with regard to friendships and homework. There are examples of schools running breakfast clubs and homework clubs and having schemes to help children struggling with friendships. Intervention could be directed at trying to help Moira Ward get up in the morning so that she could actually get Michael off to school on time.

Before considering which intervention(s) to recommend, consideration would have to be given to what the family would be most likely to be able to cooperate or engage with. Some interventions would be likely to produce more immediate benefits and some might take time. There may need to be a sequence to these interventions.

Given the immediate concern about Michael being hungry at school, the combination of a family support worker visiting to help Moira Ward to ensure Michael got to school in time to attend the Breakfast Club could be seen as an intervention which might produce an immediate benefit. Another practical intervention could be the suggestion of a discussion with Moira Ward and Ian Ross about the benefits of a nightlight to help Michael sleep.

Step 7: Identify outcomes and measures which would indicate whether interventions are successful

The key outcome of the above interventions is whether Michael has made developmental progress and is functioning at the level to be expected for his age and stage of development. This requires an assessment of whether he has progressed, in what dimensions and how the improvements or deteriorations came about. It has been hypothesized that Michael is not receiving an adequate breakfast because Moira Ward is not getting up on time because she may be depressed. An immediate intervention suggested was the involvement of a family support worker to help get Michael up so that he could attend the Breakfast Club at school. It was hypothesized that, if he attended the Breakfast Club, he would be at school on time, be less hungry and able to concentrate better in class. A longer term intervention in this area might be to refer Moira Ward to her GP with a view to obtaining help from a specialist service regarding her symptoms of depression.

Regarding measuring the outcome of the first intervention, a record could be kept of the days on which the family support worker visited the home and a commensurate record kept at the Breakfast Club of the days and times Michael attended. These would be case-specific measures. It is hypothesized that, if he attended the Breakfast Club, had something to eat and was at school on time, this would contribute to improvement in peer relationships and increase levels of self-esteem. These could be assessed by administering the *Adolescent Well-Being Scale* and SDQ before the intervention took place and at follow-up. The SDQ could be readministered to see if there was an improvement in his mood and peer problems.

Regarding measuring the outcomes of the second intervention, if Moira Ward's referral to the GP resulted in the prescription of antidepressant medication, a record could be kept of the times she got up in the mornings during the week before the intervention commenced and compared with the times she got up in the morning after. This would be a case-specific measure. Any improvement or deterioration in Moira Ward's state. For the impact of her getting up in the morning on Michael, case-specific measures such as school attendance records could be used. His attentiveness in class could be rated in conjunction with base-line and follow-up standardized measures such as the SDQ and *Adolescent Well-Being Scale.*

Conclusion

The first stage of the assessment revealed a range of met and unmet needs of Michael's, some of which were sufficiently well understood to analyse the contributory factors and processes and then plan and implement some interventions. This would have the benefit of seeing whether the family could be engaged and respond to working with the services involved and whether the interventions were effective. There were clearly other difficulties, including potential safeguarding concerns, where there were significant gaps in information requiring further assessment at the same time before deciding how best to intervene. This next stage of assessment is described in Chapter 5.

Chapter Five

Assessing Strengths and Risks with Children and Their Families

Operationalizing the Assessment Framework Where There are Safeguarding Concerns

Arnon Bentovim, Liza Bingley Miller
and Stephen Pizzey

Introduction

As set out in previous chapters, the assessment of children's health and development requires a conceptual map of information which guides the assessment and analysis of the child's current developmental functioning and needs, the care or parenting they are receiving and relevant aspects of the child's family and the wider environment in which they and their family live. The *Assessment Framework* provides such a map.

This chapter focuses on the domains of the *Assessment Framework* in greater detail to identify some of the strengths and difficulties in the different dimensions, which are of relevance when assessing children and families in the safeguarding context.

Assessing strengths and difficulties in children's developmental needs, parenting capacity and family and environmental factors

In order to further operationalize the *Assessment Framework* in a way which helps workers to make evidence-based assessments in a safeguarding context, it is helpful to focus in more detail on the dimensions of each domain and to systematize further the way they are described.

One of the key principles underpinning the development of the *Assessment Framework* is the emphasis on the importance of identifying strengths as well as areas of difficulty. The assessment is then balanced and plans for intervention can build on strengths as well as address areas of difficulty and need.

The *Assessment Framework* provides an invaluable map for collecting information. In this chapter we attempt to provide a systematic guide for assessing the degree of strength and/or difficulty in each of the dimensions of each domain. In the description of approaches to analysis of data gathered in assessments in Chapter 2, a method of evaluating the severity of impact of negative factors and weight of benefit derived from positive factors has been described. Here some particular strengths and difficulties will be highlighted that have particular relevance in a safeguarding context. This is important because of the nature of the events that occur in child abuse. They are often by their nature 'severe' because they impact on several domains of child's developmental needs, parenting capacity, and family and environmental factors. They often set in train longstanding changes in all these domains.

Descriptors for different aspects of strength and difficulty for each dimension of the *Assessment Framework* have been developed that indicate what a worker might expect to see if a child or family has strengths in any particular dimensions and what might indicate difficulties in that area. These descriptors are guides only and need to be used in the context of other information the worker has obtained about the child and family and in light of professional judgement. The descriptors can help identify gaps in information or evidence and assist the worker in looking for examples of behaviour or sequences of interaction, which help to form an evidence-based assessment.

Children's developmental needs domain

Health

In this section strengths and difficulties are defined and operationalized for each of the dimensions in the children's developmental needs domain in turn, i.e. *health, education, emotional and behavioural development, identity, family and social relationships, social presentation* and *self-care skills*. Indicators of the level of the child's functioning and how well the child's needs are being met are listed in Table 5.1.

Table 5.1 Indicators of strengths and difficulties in each dimension

Level of functioning	Area of need	Level of functioning
Strengths		Difficulties
Foetus healthy in pregnancy	**General physical health**	Foetal health or survival threatened in pregnancy; repeated injuries and/or infections at any stage of development
Good general health in perinatal period, the early years and later childhood		Chronic physical illness and/or illness or injury requiring repeated hospitalization
No injuries or illnesses requiring repeated or protracted hospitalization		Onset of soiling or enuresis after continence was firmly established
No physical genetic disorders		Physical or genetic disorders
Child takes exercise and eats a healthy diet		Takes little exercise and eats a poor diet
Child has positive health attitudes		Child has negative attitudes towards health
Positive trajectory of physical growth	**Growth and development**	Negative trajectory of physical growth and failure to thrive
No persistent developmental problems		Presence of a developmental problem, e.g. learning difficulties, autism or delay in language development
No non-accidental injury	**Injuries or illnesses possibly related to physical and sexual abuse**	Non-accidental injury
No genital injuries or infections; hymen intact		Genital injuries; ruptured hymen; genital infection
		Other evidence child has experienced sexual abuse
		Fictitious illnesses or injuries to child reported
No significant level of anxiety or depression	**Mental health**	Protracted periods of anxiety or depression
Absence of delusions or persistent hallucinations		Firmly held delusions or persistent hallucinations

No major sleep problems		Major and protracted sleep disturbance
Absence of flashbacks of abusive or traumatic experiences		Flashbacks of abusive or traumatic experiences
Capacity to mentalize and appreciate feelings and point of view of others		Lack of capacity to mentalize or appreciate feelings and point of view of others

Looking at *health* it can be seen there are four components to operationalize the *Assessment Framework*.

GENERAL PHYSICAL HEALTH

It is useful to provide a general account of the physical health of the child.

Strengths are associated with good general health, no problems during pregnancy, perinatal period, early years, later childhood and the development of appropriate attitudes to health on the child's behalf.

Difficulties may include poor general health during the pregnancy, during the perinatal period, early years, later years, with a general negative attitude to health and/or a risk-taking attitude developed by the child. Repetitive injuries and illnesses to a child raise a warning about the possibility of abuse. This can include fictitious illnesses being reported by caregivers, which are not found on medical examination and assessment.

GROWTH AND DEVELOPMENT

Strengths are usually reflected in a positive trajectory of physical growth and the child thriving.

Difficulties are often indicated by a negative trajectory of physical growth and failure to thrive. Characteristics associated with major impairment of growth and development are described at a later point under the different categories of harm, differentiating between growth failure in weight and height, or in height alone, and associations with signs of neglect. Children with developmental disorders are more vulnerable to physical and mental health problems.

INJURIES OR ILLNESSES POSSIBLY RELATED TO PHYSICAL AND SEXUAL ABUSE

Strengths are represented by there being no evidence of non-accidental injury or injuries or illnesses that may indicate abuse, fictitious illness or sexual abuse during development and currently.

Difficulties are represented by the presence of non-accidental and accidental injury or physical signs of sexual abuse. There are extensive and widespread ways in which physical and sexual abuse can present, ranging from bruising and fractures associated with physical abuse to regression and soiling, for example, associated with episodes of sexual abuse. A further example of the harmful impact of dangerous parental behaviours are the physical manifestations of the fabrication of symptoms or induction of illness state by parents.

MENTAL HEALTH

Evidence of the impact of good and poor mental health development may be reflected in all the other dimensions in the children's developmental needs domain.

Strengths are represented by the presence of a predominantly positive mood, enjoyment of activities and relationships, and the absence of persistent anxiety, depression or the symptoms of severe mental illness. The child is not unduly concerned with their own state of health, accepts the need for treatment when appropriate, and does not engage in activities that pose a serious threat to physical or mental health.

Difficulties are indicated by symptoms of mental illness or disorder such as persistent delusions, obsessions, hypochondriasis or eating problems. Of particular relevance in a safeguarding context are the signs of post-traumatic stress disorder such as flashbacks, sleep problems, anxiety or depression. Problems with the capacity to mentalize, recognize and appreciate the feelings and point of view of others may be evident. However, when making an assessment it must be remembered that such symptoms are also found in children with autistic spectrum disorder and related conditions.

Education

Indicators of the level of the child's functioning and how well the child's needs are being met are listed in Table 5.2.

Education encompasses four components, discussed below.

DEVELOPMENT OF COGNITIVE AND LANGUAGE SKILLS

The satisfactory unfolding of a child's cognitive and language skills is fundamental to successful progress in education.

Strengths include evidence of the satisfactory development of a child's cognitive and language skills, which are often protective factors for the child in the safeguarding context.

Difficulties: it is important to attempt to distinguish between cognitive, language or educational difficulties which reflect genetic or developmental factors within the child that are contributing to the delay or difficulty, and those which might be due to a failure to provide appropriate levels of stimulation and care to ensure that the child achieves his or her optimal level of development. This is difficult to do without psychometric testing and broad-ranging

Table 5.2 Indicators of strengths and difficulties in the education dimension

Level of functioning	Area of need	Level of functioning
Strengths		*Difficulties*
Satisfactory unfolding of cognitive and language skills	**Development of cognitive and language skills**	Significant delays and/or unevenness in cognitive and/or language skills
Satisfactory readiness for educational contexts; interest in learning	**Attitude to learning and work and adjustment to educational context**	Child not ready to participate in or cannot adjust to educational context
Accepts teaching; self-reinforced learning		Lack of interest in learning; rejects teaching; no self-motivation to learn
Satisfactory acquisition of educational skills and knowledge according to ability	**Educational progress**	Failure to acquire educational skills and/or knowledge at level appropriate to ability
No special educational needs	**Special educational needs**	Evidence of special educational needs
Has special educational needs but makes progress expected taking into account the nature of their specific educational difficulty		Failure to achieve at level expected for intelligence and specific educational difficulty, e.g. dyslexia

assessment, so although a history of delays in the development may in some cases suggest safeguarding concerns, it must not be assumed that they are the consequence of maltreatment.

ATTITUDE TO LEARNING AND WORK AND ADJUSTMENT TO EDUCATIONAL CONTEXT

The process of a child's adjustment to educational contexts needs to be considered across the lifespan, from functioning in pre-school contexts through transition to early school, and subsequent progress through junior and senior school and on to higher education or employment.

Strengths include curiosity and desire to learn, ability to use appropriate educational materials and work in a school context, carrying out educational tasks among peers supported and directed by a teacher. The child accepts the need for assistance and instruction. Initiative and self-motivation in educational activities are strengths. A positive attitude will be reflected in performing out-of-school assignments and the maintenance of satisfactory attendance.

Difficulties are indicated when the child shows little curiosity or desire to learn, and/or has difficulty using available educational materials or working in a school context. Rejection of the need for support and instruction can contribute to educational failure. Out-of-school assignments may not be performed, and particularly at older ages there may be poor attendance. Self-motivation and initiative in educational tasks will be lacking.

EDUCATIONAL PROGRESS

Strengths are indicated by children making progress in all aspects of education, including both skills and knowledge, at a level appropriate to their capacity. It is common for children to vary in their ability with different subjects or activities but if they are particularly successful in at least one area that is a strength.

Difficulties are characterized by persistent difficulty in acquiring educational skills or knowledge. The more widespread the difficulty, the more severe it is. Early difficulties in developing basic educational skills may set the child on a negative trajectory of lack of success, negative educational experiences and a low level of achievement, which reinforce a negative attitude to learning, leading to further failure.

SPECIAL EDUCATIONAL NEEDS

Associated with the attitude to learning and work is the issue of whether the child or young person has special needs. These may arise in a number of different ways, which may include innate cognitive and language factors as well as the influence privation and neglect. It is important to remember that it is not necessarily either innate or environmental factors that are contributing to a particular difficulty; they may be acting in combination.

Strengths are where the child is making progress consistent with their abilities. The child needs to be able to respond to any special educational input provided.

Difficulties are evident when a child is failing to make the progress that can be reasonably expected on the basis of their special needs. As indicated above resistance to necessary support and instruction can contribute to failure. This may be particularly important where there are special educational needs.

Emotional and behavioural development

Indicators of the level of the child's functioning and how well the child's needs are being met are listed in Table 5.3.

Strengths in the emotional and behavioural development dimension include evidence that a child can regulate their emotional states appropriately as well as express feelings appropriately and respond empathically. Positive emotional adjustment and a reasonable response to stressful events are relevant and the

Table 5.3 Indicators of strengths and difficulties in the emotional and behavioural dimension

Level of functioning	Area of need	Level of functioning
Strengths		*Difficulties*
Emotional states and levels of arousal well regulated, appropriate responses to age and stage of development	**Regulation of emotional states relative to age and developmental stage**	Persistent or recurrent states of arousal, frustration, distress and/or disorganized emotions
Secure attachment behaviour towards caregivers and/or other salient adults	**Early attachment behaviour**	Markedly insecure or disorganized attachment behaviours towards caregivers or other salient adults
Capacity to concentrate and maintain attention; not overactive	**Concentration and level of activity**	Difficulties with attention and concentration; marked overactivity
Feelings clearly and appropriately expressed; predominantly positive mood	**Expression of feelings and characteristic mood**	Expression of feelings lacking or inappropriate; pervasive negative mood
No persistent anxiety or depression		Persistent anxiety or depressed mood
Traumatic experiences resolved; no persistent post-traumatic symptoms	**Response to traumatic and stressful events**	Persistent unresolved traumatic symptoms
Positive emotional and behavioural adjustment and reasonable response to stressful events		Exaggerated or absent response to stressful events, mood difficulties, oppositional behaviour, aggression, self-harm, dangerous behaviour
Collaborative and pro-social; no or infrequent dangerous risk-taking behaviour	**Social behaviour** Behavioural disorders are usually included here although they get double-coded under family and social relationships if that behaviour is evident in those relationships	Severe or persistent uncooperative behaviour
No severe nor persistent aggressive behaviour, stealing		Aggressive behaviour or stealing
Shows sympathy and empathy		Lack of sympathetic and/or empathetic behaviour

capacity of the child to concentrate and maintain their attention are also elements of positive emotional and behavioural development. Pro-social behaviour is a strength and is appropriately placed on this dimension although it also appears on the family and social relationships dimension if such behaviour is displayed in those relationships.

Difficulties: it should be noted that many different factors can contribute to a child's emotional and behavioural state, so there should not be an immediate assumption that post-traumatic symptoms are indicative of abuse. In the same way, if a child has difficulties with attention or concentration, there may be underlying genetic and temperamental factors and/or a contribution from the home or school environment. It is important not to assume that disrupted attention and concentration derive from growing up in a climate of violence and abuse. Persistent and pervasive disobedience, aggression and/or lack of sympathetic or empathic behaviour can arise for many reasons including the experience of abuse. Research repeatedly points to combinations of factors and processes as determinants of children's emotional and behavioural state.

REGULATION OF EMOTIONAL STATES RELATIVE TO AGE AND DEVELOPMENTAL STAGE

Strengths are represented throughout a child's development by evidence that the child's emotional states and levels of arousal are reasonably well regulated, depending on the age and stage of development of the child, and that they gradually develop the capacity to contain and manage feeling states more satisfactorily. Strengths can be seen across the whole range of a child's emotions and behaviour from predominantly positive mood, good concentration, satisfactory eating and sleeping to pro-social actions. Many children show difficulties in at least one aspect for a period of time. The presence of satisfactory development in other areas indicates a positive outlook.

Difficulties: when there are difficulties in a child's emotional functioning and therefore higher levels of need, there is usually evidence of the child's emotional states being characterized either by high levels of arousal or extreme responses to frustration or disorganization of the child's emotional states. This may persist into later childhood and adolescence so that older children continue to show extreme responses to frustration and distress, which usually reflects a poor capacity for self-regulation.

EARLY ATTACHMENT BEHAVIOUR

Strengths include secure attachment behaviours in a young child, which are evident when a child seeks care or comfort when aroused, distressed or frightened, accepts care from their caregiver and is calmed and comforted by it. This behaviour is also evident when a child is reunited with the main caregiver following a separation.

Difficulties include disorganized attachment behaviour which is shown by a young child switching rapidly between different feelings such as distress, anger, arousal, excitement, with poor modulation, when being reunited with the caregiver or when the child is distressed, frightened or aroused.

EXPRESSION OF FEELINGS AND CHARACTERISTIC MOOD

Strengths are reflected in the child or young person having a predominantly positive mood and an ability to express their feelings in an appropriate way. States of anxiety and/or depression are not persistent nor frequently recurrent.

Difficulties may be indicated when, in circumstances where expression of certain feelings would be fitting, the child shows no feeling or inappropriate feelings. For example they may not be appreciative of praise, be intensely suspicious about the positive responses of others or have a predominant negative, angry, or distressed mood. Persistent and/or recurrent anxiety or depression indicate significant difficulties, particularly where they are pervasive across different situations and activities.

RESPONSE TO TRAUMATIC AND STRESSFUL EVENTS

A characteristic experience for children growing up in a climate of violence is the overwhelming nature of the abusive and stressful life events to which they are subject. Repetitive violent and abusive experiences have a cumulative impact generating negative processes that impair the child or young person's health and development.

Although there are patterns of development that can appear characteristic of those children or young people who have suffered such events, it must always be remembered that some are, for various reasons, more resilient and do not show serious impairment of their health and development. Furthermore many of the symptoms and behaviours can occur for other reasons. Dreams and flashbacks which portray specific abusive or violent experiences, or play and other behaviours, which re-enact such experiences explicitly are usually a strong indicator that the child has indeed encountered these events.

Strengths are indicated when a child or young person who has experienced abuse and violence shows no evidence of the emotional and behavioural difficulties usually associated with post-traumatic stress disorder described in the section below. They are able to respond to life events appropriately and be collaborative and pro-social (thoughtful and cooperative) in their responses towards others. It is particularly important to look for strengths among children who have experienced recurrent abuse or violence. While there will be some who are nevertheless developing satisfactorily in all areas, there will be many who show difficulties in some dimensions but strengths in others.

Difficulties: children or young people who have experienced multiple abuse and/or violence that has built up incrementally over time usually show two broad patterns of emotions and behaviour – internalizing and externalizing, which may develop into or trigger disorders of mood and conduct. Internalizing patterns are characterized by evidence of persistent arousal, disturbed mood, irritability, frozenness, i.e. lack of emotional response, intense recollections of abusive or violent events through nightmares or flashbacks, broken sleep, avoidance of circumstances or events associated with their traumatic experiences, disassociation from current events, dreaminess and absences. A child may experience intense fears, anxieties over falling asleep, panic or fearfulness. Children may develop emotional disorders such as depressive states, disorders of mood or exhibit self-harming behaviour.

Externalizing responses are characterized by misuse of drugs, alcohol or other substances, or the development of conduct or behavioural problems which involve excessive anger or aggression and sometimes a re-enactment of violence which they have experienced. The presence of a predominantly externalizing or internalizing pattern does not preclude a mixture. Some who are aggressive are also depressed or anxious. Some who are depressed misuse drugs.

This can affect other areas of a child's development. For example, some children suffering from emotional problems, such as depression or anxiety or being too fearful or too angry to be able to put energy into how they take care of themselves and their appearance and present themselves to the outside world.

Some children and young people show sexualized behaviour. This may be manifest as a preoccupation with drawing or enacting sexual behaviour in play, or at later age promiscuity. There may be evidence of premature sexual interests, sexualization of relationships, intensive masturbatory activities or inappropriate sexual activities with peers or adults. This may include the development of intensely eroticized and inappropriately sexualized activities with self or with others, or extreme frozenness or promiscuous patterns of relating. In extreme cases, there is the risk of the child or young person developing dangerous sexual behaviours and attitudes and a view of sexual relationships with children as being appropriate.

Other features include obsessions or obsessional behaviour. However, it should always be remembered that most behaviour of children or emotions they experience can be brought about by a wide variety of factors, not necessarily family violence or abuse.

Identity

Indicators of the level of the child's functioning and how well the child's needs are being met are listed in Table 5.4.

Identity is concerned with the following four concepts.

Table 5.4 Indicators of strengths and difficulties in the identity dimension

Level of functioning	Area of need	Level of functioning
Strengths		Difficulties
Child has secure sense of self as an individual who belongs to a family	**Sense of self as individual in family**	Child does not have a secure sense of self as individual belonging to a family
Child is able to make choices, assert their views and needs, and act as an individual at a developmentally appropriate level	**Individual choice and action**	Child unable to make choices, assert personal views or needs and cannot initiate action for self; 'omnipotent' sense of self; over-assertive
Positive sense of self as valued and of value to others; confident in where belongs socially and culturally but preserving sense of individuality	**Sense of self and others in social and cultural contexts**	Negative sense of self as unvalued or bad; unconfident or unhappy with where belongs socially or culturally; no sense of belonging or identity absorbed; no independent views or actions
Satisfactory sense of gender and/or sexual identity and comfortable with it	**Gender and/or sexual identity**	Unhappy with gender and/or sexual identity or uncertain of it

SENSE OF SELF AS INDIVIDUAL IN FAMILY

Strengths: when a child has a positive sense of identity they are clear about how they are similar and different from others, and reasonably comfortable with those similarities and differences. This includes their gender identity and the recognition that they belong to a particular family and cultural group. Satisfactory identity development also comprises a sense of personal worth and that the child feels valued and of value to others.

Difficulties: a child may be unclear or unhappy with who they are. This may be concerned with whether or where they belong in terms of family or community. There can be a sense of separateness that is so acute that the child feels that they do not belong with any social group. At the other extreme they can feel so absorbed or taken over by relationships in the family or community that they have no will of their own. All aspects of personality are relevant. It may be gender identity with which they are uncertain or uncomfortable. They may consider themselves unvalued and of no benefit to others.

INDIVIDUAL CHOICE AND ACTION

Strengths are indicated when a child is confident in expressing and making choices that reflect their individual needs and wishes.

Difficulties may be reflected in a lack of confidence in expressing personal needs or expressing or making choices. Sometimes a child may feel not just unvalued but bad; they may be preoccupied with acts that are socially disapproved and/or have a strong desire to commit them. Their sense of personal worth can be so low that the child expects to be rejected by others and/or does not expect that their needs will be met.

SENSE OF SELF AND OTHERS IN SOCIAL AND CULTURAL CONTEXTS

Strengths: a positive sense of self can be seen in a child's capacity to make choices and express individual needs and wishes with an appropriate degree of assertiveness in the different social contexts in which they live. Whether they picture themselves in a positive light can be shown by their confidence in being accepted in the family and other social groups, and having a positive sense of future possibilities and realistic hopes and expectations for the future.

Difficulties in a sense of self are often reflected by a lack of assertiveness in making choices or expressing personal needs and wishes. A negative sense of self, feeling of badness, a fear of having an 'evil' character and/or a fear and sense of foreboding about the future may be expressed. There may be an almost total lack of confidence in social interactions within and/or outside the family. Alternatively, in older children, an 'omnipotent' sense of self may be observed, which may be related to experiences of abuse and neglect. The child or young person may have impossible dreams for the future and/or a totally unrealistic view of their capacities.

GENDER AND/OR SEXUAL IDENTITY

Strengths: the child or young person develops a gender identity about which they are both clear and comfortable. This may be more difficult to achieve where gender identity or behaviour does not match physique, or where gender orientation is not heterosexual.

Difficulties are likely to be characterized by a child or young person being uncertain about their gender identity or sexual orientation.

Family and social relationships

Indicators of the level of the child's functioning and how well the child's needs are being met are listed in Table 5.5.

Family and social relationships encompass the following five concepts.

CHILD'S GROWING RELATIONSHIPS WITH FAMILY AND OTHERS

Strengths: the child relates warmly, sympathetically and empathically to others in family contexts, and cooperates constructively in family activities. The child is able to cooperate actively in school and with others outside the family.

Table 5.5 Indicators of strengths and difficulties in the family and social relationships dimension

Level of functioning	Area of need	Level of functioning
Strengths		Difficulties
Child able to participate in a network of emotionally responsive, stable, affectionate relationships inside and outside the family	**Child's growing relationships with family and others**	Child has a network of disrupted, unstable relationships or relationships marked by enmeshment, or hostility, absence of warmth inside and outside the family
Child able to relate to, be responsive towards and show affection and empathy for others		Child withdrawn, hostile or unable to be responsive and empathic towards others in family
Child has a network of secure organized attachment figures	**Development of network of attachments**	Child has a network of insecure, disorganized or indiscriminate attachments
Collaborative relationships with parents, reasonable demands made by child; child protective towards and protected by siblings and peers, older and younger	**Relationships with parents, siblings and peers**	Exploitative, avoidant, over/under-dependent relationships with parents, unreasonable demands made by child; child fighting and/or rivalrous with siblings, abusive towards or abused by peers and siblings
Positive relationships with teachers and peers	**Relationships in school**	Negative relationships with teachers and peers
Child connected, responsive, independent, pro-social attitudes and relationships, respects diversity	**Attitudes to family, social and cultural contexts**	Child isolated, dominating, controlling, dependent, antisocial attitudes and relationships, prejudiced

The child does not persistently bully or manipulate others, or isolate themselves. There will always be occasions when a child acts or responds disobediently, angrily or in uncaring way, but the predominant picture is one of warmth and cooperation.

Difficulties: disorganized attachment behaviour in early childhood predicts difficulty in later relationships. Difficulties include a child persistently or recurrently engaging in disobedient, uncooperative or aggressive behaviour towards others. Such behaviour may not occur in all contexts or with all people, but in severe cases it will be more pervasive. Other difficulties include bullying, manipulation and avoidance of interaction within the family or with significant others such as teachers or school peers.

DEVELOPMENT OF NETWORK OF ATTACHMENTS

The establishment of satisfactory early attachment relationships with care-givers is a key factor in ensuring a child's emotional and behaviour adjustment, and their capacity for relating to others.

Strengths: secure attachment behaviour with a main caregiver and respon-sive social behaviour in a young child are strengths. However, such behaviour may not be shown on all occasions, and certainly not with all people. Children with developmental problems often have a different pacing and pattern of evo-lution of early social relationships, which may constitute a vulnerability but does not necessarily predict major later problems in relationships.

Difficulties: disorganized attachment behaviour in early childhood predicts later difficulty in relationships with peers and adults. Such behaviour is shown by the child fluctuating between clinging and rejection or avoidance of care-givers and other people they know well, or indiscriminate seeking of attention from strangers. It may also be associated with children who 'freeze' under situa-tions of stress and neither go towards their caregiver nor avoid contact with them nor seek or accept comfort from others.

RELATIONSHIPS WITH PARENTS, SIBLINGS AND PEERS

Strengths are represented by the child having a sense of themselves as being emotionally close to their immediate family members and others in their world. The child or young person has a reasonably collaborative relationship with parents with evidence of a positive set of alliances with parental figures, siblings and peers and the capacity for being able to communicate effectively with others, demonstrate and respond to emotional warmth and accept guidance and boundaries set by caregivers. A child or young person with strengths in this area is likely to show reasonable levels of protective responses to younger siblings.

Considerable *difficulties* may be demonstrated by the child or young person exploiting family relationships and alliances, manipulating peers, and/or having difficulties in communicating and managing emotional responses with family members and peers and others. Their behaviour may include making unreasonable demands, rejecting boundaries and guidance offered by care-givers, being unable to accept or demonstrate emotional warmth, getting involved in fights, and exhibiting rivalrous behaviour with siblings, abusive behaviour towards peers or extensive bullying, victimization or disrupted boundaries. Persistent disobedience, non-cooperation or withdrawal from interaction with others are also evidence of difficulties.

RELATIONSHIPS IN SCHOOL

Strengths: positive relationships between the child and their peers and teachers can be a protective factor with regard to the child's development. Acceptance of teaching, reasonable obedience and cooperation with the teacher and peers both in and out of class are all strengths, as is any pro-social behaviour, e.g. caring for others.

Difficulties: conversely, poor relationships between children and their peers or teachers can have a negative impact on the child's overall development. Bullying, aggression, manipulation and, on the other hand, excessive anxiety in relationships or avoidance of interaction with others may all present difficulties.

ATTITUDES TO FAMILY, SOCIAL AND CULTURAL CONTEXTS

Strengths: a child or young person with strengths in this area is likely to be connected, responsive, independent, pro-social, i.e. cooperative and helpful in their responses to others, and respectful of diversity and valuing of relationships with others.

Difficulties in functioning are indicated when children or young people are isolated, dominating in their responses, controlling or overly dependent. They may well develop antisocial attitudes and relationships and show evidence of considerable prejudice and intolerance of others and of difference. This can be a feature of children who have grown up in a context of violence and neglect.

Social presentation

Indicators of the level of the child's functioning and how well the child's needs are being met are listed in Table 5.6.

Social presentation is concerned with three main concepts, as follows.

UNDERSTANDING THE NEED TO PAY ATTENTION TO APPEARANCE,
DRESS, BEHAVIOUR AND HYGIENE

Children develop a growing understanding of the need to pay attention to their appearance and to dress and behave in ways which are appropriate to the different social contexts they take part in. They gradually recognize that the way they present themselves has an impact on the attitude of others towards them.

Strengths: are reflected when a child or young person has a growing understanding of the impact of their appearance, dress, behaviour and level of hygiene on how others respond to them and take steps to dress and behave in ways that are appropriate to each setting they find themselves in.

Difficulties: some children and young people are unaware, resistant to or unable to understand how others respond to them and do not adjust their dress, behaviour and level of hygiene in a fashion appropriate to the social context. This can be found among children who have suffered neglect, or experienced abuse, but is not necessarily for those reasons.

Table 5.6 Indicators of strengths and difficulties in the social presentation dimension

Level of functioning	Area of need	Level of functioning
Strengths		Difficulties
Awareness of and capacity to present self positively, with pride in appearance, dress, hygiene and behaviour, appropriate to age, gender and culture	**Understanding the need to pay attention to appearance, dress, behaviour and hygiene (as appropriate for their age, gender and culture)**	Lack of awareness or capacity to present self in positive light, with pride in appearance, dress, hygiene and behaviour, appropriate to age, gender and culture
Impairments adjusted to and managed, copes with discrimination by others	**Adjustment and attitudes to impairment and discrimination by others**	Failure to adjust or manage impairment, child rejects impairment and/or diversity in self or others; child unable to cope with discrimination by others
Evidence of respect for family, cultural, religious and spiritual values and diversity in own social presentation	**Respect for family, cultural, religious and spiritual values and diversity**	Shows lack of respect for family, cultural, religious and spiritual values in self-presentation

ADJUSTMENT AND ATTITUDES TO IMPAIRMENT AND DISCRIMINATION BY OTHERS

In terms of the child's developmental needs domain, children also need to learn ways of adjusting to and managing their own impairment and difference within themselves and managing expressions of discrimination in ways which reduce the impact on their own self-esteem and potential. This difficulty occurs among children who have suffered abuse but is not confined to children in that predicament.

Strengths are evidenced when a child or young person can acknowledge their impairment or other difference from others, present themselves and manage the responses of others with self-respect and assertiveness while maintaining a capacity to value diversity and difference in others.

Difficulties: some children find it difficult to adjust to their impairment so that they present themselves and respond to others in ways which adds to their difficulties. They may demonstrate a lack of self-worth and find it hard to be self-assertive or be rejecting or angry and confrontational in their behaviour towards others. These patterns of behaviour can impact negatively on aspects of their own development such as their family and social relationships and education.

RESPECT FOR FAMILY, CULTURAL, RELIGIOUS AND SPIRITUAL VALUES
AND DIVERSITY

Learning to demonstrate an appropriate degree of respect for family, cultural, spiritual and religious values is part of positive child development.

Strengths include evidence of a child or young person's respect and regard for positive values held by their family and the beliefs and values embedded in the cultural, religious and/or spiritual aspects of their family life and community. The child or young person shows evidence of developing their own internal set of values to guide their life and behaviour and ways of relating to others including a respect for diversity and difference.

Difficulties: a child or young person may show lack of respect for family, cultural and religious and/or spiritual values and have difficulty fitting into their immediate family and community. Alternatively, a child or young person may be unable to manage critical/punitive responses from others. Some children and young people may reject or feel unable to follow demands from their family and community to adhere to cultural and other values.

Self-care skills

Indicators of the level of the child's functioning and how well the child's needs are being met are listed in Table 5.7.

Table 5.7 Indicators of strengths and difficulties in the self-care skills dimension

Level of functioning	*Area of need*	*Level of functioning*
Strengths		*Difficulties*
Positive self-care, emotional and communication skills unfolding in sequence of competencies leading to increasing independence within child's capacity	**Developing a capacity for independent living skills**	Poor self-care skills, uneven pattern of development of emotional and communication skills so that the child fails to achieve independence given their capacity
Positive capacity to problem-solve in family, school and community	**Developing a capacity to problem-solve in family and community contexts**	Failure to problem-solve in family, school or community; child helpless or over-confident
Appreciates contexts of danger and risk, realistic sense of safety and an ability to keep self safe, capacity for exploration	**Appreciation of risks and safety**	Failure to appreciate risks, over-anxious or puts self in danger

Self-care is concerned with the following three concepts.

DEVELOPING A CAPACITY FOR INDEPENDENT LIVING SKILLS

Strengths are indicated when a child or young person demonstrates having acquired competence in practical self-care skills, emotional literacy and competence in communicating with others which is enabling them to develop autonomy and independence in line with their age and stage of development.

Difficulties are evidenced when children are not able to care for themselves and are not developing the self-care skills at the level to be expected for their age and stage of development or who are more self-sufficient than normally expected.

DEVELOPING A CAPACITY TO PROBLEM-SOLVE IN FAMILY AND COMMUNITY CONTEXTS

Children and young people have to learn to problem-solve, deal with difficulties and with the unexpected, including crises in school and in family life on a daily basis.

Strengths are indicated if a child shows resilience in coping with stressful events; this may give an indication of their capacity for self-care with strengths being demonstrated by a positive capacity to problem-solve in a variety of contexts.

Difficulties, on the other hand, are often shown by a failure to problem-solve, or a child or young person is helpless, overwhelmed or perhaps over-confident in one or more settings.

APPRECIATION OF RISKS AND SAFETY

An important aspect of self-care is a child or young person being able to recognize the need to keep oneself safe, gradually acquiring an appreciation of risks in the various social contexts they encounter, e.g. family, peer group, school and wider community.

Strengths are often shown by a child or young person being able to take appropriate care, being aware of stranger danger, knowing how to behave when both within and outside the family. This includes an appreciation of contexts which present danger and risks and having a realistic sense of safety and a capacity to explore and know how to keep themselves safe in new or potentially difficult social contexts.

Difficulties in this area include when children or young people fail to appreciate risks or when they demonstrate undue or excessive anxiety about any appropriate degree of exploration, or alternatively when children are putting themselves in contexts of danger.

Parenting capacity domain

In this section, the parenting capacity domain is examined in a similar way by defining and operationalizing strengths and difficulties for each of the dimensions of parenting capacity, which involves the provision of *basic care, ensuring safety, emotional warmth, stimulation, guidance and boundaries* and *stability* by the parent(s) or carer(s) of the child.

Basic care

Indicators of strengths and difficulties in the *basic care* dimension of parenting capacity are listed in Table 5.8.

Table 5.8 Indicators of strengths and difficulties in the basic care dimension

Strengths	*Parenting capacity*	*Difficulties*
Parents work well together to provide adequate, reasonably organized, effective basic care	**Parents' capacity to provide effective basic care**	Parents fail to provide adequate basic care, parents divided and provide ineffective, inadequately organized basic care
Parents reasonably adaptable to child's changing needs, basic care consistent over time	**Adaptability to changing needs and consistency of basic care over time**	Parents fail to adapt to child's changing needs; basic care inconsistent over time
Parents able to place appropriate reliance and support from extended family and community agencies to provide basic care	**Parents' ability to use extended family and community resources to provide basic care**	Parents place undue reliance of family and community or unable to use family or community resources to enable them to provide basic care

Basic care looks at three main concepts.

PARENTS' CAPACITY TO PROVIDE EFFECTIVE BASIC CARE

The complexity of the parenting tasks involved in providing basic care depends on the nature of the particular child's needs, the number of children and the context in which the family is living. The challenges are particularly great when there are the major changes and disruptions associated with living in a context of family violence. The capacity of the parents to work together to provide basic care, or of a lone parent to work with appropriate family members or external assistance when required, is key to being able to respond to a child's needs. As children grow older, organization of the family's arrangements becomes more complex because there are different demands to ensure children's basic care is adequately provided for and that their health and care needs are appropriately organized and managed by parents.

Strengths are represented when good basic care is provided by parents working well together to provide adequate effective care. When an individual parent is caring alone, strengths are reflected in their being able to manage the complex tasks associated with ensuring that the basic care needs of children are being met single-handed or eliciting the help of others when required.

Difficulties are represented when parents fail to provide adequate basic care in terms of providing food, regular meals, adequate clothing, care over washing, dressing, managing hygiene, ensuring children receive necessary medical care and so on. The delivery of basic care may be inconsistent, chaotic, disrupted or dominated by arguments or attention to the adults' needs or there may be ineffective management of the children's activities, for example, in relation to self-care and social presentation. Parents may have extensive or persistent battles with children about basic care activities such as dressing, washing and behaviour at mealtimes or a child may be expected to care for themselves or care for others in the family, including their parents, in a way not appropriate to their age and stage of development.

ADAPTABILITY TO CHANGING NEEDS AND CONSISTENCY OF BASIC CARE OVER TIME

Parents need to be able to maintain the organization of family arrangements and provide basic care with a reasonable degree of consistency while adapting to the changing needs of children at different ages and stages of development and the specific needs of each individual child.

Strengths: positive features include evidence of parents having a reasonable ability to meet children's changing needs and provide consistent care at different phases of their development.

Difficulties are represented when parents fail to adapt to the changing needs of children. The parenting that might be appropriate for the care of an infant will not meet the needs of that same child moving through school age or into adolescence. There may therefore be an inconsistency in the quality of the parenting provided, with phases of reasonable basic care and adaptability to changing needs and phases where there are significant failures in parenting.

PARENTS' ABILITY TO USE EXTENDED FAMILY AND COMMUNITY RESOURCES TO PROVIDE BASIC CARE

Parents need to be able to use the extended family, when it is a potential source of support, to help provide basic care if required. When parents are separated, the capacity of parents to work together despite separation is an important aspect of parenting to assess. The use of extended family and community agencies is often key for parents to be able to maintain adequate basic care, especially if they have difficulties of their own such as mental health or substance misuse problems, episodes of conflict or domestic violence or other forms of disruption.

Strengths are represented when parents are able to place appropriate reliance and support in providing basic care from extended family and community agencies.

Difficulties include when parents place undue reliance on family or community agencies to provide basic care, or fail to use separated parent figures or family members or community agencies in time of considerable need.

Ensuring safety

Indicators of strengths and difficulties in the *ensuring safety* dimension of parenting capacity are listed in Table 5.9.

**Table 5.9 Indicators of strengths and difficulties
in the ensuring safety dimension**

Strengths	*Parenting capacity*	*Difficulties*
Parents provide positive caregiving responses to care-seeking behaviour by child, evidence of establishment of secure attachments	**Establishment of secure attachments**	Unresponsive caregiving by parents or rejection of care-seeking behaviour by child, evidence of insecure or disorganized attachments
Parents have reasonable expectations of child in respect of protection and ensuring safety, appropriate handling, reliable caregiving and protection	**Parents' expectations of children and handling of protection issues**	Parents have inappropriate expectations in relation to protection and safety of child, unreliable, fragmented caregiving and handling of protection issues
Parents ensure adequate care and safety for children in home and environment	**Provision of safety in the home and in the environment (relative to risks and developmental stage)**	Parents fail to protect children from hazards in the home and environment
Parents protect children from individuals who present a risk to them	**Protection from individuals who present a risk to children**	Parents fail to protect children from individual(s) who present a risk to them in the home environment or elsewhere

Ensuring safety is operationalized to include the following four concepts.

ESTABLISHMENT OF SECURE ATTACHMENTS

The establishment of secure attachments is a key factor in safety. Ensuring safety relies on the core attachment relationships established between children and parents and other appropriate family members. In families where parents have fostered the development of secure attachment relationships and children are securely attached to their parents, the family provides a secure base from which the children can explore, checking back and returning when in need of proximity, keeping safe or reassurance about whether the situation is safe. Parents therefore need to maintain an appropriate level of closeness and distance between themselves and their children in order to maintain the basic safety of the growing child.

Strengths are demonstrated by a child growing up in a context where their parents and other carers provide positive caregiving responses to their care-seeking behaviour and with whom they have established secure attachments. Parents need to ensure these are reinforced and developed with a network of attachment figures both within and outside the family over time. Parents need to provide children with a consistent place of safety and the expectation that their care-seeking needs will be reliably met.

Difficulties occur when parents or carers demonstrate unresponsive caregiving and/or reject care-seeking behaviour by their children. There is a spectrum of more insecure attachments including patterns of clinging or ambivalent care-seeking behaviour by the child, which are associated with unpredictable or inconsistent parenting, or avoidant behaviour, which develops as a result of rejecting and punitive responses to care-seeking. More disorganized attachment patterns emerge in the context of disrupted care or abuse by the child's caregiver. In this way, a network of insecure or disorganized attachments can result in the creation of a context of danger and risk for the child(ren) instead of providing safety.

PARENTS' EXPECTATIONS OF CHILDREN AND HANDLING OF PROTECTION ISSUES

Parents need to adapt the ways they handle protection issues and establish safe boundaries and their expectations of children in response to their growing capacity to care for themselves. They need to adapt. How parents handle their own protection and keeping themselves safe and setting boundaries for themselves and their behaviour is also an important factor, as this provides a model for children in developing an adequate sense of safety and self-management.

Strengths are represented when parents have reasonable expectations of a child in terms of the degree of dependence or independence they develop at different ages and stages of development. When parents are reliable and provide appropriate caregiving and protection and are generally 'there' for the child, it helps to create a context of safety for the child and a model for their own developing capacity to keep themselves safe.

Difficulties are evident in contexts where parents or carers have inappropriate expectations such as, for example, when children are expected to be inappropriately adult and self-caring or are not encouraged to take responsibility for themselves, which can lead to the child failing to develop an appropriate model of self-safety. When care is unreliable, fragmented or the parents' caregiving and handling of their children is rejecting or negative, then a context of both physical and emotional danger exists for the child.

PROVISION OF SAFETY IN THE HOME AND IN THE ENVIRONMENT

Awareness and consciousness about the need to make sure the home is safe for the child and that they are not at risk in the wider environment is an important component of appropriate parenting.

Strengths are represented when parents take steps to ensure the child is safe in the home. Parents and carers demonstrate a constant and continuing awareness of the risks presented to the child and in the wider environment protect them from and prepare them for areas of danger.

Difficulties are indicated when parents ignore or fail to recognize hazards and fail to protect children as a result and do not ensure the child is safe in the wider environment and do not teach the child to recognize risks and potential areas of danger to them.

PROTECTION FROM INDIVIDUALS WHO PRESENT A RISK TO CHILDREN

It is important that parents protect children from individuals who represent a risk to them both inside and outside the home, including, where relevant, former or current partners.

Strengths are evident when the child is not exposed to individuals who present a risk to them because parents or carers are able to recognize concerns about the dangers represented by potentially dangerous individuals or groups and provide an appropriate degree of protection both inside the family and in the wider social context so that the child is not put at risk of harm.

Difficulties in this area of parenting are often indicated by the presence in the family of individuals who present a significant degree of risk to the child or when parents fail to take note of or respond to concerns raised by children or by those outside the family. This often includes parents failing to draw attention to the presence of such individuals to the relevant authorities. In families who are living in a climate of violence, this may include parents having frequent and brief liaisons, partnerships which are made despite concerns about the risk that particular individuals pose. Parents may also ignore worries raised by children and others about individuals caring for the child at home or in the family. If children are exposed to their parents having multiple partners or if their parents have confused gender identity, or if the child is abused by being used as a sexual partner or if they come to associate sexuality with violence, they may become confused about sexual roles and relationships.

Emotional warmth

Indicators of strengths and difficulties in the *emotional warmth* dimension of parenting capacity are listed in Table 5.10.

Emotional warmth looks at a number of areas including the following.

PARENTAL CONSISTENCY, RESPONSIVENESS, EMPATHY AND UNDERSTANDING OF CHILDREN'S VARYING EMOTIONAL STATES

A key component of emotional warmth is concerned with how parents express feelings towards children and their capacity to respond appropriately to varying emotional states shown by children. It is important they are able to provide emotional consistency and that they are receptive and responsive to the child's feelings and are able to show empathy and understanding of children's emotional needs at different ages and stages of development.

Strengths are demonstrated when there is evidence of the parents showing clarity of emotional expression, warmth and consistency towards the children. This is usually reflected by the parents showing warmth, attunement, empathy and understanding with a general sense of tolerance towards the children, and parental responses being appropriate to the feeling states shown by children. If carers reinforce and manage the child's communicated needs effectively, this creates a sense of internal security for the child and a positive sense of their own identity. Containing a child's emotional distress strengthens their expectation that their needs will be met and this helps them to form a core identity built on acceptance and care.

Difficulties: families growing up in a context of violence and abuse may be characterized by a pattern of parents expressing feelings in an intense or over-whelming or inconsistent way. This may include parental coldness, criticism, humiliation and/or and punitiveness towards the children, or a lack of empathy, attunement or understanding or an absence of expression of feelings.

PARENTS' VALUING OF CHILDREN AND PARENTS' EMOTIONAL TONE

Allied to the expression and responsiveness to feeling states of the children is the degree of which children are valued and the general emotional tone of the parents towards the children.

Strengths are represented when the parents have a supportive and mutually valuing approach towards the children, a positive emotional tone and provide a context of calmness and positive coping with parenting.

Difficulties are indicated when parental emotional responses towards the children are attacking, rejecting, scapegoating and/or devaluing, creating a negative chaotic, cold or panicky atmosphere related to parenting, rather than one of calmness and coping with parenting.

Table 5.10 Indicators of strengths and difficulties in the emotional warmth dimension

Strengths	Parenting capacity	Difficulties
Parents express feelings clearly and with consistency, parental warmth, tolerance, receptiveness, attunement, empathy and understanding towards children and appropriate responses to children's feeling states	**Parental consistency, responsiveness, empathy and understanding of children's varying emotional states**	Overwhelming or absent expression of feelings by parents, parents unreceptive, cold, critical or punitive towards children and lack of empathy, attunement and/or understanding, parental inconsistency in responses to children's feeling states
Parents' valuing of child, positive emotional tone, calmness, atmosphere warm	**Parents' valuing of children and parents' emotional tone**	Parents attacking, rejecting, scapegoating, devaluing, undermining towards children with negative emotional tone, negative parental emotions predominate and atmosphere negative, chaotic or panicky
Parents supportive towards children, engaged and involved, respect child, maintain balance of dependence and independence	**Degree of parental support, engagement and participation and management of balance of dependence and independence**	Parents unsupportive, over-involved or under-involved with child, enmeshed with or ignore, exploit, disqualify or humiliate the child; parents promote either under-dependence or over-dependence of child

DEGREE OF PARENTAL SUPPORT, ENGAGEMENT AND PARTICIPATION AND MANAGEMENT OF BALANCE OF DEPENDENCE AND INDEPENDENCE

The degree of support, engagement and participation of parents in the children's lives and managing the balance between dependence and increasing independence is the final aspect of emotional warmth.

Strengths are shown where there is evidence of parental support, engagement and participation with their child while ensuring an appropriate balance of dependence and independence and respect for the child.

Difficulties are shown when there is evidence that parents are either over-involved or under-involved with their children. This may take the form of parents being enmeshed or over-involved with and/or over-dependent on their children with associated conflict avoidance. Alternatively there may be evidence of parents being uninvolved with their children or exploitative, disqualifying or humiliating towards them. They may require the children to be more independent than appropriate for their age and stage of development.

Stimulation

Indicators of strengths and difficulties in the *stimulation* dimension of parenting capacity are listed in Table 5.11.

Table 5.11 Indicators of strengths and difficulties in the stimulation dimension

Strengths	Parenting capacity	Difficulties
Parents provide stimulation, praise and encouragement, responsive to child's learning needs	**Degree of parental stimulation and praise, encouragement and responsiveness to child's learning needs**	Little stimulation provided by parents for child's learning and social development; parents cold, rejecting, undermining, critical atmosphere, unresponsive to child's learning needs
Parents provide clear communication, attentive listening, acknowledgement and responsiveness towards children	**Parents' ability to communicate with children and listen, acknowledge and respond to them**	Parents fail to acknowledge or listen to child, parents controlling, directive, stifling towards children or ignore them; minimal interchange between parents and children
Parents provide challenging tasks and activities in home and social contexts and support learning and social development; parents involved, sharing, focused, and creative in relation to children's play, learning and social activities, provide encouragement, persistence and continuity	**Provision of opportunities for learning and social development and parental participation**	Parents provide few or inappropriate opportunities for learning and social development in family or social context, lack of parental involvement, focus or sharing in relation to children's play, learning or social activities, failure to provide encouragement or continuity
Child well prepared and supported for and parents involved in educational contexts	**Preparation and support for child for educational contexts**	Poor preparation and support for attendance and involvement in educational contexts and parents not involved

Stimulation is concerned with the following four concepts.

DEGREE OF PARENTAL STIMULATION AND PRAISE, ENCOURAGEMENT AND RESPONSIVENESS TO CHILD'S LEARNING NEEDS

Strengths: parents provide a stimulating and enriching environment for the children which is responsive to their learning needs along with encouragement, praise and reassurance to children to help them develop their potential.

Difficulties are characterized by parents failing to provide adequate stimulation for the children so that there is an impoverished environment for their intellectual and social development. Parents may be critical, cold, rejecting and undermining towards the children and unresponsive towards the children's learning needs.

PARENTS' ABILITY TO COMMUNICATE WITH CHILDREN AND LISTEN, ACKNOWLEDGE AND RESPOND TO THEM

Children's educational and social development is enhanced if parents are able to communicate effectively and take part in conversations with their children and children are not excluded or ignored.

Strengths: parents having skills in communicating clearly, and being able to share and pursue a topic of conversation with the children. They can also acknowledge and listen carefully to children when they talk and respond appropriately.

Difficulties include when parents are over-controlling or directive in their communications with children, or when they fail to listen to them or stifle or ignore their communications or when there is minimal interchange.

PROVISION OF OPPORTUNITIES FOR LEARNING AND SOCIAL DEVELOPMENT AND PARENTAL PARTICIPATION

Children's development is likely to be enhanced when parents ensure that they have access to a range of activities which help them develop their knowledge and skills at an appropriate level for their age and stage of development.

Strengths: parents are able to provide adequate opportunities and experiences for learning and social development in different social contexts which reflect appropriate expectations of achievement by their children. This is often achieved by parents creating learning and social opportunities and then participating in activities together where children learn to share, focus and maintain their involvement in an activity or interest, including creative play.

Difficulties may be indicated when parents may provide few appropriate learning or social opportunities for the children and little encouragement or support for the child in relation to their involvement and achievement in schools and other educational contexts. Parents may fail to expect children to achieve, disrupt or abandon tasks relating to learning and social development or fail to participate in social and learning opportunities with the children when appropriate.

PREPARATION AND SUPPORT FOR CHILD FOR EDUCATIONAL CONTEXTS

It is well established that careful preparation of a child for their nursery, school and other educational contexts has a significant impact on the child's educational achievement.

Strengths are reflected if parents take care to provide opportunities for learning and social development as the child grows in ways which prepare them for the different educational contexts they are going to encounter. This includes parents providing structure and support for school work, having expectations of the child achieving at school which helps them maximize their potential and helping them find a balance between the demands of school, relationship with peers and family life.

Difficulties may be indicated when parents fail to provide adequate support for children's learning and social development, have low expectations for their children's achievement or do not help them with managing their school work and balance their friendships, their school commitments and involvement in family life.

This may be particularly important when children have special educational needs which are unrecognized by parents or where they reject concerns about the child's progress. In some cases, parents may perceive children as having far greater difficulties than they in fact have, so that an increasingly negative view of the child may develop over time. Parents may demand more special attention from services than required or fail to provide enough support with education so the young person may reject the idea he or she has special needs, disrupt attempts to support them or reject the learning context altogether. Clearly this can lead to a child or young person failing to achieve their potential with the parents having contributed to failing to address their special needs.

Guidance and boundaries

Indicators of strengths and difficulties in the *guidance and boundaries* dimension of parenting capacity are listed in Table 5.12.

Guidance and boundaries focuses on four main areas.

GUIDANCE AND BEHAVIOURAL MANAGEMENT

Strengths are indicated when appropriate parental guidance and behavioural management of the child can be observed and parental expectations of the child are realistic and there is appropriate use of rewards and sanctions.

Difficulties are present when oppressive behavioural control by parents can be observed. Parents may show excessively punitive response towards their children or have inappropriate expectations of them. Alternatively behavioural management by parents may be absent or inconsistent.

Table 5.12 Indicators of strengths and difficulties in the guidance and boundaries dimension

Strengths	Parenting capacity	Difficulties
Parents provide positive and reflective guidance and behavioural management and adequate care, realistic expectations of children, appropriate use of reward and sanctions	**Guidance and behavioural management**	Absent or oppressive parental guidance and behavioural control, unrealistic expectations of children, inappropriate, punitiveness and use of sanctions and rewards
Parents help child to manage or distract child from frustration	**Helping children manage frustration**	Parental intolerance or reinforcement of frustration or negative states in child
Parents provide flexible boundaries and rules, parents maintain structures and adult and child distinction	**Clarity and flexibility of boundaries, rules and expectations**	Parents set rigid boundaries, lack of boundaries or rules, over-protection or child expected to care for parent
Parents manage decision-making collaboratively in relation to providing guidance and boundaries for children, oppositional behaviours managed without undue conflict with child	**Management of conflict and oppositional behaviour**	Parental provision of guidance and boundaries marked by frequent futile arguments with child, failure to resolve conflicts with or manage oppositional behaviour by child

HELPING CHILDREN MANAGE FRUSTRATION

A key aspect of guidance and boundaries is how parents manage the children's response to frustration. This includes tantrum behaviour in younger children and forceful, aggressive, demanding responses or a significant degree of distress in children and young people at later stages.

Strengths are indicated by parenting which helps children manage or be distracted away from frustration represents a strength. Parents will be observed containing and managing children's frustration with calmness and finding appropriate ways of providing reassurance.

Difficulties are often evidenced by parents showing intolerance of children's frustration and reinforcing their children's negative states through anger, rejection or inappropriate levels of ignoring them.

CLARITY AND FLEXIBILITY OF BOUNDARIES, RULES AND EXPECTATIONS

Strengths are evident when parents provide flexible boundaries while maintaining structures and reasonable expectations for their children. Parents maintain a clear distinction between adults and children, with children being encouraged to take increasing amounts of responsibility without having to take on inappropriate responsibilities.

Difficulties are indicated when parents set rigid boundaries and are inflexible and unresponsive to children's needs. This is often marked by their inability to perceive, understand and manage a child's areas of frustration and behaviour, so that their responses as parents are punitive and rejecting, which then increases the level of the child's difficulties. Alternatively, in situations where children and parents are functioning at a similar level, or where the child is expected to take on a parental role, parents often find it extremely difficult to provide appropriate guidance, and boundaries are often unclear or absent. Parents may give children powerful parental roles and fail to provide management of the children's behaviour or assistance in managing frustrations so that the children fail to develop an appropriate capacity to manage anger and frustration.

MANAGEMENT OF CONFLICT AND OPPOSITIONAL BEHAVIOUR

Strengths are evident in families where guidance and boundaries have been managed adequately, parents help children to manage conflicts appropriately and decision-making is made collaboratively and on the basis of considering the needs of all family members.

Difficulties: in family contexts where there are considerable difficulties, there are frequent, futile arguments between parents and children. Parents may fail to resolve conflicts with children or to make decisions collaboratively and often an atmosphere of considerable discomfort and unhappiness is maintained.

Stability

Indicators of strengths and difficulties in the *stability* dimension of parenting capacity are listed in Table 5.13.

Stability is to do with five main concepts.

DEGREE OF STABILITY OF PARENTING DURING DEVELOPMENTAL AND FAMILY LIFE CYCLE

Strengths: in families where there is a reasonable degree of strength, there is evidence that the parenting has been reasonably stable over the family life cycle and that the parenting provided has remained appropriately focused on providing stability for the children even during times of stress and during potentially destabilizing events.

Difficulties are represented by family contexts where there are significant imbalances or distortions within the parenting partnership and a network of disrupted, unstable relationships. The family structure may transient so that

Table 5.13 Indicators of strengths and difficulties in the stability dimension

Strengths	Parenting capacity	Difficulties
Parents ensure stability provided during development	**Degree of stability of parenting during developmental and family life cycle**	Transient family structure, disruption, no adaptation to changes in family and social contexts
Parents maintain appropriate contact with key members despite separation	**Maintaining contact with known family members**	Isolation of parents and children, contacts not sustained, or distorted
Parents maintain stable network of parents and parent substitutes for children	**Stability of a network of important figures**	Unstable network of parents and parent substitutes
Parents help child to develop social responsibility and a sense of their identity in family, cultural and social contexts	**Developing child's sense of social responsibility and family, cultural and social identity**	Parents expect child to be inappropriately adult or treat them as much younger child, parents fail to help their child to develop sense of their identity in family, cultural and social contexts
Parents maintain consistency and stability in the face of significantly stressful and potentially destabilizing events	**Managing stability in the face of adversity and major family changes**	Children exposed to variations of parental involvement and disruption in the face of stressful and destabilizing events

there are frequent disruptions in parenting, partnerships are unsustained, and there may be high levels of enmeshment, hostility and an absence of warmth inside and outside the family.

MAINTAINING CONTACT WITH KNOWN FAMILY MEMBERS
Strengths: where there are strengths, even though there may be family break-down, nonetheless parents work together to ensure that consistent and adequate contact is maintained with significant family members to enable the children to sustain their attachments.

Difficulties occur when children experience significant separation and isolation from parent figures. Parents may have had a number of partners with whom there is no ongoing contact or support. Relationships may have been disrupted and parents have not maintained contact for the children with key family members.

STABILITY OF A NETWORK OF IMPORTANT FIGURES

This aspect of stability involves parents providing a context in which children can develop secure attachments through being able to rely on the presence of attachment figures who provide attuned, responsive and sensitive caregiving over time.

Strengths: parents ensure that they and other attachment figures for the child are available to the child and provide consistent caregiving over time, even when there are separations or changes in significant adults caring for the child, so that the child has access to a stable network of parents and parent substitutes.

Difficulties: are represented by contexts where there is instability as far as parents and parent substitutes are concerned and children have no network of stable figures on whom they can rely. Parents may not ensure that the child's relationship with key attachment figures is maintained or that they provide attuned and responsive caregiving when the child is with them.

DEVELOPING CHILD'S SENSE OF SOCIAL RESPONSIBILITY AND FAMILY, CULTURAL AND SOCIAL IDENTITY

Strengths: stability ensures that children are helped to develop a sense of social responsibility and are made aware of and helped to feel connected with family, cultural and social contexts as one aspect of a positive sense of their own identity.

Difficulties: in unstable contexts, parents may not ensure appropriate connection with the wider family, or social and cultural contexts so that stability is not provided either from within or outside the family. Parents may expect a child to be inappropriately adult, or to remain in an over-dependent role so that they do not develop a sense of social responsibility or involvement in their family, cultural and social contexts.

MANAGING STABILITY IN THE FACE OF ADVERSITY AND MAJOR FAMILY CHANGES

Strengths: it is characteristic of families where there are strengths that parents can manage to maintain a stable life for children in the face of adversity of major social change, stressful and potentially destabilizing events. This means that despite events in the parents' own lives or in the family social environment, parenting arrangements are maintained with consistency.

Difficulties: considerable difficulties occur when there is extreme variation in parental involvement with children and/or disruption in the face of major stressful and destabilizing events. This may occur as a result of individual parental mental health or other problems, or because of disruptions within the family and social context and environment.

Family and environmental factors domain

Family history and family functioning

In this section strengths and difficulties are defined and operationalized for each of the dimensions in the family and environmental factors domain in turn, i.e. *family history and family functioning, wider family, housing, employment, income, family's social integration* and *community resources*. Indicators of strengths and difficulties in the *family history and family functioning* dimension of family and environmental factors are listed in Table 5.14.

Table 5.14 Indicators of strengths and difficulties in the family history and family functioning dimension

Strengths	Family history and functioning	Difficulties
Stable household, maintenance of significant relationships despite separation and change, family and social support	**Stability of the household**	Unstable changing household, relationships disrupted, not maintained or destabilized by extended family and social context
Stable childhood and protected from major losses or disruption; traumatic events processed, so autonomous functioning achieved	**Parents' childhood**	Unstable family environment in childhood; exposure to violence, abuse, rejection, loss, illness; traumatic events unprocessed and attachments dismissive or preoccupied or entangled
Recognition and acknowledgement of significant past events, relationships and circumstances and appropriate 'coming to terms' with traumatic or distressing experiences	**Impact of family history**	Unresolved past significant events, relationships or circumstances having major impact on current individual emotional states and family functioning
Adequate functioning, reasonable health, acknowledgement and management of physical and mental illness or impairments, or personality difficulties, appropriate management of drugs and alcohol	**Individual functioning of the parents during development and currently, physical and mental health, management of impairments, personality difficulties, criminality, substance misuse**	Negative functioning with regard to physical and mental health, impairments and disability, personality problems, criminal activities, substance misuse
Family members use appropriate treatment; community support is used	**Family's use of treatment and community support**	Family members fail to engage in treatment and social support or reject appropriate services

Table 15.4 cont.

Strengths	Family history and functioning	Difficulties
Couple supportive, respectful, confiding, balance of assertiveness and ability to compromise	**Couple relationship**	Couple isolated, unsupportive, unconfiding, unbalanced, dominant or submissive pattern, destructive, at war
Violent partner ceases domestic violence, acknowledges responsibility, aware of consequences for partner and children; collaborative, sharing, motivation to change	**Domestic violence issues**	Violent partner denies or legitimizes violence, continues to be violent, fails to take responsibility or blames victim, impact on children ignored, uncollaborative, resistance to intervention
Reasonably flexible yet stable family organization meeting individual needs and adaptable to changing circumstances and life cycle stages	**Family organization to meet family members' basic needs and respond to changing needs and stressful events over life cycle**	Family rigid, chaotic, disrupted by stress, minimal adaptation to changing individual needs, inconsistent provision of care for family members
Family members have reasonable strengths in ability to communicate, listen and respond to each other, to express and respond to feelings appropriately, to maintain positive family alliances and a sense of individual and family identity over time	**Nature and stability of family functioning**	Family members have considerable difficulties in communicating clearly and listening to one another and responding appropriately and expressing and responding to emotions positively; family alliances divide or disempower some family members, negative sense of individual and famiy identity

Family history and family functioning is a key area and there are a number of factors that can have a major impact on family life and relationships. *Family history and family functioning* has been operationalized in the following elements.

STABILITY OF THE HOUSEHOLD

This element looks at the way in which significant relationships have been managed in the household, despite separation and change.

Strengths in this area are represented by the maintenance by a stable household and are associated with stability of parenting. If there have been separations or changes, significant relationships have been maintained and adequate support provided to the family members despite separation.

Difficulties arise when there is considerable instability and disruptions are such that close relationships, including children's relationships with significant attachment figures, are not maintained, or the household has been destabilized.

PARENTS' CHILDHOOD

The degree of stability and protection the parents had as children in their own development, and the range of adverse experiences they suffered including exposure to violence and abuse and loss and the way they relate to past experiences can affect their current functioning.

Strengths are represented by the parents having experienced stability in their own childhoods, where they were reasonably protected from major loss or disruption. If traumatic events occurred in their childhood, it is a protective factor if the parents have been able to process them and can describe them using the language of the adult adverse experiences in their childhood with a coherent narrative with congruent emotions linked with those experiences. This is linked to parents having a reasonable degree of autonomous functioning where they are neither preoccupied by nor dismissive about their childhood experiences.

Difficulties are associated with the parents' childhood having been unstable, especially when they have grown up in a family environment where they were exposed to violence, abuse, rejection and illness. It is of concern when it is clear that these experiences have not been adequately dealt with and remain unprocessed in the form of either dismissive attitudes to experiences or when it is evident that the parent remains preoccupied about or entangled with his or her past or idealizes of what may be seen to have been highly stressful.

IMPACT OF FAMILY HISTORY

It is then important to identify whether and how significant events, circumstances and relationships are affecting the current functioning and relationships of family members.

Strengths are indicated when parents recognize and acknowledge the role of significant past events and relationships. They have been able to come to terms with adverse past experiences in an appropriate way and there is evidence that such events are not influencing their current individual functioning, including their mental and physical heath, and their relationships with others in the family and in terms of their capacities to parent adequately.

Difficulties are indicated when parents have been unable to resolve significant events in an emotional sense and it is evident that difficult relationships or circumstances continue to have a major impact on the parents' current physical or mental health and/or emotional state, their capacity to parent and on family functioning.

INDIVIDUAL FUNCTIONING OF THE PARENTS

It is important to assess the individual functioning of the parents, including physical and mental illness, impairments or disability, personality difficulties or involvement with antisocial activities. It is important to know what sort of treatment and community support each individual has had, both in the past and currently, including hospitalization and periods in prison and how they have responded to it.

Strengths are reflected when individuals are able to function adequately in their different roles inside and outside the family. Where individuals have physical or mental health difficulties, they acknowledge and manage them and use and cooperate with appropriate treatment and community support.

Difficulties in this area are indicated when parents' physical or mental health problems are impacting on their current functioning, including their capacity to parent. This may also involve parents having personality problems, or major problems with substance misuse, both drugs and alcohol, and addiction problems. Parents may have difficulty in adapting to physical or mental health problems or impairments or be disabled in ways that affect their capacity to parent. They may be reluctant to cooperate with appropriate treatment provision or to use support within their family or the local community.

COUPLE RELATIONSHIP

Where there are two adults in a family, it can be helpful to assess the couple relationship in terms of the balance of support, respect, the pattern of dominance and submission in relationships and whether the couple can confide in each other.

Strengths: when relationships are supportive, confiding, and appropriately respectful with a balance of assertiveness and compromise, children's welfare is likely to be enhanced. Where one or other parent has significant personal difficulties, a strong couple relationship can serve to neutralize the potential impact on the children and therefore protect them. Even when one of the couple has significant difficulties with parenting, their partner can provide sometimes important support for their individual development in ways which help them develop their parenting skills.

Difficulties are represented when the couple are isolated from each other and fail to acknowledge, confide in or support each other. This includes failing to acknowledge their responsibility to work together as parents in the best interests of the children, even when they may have difficulties as a couple, whether living together or separately. The relationship may be unbalanced with one person being markedly dominant and the other submissive. There may be high levels of destructiveness with a couple being at war and in major conflict about issues such as contact or roles. These factors can have a highly deleterious effect on the capacity to provide adequate parenting.

DOMESTIC VIOLENCE ISSUES

It is important to look carefully at any issues of domestic violence, and the way in which such issues are dealt with in the family as a potentially key factor affecting the parents' response to their children's needs. Domestic violence is a factor often associated with other family and environmental factors, such as individual mental health issues and negative attitudes from the families of origin.

Strengths: where violence has occurred, it is sign of strength when the perpetrator stops being violent, acknowledges appropriate responsibility for the violence and is aware of the consequences for their partner and for their children and is motivated to change. The welfare of the children is more likely to be protected when the couple accept the importance of ensuring the safety of the children, are able to be collaborative and are ready to be involved in appropriate therapeutic programmes.

Difficulties: where there are difficulties the violent partner often legitimizes the violence, justifies, denies or minimizes the extensiveness of the violence. They may fail to cease being violent, blame the victim, fail to take responsibility themselves and ignore the impact on children. They are likely to resist intervention and fail to be collaborative with families and professionals, thus creating contexts of danger and anxiety.

FAMILY ORGANIZATION TO MEET FAMILY MEMBERS' BASIC NEEDS AND RESPOND TO CHANGING NEEDS AND STRESSFUL EVENTS OVER LIFE CYCLE

The family as a system also has to be sufficiently flexible to adapt to the changing needs of family members and the different family life cycle stages over time. This involves the way the family is organized to meet the needs of family members and whether they can respond effectively to any challenging or stressful events they encounter.

Strengths: in family contexts where there are adequate strengths, reasonable family functioning and stability is maintained despite disruptive events. Family functioning and relationships are such that even if an illness, major difficulty or life event arises, there are adequate family and other resources available to cope.

Difficulties: where there are difficulties, it is evident that the family functioning is overwhelmed and disorganized by major events resulting in a chaotic and disrupted family environment.

NATURE AND STABILITY OF FAMILY FUNCTIONING

To meet the changing needs of children and young people through their development family functioning needs to be at an optimal level in terms of the alliances between parents and between parents and children, the capacity for communication and emotional responsiveness and the ability to manage closeness and distance between family members. These aspects of family functioning are central to the parents being able to get their own emotional and other needs met and respond to the needs of their children.

Strengths: when there are strengths, the key aspects of family functioning are well managed including boundaries and closeness and distance between family members, communication and emotional responsiveness so that the changing needs of children are met throughout their development.

Difficulties: where there are difficulties, family functioning is rigid or chaotic and the family is disorganized and disrupted by stress. There are usually significant difficulties in aspects of family relationships such the alliance between the parents, parent–child relationships and the way talking and listening and feelings are handled. This may mean that parenting cannot be provided on a consistent basis and there is not enough flexibility to enable the parents to adequately respond to the changing needs of the children.

Wider family

Indicators of strengths and difficulties in the *wider family* dimension of family and environmental factors are listed in Table 5.15.

**Table 5.15 Indicators of strengths and difficulties
in the wider family dimension**

Strengths	*Wider family*	*Difficulties*
Network of supportive family members; support available when needed with disability, illness and times of stress; caregiving provided and practical and emotional support	**Relationship with the wider family**	Wider family intrusive, over-involved, abandoning or ineffective; failure to provide caregiving or practical or emotional support when needed with disability, illness or times of stress
Protection from individuals presenting risks to family members provided	**Protection of family members from individuals who present a risk to them**	Failure to protect from individuals who present risks to family members

RELATIONSHIP WITH THE WIDER FAMILY

Supportive family members in the wider family can provide a major protective factor in families living with violence. The involvement of unsupportive family members may add to the difficulties for both parents and children and in some cases raise the level of concern about the safety of the children. It is therefore important to understand how far the family is connected to their wider family and whether the adults in the family can take appropriate responsibility for maintaining and managing those relationships.

Strengths: families with strengths in this area have a network of supportive family members in their wider family who provide help and assistance especially in times of stress. Family members, including children, are also protected by the wider family from individuals or potential partners who might represent a risk to them.

Difficulties: in families with difficulties, members of the wider family may be intrusive and over-involved or, alternatively, they may be hostile, critical or disengaged. They may fail to caregive when the need arises or to offer emotional support or practical assistance in times of crisis. The adults may also fail to protect the children from individuals and potential partners who present a risk to them.

There is then a set of issues to do with the supportive infrastructure surrounding the family concerned with housing, employment and income which may interfere with the child's needs for care or contact and ensuring adequate substitute arrangements.

Housing

Indicators of strengths and difficulties in the *housing* dimension of family and environmental factors are listed in Table 5.16.

Table 5.16 Indicators of strengths and difficulties in the housing dimension

Strengths	Housing	Difficulties
Stable housing availability, suitable for needs of child and other family members, maintained by owner or family, child and parent friendly, adapted for disability	**Availability, quality, maintenance and adaptations**	Unstable housing circumstances, unsuitable for needs of child and other family members, poorly maintained by owner or family, poorly adapted for children and/or disability

Housing includes looking at the availability, quality, maintenance and consistency of housing available.

Strengths: with housing it is clearly beneficial for all family members, especially children, when there is stable, suitably maintained housing appropriately adapted to the family and individual children's needs, particularly if there is disability.

Difficulties are present when housing is temporary, poorly maintained or not adequately adapted to the children's specific needs, for example, if there is a large sibling group or if any of the children have a disability, this can significantly increase the difficulties for parents trying to bring up their children.

Employment

Indicators of strengths and difficulties in the *employment* dimension of family and environmental factors are listed in Table 5.17.

**Table 5.17 Indicators of strengths and difficulties
in the employment dimension**

Strengths	Employment	Difficulties
Work available, working patterns consistent with supporting family life and providing adequate consistent care	**Nature and pattern of work**	Inconsistency of work availability, unpredictability of working patterns, work patterns fail to support and provide for family life
Balance between work hours or pattern and child's needs for care or contact and substitute care arrangements adequate	**Balance of work and parenting**	Hours or work pattern undermines family life, or interferes with child's needs for care or contact and substitute care arrangements inadequate
Unemployment managed in way which does not undermine family life	**Issues associated with unemployment**	Unemployment disrupts and undermines family life
Work undertaken by young people or associated responsibilities appropriate	**Child's experience of work**	Undue pressure on children and young people to work or take responsibility for care due to parents' work patterns

Issues of *employment* are central including the nature and pattern of the adult's work and how they balance work with parenting, the child's experience of their parents being at work and how this impacts on income and the use of available resources.

Strengths: there are strengths in this area when working patterns are consistent with supporting family life and providing adequate care for the children. It helps when there is reasonable balance between children's and parents' needs, in terms of work arrangements, and the parents' work patterns do not result in undue responsibility being placed on the children to care for themselves or each other. It is also a strength when periods of unemployment do not undermine family life.

Difficulties: in families with employment difficulties, unpredictable work patterns, long or unreasonable work hours or unemployment disrupts family life and undermines the parents' ability to care effectively for the children. Children may be left to care for themselves while their parents are at work or be required to care for younger siblings on their own.

Income

Indicators of strengths and difficulties in the *income* dimension of family and environmental factors are listed in Table 5.18.

Table 5.18 Indicators of strengths and difficulties in the income dimension

Strengths	Income	Difficulties
Sustained and adequate income, entitlements claimed and utilized	**Availability of income**	Income inadequate, inconsistent or unsustained leading to privation; entitlements not claimed or used inappropriately
Primary focus for use of available resources is on child and family needs	**Use of available resources**	Available resources used on adult needs, children and family needs neglected
Children buffered from variations in income		Children not protected from impact of variations in income
Resources well-managed and adequate standard of care maintained within income		Available resources poorly managed and inadequate standard of care maintained

Strengths are indicated when the income coming into the family is reasonably sustained with adequate standards of care maintained within the family income. Any state entitlements are used with a primary focus on child and family rather than meeting individual adult needs or wishes.

Difficulties are indicated when there are financial problems in families. The income coming into the household may be inadequate, inconsistent or not sustained, leading to family members being deprived of basic requirements. The available financial resources may be poorly managed or used on adult needs or wishes rather than targeted towards the needs of the children and the family as a whole.

Family's social integration

Indicators of strengths and difficulties in the *social integration* dimension of family and environmental factors are listed in Table 5.19.

INTEGRATION OF CHILDREN AND PARENTS INTO LOCAL NEIGHBOURHOOD AND COMMUNITY CONTEXT

The family's *social integration* looks at the integration of children and parents into the local neighbourhood and community context, including the avail-

**Table 5.19 Indicators of strengths and difficulties
in the family's social integration dimension**

Strengths	Family's social integration	Difficulties
Family accepted by and integrated into neighbourhood and wider community	**Integration of children and parents into local neighbourhood and community context**	Children and family isolated, not accepted by or integrated into neighbourhood or wider community
Family uses available resources, educational and social opportunities to support development of children's sense of identity, social skills, independence and sense of responsibility	**Family use of available resources, social and educational opportunities to develop social skills, identity and independence of children**	Family does not use available resources and opportunities for development of child's identity, social skills, independence and sense of responsibility
Acceptance and valuing of diversity; discrimination actively discouraged	**Community attitude to diversity**	Climate of threat, discrimination, absence of tolerance, antisocial influence in neighbourhood and wider community
Peer group and friendship networks available and used by children and adults in family	**Availability and use of peer group and friendship networks**	Peer group and friendship networks unavailable or not used by children and adults in family

ability of peer groups, friendships and social networks and how the adults and children in the family use such resources in the wider family and community. The level of the family's social integration will be affected by the attitudes and climate of neighbourhood and community, for example in relation to diversity and disadvantage and affect their own relationships and capacity to use support.

Children and young people have a right to be accepted and valued whatever their cultural, ethnic, spiritual or religious identity and whether or not they have an impairment. The responses of those around a child to any difference, including to any impairment they may have, can serve to disable a child and reduce their chances of reaching their potential. Interventions need to target such disabling responses in others.

Strengths are represented by the families who are integrated and accepted by the neighbourhood and wider community. The family is able to use the available resources to support the children's development, including building up a positive sense of their identity, their social skills and independence. In the community, there is a climate of acceptance and valuing of diversity and active prevention of discrimination. In addition, peer groups and friendship networks are available for both children and adults in the family.

Difficulties may be indicated when children and other family members are isolated within their community. This may be because they have not actively tried to become integrated into the local neighbourhood and community or because they have not been accepted by others. Peer groups and social and friendship networks may be unavailable. There may be difficulties with specific services. For example, a key factor in how children function in educational contexts is the nature of relationships the child and young person makes with both peers and teachers throughout his or her educational career. If the quality of family–school relationships is poor, this impacts on the relationships between the child and teachers and peers. In addition, the family may not take up the available opportunities that would help to foster the children's sense of identity, or they may not have adequate resources to do so. Alternatively, the family may be living in a climate of threat and discrimination. It may be that family members themselves are an antisocial influence in the neighbourhood.

Community resources

Indicators of strengths and difficulties in the *community resources* dimension of family and environmental factors are listed in Table 5.20.

Table 5.20 Indicators of strengths and difficulties in the community resources dimension

Strengths	Community resources	Difficulties
Availability of accessible community resources and facilities to fit needs of child and other family members	**Community resources and facilities**	Absent or inadequate or inaccessible community resources and facilities which do not fit needs of the child and other family members
Threshold for services reasonable; recognition by services of needs related to child living in context of family violence	**Access to universal services**	High threshold for services; little or no recognition by services of needs related to child living in context of family violence
Specialist resources available and accessible	**Accessibility and availability of specialist resources and services**	Lack of availability of or access to specialist resources and services
Recognition by services of needs related to child living in context of family violence		Little recognition by services of needs related to child living in context of family violence
Good communication between services and family		Poor communication between services and family

COMMUNITY RESOURCES AND FACILITIES

It is important to assess what community resources are available to the family, how accessible they are and whether they fit the needs of the family. This includes the threshold for universal services, and the availability of and access to specialist services. Services have to be able to recognize the needs of children and families living in a context of family violence to provide an effective input. In terms of children with special educational needs, their additional or special needs, whatever their origin, need to be recognized and properly assessed so that adequate intervention and support can be provided. This is linked to how well the professionals providing services communicate with the family and the family's relationship with the professionals with whom they are involved. This is a key factor in the longer term risks of future abuse or neglect for a child remaining in their family, the prognosis for achieving change and the likelihood of interventions being successful.

Strengths: it is clearly helpful when families live in contexts with reasonable community services, where the resources which fit the needs of children or families are available, the threshold for services are reasonable and specialist resources are available and accessible. Good communication and cooperation between the professionals providing services and the family also benefits the children and their development. Where professionals understand the links between children's needs and any current problems they may have and their experiences of abuse, neglect and/or family violence, the support and services provided are likely to be more effective.

Difficulties are indicated when there are few community resources or those which are available are inadequate and do not fit the needs of the family members. In addition, there may be a high threshold for access to services and a lack of specialist resources. Additional needs of children living with family violence may not be recognized. For example, a school may fail to understand the links between a child's experiences of abuse and neglect or other traumatic experiences and current educational difficulties. They therefore may not provide the additional support and specialist input a child requires to begin to be able to achieve more in school. There may be poor communication between those delivering services and the family, with little understanding or flexibility on the part of those providing services and a lack of cooperation from family members.

Case example: The Ward family

The Ward family is used as a case example in Chapter 4 to illustrate the process of assessment, analysis and planning described in earlier chapters. Here the family is referred to again to illustrate the use of the *Family Assessment* and how operationalizing the *Assessment Framework* by focusing further on strengths and difficulties in each dimension can help to explore and highlight the safeguarding concerns, which have been raised by the core assessment.

It became apparent during the interviews set out in Chapter 4 that family history and family functioning was having a significant impact on the situation and it was decided to use the *Family Assessment* to explore these aspects. The *Family Assessment* has been described in Chapter 3 (pp.116–118). It uses semi-structured interviews and family tasks for the assessor to gather the relevant information and can be used as part of a core assessment or as a specialist assessment conducted by professionals from a range of disciplines.

A family meeting was held with Moira Ward, Ian Ross, Laura and Michael Ward present. The interviewer explained the purpose of the interview and explored a range of areas of family life and relationships. The interviewer worked to involve all the family members so that they could have a 'voice' and their perspective could be understood. Some of the key information emerging from the family interview is described below.

When asked who was the main carer of the children, Moira Ward replied that it was her and that she provided comfort to the children. She said that Ian Ross was often not there. The handling of boundaries, parents' expectations of the children and adequate protection, and punishments and rewards was discussed. Ian Ross was emphatic about punishment, stating that 'grounding' was his approach. Moira Ward spoke about Laura being put in her room because she was so argumentative. Laura asserted that it was not just her who was argumentative, indicating that Ian Ross was also 'loud'. Laura and Ian Ross challenged each other. Ian Ross justified his control, shouting and forcefulness, claiming that the way the family worked beforehand was wrong. He said he wanted 'a nice family and that everybody had to obey the rules'.

Moira Ward said there was an unacceptably high level of conflict in the home, which involved Laura and Ian Ross. Michael exhibited considerable distress, covering his ears and head with his arms and tucking his legs up. Moira Ward tried to explain that talking might help the family. Laura and Ian Ross cut across her and did not listen. Ian Ross leant across with a controlling, aggressive, blaming response to Laura, who tried to assert the reality of what she saw happening at home.

The interviewer explored who in the family wanted the situation to be different. Both adults agreed that peace would be a desirable outcome. Ian Ross indicated that peace would occur when people agreed with his approach, which he emphasized with powerful gestures of the hands and arms. Laura asserted that the family unit had worked in the past and that they could live in peace again without the presence of Ian Ross.

The children were able to respond to a question about Ian Ross's smacking. Michael pointed at Ian Ross and Laura said firmly that it was Ian

Ross who had the hardest hand. The interviewer asked the parents about times when they might have lost control, and whether they had been concerned about the children getting hurt. Ian Ross forcefully stated that he had never laid a finger on the children, challenging anyone to dispute this. He acknowledged shouting, but not physical punishment.

Laura confronted Ian Ross by bringing up the subject of his physical abuse of her mother. She demonstrated a strong alliance with her mother, wanting to speak for her and for her to be protected. Moira Ward attempted to say that the conflict had been forgotten and patched over, although she accepted the fact that this does not guarantee that violence will never happen again. Attempts were made to silence Laura, who was labelled by Ian Ross as vindictive.

The interviewer asked whether 'some hitting' happened, noted that Michael had curled up even more when the subject was raised, and connected it with the initial problem, which they had identified as high levels of argument. Moira Ward asserted that there had been one incident early in her relationship with Ian Ross when he had hit her, partly attributing it to drink and acknowledged that she had been accused of 'asking for it', adding, 'perhaps I was'. She indicated her own strength and resources – she was not going to accept his violence and so 'chucked him out'. She asserted somewhat anxiously that Ian Ross had learnt his lesson. Ian Ross stated that it was 'a stupid mistake'; while not blaming alcohol he indicated that he was 'the worse for wear' and the 'violence was out of character'. He stated that he 'had to plead' to be accepted back into the family.

Laura pointed out that Michael was sitting in the interview crying. The interviewer invited Moira Ward to give him a cuddle. Laura described the process of arguments leading to her mother's stress, and her going to get a drink. Ian Ross minimized the situation, saying, 'We all like a bit of a drink'. Moira Ward focused on drink as a means of helping her 'unwind' rather than helping her cope with conflicts or avoid her need for external support. Laura voiced concern for her mother. Michael remained curled up, withdrawn and avoided eye contact.

The interviewer asked about various aspects of the family's care and how they managed the day. Laura described how she got Michael up each morning. Michael said that he had to 'make himself ready, brush his teeth, remember everything and get to school'. Moira Ward described this as an aspect of the new regime, 'the new rules' and the need for the children to be independent. In saying this, Moira Ward said they were Ian's 'new rules' and reflected Ian Ross's view of Michael and the need to 'toughen him up'. Laura asserted that Michael was only eight years old.

The family were asked to undertake a task without the interviewer being directly involved. They were asked to imagine they were going on an outing together and plan a day out together. The task started positively. Ian Ross brought up what seemed to be a positive idea – they could all go on an outing to Hastings, by the sea. Moira Ward smiled and Michael showed a warm response. Laura cut across saying that Michael could not do 'that many things'. Both Moira Ward and Ian Ross then asked Laura what she would want to do. Both cut across each other and across Laura, creating an uncomfortable atmosphere. Michael curled up. Laura refused to take the lead, or make any suggestions. Her negative response evoked a negative, critical comment from her mother.

Moira Ward and Ian Ross joined together in criticism of Laura. Then Laura and Ian Ross confronted each other in a 'head to head' – Ian Ross told Laura not to 'grit her teeth' at him as she challenged his authority. Moira Ward desperately tried to reduce the tension, saying they should just drive anywhere. Laura said they just would not 'survive together in a car for any length of time'. She revealed her concern about the uncomfortable nature of current family life.

Moira Ward then took the initiative and, indicating her negotiating skills, tried to suggest an activity, which would be caring and positive for both children. She suggested that they should get their rooms decorated and sorted out. Ian Ross was unable to agree with this suggestion. He asserted that Moira Ward's ideas were impractical, that the cost would be too great, and implied once more that she would allow the children to be in control rather than herself. Moira Ward challenged this in a minor way, saying that a pot of paint cost eight pounds rather than the hundreds of pounds he implied. Laura asserted Ian Ross was 'tight-fisted'. There ensued an escalating battle between Laura and Ian Ross, with mother opting out and Michael being withdrawn.

The interviewer talked to the family about the theme of family likes and dislikes in order to explore issues of identity, family alliances and the emotional life of the family. Moira Ward was initially asked about what she likes about Ian Ross. She talks about liking Ian Ross's strength. The interviewer asked Ian Ross what he thought Moira Ward would say if she were asked what she found more difficult about him – following the principle of not putting potentially vulnerable family members, in this case Moira Ward, in a difficult position by directly inviting them to talk about negative aspects of their partner. He said he knew she found the arguments difficult. Moira Ward was then able to make quite a forceful statement about the fact that Ian Ross has a son who is very different to Michael. She tries to tell Ian Ross that he should not make comparisons between his son and Michael. She went on to say that she wished that he would not make comparisons because Michael was not quite as strong as other boys. She put her arm around Michael's shoulders.

Turning to the children, the interviewer asked them what they like about their mother as a mother. Laura picks up on her mother's attempts to keep the peace in her house as something she likes – she recognized that her mother attempts to defuse arguments. Michael was also asked about what he liked about his mum, and as he talked about liking a cuddle with her, he wraps himself up, holding his arms and almost seeming to sink into his tee-shirt. Moira Ward put her arm around him. Michael emphasized that he liked time with her, when this was possible.

The interviewer asked indirectly what the family might dislike, again following the principle that to put children into a position where they have to challenge the adult or parent is usually unacceptable. She asked Moira Ward and Ian Ross to consider what they imagine the children might find difficult. Moira Ward referred to herself and talked about 'being preoccupied' – the arguments were on her mind and the start of each day did not feel fresh as the difficulties from the day before pressed in on her. Laura stated that this was not the case before Ian Ross came on the scene. Her mother did not respond to this and talked about Laura arguing.

The interviewer then tried to get confirmation from both children, asking them for feedback on the mother's statement that she was preoccupied. They agreed with this. Michael's body language and emphatic non-verbal agreement gave a clear indication that he found the change in his mother, her preoccupation, withdrawal and associated difficulties problematic. The interviewer then asked whether he felt his mother worries about him too much. He said he wanted more rather than less of his mother's attention and indicated that too much of her energy is being taken up with arguments between Laura and Ian Ross.

Another family task was used to explore the nature of the family relationships further. In contrast to asking the family directly about their likes and dislikes, the family were asked to talk to each other about their likes and dislikes while the interviewer remained silent. This task provided an alternative way of understanding the family's sense of themselves as a family. This revealed very similar patterns to the interview. Moira Ward started by trying to urge the family to take part, which there seemed to be a reluctance to do. Ian Ross, with some reluctance to joining in the task, rather jokingly said that he did not like Brussel sprouts. Moira Ward talked about not liking football. Michael revealed an important dislike, saying that he did not like sleeping with the light off. Laura said very forcefully that she did not like Ian Ross and he responded to this by indicating that this was a blunt statement.

As if thinking further about Michael's statement, Laura asked Michael whether having the light off was the reason why he could not go to sleep, and Michael confirmed that he did not like the light off. This immediately provoked a response from Ian Ross, confirmed by Moira Ward, that Michael should not be 'wrapped in cotton wool' as he was old enough to have the light off. Moira Ward sided with Ian Ross, agreeing with him. Laura then got into an argument; she pointed out that Michael was not sleeping. He looked scruffy. He was not his usual self. He was not coping. She noted that 'then you shout at him for being tired'. The task ended with Moira Ward joining Ian Ross in his criticism of Laura's attitude and with Laura asserting that she didn't care what Ian Ross thought.

The above section of the interview was brought to a conclusion and Moira Ward and Ian Ross were subsequently interviewed about their background and history. Moira Ward's family background was characterized by punitive, parental attitudes and domestic violence. She had had a number of partners herself and had used alcohol in the past as a coping strategy. This seemed to have had the effect of evoking Laura's support and Michael's anxious clinging attachment. Ian Ross came from a hard-drinking, male-orientated family in which his father used domestic violence as a way of maintaining control. Moira Ward was further interviewed on her own about the episode of domestic violence and her use of alcohol referred to earlier in the interview. She confirmed that there had been one incident that had been associated with Ian Ross drinking and as stated in the interview she told him to leave, which he did. She acknowledged her use of alcohol had increased. When asked about her difficulty getting up in the morning, she thought the alcohol might be contributing to this.

Michael and Laura were spoken with together. Regarding being hit by Ian Ross, Michael confirmed the account he had given in the earlier interview with his mother (using the *HOME Inventory*, see Chapter 4), namely that Ian Ross has recently been hitting him about two or three times a week. Michael said that Ian Ross hit him on the legs as a punishment. Both Michael and Laura confirmed they had witnessed Ian Ross hit their mother on the occasion referred to earlier. Michael said he was frightened when this happened. They both reported Moira Ward drinking more heavily than usual. They contrasted the present situation with how things had been when their mother lived with Gary Wills, her previous partner. Then their mother drank less and seemed less worried. They both reported that they had liked Gary Wills very much and were very sad when he left.

Examination of social work and medical records indicate concerns about previous episodes of neglect and instances of violence between Moira Ward and previous partners.

Categorizing information and identifying strengths and difficulties

Having obtained further information the next task is to add the information to that which has been previously obtained and categorized in Chapter 4 and thereafter analyse it in the manner set out in Chapters 2 and 4. Rather than repeat the exercise entirely here we have chosen to select certain dimensions from each domain to demonstrate this approach to categorizing the information and identifying strengths and difficulties in each dimension gathered in more complex cases particularly those involving safeguarding concerns. For clarity, we have also continued to focus the example on Michael, though Laura's needs are obviously also important.

Children's developmental needs domain

Health

GENERAL PHYSICAL HEALTH AND GROWTH AND DEVELOPMENT

Michael aged eight has a generally reasonable health history and has thrived. There are no persistent developmental problems. Concerns about health have been more recent given Michael's neglected appearance. He is reported to be tired on arrival at school so may have suffered lack of sleep. Michael is reported to complain of headaches and stomach-aches at school.

PHYSICAL AND SEXUAL ABUSE AND NEGLECT

Michael has a consistent evening meal but he either goes without breakfast or has very little. He is reported to be hungry at school in the morning. Over recent months where there has been a degree of neglect, concerns about appearance, lateness at school, not having regular meals, a change in levels of functioning consistent with recent neglect in a child who had previously functioned more satisfactorily.

More recently Michael and Moira Ward have reported that he has been hit by Ian Ross two or three times a week. Michael has been exposed to physical violence perpetrated by Ian Ross against Moira Ward.

MENTAL HEALTH

The results of the *Adolescent Well-Being Scale* suggest that Michael may be suffering from a depressive disorder.

Level of strengths, difficulties and risk

Strengths				*Difficulties*
			X	

Education

DEVELOPMENTAL, COGNITIVE AND LANGUAGE SKILLS

There has been satisfactory unfolding of skills, and evidence of generally positive development until recent concerns about Michael's development.

ATTITUDE TO LEARNING AND WORK AND ADJUSTMENT TO EDUCATIONAL CONTEXT

Michael is showing developmental difficulties and poor adjustment to educational contexts. Key concerns include Michael's poor attendance at school, arriving late, poor concentration, appearing hungry, unkempt, a significant change in educational response, and his current negative response to learning.

EDUCATIONAL PROGRESS

Michael's performance at school has deteriorated. Previously he had been performing at an average level. Michael had been positive about learning and work, previously, Michael's failure of progress has led to concerns.

SPECIAL EDUCATIONAL NEEDS

Michael has basically good potential, and has not required specific intervention and support for special needs.

Level of strengths, difficulties and risk

Strengths				Difficulties
			X	

Emotional and behavioural development

REGULATION OF EMOTIONAL STATES, RELATIVE TO AGE AND DEVELOPMENTAL STAGE

There is evidence from the SDQ that Michael is at high risk of having an emotional disorder and from the *Adolescent Well-Being Scale* that he is at risk of developing a depressive disorder. Michael was observed to cover his ears and head with his arms and tucking his legs up during sections of the *Family Assessment* interview. Michael curled up even more when the subject of 'hitting' was raised. He was observed to be crying, withdrawn and avoiding eye contact during sections of the interview. Michael's emotional responses are to be withdrawn, highly distressed, frozen, with a pervasive depressed mood.

EARLY ATTACHMENT BEHAVIOUR

Michael has a history of an anxious clinging attachment to his mother at times of stress, e.g. when his mother was suffering domestic violence by her partners, and/or when she was drinking heavily.

CONCENTRATION AND LEVEL OF ACTIVITY

There is evidence from the SDQ that Michael is at medium risk of having hyperactivity or concentration disorder. His concentration at school has deteriorated during the course of the last year.

EXPRESSION OF FEELINGS AND CHARACTERISTIC MOOD

Michael shows evidence of a presence of a pervasive, negative mood and withdrawal.

RESPONSE TO TRAUMATIC AND STRESSFUL EVENTS

During the family meeting Michael was observed to be curled up and withdrawn and he avoided eye contact. When an argument took place between Ian Ross and Laura, Michael exhibited considerable distress, covering his ears and head with his arms and tucking his legs up. There is concern about Michael's recent exposure to domestic abuse perpetrated against their mother by Ian Ross, fuelled by his use of alcohol and the impact of his mother's withdrawal associated with alcohol misuse. This is contributing to Michael's withdrawal, depressed affect and neglected appearance.

SOCIAL BEHAVIOUR

There is evidence from the SDQ that Michael is at low risk of having a conduct disorder. He was also found to have 'low needs' in terms of his pro-social behaviour.

Level of strengths, difficulties and risk

Strengths				Difficulties
			X	

Identity

SENSE OF SELF AS INDIVIDUAL IN FAMILY

Michael is showing evidence of disruption of his closeness to his mother. He said he wanted more cuddles with his mother and wanted her to think about him more. He regrets the loss of Gary Wills, his mother's previous partner, with whom he had a positive identification. He is distant from Ian Ross. He is notably quieter and more withdrawn in the presence of Ian Ross.

INDIVIDUAL CHOICE AND ACTION

Michael was consistently able to assert his views when he was interviewed with his mother and his sister. In contrast he was rarely able to do this when interviewed in the presence of Ian Ross.

SENSE OF SELF AND OTHERS, FAMILY, SOCIAL AND CULTURAL

Generally Michael is showing increasing difficulties in being appropriately assertive and this is related to his pattern of withdrawal. He is not as confident or happy as he used to be in both social contexts, e.g. school, where is withdrawing from peer relationships, and in the family home.

GENDER AND/OR SEXUAL IDENTITY OF RELATIONSHIPS

Michael does not exhibit any particular problems in terms of sexual identity and relationships.

Level of strengths, difficulties and risk

Strengths				*Difficulties*
			X	

Family and social relationships

CHILD'S GROWING RELATIONSHIPS WITH FAMILY AND OTHERS

Within the family context in the past, Michael had more satisfactory relationships with both his mother and her former partner than he does now. While there is evidence of warmth in Michael's relationship with his mother, his family relationships are now marked by disruption, unstable relationships and hostility. He interacted with his mother when they were alone together but did not participate in a family meeting, remaining largely quiet throughout. Michael is showing a degree of both clinging to his mother and withdrawal from the family.

DEVELOPMENT OF NETWORK OF ATTACHMENTS

Michael has a history of an anxious clinging attachment to his mother. There have been disruptions of attachments with his father, and with Gary Wills, his mother's previous partner. Michael has indicated feelings of sadness and loss about Gary's departure. He has no contact with either his father or Gary. Relationships with paternal figures and partners have been disrupted including separation from a partner who had provided positive interaction. He has a poor relationship with Ian Ross and has not made an attachment to him.

RELATIONSHIP WITH PARENTS, SIBLINGS AND PEERS

The results of the SDQ regarding Michael's pro-social behaviour suggest that he has developed social skills and has an ability to relate to others. During the *HOME Inventory* interview Michael made persistent demands of his mother for food, His mother described him as a child who whined a lot. The *Family Activity Scale* showed that he had not had a friend visit him in the last month. He is not able to get out and see friends.

RELATIONSHIPS IN SCHOOL

Michael withdraws from social relationships in educational contexts. Michael is lonely among his peers at school. Over the last year, his number of friends at school has reduced.

ATTITUDES OF FAMILY, SOCIAL AND CULTURAL CONTEXTS

While Michael has a history of well-developed pro-social skills, he is presently quite isolated within the family and at school. He has little contact with his extended family.

Level of strengths, difficulties and risks

Strengths				Difficulties
				X

Social presentation

UNDERSTANDING THE NEED TO PAY ATTENTION TO APPEARANCE, DRESS, BEHAVIOUR HYGIENE AS APPROPRIATE FOR THEIR AGE, GENDER AND CULTURE

Michael's physical appearance has changed over the last year. He used to be well turned out at school. Michael is showing increasing failure to pay attention to appearance, dress and hygiene, with an increasingly neglected presentation.

Level of strengths, difficulties and risk

Strengths				Difficulties
			X	

Self-care skills

DEVELOPING A CAPACITY FOR INDEPENDENT LIVING SKILLS

There are concerns about Michael's poor self-care skills, difficulties in meeting parental expectations. His response is to become less competent in terms of his self-care skills. Michael's problem-solving skills in family and community are showing increasing signs of difficulty, including his failure to attend school on time, or to make sure that he has adequate nutrition, and his not being able to organize and manage himself at home or in the community. His needs for support, guidance and care are considerable.

DEVELOPING A CAPACITY TO PROBLEM-SOLVE IN FAMILY AND
COMMUNITY CONTEXTS

Michael is not able to perform some of the self-care tasks expected of him by his mother and Ian Ross, such as taking a bath, washing himself in the morning or getting his own breakfast and getting to school on time.

APPRECIATION OF RISKS AND SAFETY

Michael is generally anxious and fearful.

Level of strengths, difficulties and risk

Strengths				*Difficulties*
			X	

Parenting capacity domain

Basic care

PARENTS' CAPACITY TO PROVIDE EFFECTIVE BASIC CARE

Moira Ward has in the past demonstrated a reasonable capacity to provide basic care for the home and the children and that she has been a competent home-maker. Evidence from school and the *HOME Inventory* interview suggests that the standards of the basic care provided to the children has deteriorated. The provision of breakfast in the morning is variable. Moira Ward does not always ensure there are the basic supplies necessary for breakfast available and has been sleeping in and not able to prepare breakfast for Michael. She has not been able to supervise his personal hygiene or ensure the availability of clean clothing. The couple have been able to ensure the provision of warmth and shelter for the children. However, they appear unable to ensure that Michael has adequate sleep at night. Ian Ross's expectations and views about Michael caring more independently for himself have led to increasing conflicts between himself and Moira Ward, who feels caught between him and the children. As a result there has been a failure of provision of adequate care, with inappropriate expectations of Michael for self-care and self-organization. His appearance is neglected, there are inadequate meals, inappropriate expectations of self-care and he is late and failing in school.

ADAPTABILITY TO CHANGING NEEDS AND CONSISTENCY OF BASIC CARE OVER TIME

Conflict between Ian Ross and Moira Ward about what it is reasonable to expect Michael to do for himself prevents Moira Ward responding to Michael. She has become less aware of and responsive to his basic needs. Her basic capacity to provide care adequately becomes increasingly less effective.

Moira Ward is becoming less sensitive to Michael's needs, as Ian Ross becomes more critical and demanding he focuses on work rather than support Moira's basic care of children. His expectations distort the views of what is required to adapt to the children's needs.

PARENT'S ABILITY TO USE EXTENDED FAMILY AND COMMUNITY RESOURCES TO PROVIDE BASIC CARE

With the family's recent move there has been limited use of the extended family support. Also, in contrast to Moira Ward's previous behaviour, there has been a reluctance on her and Ian Ross's part to be involved with community agencies in response to the concerns expressed by the school about Michael's poor attendance and neglected appearance.

Level of strengths, difficulties and risk

Strengths				*Difficulties*
			X	

Ensuring safety
ESTABLISHMENT OF SECURE ATTACHMENTS

The past history of the family is a one of reasonably secure attachments between Moira Ward and her children, particularly reinforced by her relationship with a previous partner. Michael has always been more clingy. In response to Ian Ross's views about Michael being over-protected, Moira Ward's caregiving is less responsive resulting in the degree of neglect experienced by Michael and a context of considerable insecurity for him and Laura. In terms of the analysis of the processes taking place in the family, Moira Ward's increasing drinking makes her less sensitive to safety issues.

PARENTS' EXPECTATIONS OF CHILDREN AND HANDLING OF
PROTECTION ISSUES

There are inappropriate expectations of Michael in terms of his age and
stage of development, expectations of self-care and independence.
Boundaries are ineffectively managed; there is a failure to protect the family
environment given Moira Ward's increasing pattern of heavy drinking.

SAFETY IN THE HOME AND IN THE ENVIRONMENT RELATIVE TO RISKS
AND DEVELOPMENTAL STAGE

There has been a failure of protection of the children from Ian Ross as a
potentially punitive individual who is attempting to influence family life
towards his expectations of a change from the laissez-faire but emotionally
positive response to an atmosphere of tension and a punitive parenting style
which reduces the sense of safety for both children.

PROTECTION FROM INDIVIDUALS WHO PRESENT A RISK TO CHILDREN

There is evidence that Michael has been hit or 'clipped' by Ian Ross, and
that Moira has not been able to prevent it happening. This was reported by
Michael and Moira Ward in the *HOME Inventory* interview. The results of
the *emotional climate* subscale of the *HOME Inventory*, which indicates the
amount of restriction and punishment experienced by the child, showed a
raised level of concern. The results of the *Family Assessment* interview reveal
that Ian Ross denies 'hitting/clipping' Michael. Moira Ward did not
challenge him about this denial despite having told the social worker in the
HOME interview, in the presence of Michael, that 'hitting/clipping' of
Michael by Ian Ross took place as frequently as two or three times a week.
Moira Ward's inability to challenge Ian Ross about this increases concerns
about her capacity to protect Michael from Ian Ross.

Level of strengths, difficulties and risk

Strengths				*Difficulties*
			X	

Emotional warmth

PARENTAL CONSISTENCY, RESPONSIVENESS, EMPATHY AND
UNDERSTANDING OF CHILDREN'S VARYING EMOTIONAL STATES

There is evidence that the family unit of Moira, Laura and Michael Ward
and Gary Wills was one where there was effective emotional responsiveness,
a reasonable degree of warmth and understanding. While Moira Ward has
demonstrated a capacity to provide emotional warmth in the past and to a
limited degree in the present, there is evidence that this capacity has been

influenced by Ian Ross's more rigid attitude and has led to the couple deciding to implement a somewhat stricter parenting regime.

The change in the family make-up with the arrival of Ian Ross has led to a significant change in emotional warmth. Michael is being required to 'grow up'. An example of this is Ian Ross's insistence, supported by Moira Ward, that the hall light is turned off at night when Michael goes to bed, something which means he is scared at night and does not sleep well. Moira Ward demonstrated more physical warmth towards Michael when they were interviewed together than she did when the family, including Ian Ross, were interviewed. The score for the *responsivity* subscale of the *HOME Inventory* raised a concern regarding parental warmth and affection. With a different level of expectation, there is a greater criticism, punitiveness, a failure of understanding and responsiveness.

PARENTS' VALUING OF CHILDREN AND PARENTS' EMOTIONAL TONE

When Michael and Moira Ward were interviewed together, there was evidence of Moira Ward exhibiting a mixture of warmth and positive emotional tone with devaluing and negative comments. When the family were interviewed together there was a serious increase in negative tone, criticism, attack and hostility within the family, although this was mostly directed towards Laura and principally by Ian Ross, with some agreement by Moira Ward. Moira Ward reports that Ian Ross compares Michael unfavourably to his son of the same age by another relationship, which she comments she wishes Ian Ross would not do: it is clear she is aware that this is not helpful for Michael.

DEGREE OF PARENTAL SUPPORT, ENGAGEMENT AND PARTICIPATION
AND MANAGEMENT OF BALANCE OF DEPENDENCE AND
INDEPENDENCE

The context prior to Ian Ross' arrival, when there was support, valuation, participation between mother, her previous partner and the children, has now changed. The score for the *encouragement of maturity, enrichment* and *family companionship* subscales of the *HOME Inventory* raised a concern regarding the participation of Moira Ward and Ian Ross in any activities with Michael and the lack of supportive guidance being given to Michael to help him mature. Expectations are set about the completion of homework but no help is given to Michael to help him comply with this expectation.

Level of strengths, difficulties and risk

Strengths				*Difficulties*
				X

Stimulation

DEGREE OF PARENTAL PRAISE, ENCOURAGEMENT, ENRICHMENT AND
RESPONSIVENESS

Originally the family appeared to be a context where there was reasonable
parental praise, warmth and responsiveness, with Michael responding
reasonably to his educational context. With the change there has been far
more parental criticism, rejection, undermining, a gradual failure of
appropriate stimulation and support for Michael. The results of the *HOME
Inventory* interview showed a lack of involvement on the part of Moira Ward
and Ian Ross in any activities with Michael or, indeed, in supervising his
homework.

PARENTS' ABILITY TO COMMUNICATE WITH CHILDREN AND LISTEN,
ACKNOWLEDGE AND RESPOND TO THEM

During the *Family Assessment* it was evident that communication between
Moira Ross and Ian Ward and the children is now disrupted, characterized
by forceful statements, withdrawal, high levels of conflict, failure to listen
and failure to develop a constructive dialogue. There are some exceptions to
this when Moira Ward responds to Michael's expressions of his wish to
spend more time with his mother and his wish that she worried more about
him and less about Ian Ross and Laura. On these occasions, she put an arm
round him and leaned towards him.

PROVISION OF OPPORTUNITIES FOR LEARNING AND SOCIAL
DEVELOPMENT AND PARENTAL PARTICIPATION,

Although there was an adequate supply of *learning materials* and *opportunities*
provided in the home, as measured by the *HOME Inventory*, the subscale of
enrichment, which is the extent to which Moira Ward and Ian Ross
consciously utilize family and community resources to enrich the
development of Michael in activities outside of the home, showed an
elevated level of concern. Michael appears to be frequently grounded and
has few opportunities for socializing with friends. He is not allowed to have
friends in the home. Discussion of the *Family Activity Scale* revealed that
Michael used to be engaging in more activities a year ago than he does now.
This has been in terms of family activities together outside the home, and an
increasing withdrawal of Michael from outside activities.

PREPARATION AND SUPPORT FOR CHILD FOR EDUCATIONAL
CONTEXTS

In the past Moira Ward participated and supported the children's
educational participation. She used to have regular involvement with the
school. Now there is a significant failure in ensuring that Michael is being

adequately prepared for educational provision which is manifested in Moira Ward and Ian Ross not ensuring Michael's attendance at school on time, failing to ensure he has enough sleep to concentrate, and failing to provide adequate nutrition, or support for homework.

Level of strengths, difficulties and risk

Strengths				*Difficulties*
			X	

Guidance and boundaries

GUIDANCE AND BEHAVIOURAL MANAGEMENT

There has been significant change within the family life as far as guidance, care and management are concerned. There is evidence from the *encouragement of maturity* subscale of the *HOME Inventory* of an elevated level of concern about Moira Ward and Ian Ross's capacity to help Michael in this area. They clearly expect Michael to get his own breakfast, attend to his own personal hygiene, tidy his room and so forth, but provide him with little support to help him do this. These expectations have changed substantially with the arrival of Ian Ross and are not consistent with what had been previously expected of him. In the *Family Assessment* interview it was clear that Ian Ross perceives discipline and control as having being absent and he asserted that Moira Ward was failing to maintain appropriate boundaries and discipline. His expectations are higher and failure on the part of Michael (and Laura) to comply evokes increasingly punitive responses. He also has expectations that Michael should be more independent, take on self-care capacities, which Moira Ward is complying with. Firmness, use of time out 'groundings', 'hitting/clipping' are being used extensively, as well as punitive rejecting responses.

HELPING CHILDREN MANAGE FRUSTRATION

Ian Ross is intolerant of distress and anger and oppositional responses and fails to appreciate and understand Michael's responses to considerable change in the household. Moira Ward is able to be more sympathetic to Michael when interviewed on her own with him than she is when interviewed with Ian Ross present. She is also, despite her pattern of complying with Ian Ross, able to stick up for Michael occasionally during the *Family Assessment* interview.

CLARITY AND FLEXIBILITY OF BOUNDARIES, RULES AND EXPECTATIONS

There is therefore a confusion of boundaries which are rigid but get poorly maintained, with a failure of protection and responsiveness. Michael is expected to care for himself without adequate support or guidance, resulting in failure to complete homework or have a bath at night. There are frequent arguments and failure of conflict resolution, and an absence of agreement and development of an appropriate agreed set of rules and expectations.

MANAGEMENT OF CONFLICT AND OPPOSITIONAL BEHAVIOUR

Conflict is poorly managed. When Michael's school sends notes regarding his late arrival, Ian Ross's response is to 'clip' him and then for Moira Ward and Ian Ross to 'ground' Michael. The responses of Ian Ross and Moira Ward include an increase in their expression of anger towards Michael. There is evidence of an increasing risk of physical abuse. Overall there is a marked absence of adequate guidance for Michael and a marked presence of punitive responses.

Level of strengths, difficulties and risk

Strengths				*Difficulties*
			X	

Stability

DEGREE OF STABILITY DURING DEVELOPMENTAL AND FAMILY CYCLE

The relationship between the mother and the two children has been stable, but has been undermined by the breakdown of Moira Ward's relationship with her previous partner, Gary Wills, and her attempt to maintain the relationship with her new partner. Michael has had at least three significant male father figures in his life. He had developed a positive relationship with Moira Ward's former partner, Gary Wills, which is in marked contrast to Ian Ross's relationship with Michael. Ian Ross is unyielding towards Michael and displayed little evident affection towards him. Moira Ward has always cared for her children and they have never lived separately from her.

MAINTAINING CONTACT WITH KNOWN FAMILY MEMBERS

There has been a failure of maintenance of contact for the children with parental figures, which has added to the sense of instability, a lack of contact with extended family members or parental figures.

STABILITY IN THE FACE OF ADVERSITY AND MAJOR FAMILY CHANGE

Moira Ward is attempting to introduce change into the family to support her relationship with Ian Ross, with the risk of the children becoming isolated from her, the likelihood of an increased use of controlling behaviour by Ian Ward and an increased risk of further violence and family breakdown. There is a resultant general instability in the family network, confusion about expectations of the children in terms of their roles and expectations.

There has therefore been considerable stress associated with the change of family structure, violence between Moira Ward and her new partner, leading to her excess drinking, plus withdrawal and oppositional behaviour by Michael and Laura respectively. There is a feeling of instability and risk of family breakdown.

Level of strengths, difficulties and risk

Strengths				Difficulties
			X	

Family and environmental factors domain
Family history and family functioning
STABILITY OF THE HOUSEHOLD

Moira Ward and Ian Ross have both had a number of relationships, Ian Ross having a son by a previous partner, and Moira Ward having separated from Michael and Laura's father, also having a number of partners including a positive relationship for three years with Gary Wills before her relationship commenced with Ian Ross, some 12 months before the assessment.

Thus both parents have had a degree of instability of household, attachments disrupted and not maintained, to the distress of Michael and Laura. Ian Ross's rigid, high expectations appear to mirror his previous family relationships, his son being a very different child to Michael. Ian Ross has attempted to recreate his previous family context. A struggle to maintain stability is a common factor to both parents. There is considerable instability of the current household for Michael and Laura.

PARENTS' CHILDHOOD

Moira Ward's family background was characterized by punitive, parental attitudes and domestic violence. She has had a number of partners herself and has used alcohol in the past as a coping strategy. This has had the effect of evoking Laura's support and Michael's anxious clinging attachment.

Looking at Ian Ross's family background, he comes from a hard-drinking, male-orientated family, where domestic violence was used by his father as a way of maintaining control.

IMPACT OF FAMILY HISTORY

Models from the family of origin play a part in partner choice, partner relationship and parenting responses. Ian Ross recreated the punitive paternal style, while Moira Ward attempted to reverse the punitive and controlling style of her own upbringing, which makes her vulnerable to her partners who employ abusive controlling modes of relating.

INDIVIDUAL FUNCTIONING OF PARENT DURING DEVELOPMENT AND CURRENTLY, PHYSICAL AND MENTAL HEALTH, MANAGEMENT OF IMPAIRMENTS, PERSONALITY DIFFICULTIES

The results of the *Adult Wellbeing Scale* show that Moira Ward was above the borderline for depression and that Ian Ross was at the top of the borderline area for outward-directed irritability. Moira Ward was also in the borderline for anxiety, outward-directed irritability and inward-directed irritability and may well be experiencing mental health difficulties at the moment.

The results of the *Alcohol Use Questionnaire* did not raise concerns about current levels of drinking but did highlight that there have been concerns in the past about Moira Ward's level of alcohol consumption. The *Family Assessment* interview revealed that in contrast to Moira Ward's earlier account, she is in fact drinking to excess and that this is having a significant impact on how she is presently coping. Ian Ross's use of alcohol was associated with his violence to Moira Ward.

Both parents use alcohol as a coping strategy, with Moira Ward being caught in a cycle of anxiety, tension, attempts to comply with Ian Ross's expectations, Laura's defiance, Michael's withdrawal and Ian Ross's expectations by drinking with increasing frequency and intensity. Moira is at risk of an alcohol dependency disorder.

FAMILY'S USE OF TREATMENT AND COMMUNITY SUPPORT

In the past Moira Ward has maintained good contact with Michael's school. Recently she has not responded to the school's request for her to come in to speak to staff about Michael.

Level of strengths, difficulties and risk

Strengths				*Difficulties*
			X	

COUPLE RELATIONSHIP

The couple relationship between Ian Ross and Moira Ward is conflictual; however, both partners are committed to the relationship. Moira Ward has considerable difficulties in influencing Ian Ross's forceful strong opinions concerning the children, and is forced to sacrifice her own and her children's needs for the sake of the couple's relationship. Despite reservations she is working with Ian Ross in attempting to change the family culture to fit into his ideas. Ian Ross asserts and needs to change in an adversarial way, demanding compliance, using blame to justify his attitudes.

DOMESTIC VIOLENCE ISSUES

There has been an episode of domestic violence, Moira Ward's response was to insist on Ian Ross leaving the family home. He reluctantly acknowledges responsibility and blames alcohol. Moira Ward blames herself and also drink. They both exhibit limited awareness of the impact on the children, and associated physical punitiveness towards Michael is minimized.

FAMILY ORGANIZATION AND NATURE AND STABILITY OF FAMILY FUNCTIONING

There are high levels of family conflicts and difficulties with multiple determinants. There is a history of Moira Ward coping better with the children's needs. Family organization has been disrupted by Ian Ross attempting to improve on what he perceives to be Moira Ward's lack of discipline and control. He believes the children are controlling her.

Resulting conflict and high levels of disagreement between family members has meant that Michael's needs are not being met. Laura is attempting to fulfil her mother's parental tasks and Michael's needs are continuing to be neglected. There is an absence of involvement with wider family and a reluctance to be involved with the community agencies.

Level of strengths, difficulties and risk

Strengths				Difficulties
				X

Summary of other relevant dimensions

The family do not have contact with members of the wider family. In respect of Moira Ward and her extended family, this appears to be because they disapprove of her relationship with Ian Ross. The family has not seen Moira Ward's mother for over a year. The *HOME Inventory* interview and the

Family Activity Scale revealed the family has little contact with neighbours and a relatively restricted social life.

The family home is a rented council house, which is adequately maintained. The *Home Conditions Scale* did not reveal any concerns about domestic hygiene apart from a general lack of cleanliness in Michael's room.

Ian Ross is an individual who has a good earning potential. There is adequate income available.

Michael attends the local school. Moira Ward used to visit school regularly for parents' evenings and generally maintained good contact, but of late she has been noted not to respond to school letters. Teaching staff have been responsive to Michael's current situation both by writing to Moira Ward and by making a referral to children's social care. The family is registered with a local GP. With the increasing conflict within the family context, increasing neglect of Michael, Laura's opposition and separating herself, there is conflict between the family and community resources and the school, and a reluctance to be involved with health and social services. They have agreed to a family meeting, and there has been a reasonable revealing of the extensiveness of difficulties.

Level of strengths, difficulties and risk

Strengths				*Difficulties*
		X		

Summary in terms of Assessment Framework dimensions

In terms of Michael's developmental needs, he appears to be receiving inadequate nutrition and exercise. He appeared unhappy and there are indicators that he is depressed. There is evidence he is being physically chastised. There was a history of him making reasonable educational progress but recently he has begun to struggle at school. There are concerns about his emotional development. He appears clingy and rather timid and seems to lack self-esteem. He has restricted family and social relationships. He appears to have few friends and to have little contact with members of his extended family. His appearance has worsened over the past few months, resulting in him looking rather dishevelled and unkempt.

In terms of *parenting capacity*, there is evidence that Moira Ward and Ian Ross are failing to meet Michael's physical needs, particularly regarding the adequacy and consistency of diet provided for him. There is also evidence of increasing lack of supervision of his hygiene, clothing and so on. Michael and Moira Ward have revealed that Ian Ross has hit Michael, although Ian

Ross has denied this. Michael has also witnessed the domestic violence exhibited by Ian Ross towards his mother.

There is a history of Michael enjoying a closeness in his relationship with his mother. This appears to be changing, particularly in the presence of Ian Ross. The parenting response to Michael's clingy and unhappy presentation appears marked by a rather harsh regime designed to 'toughen him up'. Evidence of this is the requirement that the hall light should be turned off at night when he goes to sleep. Michael appears to enjoy some physical contact with his mother.

While there is evidence of a limited range of learning materials being available, there is little evidence of encouragement given to Michael to help him use them. Moira Ward and Ian Ross appear to be finding it difficult to ensure Michael's attendance at school on time. There is little evidence of Michael being encouraged to join after-school clubs or, indeed, other clubs outside of school.

Moira Ward and Ian Ross provide Michael with guidance and boundaries in an extremely rigid fashion, which does not appear to have been the case before Ian Ross moved in to live with Moira Ward. Michael is increasingly exposed to a limited, rigid environment where there is little opportunity for discussion and consideration of issues affecting him. There appears to be inappropriate demonstration and modelling of behaviour, control of emotions and interactions with others by Moira Ward and Ian Ross and, indeed, Laura. This environment does not help Michael develop his own capacities for problem-solving, regulation of emotions and so on.

The environment currently provided is rather unstable. Although there is evidence of Moira Ward having provided adequate parenting for Michael in the past, the benefit of this is being tested in the face of the demands from Ian Ross for a different way of managing Michael. While Michael's attachment to his mother has not been disrupted, it is noticeable that the consistency of emotional warmth which he previously enjoyed has now changed and become rather more limited. Parental responses appear to be more punitive and there is a marked absence of support and encouragement for Michael.

In terms of *family and environmental factors*, there is evidence that, in the past when Moira Ward lived with her previous partner, the care of Michael and, indeed, his sister Laura was better. There is also evidence that these were happier times for the family. Moira Ward has had in the past a series of difficult relationships, sometimes marked by violence. Ian Ross comes from a rigid background in which there was domestic violence in his family perpetrated by his father. Ian Ross appears to have a tendency towards outward-directed irritability. Moira Ward appears rather depressed and there is evidence of her drinking alcohol excessively. There is evidence of domestic violence between Ian Ross and Moira Ward. The couple appears to be committed to being with one another but find agreeing about how to parent the children difficult. The family appears dominated by the conflicting relationship between Ian Ross and Laura and the rather submissive presentation of Michael. Moira Ward appears overwhelmed by the family's difficulties. There appears to be little support available to the family from the wider family.

The family appears to benefit from reasonable housing that is presently kept to a reasonable standard. Ian Ross works and provides money for the family. The family appears to have little contact with other people in the neighbourhood. Apart from school, Moira Ward appears to have little contact with agencies in the area.

Chapter Six

Assessments Where There are Continuing Safeguarding Concerns

Arnon Bentovim

Introduction

In Chapter 2 a generic model of evidence-based assessment, analysis, planning interventions and identifying outcomes and measures is described. The model incorporates the *Assessment Framework* triangle and the use of the DCSF recommended *Standardized Assessment Tools* (see Chapter 3) and is relevant to all children whether in need or those in need of protection or thought to be at risk of significant harm. The process includes:

- considering the safety of the child, the referral and the aims of the assessment
- gathering additional information
- categorizing available information and organizing it within the *Assessment Framework* triangle
- analysing the processes influencing the child's development
- predicting the outlook for the child
- planning interventions
- identifying outcomes and measures which would indicate whether interventions are successful.

Assessing children's needs in a safeguarding context

There are additional considerations in assessing the needs of children growing up in a context of trauma and family violence. This chapter explores seven stages of assessment required in situations where harm to a child's development has already occurred or is likely to occur as a result of being exposed to a cumulative set of traumatic and stressful events.

In this chapter:

- Seven stages of assessment in the safeguarding context are explored.

- A crucial stage in the process is the assessment of the likelihood of successful rehabilitation and the risks of re-abuse. A 12-step process for assessing the risk of re-abuse to a child, parenting capacity and prospects of rehabilitation is presented.

- The Ward family is used as a case example to illustrate the assessment stages and the 12-step process.

When initial investigation gives rise to significant levels of concern, a core assessment is carried out following guidelines set out in *Working Together* (HM Government 2006) and the *Assessment Framework*. *Every Child Matters* (Department for Education and Skills 2004b) delineates the five outcomes for children which interventions involving children should aim to achieve and incorporates the *Integrated Children's System*. This provides the structure, guidance and protocol for assessment and planning for children and their families and integrates the model of assessment and the assessment tools. The Public Law Outline (2008) lays down the statutory requirements for reports submitted to court in care proceedings identifying the *Assessment Framework* triangle as the core framework for assessment and planning.

Definition of significant harm

Definitions of 'significant harm' included in the UK legal framework regarding safeguarding children was referred to in Chapter 1 (see p21). The definition has developed over a period of time to include a wide variety of forms of harm, so that children exposed to the variety of harmful contexts referred to are included. The key issue is the threshold at which intervention in family life is justified. This requires the establishment of criteria for the court to intervene and put in place legally binding arrangements and for the state to share care with parents and make decisions which would ensure protection of the children, their recovery and meeting their potential for future health and development.

Legal definition of harm

As discussed in Chapter 1, it is important to be aware of the distinctions made in legal contexts where the issue of harm is being assessed. The notion of significant harm is a threshold which needs to be established to justify compulsory intervention in family life. It is established by the courts, and the local authority social services departments and their legal departments are the prime movers in drawing attention to the concern about the needs of a child.

As mentioned in Chapter 1, the Children Act 1989 – Section 31(9) in England and Wales provides the following definitions:

- '*Harm*' means ill treatment, or the impairment of health or development, including for example impairment suffered from seeing or hearing the ill treatment of another.

- '*Development' means physical, intellectual, emotional, social or behavioural development.*

- '*Health*' means physical or mental health.

- '*Ill treatment' includes sexual abuse and forms of ill treatment which are not physical – including emotional abuse.*

Section 31(10) states that:

> Where the question of whether harm suffered by a child is significant turns on the child's health or development, his health or development shall be compared with that which could reasonably be expected of a similar child.

It will be noted that there needs to be the establishment of a *specific form of harm, ill treatment, impairment of health or development*, including mental health.

Section 120 of the Adoption and Children Act 2002 updates the definition of 'harm' in the Children Act 1989 – Section 31(9). The addition is 'including, for example, impairment suffered from seeing or hearing the ill-treatment of another' and has the effect of strengthening the case for significant harm through domestic violence, or the abuse of another in the household.

In Scotland and Ireland, the definitions of harm and maltreatment used in the comparable legislation need to inform assessments in the safeguarding context.

Seven stages of assessment in the safeguarding process

The stages in the process of safeguarding children include the following:

- Stage 1: The phase of identification of harm and initial safeguarding.

- Stage 2: Making a full assessment of the child's needs, parenting capacity, family and environmental factors.

- Stage 3: Establishing the nature and level of harm and harmful effects.

- Stage 4: Assessing the likelihood of response to professional intervention in the context of the level of the child's needs and the level of parenting capacity and family and environmental difficulties.

- Stage 5: Developing a plan of intervention to include therapeutic work in a context of safety and protection from harm.

- Stage 6: Rehabilitation of the child to the family when living separately or moving on from a context of protection and support.

- Stage 7: Placement of children in new family contexts where rehabilitation is not possible.

Stage 1: The phase of identification of harm and initial safeguarding

The initial step is to recognize when a child is being harmed. This awareness arises in many contexts – family, community and professionals, and requires a variety of routes and established ways for such awareness to be communicated (e.g. *Working Together to Safeguard Children:* HM Government 2006).

Looking at physical and sexual abuse as two examples, it is possible to identify some key signs and patterns which can help to alert professionals to the possibility that a child is being harmed.

Physical abuse

Physical abuse is usually presented either directly by a child or parent or by an interested third party, as described in Box 6.1.

Box 6.1 Presentation of physical abuse

- Repetitive patterns of injury, parents using different hospitals to avoid detection.
- Injuries not consistent with the history, too many, too severe, the wrong kind, the wrong distribution, wrong age.
- A pattern of injury, which strongly suggests abuse, for example bruising to a young baby. Few reasonable explanations for the injuries. Multiple injuries may be observed following what is described as moderate fall. Severe head injuries in babies and toddlers, rib fractures; subdural haematoma and retinal haemorrhage associated with violent shaking, multiple cigarette burns; fractures in infants and toddlers are all characteristic of severe child abuse.

- The presence of other signs of abuse, e.g. neglect, failure to thrive, sexual abuse.
- Unusual behaviour in parents, e.g. delay in seeking medical advice, refusal to allow proper treatment or admission to hospital, unprovoked aggression towards staff.

(Bentovim 2006a)

Injuries may be discovered incidentally, for example a child being allowed to go to school or nursery or to another person's care, when injuries may be found and reported. In such situations parents often deny knowledge of the injury and no satisfactory explanations are given – although there may be a covert wish for discovery. This may be a way of drawing attention to overwhelming family stress, which cannot be openly acknowledged.

Some of the important features in the history are illustrated in Box 6.2.

Box 6.2 Important features in the history

- The parents give a discrepant history which changes with the telling or who tells it. Details are vague or unclear. Exact details of time, place, persons and actions are required to clarify the presentation. There needs to be a comparison of the accounts of various professionals, with major differences needing explanations. Parents may not give the same story.
- An unreasonable delay in seeking help or care, especially following a fracture or serious burn or scald, is a strong indicator of an abusive situation. Denial that a child is in pain and minimization of symptoms are common. A baby may be left tucked in a cot, only to be brought hours later when he or she refuses a feed or begins to have a seizure.
- Trigger factors are behaviour in the child which precipitated a parent's violence; inconsolable crying, difficult feeding or wetting, stealing or lying may all provoke an angry outburst on a stressed parent's part.
- As abuse escalates, parents find it increasingly difficult to allow anyone into their lives for fear of discovery, and the isolation grows.
- Past history of high levels of parental anxiety, frequent admissions to hospitals in the first months of life, frequent accidents, behavioural difficulties, growth and development delays all may be sources of anxiety, and the source of stress, and the result of poor care.

Poisoning, suffocation and induced or fabricated illness are forms of dangerous physical abuse, which are not characterized by the loss of control, punitiveness and anger, associated with physical abuse, but more with a perception or a belief that the child has a physical illness. The parent believes he or she has to convince the medical team that this is the case and does so by describing or inducing symptoms, requesting investigation or intervention. Behavioural difficulties may be interpreted as having physical causes. While the child becomes the focus of medical attention, the parent gains the support and comfort of being the parent of a sick child, receiving care and support by proxy. Death may result from any of these forms of physical abuse, long-term physical or psychological harm. These patterns need to be recognized by the relevant professional, and reported (HM Government 2006).

Sexual abuse

Sexual abuse presents in a variety of different contexts, and different presentations, as in Box 6.3 9 (adapted from Vizard and Tranter 1988).

Box 6.3 Presentation of sexual abuse

• Disclosure	By child or third party
• Physical indicators	Rectal or vaginal bleeding, pain on defecation
	Sexually transmitted disease (STD)
	Vulvovaginitis (inflamation of the skin around the vagina) or vaginal discharge or 'sore'
	Dysuria (painful passing of urine) and frequency, urinary tract infections
	Physical abuse, note association of burns, pattern of injury, death
	Pregnancy
• Psychosomatic indicators	Recurrent abdominal pain
	Headache, migraine
	Eating disorders, bulimic variety
	Encopresis (involuntary faecal soiling)
	Secondary enuresis (involuntary passing of urine)
	Total refusal syndrome

- Behavioural indicators
  - (a) Pre-school   Sexually explicit play, 'excessive' masturbation, insertion of foreign bodies (girls), self-mutilation, withdrawn, poor appetite, sleep disturbance, clingy, delayed development, aggression
  - (b) Middle years   Sexualized play, sexually explicit drawing or sexual precocity, self-mutilation, anxiety, depression, anger, poor school performance, mute
  - (c) Teenagers   Sexually precocious, prostitution, anxiety, anger, aggression, depression, truancy, running away, solvent/alcohol/drug abuse, self-destructive behaviour, overdoses, self-mutilation, suicide
- Learning difficulties or severe learning problems
      May present with depression, disturbed (including aggressive) behaviour

      Sexualized behaviour
- Physical handicap   Attempts at disclosure not understood; may be physical and psychosomatic indicators as above
- Social indicators   Concern by parent or third party, sibling, relative or friend of abused child

      Known offender in close contact with child

Each of the particular forms of abuse, failure to thrive, physical abuse and neglect has characteristic patterns, e.g. the poor growth, skin quality and development of neglected children who are failing to thrive, the pattern of emotional responses, depressive symptoms, self-harming, anxious or angry responses of children who are emotionally abused. Neglect and emotional abuse are more subtle and are not recognized as acutely by professionals. The nature and impact of experiences of neglect and emotional abuse emerge in the context of the comprehensive assessment described later in this chapter. Different forms of abuse often present in the same family and present at different times in differing ways. The analogy of an iceberg with multiple impact points describes child abuse aptly.

Social work, health, police and education professionals will be involved, through a process of strategy meetings, child protection conferences, initial and core assessments and reviews (DOH 2000, 2002) with action following to safeguard the child depending on the level of current risk and future harm.

The full extent of harm of a child may not be known initially, nor the extent of the trauma or the effects (Cicchetti and Carlson 1989). For instance, when one child has been identified as being harmed sexually or physically in a family, it is not unusual to find that other children in the family have been harmed. The impact of a parent with a psychiatric illness, or prone to substance abuse or domestic violence, may differ substantially depending on the age or develop-mental stage of children. It may emerge that a parent, who is initially perceived as protective, may also have been involved or have condoned abusive action. There may be considerable uncertainty about parents' capacity to protect their children, or the extent of abuse and safeguarding requirements until further assessments are completed.

The presence of severe or extensive abuse of a child, for example sexual abuse associated with physical abuse and neglect, will make it more likely that there will be major difficulties associated with parenting capacity and family and environmental factors. The emergence of mental health difficulties in parents, domestic violence which has not been reported earlier or addiction (Cleaver *et al.* 1999) are all likely to indicate a higher level of complexity and requiring more extensive professional and legal intervention. In such situations, it may be necessary to use interventions, which are supported through child protection conference decisions, or a court order to adequately safeguard the child and address their needs. This can include having to work with and motivate parents who themselves may have considerable difficulties and require extensive services.

Stage 2: Making a full assessment of the child's needs, parenting capacity, family and environmental factors

Standardized Assessment Tools

In Chapter 3, a range of *Standardized Assessment Tools* were described and their role in making evidence-based assessments of children's developmental needs and functioning, the capacity of parents to meet their needs, and family and environmental factors which impact on parenting, family life or the children directly.

Specialist assessments

Specialist or further assessments may be required depending on the need for further information on specific aspects of children's developmental functioning, parenting capacity or family and environmental factors which emerges from the initial and core assessments with children and their families. Initial assessments must be completed in 7 working days and the regulations require that the core assessment process takes place over 35 days.

Other assessments can include paediatric assessments to make detailed examination of health and development; child mental health assessments of post-traumatic states, or offending behaviour; adult mental health assessments of parents as individuals and couples, drug and substance misuse assessments; psychological assessments of children's and parents' intellectual and general functioning; educational assessments, and adult offending assessments. A variety of different professionals in the social work and health fields have the skills to make specialist assessments and such assessments have an important role in assessing the impact of harm on a child and understanding and assessing the factors associated with harm and harmful parenting as well as the potential for change. This includes gauging the modifiability of any difficulties in parenting and/or family and environmental factors which have contributed to the harm experienced by the child.

Constructing a comprehensive chronology

An important element of a specialist assessment is the recommendation to construct a comprehensive chronology of significant information from medical, social services and educational contexts which helps to establish the nature of risk and protective factors experienced by the young person and the family.

It is often a challenge to gather and analyse information about a child's history and map the interventions and outcomes in previous work with the child and family. But such information is central to establishing the harm and protective factors a child has already experienced and to assessing the potential for change. Systems for collecting and analysing information from documents are useful to ensure a full picture is obtained. Cross-sectional research at Great Ormond Street Hospital for Children, London (Skuse *et al.* 1998), which looked at the history of young people who had displayed sexually abusive behaviour, showed that information from case notes etc. could be reliably analysed using descriptors. Bifulco, Brown and Harris (1994) have demonstrated that an instrument, the *Childhood Experience of Care and Abuse* (CECA), used to assess the presence of physical, sexual or emotional abuse and neglect, can be applied to chronological or historical data from case files or elsewhere in order to construct a chronology for a child or young person.

Contexts for assessment

Depending on the level of concern, assessments may need to take place while a child is accommodated in a place of safety, for example, due to the nature and severity of possible harm or risk of harm or the severity of parental mental health or substance or alcohol abuse problems. A foster placement provides the opportunity for observing the state of the child immediately after being in parental care, establishing needs and assessing the child's response to a context of more adequate care.

Observing a child's response to parental contact provides opportunities for establishing the nature of parenting capacity and family relationships and other family and environmental factors. A family centre provides the opportunity for extensive observations, and testing the child and family's response to interventions (e.g. the Marlborough Family Day Hospital: see Asen *et al.* 1989). Residential settings for the family (Healy, Kennedy and Sinclair 1991) or fostering placements for a mother or father and baby allow for 24-hour observation of a wide range of parent–child and other relationships and interactions. It is often necessary to combine different contexts to establish a comprehensive understanding of children's needs, parenting capacity and family and environmental factors, and integrate assessments from a number of perspectives.

Capacity of parents and family to acknowledge responsibility and need for change

An essential component of the assessment process is the reflection on the assessment process by parents and professionals. The use of the *Standardized Assessment Tools* requires a consistent and continuous reflective process with parents, children and young people which facilitate an exploration of the parents' and other family members' capacity to reflect on the findings of the assessment as it takes place and recognize the need for change. Central questions are:

- Do parents acknowledge the extensiveness of their child's difficulties, and need for intervention?

- Do they acknowledge responsibility for harm they may have been responsible for?

- Is there willingness to address individual, family and environmental issues which may be having a deleterious impact on parenting capacities?

- Is there a prospect for positive change within the young person's timeframe?

Stage 3: Establishing the nature and level of harm and harmful effects

In considering the issue of harm, a broad-based, integrated approach is required to assessing whether a child has suffered harm or is likely to suffer harm in the future. The *Assessment Framework* is the conceptual map used in the UK to guide assessments of children's needs and the factors influencing whether they are met, and in Chapter 5, the *Assessment Framework* has been operationalized to facilitate gathering information in the safeguarding context about strengths and difficulties in each dimension of the three domains.

Assessing the impact of parenting capacities on children's developmental needs

To assess the needs of children who are at risk of being harmed as a result of abusive parenting, it is useful to focus on the parenting capacity domain of the *Assessment Framework* to define the range of parental strengths and difficulties and the potential resulting effects on children's functioning and the potential harm which may result.

By looking at each dimension of the parenting capacity domain in turn, it is possible to draw out some key themes and connections between strengths and difficulties in specific dimensions of parenting capacity and the impact on particular dimensions of children's developmental needs. The themes have particular relevance in the safeguarding context. It is essential to note, however, that there are many other themes which could be included and also that the dimensions are interrelated so that different aspects of parenting may impact on one or more several areas of a child's developmental needs. In addition, of course, the impact of family and environmental factors must always be taken into account.

CYCLES OF POSITIVE PARENTING

In a family with parenting strengths, it is possible to map some links between the provision of positive parenting in each dimension and the predominant potential impact on the child's health and development.

Basic care

The provision of good quality *basic care* which includes attention to children's health needs facilitates the child's growth, self-care and health, promoting the healthy development of the child and helping them develop a capacity for adequate self-care.

Ensuring safety

Providing adequate *responsiveness, safety and protection* ensures that there is protection at home and away from home, including protection from all types of abuse, including physical and sexual abuse. It also promotes the development of secure attachments is supported so that the child is confident and free from harm.

Emotional warmth

The provision of adequate *emotional warmth and containment* supports emotional development, facilitates the regulation of the child's emotional states and the development of their emotional coping capacities and positive emotional adjustment.

Stimulation

Positive *stimulation* and effective *communication* ensures the development of the child's cognitive, motor and language skills which are the building blocks for future education.

Guidance and boundaries

Providing adequate *guidance and boundaries* for children and *managing their behaviour* effectively ensures that they develop an appropriate level of cooperative behaviour in their relationships with others, self-assertiveness and pro-social attitudes.

Stability

Stability of family relationships promotes the building of secure attachments and ensures the satisfactory development of the child's sense of identity, and their capacity for family and social relating.

Figure 6.1 represents a benign developmental cycle related to positive parenting. It illustrates the way that *positive family and environmental factors* provide the background for parents to develop *adequate parenting skills*. Linking these parental capacities in a circular fashion indicates that there is an interactional process which involves each of these particular parental qualities.

The positive parenting skills impact in turn on *children's health and development* resulting in the child thriving with healthy development and good self-care skills and freedom from harm, as well as having a sense of security and confidence, maximizing their educational skills, capacities and potential and developing emotional coping skills and resilience and collaborative and pro-social behaviour, and having a positive sense of identity and social and

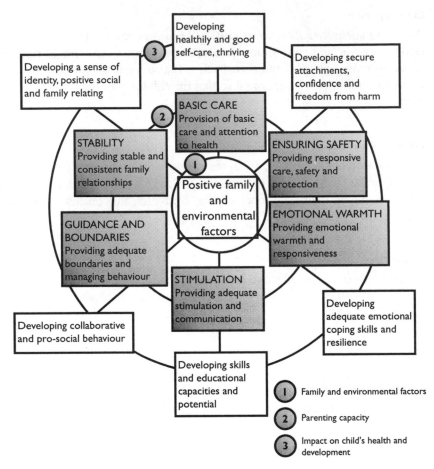

Figure 6.1: Parenting strengths and positive impacts on child health and development

family relationships. These are linked in the outer ring of the circle, again indicating the interaction between these different aspects of development.

CYCLES OF HARMFUL PARENTING

Cycles of more harmful impacts on children resulting from parenting difficulties are represented in Figure 6.2. Here *negative family and environmental factors* are associated with *difficulties in parenting capacities*. These difficulties affect the provision of basic care and attention to health needs, parental responsiveness, protection and security, consistency of emotional warmth, stimulation and communication, providing guidance, boundaries and managing children's behaviour and maintaining stable relationships. In turn, parenting difficulties in each

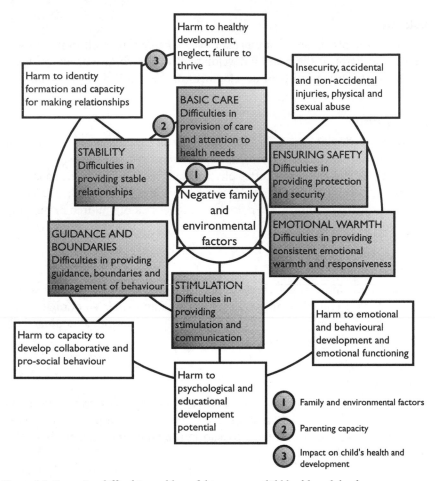

Figure 6.2: Parenting difficulties and harmful impacts on child health and development

of these dimensions relate to potentially harmful impacts on children's development and well-being.

Representing the domains in a circular fashion indicates the interaction between these various parenting difficulties which reinforce, interact and are cumulative in their impact on children's development. Each form of potentially harmful parenting may be associated with recognized patterns of harm to children and young people.

Basic care

Failures in the provision of *care and attention to health* can result in patterns of neglect and harm to the healthy development of the child with poor health care, failure to thrive and poor development of the child's self-care skills.

Ensuring safety

When parents do not ensure the child's *safety in the home and in the community* or fail to provide adequate *supervision, responsiveness and protection* there is an increased risk the child will suffer physical and sexual harm, be exposed to violence or become involved in risk-taking behaviour related to drug, alcohol and other substance misuse. There is also a higher risk of children developing of disordered attachments.

Emotional warmth

A failure to provide *consistent emotional warmth, containment and empathic responses* may result in a child having problems in managing their emotional states, having disordered expression of emotions and poor emotional coping skills and being emotionally vulnerable.

Stimulation

When parents do not provide *adequate stimulation, effective communication* and *attention* to a child's educational and social learning needs, this can result in the child developing negative attitudes to learning and failing to achieve their educational potential.

Guidance and boundaries

Parental difficulties in providing *adequate guidance, boundaries and management of behaviour* can result in the child failing to develop pro-social and collaborative behaviour with the risk of antisocial behaviour and disorders of conduct and oppositional behaviour.

Stability

Failures in providing *stable family and social relationships* can result in harm to the formation of child's sense of identity and potential problems for them in interpersonal relationships and maintaining attachments.

Impact of family history and family functioning

It is also always important to consider the impact of family history and family functioning on development of parenting capacities, as well as the other dimensions of family and environmental factors, as discussed in more detail in Chapter 2.

Detailed analysis of the specific effects of harmful parenting on the child

Having identified the broad themes and connections between positive and negative patterns of parenting and their potential impact on children's developmental needs, it is helpful to take each area of parenting and look in detail at whether it is possible to relate the elements of parenting difficulties to specific harmful effects. Building on the operationalization of the *Assessment Framework* in Chapter 4, the following descriptors are adapted for contexts when children are in need of protection, and decisions about intervention need to be taken. Descriptions of strengths and difficulties in parenting capacity are juxtaposed with descriptions of the potential impact on the child's developmental needs, when needs are met adequately or when there is a risk of harm.

Basic care: failure by parents or carers to provide adequate care and attention to health needs

Box 6.4 lists parental strengths and difficulties and the impact on the child when providing basic care.

Box 6.4 Providing basic care and attention to health needs

Parental strengths

- Provides adequate, effective basic care and attention to health needs reasonably organized.
- Adapting successfully to children's changing needs.
- Appropriate reliance and support on extended family and community.
- Appropriate attention to health and disability issues.

Parental difficulties

- Lack of basic care and attention to health needs inconsistent poorly organized over time.
- Failure to adapt to children's changing needs.
- Undue reliance or unable to use extended family and community.
- Failure to attend to physical health or disability.

- Focus on health and maximizing of physical potential.

- Invalidism, beliefs about illness, induction of illness states.

Impact on child when basic care provided and health needs adequately met

- Good general health and positive health attitudes.
- Child thriving, healthy, growing well.
- Satisfactory care and attention to health throughout development.
- Health and disability issues responded to adequately, functioning to potential.
- Child has capacity to care and present self positively, potential, positive health attitudes.
- Appropriate reliance on extended family and community resources.

Risk of harm: impact on the child when failure to provide basic care or meet health needs adequately

- Poor standards of care, general health.
- Child not thriving, evidence of neglect, poor growth, poor health care, skin care, failure to thrive.
- Lack of attention to care and health needs during development.
- Health and disability, not functioning to potential, lack of care.
- Poor capacity to care and present self within potential, negative health attitudes.
- Over- or under-reliance on family and community resources.

HARMFUL PARENTING PATTERNS

In this dimension of parenting capacity, difficulties include a lack of basic care, inconsistent or poorly organized parenting, the provision of inadequate nutrition or failure to attend to a child's needs for feeding, failure to attend to health or disability needs, distorted beliefs about illness states of the child and/or a degree of invalidism (treating the child as an invalid) and failure to adapt to children's changing needs over time. Parents may fail to utilize or to be unduly reliant on extended family and community resources.

IMPACT ON CHILD

Evidence for harmful effects includes children showing signs of poor care, including having neglected appearance, poorly cared-for skin, hair and clothing and/or non-organic failure to thrive. This might be associated with a 'Cinderella' appearance; there may be evidence of deprivation, noted through characteristic skin and hair changes and a degree of growth failure in both height and weight. In severe forms of non-organic failure to thrive, this may include the unusual state of 'derivational dwarfism', a state associated with endocrine abnormalities of the production of growth hormone. In less severe cases, height may be more affected than weight. Reviewing health records over a number of years can be helpful as there may be a longstanding evidence of poor care and failure to help the child develop self-care skills. Alternatively, the child may take more responsibility for their own self-care than would usually be expected for their age and stage of development, i.e. 'pseudo-adult' functioning, as a form of compensation.

A parental context of invalidism, distorted beliefs or induction into illness states results in a range of processes which negatively impact on the child's health. This includes the most severe cases, when the child might be subject to life-threatening induction of illness states, for example suffocation or attempted drowning, administration of noxious substances and medication, or interference with medical procedures (Gray and Bentovim 1996). Moderate forms of induction or fabrication of illness states would include fabrication of symptoms leading to extensive medical investigations, or major anxieties about the child's health with associated 'doctor shopping'.

Evidence of a poor state of health in a child is noted through failure to attend for medical examinations or the regular immunization of children. A failure to attend to a child's disability needs may be indicated when the child level of disability is greater than the potential which could be expected, given the child's impairment(s).

INTEGRATED INTERDISCIPLINARY ASSESSMENTS

These are complex judgements and require integrated interdisciplinary assessments from health, social work and psychological professionals. Baseline information can be obtained from the evidence-based assessment tools, particularly the *HOME Inventory*. These assessments may need to be reinforced and elaborated upon through specialist assessments to define the nature and extent of harm to the child's health, the contribution of the parenting difficulties to the problems experienced by the child and the potential for adequate care.

Ensuring safety: failure by parents or carers to provide security and protection from harm

Box 6.5 lists parental strengths and difficulties and the impact on the child when providing security.

Box 6.5 Parental provision of safety, responsiveness and protection

Parental strengths

- Attuned, responsive, reliable, coherent caregiving.
- Safe environment, appropriate discipline and relating.
- Reasonable expectation of children dependence or independence, self-care, care of others.
- Adequate supervision of activities inside and outside the home.
- Provision of safe environment and protection from physical hazards, risky individuals inside and outside home.

Parental difficulties

- Unresponsive, unreliable, fragmented caregiving.
- Unsafe environment inappropriate punitiveness, sexualized relating, risk of physical and/or sexual abuse.
- Unreasonable expectation of children's dependence or independence, self-care and care of others.
- Inadequate supervision of activities inside and outside the home.
- Environment unsafe, failure of protection from physical hazards and risky individuals inside and outside the home.

Impact on the child when adequate safety and protection ensured

- Developing secure primary and secondary attachment responses.
- Age-appropriate capacity for safe independent behaviour, care of self and others at home and in the environment.
- No evidence of physical or sexual harm sustained at home or environment.
- Injuries sustained consistent with age and developmental stage.

Risk of harm: impact on the child when failure to ensure adequate safety and protection

- Developing insecure, disorganized or indiscriminate attachment responses.
- A lack of age-appropriate capacities for safe independent care of self – at home and in the environment – over-dependent, pseudo-mature.
- Evidence of physical or sexual harm sustained at home or in the environment.
- Injuries sustained not consistent with age and developmental stage.

HARMFUL PARENTING PATTERNS

This area of parenting failure can result in the most severe forms of harm. Parenting difficulties in this area focuses on the failure to provide security and protection from harm. This includes unresponsive, unreliable, fragmented caregiving, the child living in an unsafe environment and the parents failing to provide protection from inappropriate punitiveness or sexual experiences. An unsafe physical environment includes failure of protection from physical hazards inside or outside the home and the child not being kept safe, including exposure to risky individuals or contexts. This may be associated with inappropriate parental expectations either of dependence or independence in a child.

IMPACT ON CHILD

This can, in turn, result in evidence of physical or sexual abuse of a child and/or a child exhibiting sexualized behaviour. The most severe levels of harm include fractures and other injuries which are multiple and found in different sites and which may have occurred over a period of time. Fractures around the head and neck in a baby under six months are, of course, of particular concern.

The most severe forms of sexual abuse include children or young people being involved in longstanding attempted or actual genital or anal intercourse, especially younger children and/or involvement in prostitute sex rings. Less severe forms of sexual abuse involve exposure and sexual contact without penetration.

In terms of physical harm when children are not kept safe, failure to protect children from danger can result in severe injuries, poisoning, burns or scalds, preventable accidents, whether in the home or outside the home.

A key negative impact when there is a failure of parental attunement to the child is the development of insecure, disorganized or indiscriminate attachments. As children get older they may develop compliant or controlling angry, dismissive responses and be unable to develop appropriate dependence or independence in their relationships with others.

Exposure to harmful or risky individuals inside or outside the home can result in abusive action perpetrated against the child. The impact of physical and sexual abuse includes children developing patterns of arousal which cannot be easily managed by the child or caregiver, premature sexualized behaviour, frozen emotional states, dissociation or compliant or explosive responses.

INTEGRATED INTERDISCIPLINARY ASSESSMENTS

The assessment of children exposed to a context which fails to provide adequate security and protection requires a well-coordinated health, social work and police response.

The use of the evidence-based assessment tools provides a comprehensive assessment of functioning of the child, the level of parenting capacity and the impact of individual and family functioning strengths and difficulties and other relevant family and environmental factors. The use of the *In My Shoes* interview for children provides a useful tool for skilled specialist interviews of the child. It is essential when more serious harm has occurred to construct a full chronology of health, social work, criminal records to explore past concerns, and intergenerational patterns of harm. Specialist assessments of children, young people, abusive parents and partners may be required from the perspective of mental health or offending services. Integration of information requires an interdisciplinary approach to analysis and care planning.

Emotional warmth: failure by parents or carers to provide adequate emotional warmth and responsiveness

Box 6.6 lists parental strengths and difficulties and the impact on the child when providing emotional warmth.

Box 6.6 Emotional warmth and containment

Parental strengths

- Satisfactory expression and reception of feelings, valuing, respecting consistent.
- General emotional tone, warmth, calmness, humour, support, engagement.
- Empathy, understanding of child's emotional responses and states, containment and tolerance, non-punitive responses.
- Protection of child from current traumatic losses and stressful events and situations, mental health, parental conflict, or personality issues currently and in early development.

Parental difficulties

- Failure to express or respond to feeling, critical, humiliating, rejecting, inconsistent.
- General emotional tone, negative, undermining, exploiting, disqualifying, coldness, lack of support, disengaged.
- Lack of empathy, failure to understand child's emotional states, lack of containment, intolerance, punitive responses.
- Failure to protect child from current traumatic losses, situations, stressful events, parental conflict, mental health, or personality issues, currently and in early development.

Impact on the child when provision of emotional warmth and containment adequate	Risk of harm: impact on the child when failure to provide adequate emotional warmth and containment
• Child is part of a network of secure, organized attachments. • Capacity to respond appropriately to emotional communication, emotional states well regulated. • Shows basic positive emotional mood, brief appropriate responses to disappointment and change. • Traumatic and stressful events have been processed without lasting effects. • Positive emotional adjustment.	• Child is part of a network of insecure, disorganized attachments, clinging, indiscriminate, avoiding or controlling responses. • Lack of a capacity to respond to emotional communication, arousal, frozenness results, and emotional states poorly regulated. • Pervasive negative mood, failure to cope with disappointment, change. • Persistent fear, distress, traumatic responses, failure of processing. • Negative emotional adjustment, mood difficulties, anxiety states and self-harm.

HARMFUL PARENTING PATTERNS

Parental difficulties in providing *emotional warmth and containment* are associated with the risk of emotional abuse. Difficulties in parenting capacities associated with potentially emotionally abusive actions include parents who fail to express or respond to feelings and the presence of predominant, critical, humiliating, rejecting tone in the relationship between parent and child. Associated with a failure of empathic, emotional understanding, parents may ignore or respond punitively to a child's expression of their emotional needs. Parents may also perceive the child's normal assertiveness as oppositional, defiant, rebellious and aggressive leading to disqualification and lack of support of the child.

Two major areas of potentially abusive aspects of parenting capacity in this dimension are the failure to protect children from potentially traumatically stressful events or from the extremes of inconsistent parental emotional states and distorted perceptions. This can include exposure to physical and sexual abuse of a child or other family members, traumatic loss or witnessing violence. Parents may fail to protect children from the impact of parental relationship conflicts or their own substance misuse, alcoholism or serious mental health difficulties.

IMPACT ON CHILD

The responses of children to these emotionally highly stressful experiences can result in children being unable to develop normal emotional responsiveness or to regulate their emotional states. This may be demonstrated in the child by frozen emotional responses, high emotional arousal states, marked anger or oppositional responses, avoidance or a fear of closeness. A child may have a pervasive negative mood and low self-perception and be unable to cope with disappointment.

A child experiencing an absence of emotional warmth from their parents or caregivers, may also have difficulty in developing a capacity for empathy and present as unfeeling, aggressive, withdrawn or distancing in response to others. There may be evidence of persistent grief, unresolved traumatic symptoms and failure of emotional adjustment, linked with persistent fear, distress, anxiety, anger and regression Responses can include the child or young person taking on a predominately caretaking role or having self-perceptions organized by parental reality.

INTEGRATED INTERDISCIPLINARY ASSESSMENTS

The use of a combination of evidence-based assessment tools can provide a picture of the parents' capacity to provide adequate emotional warmth and containment and the extent to which children's emotional needs are being met.

Assessment of this key area of harm requires coordination between social work and mental health teams, including those focusing on child, family and adult health issues. To establish the child or young person's emotional needs may require a child and adolescent mental health service assessment associated with adult mental health assessments for individuals or the couple. The contribution of assessments by domestic violence, substance or alcohol abuse services may need to be integrated into the overall assessment process to determine level of parents' needs and difficulties as individuals and/or as a couple and to establish the potential for change.

Stimulation: failure by parents or carers to provide stimulation and communication

Box 6.7 lists parental strengths and difficulties and the impact on the child when providing stimulation.

Box 6.7 Stimulation and communication

Parental strengths

- Praise, warmth, encouragement, stimulating, responsive, enriching environment.
- Clear communication, good listening, acknowledge, responsive.
- Participating, sharing, focusing, interacting, creating, persistence, continuity.
- Provides challenging tasks, supports learning.
- Well-prepared and supported, involved in educational settings.

Parental difficulties

- Critical, cold, rejecting, undermining, impoverished environment.
- Minimal interchange, failure of listening, controlling, directive, stifling, ignoring, unresponsive.
- Few or inappropriate opportunities for play and activities, lack of involvement, participation, failure to focus, share, lack of persistence.
- Poor preparation, support, uninvolved in educational settings.

Impact on child when adequate provision of stimulation and communication

- Satisfactory unfolding of skills, cognitive, motor and language.
- Capacity to develop positive communicational and interactional skills with family members, siblings and peers.
- Satisfactory attendance, achievement, attention in educational settings.
- Positive peer, teacher and family relationships.
- Satisfactory progress along the line of play to work.
- Special needs recognized, positive intervention, support.

Risk of harm: impact on the child when failure to provide adequate stimulation and communication

- Significant delays and unevenness in unfolding of cognitive, motor and language skills.
- Poor capacity to communicate or interact with family members, siblings and peers.
- Unsatisfactory attendance, educational failure, disrupted attentional capacities.
- Poor peer, teacher and family relationships.
- Failure to progress along the line of play to work.
- Special needs unrecognized, poorly assessed, failed intervention and support.

HARMFUL PARENTING PATTERNS

Parents who are failing to provide adequate *stimulation and communication* may be recognized through observation of markedly critical, cold, inconsistent and undermining responses towards their children. They may be providing an impoverished environment for the child with few learning or social opportunities. There may be a lack of communicational interchange, with parents failing to listen or respond to the children, and a lack of parental involvement and participation in play or sharing activities inside and outside the home.

Educational needs in general are likely to be ignored or minimized. There may be poor support for pre-school and school activities and limited concern about the child's educational achievements or sustaining school liaison. When the child has a disability, parents may not be responding to the child's special needs or may be failing to sustain necessary interventions.

IMPACT ON CHILD

The impact on a child of these considerable parenting difficulties in this dimension can include significant developmental delays or unevenness in the development of the child's cognitive and motor language skills. The child may have a poor capacity for communication, fail to develop a capacity for play and/or show an absence of curiosity. They may not perform to potential exhibiting difficulties such as rejecting special needs arrangements, unsatisfactory attendance at school, problems with learning, educational failure and disruptive behaviour, inattentive responses and problems in peer and teacher relationships.

INTEGRATED INTERDISCIPLINARY ASSESSMENTS

The use of the evidence-based assessment tools provides a picture of whether there is the parenting capacity in place to provide adequate stimulation and communication and children's responses. To fully assess the processes may require specialist assessments of children's potential through specialist health and psychological assessments, liaison with educational professionals, and scrutiny of educational and health records.

Making a distinction between the contribution of environmental and genetic factors to children's restlessness, inattentiveness, communicational and learning difficulties can be complex and requires interdisciplinary approaches. Assessments of parents' cognitive and psychological functioning may be relevant in the evaluation of parenting capacity and the ability of parents to respond to specific interventions, especially when children's needs for services and support are considerable if they are to achieve their potential.

Guidance and boundaries: failure by parents or carers to provide guidance, boundaries and management of behaviour

Box 6.8 lists parental strengths and difficulties and the impact on the child when providing guidance and boundaries.

Box 6.8 Guidance, boundaries and management of behaviour

Parental strengths

- Good management, realistic expectation, appropriate reward and sanctions, moderate use of discipline and punitiveness.
- Manages or distracts from frustration or negative states, tolerates firmness without battles.
- Flexible boundaries, rules, structures, appropriate adult and child distinction.
- Conflict and oppositional behaviour managed adequately and resolved, basic collaborative responses.

Parental difficulties

- Poor management, absent or oppressive behavioural control, punitiveness, inappropriate expectations.
- Intolerance or over-reinforcement of negative states and frustration, punitiveness or controlled by child's response.
- Rigid or absent boundaries, 'parentified' children, over-protection, child having to care for parent.
- Conflicts and oppositional behaviour managed inconsistently, frequent futile arguments, failed resolution, non-collaborative approach.

Impact on child when adequate provision of guidance, boundaries and management of behaviour

- Predominantly collaborative, compliant, pro-social behaviour in home, school and social context, controllable and manageable.
- Protective and protected to parents and siblings, tolerant, responsive, accepts rules and boundaries.

Risk of harm: impact on child when failure to provide adequate guidance, boundaries and management of behaviour

- Predominantly oppositional or over-compliant, aggressive, antisocial behaviour, home, school and social context, bad-tempered and controlling, unmanageable.

- Connected, responsive, independent, respectful to cultural and racial differences.
- Appropriate drug and alcohol use.

- Exploitive, avoidant, passive, fighting, bullying or bullies, rivalrous, abusive physically and sexually, rejects rules and boundaries.
- Isolated, dominating, controlling, antisocial, sexually and prejudiced to cultural and racial differences.
- Inappropriate drug and alcohol use.

HARMFUL PARENTING PATTERNS

Potentially harmful parenting difficulties in this dimension can include inappropriate expectations of children's behaviour relative to their developmental stage, absent or oppressive behavioural control and antisocial models of response by the parents in the community and neighbourhood and in the family itself. There may be either high levels of punitive reinforcement or inappropriate indulgence of children's needs. Parents may be intolerant of children's emotional states, ignoring or blaming the child rather than understanding the child's level of appropriate distress. Parents may allow themselves to be controlled by the child.

These responses may be associated with the failure to manage intergenerational boundaries which may be rigid or absent. Parents may be overprotective or 'infantilize' a child or, alternatively, have inappropriate expectations of independence and self-reliance. There may be a climate of futile arguments and a failure to resolve conflicts.

IMPACT ON CHILD

The impact on children and young people's development includes oppositional, over-compliant behaviour, passive responses, or unmanageable, antisocial risk-taking behaviour, alcohol and drug misuse. Children may be unable to cope with frustration so that there is evidence of temper tantrums, frozen emotional responses, inappropriate feelings of guilt and/or being responsible for the parents' states. Boundary problems may result in a child becoming a 'parental' or caregiver child or a 'pseudo-mature' individual who has had to take responsibility for him- or herself than they are developmentally ready to do. Children and young people may therefore exhibit infantile, enmeshed, sexualized or aggressive responses. This can include being excessively argumentative or exploiting parents, siblings, other family members or peers in either a passive or active role. A child may re-enact sexual or aggressive behavioural responses as a result of previous failures by parents to set clear boundaries, manage behaviour and avoid using antisocial models of response themselves.

INTEGRATED INTERDISCIPLINARY ASSESSMENT

In addition to the evidence-based assessment tools which can provide a comprehensive picture of the parental capacities to provide adequate guidance, boundaries and management of the children's behaviour, specialist assessments may be required to fully understand the impact on children and young people's behavioural control in complex cases. These may include assessments of young people's needs and the risk of them exhibiting aggressive, or antisocial responses, e.g. sexually or physically offending behaviour, in collaboration with youth offending services, mental health services or services for sexually abusive young people (Edwards *et al.* 2007). Assessments of parents' antisocial behaviour and mental health histories and current functioning may also be required to clarify the level of risk of harm and assess the prognosis for change.

Stability: failure by parents or carers to ensure stable family relationships and a sense of identity

Box 6.9 lists parental strengths and difficulties and the impact on the child when providing stability.

Box 6.9 Stability and family relationships

Parental strengths

- Stability of parenting currently and during development.
- Stability of parental partnerships and family relationships.
- Maintaining of a network of relationships despite separation.
- The development of a family sense of togetherness, social and cultural identity, supporting appropriate individuals.
- Support for individuation, maintaining separation and connectedness.
- Resilient response to adversity and major family change.

Parental difficulties

- A lack of stability of parenting currently and during development.
- A lack of stability of parental partnerships and family relationships.
- A failure to maintain a network of relationships following separation.
- The lack of a sense of family togetherness, failure to provide a social and cultural identity.
- Failure to support individuation and premature separation or enmeshed relationships.
- Lack of a supportive response to adversity or family change.

Impact on child when adequate stability and family relationships provided

- Child is a member of a network of emotionally stable and affectionate relationships.
- Reasonably assertive, clear role and identity.
- Optimal relationships with family and external world.
- Satisfactory sexual identity and relationships.
- Child has an appropriate degree of closeness and distance with parental sibling and family members.
- Child connects with separated parent.
- Child developing a positive sense of self, assertive and is developing a sense of family and cultural identity with appropriate individuation and avoidance of negative identification.
- Child copes with adversity and negative events.

Risk of harm: impact on the child when failure to provide adequate stability and family relationships

- Child is a member of a disrupted, network of unstable relationships, enmeshed or hostile.
- Lack of assertive skills, under-assertive or over-assertive, confused role and identity.
- Destructive relationships with the family and external world.
- Uncertain gender, sexual identity, relationships.
- Child has an inappropriate, enmeshed or excluded relationship with parental, sibling or family member.
- Child fails to connect with separated parental or family members.
- Child has an absent or omnipotent sense of self; absence or over-assertiveness. Failure to develop a sense of family cultural identity, identifies with negative family figures.
- Child cannot cope with adversity and negative events.

HARMFUL PARENTING PATTERNS

The final section looks at strengths and difficulties in the parenting capacity dimension covering the need to provide stable family relationships and a sense of identity for children and looks at the harmful impacts that parenting difficulties in this area can have on children's development.

Harmful parenting in this dimension includes there being a marked lack of stability in family relationships and adult partnerships or relationships which may be disruptive, abusive or disconnected. Parents' failure to acknowledge their parental role in the context of separation has significant disruptive effects. It can lead to breakdown and loss of stable family relationships, attachments and, consequently, a loss of a sense of family identity. A failure to maintain a network of social, educational and cultural relationships can lead to prejudice, isolation, antisocial responses and withdrawal. Children require support to move towards becoming more independent, developing relationships with peers and others and taking appropriate adolescent roles. Family breakdown adversity may result in lack of coping, being overwhelmed by moves and losses in the face of major changes.

IMPACT ON CHILD

The result of parenting difficulties in this dimension for the child can be the child developing a fragmented sense of their identity. They may become enmeshed in the identity of a particular family member or isolated from parental figures. Any sense of developing an integrated family identity is disrupted through breakdown and the child may display clinging, rivalrous or oppositional behaviour.

The child's sense of cultural identity may be also become fragmented and the child may develop prejudiced, abusive, isolated, antisocial behavioural responses which again can lead into significant, dangerous situations outside the home.

Above all, the child or young person can fail to develop a resilient capacity to cope with change or move through the developmental processes which would be expected to form part of most children and young person's experiences as they move from childhood to adult life.

INTEGRATED AND INTERDISCIPLINARY ASSESSMENT

In addition to the use of the evidence-based assessment tools, a variety of individual and family assessments may be required to understand the complex factors of family breakdown and its impact on children's functioning and the extent to which their needs are met or harm is being caused.

Assessment of strengths and difficulties in family and environmental factors

Box 6.10 lists strengths and difficulties in family history and family functioning. Later in this section, Box 6.11 lists strengths and difficulties in other family and environmental factors. Strengths and difficulties in these and other dimensions are more fully described in Chapter 5.

Box 6.10 Family history, family functioning and wider family

Strengths

- Stable and protected childhood from major losses, disruption, traumatic events processed, autonomous functioning.
- Recognition and acknowledgement of significant past events, relationships and circumstances.
- Adequate functioning, reasonable health management of physical or mental illness, personality difficulties, impairments, appropriate treatment and support.
- Supportive, respectful, confiding and balance of assertiveness and compromise.
- Violent partner acknowledges responsibility, supports partner and children. Collaborative, sharing motivation to change.
- Network of supportive family members, supportive and substitute.

Difficulties

- Unstable family environment, exposure to violence, abuse, rejection, loss, illness, unprocessed, dismissive, preoccupied or entangled.
- Unresolved significant events, relationships or circumstances, major impact on current family functioning.
- Negative functioning, physical and mental ill health, disability, personality problems, criminality, drug and alcohol misuse, failure of treatment and social support.
- Isolated, unsupportive, unconfiding, unbalanced, dominant or submissive pattern, destructive, at war.
- Violent partner legitimizes violence, fails to take responsibility, blames victim, children ignored, uncollaborative, resistant.
- Family members intrusive, over-involved, abandoning, ineffective, fail to caregive, support or substitute.

INTEGRATED AND INTERDISCIPLINARY ASSESSMENT

The use of the evidence-based assessment tools can provide an account of individual, couple and family functioning. Depending on the nature of these elements it may be necessary to carry out specialist assessments, e.g. of parental mental health or issues of domestic violence. Services specializing in substance or alcohol misuse can assist in establishing the extent of strengths and difficulties, determining the need for intervention and assessing the prospect for recovery or more adequate functioning within a child's timeframe.

Box 6.11 Other family and environmental factors

Strengths

- Stable well-maintained housing fits family needs.
- Working patterns sustain family life.
- Reasonable balance of child and parent needs.
- Appropriate responsibilities for children.
- Sustained adequate income, focused on children's needs.
- Family integrated, using resources and having appropriate network.
- Adequate resources available.

Difficulties

- Unstable, disruptive housing, poorly maintained, poor fit for needs.
- Unpredictability, inconsistency of work, failure to sustain family life.
- Work patterns undermine family life.
- Undue pressure on children to work.
- Inadequate income, unsustained, used for adult needs, children's needs neglected.
- Poor integration, excluded.
- Poor use of resources, failure to use network.
- Lack of adequate resources.

INTEGRATED AND INTERDISCIPLINARY ASSESSMENT

The use of the evidence-based assessment tools should help establish strengths and difficulties in the further dimensions of family and environmental factors. Social work investigation, integrating information from community agencies, such as housing, benefits offices and community health, reinforces and provides a fuller picture of the impact of elements.

Creating a profile of harm

Given the picture of harm which emerges from the evidence-based assessments of the strengths and difficulties in each dimension of parenting capacity, the identification of any harmful parenting and the analysis of the impact on children's developmental needs, it then becomes feasible to create a profile of harm.

Although the different forms of harm are described as though they are discrete, they often co-occur, as described in Chapter 1, and it is the interaction and cumulative impact of multiple forms of harm that has the most significant impact on a child's development and functioning.

Stage 4: Assessing the likelihood of response to professional intervention in the context of the level of the child's needs and the level of parenting capacity and family and environmental difficulties

There are two key steps to this stage of assessment in the safeguarding process. The first step, based on the principles in Chapter 2, is to make a *functional systemic analysis of the processes which have led* to the occurrence of patterns of *significant harm*. This includes understanding the way the dimensions in each domain of the *Assessment Framework* may contribute, and the interaction between dimensions and domains. It also requires a consideration of circular and linear processes, the severity of difficulties (the weight of negative processes which may be acting as maintaining factors and the magnitude of strengths), and the weight of positive processes, which are potentially protective factors. In Chapter 2 it was observed that significant harm was more likely if there were difficulties in a number of dimensions, difficulties were manifested frequently, have existed over a long period, were strikingly intrusive and resistant to modification.

The second step is to establish a prognosis for change, i.e. an assessment of the likelihood of achieving change within the child's timeframe, using information about *factors associated with the risk of re-abuse*, and knowledge about the likelihood of *response to intervention*. This requires a consideration of each domain, an assessment of the level of difficulty in each of the dimensions, the recognition of difficulty by parents, children and young people, and the likelihood of response within the child's timescale. Based on a review of each domain, an overall assessment of prognosis can be made, and an appropriate intervention plan made.

Functional systemic analysis of processes leading to patterns of significant harm

It is helpful to gather information in the following areas.

PREDISPOSING FACTORS

Predisposing factors can impact negatively on parenting capacity through circular and linear processes involving family and environmental factors, e.g. mental health issues, factors associated with unresolved abusive events in the lives of parents. Parenting capacity may be characterized by significant difficulties in key areas, e.g. providing safety and emotional warmth, maintaining boundaries and managing behaviour. The child or young person's functioning may indicate longstanding difficulties in the area of health, education, emotional and behavioural development and so on. There may be significant areas of unmet needs in relation to disability or special needs.

PRECIPITATING OR TRIGGERING FACTORS

There are precipitating or triggering factors which may be associated with changes in dimensions in the child's developmental needs domain, in relation to the child's functioning or development, for example, a child entering puberty, the development of oppositional behaviour, the increasing needs of a number of children in the family. This may have a circular impact on the dimensions of the parenting capacity, e.g. difficulties in the provision of basic care or guidance and boundaries and management of behaviour becoming increasingly negative in character. Changes in family and environmental factors may change the pressure being placed on parenting capacity or on the child directly, e.g. breakdown in relationships, which stresses a single parent and reinforces parental capacity difficulties in providing adequate safety or stability.

PROFILE OF HARMFUL RESPONSES

This information can be drawn together to create a profile of harmful responses which helps to identify the harm which can be associated with each area of parental capacity. These can be divided into maintaining factors and protective factors.

Maintaining factors

Maintaining factors are associated with the continuation and reinforcement of negative factors and circular processes associated with each domain. For example, anger and arousal in a child, associated with high levels of punitive parenting, is affecting their behaviour in school and undermining relationships with siblings and peers which in turn results in further punitiveness and rejection. Parenting difficulties in providing adequate basic care, for example, may affect capacity to provide adequate emotional warmth, support education, and provide safety for a child with the child's response affecting each area of parenting capacity in turn. Current difficulties in the family and environmental factors dimension can reinforce difficulties, e.g. the breakdown in a relationship can trigger unresolved areas of early history, which may lead to abuse of alcohol or self-harming behaviour, with a circular impact on parenting and risks of increasing difficulties in meeting children's needs.

Protective factors

Protective factors will include the maintenance of areas where children's needs are being met despite difficulties, e.g. continuing attendance at school, or attention being paid to health needs. The role of extended family support can be important, for example, a grandparent who provides temporary care can prevent the circular impact of negative factors. There may be an openness to acknowledge and seek help from services and other community resources to bolster limited capacities to meet children's needs such as parents actively seeking for help for their individual and/or couple difficulties.

In Chapter 8, the Green family will be described and a functional systemic analysis of factors leading to significant harm will be made.

Factors associated with the risk of re-abuse and the prognosis for intervention

This section demonstrates factors associated with the risk of re-abuse and the prognosis for intervention. These judgements have been drawn from a number of sources. Work carried out at Great Ormond Street Hospital for Children (Bentovim, Elton and Tranter 1987) introduced the notion of the prospects for successful rehabilitation of a child who has required protection to their family. These range from a *hopeful prognosis* where factors related to the child, family and context indicated that it was likely that rehabilitation could be achieved to a *poor prognosis* which was associated with a child who has suffered a severe level of abuse, parents not taking adequate responsibility for the level of harm and factors such as severe personality disorder or substance abuse being present, making it unlikely that rehabilitation could be achieved in the child's timeframe. A *doubtful prognosis* was identified when there was a lack of clarity, whether there were sufficient protective factors to make the prognosis hopeful, or the balance of negative factors made the prognosis poor. This is a situation where further work needed to be carried out to determine whether rehabilitation can be achieved or not.

Subsequent work by David Jones (1998) and Jones, Hindley and Ramchandani (2006) summarized factors associated with re-abuse in family contexts. These factors are associated with hopeful or poorer prognosis in terms of the prospects of rehabilitation where there had been safeguarding concerns. They noted a group of factors where there was significant risk of re-abuse if a child continued to live in the family. These factors were associated with denial, antisocial personality disorders and learning disability associated with mental health problems. Rehabilitation was less likely to be achieved in these situations with a high risk of re-abuse.

An assessment using the Great Ormond Street model (Sylvester *et al.* 1995) noted that a key issue associated with the prognosis for rehabilitation was the attribution of blame to children when the child was being perceived by the parent as being responsible for the parent's abusive action. This concept is related to the way relationships can be 'organized' by traumatic events.

A 12-step process for assessing the risk of re-abuse to a child, parenting capacity and prospects of rehabilitation

Based on these findings, a 12-step process is described to determine the risk of re-abuse and the prospect for rehabilitation. The stages suggested are in Box 6.12.

Box 6.12 A 12-step process for assessing the risk of re-abuse to a child, parenting capacity and prospects of rehabilitation

Step 1: Examine the overall levels of harm, past and present, and examine the impact on the child's health and safety, educational issues, emotional life, behaviour and identity and how the child's needs were met in the past and currently.

Step 2: Assess the level of parenting, protection and therapeutic work the child requires, considering the levels and extensiveness of harm, and factors which would act as an additional factor requiring particular parenting skills, e.g. disability.

Step 3: Establish the following: do parents acknowledge the level of harm? Can they take appropriate responsibility for harm? Do they acknowledge the need for protection and therapeutic work to ensure the child's future safety and recovery?

Step 4: Consider the level of parenting capacity in the areas of provision of basic care, ensuring safety and providing emotional warmth, stimulation, guidance, boundaries and stability.

Step 5: Establish whether parents acknowledge the nature and level of current difficulties in parenting capacity and whether they have the motivation to achieve change.

Step 6: Assess the parents' potential to respond to the child's needs and to develop their parenting capacity to help children recover from abusive effects and achieve their potential.

Step 7: Identify the influence of individual and family factors on parenting capacity, considering factors from the parents' childhood, health, relationships, family organization and family relationships, including with the wider family.

Step 8: Find out whether the parents acknowledge the role of individual and family factors and their effect on parenting and their level of motivation to change.

Step 9: Assess the potential for change in individual and family factors and to respond to intervention and improve parenting to meet the children's needs.

Step 10: Consider the role of environmental factors such as housing, employment, income and family integration and their impact on parenting, individual and family functioning and the parents' capacity to meet the children's needs.

Step 11: Establish whether parents recognize the role of environmental factors and the potential for change.

Step 12: Explore the nature of family–professional relationships, and establish whether there is a potential for working together and the availability of resources to achieve change within the child's timeframe.

The tables and descriptive text which follow have been constructed using the *Assessment Framework*. A description is provided of factors which can usefully be observed in each of the areas. The factors included are those which have been shown to have a better or worse implication for prognosis. The 12-step process will now be described in more detail.

Step 1: Overall levels of harm, impact on the child and how the child's needs were met

The first stage is to analyse information available to assess the overall level of harm to the child.

Table 6.1 provides a descriptive range from those children who are subject to least severe levels of harm, less risk of re-abuse and a better prospect for rehabilitation, to those children who have suffered higher levels of harm, higher risks of re-abuse and a poorer prospect of rehabilitation. Overall levels of harm, past and present, need to be considered, severity of harm, different forms of harm, extensiveness of traumatic effects, the impact on health, emotional development, behaviour, educational achievement, identity and relationship difficulties. There also needs to be consideration of whether needs have been met previously during the child's development, and the history of previous harm.

Table 6.1 Step 1: Areas to be considered and prospects for rehabilitation

Areas to be considered	Better prospect for rehabilitation	Poor prospect for rehabilitation
Level of harm sustained	Child with single forms of harm	Child subject of severe levels of harm, or multiple areas
Traumatic effects	Limited traumatic effects	Extensive traumatic effects
Emotional and behavioural development, identity and relationship harm	Limited evidence of impact on emotional, behaviour, identity and relationship functioning	Evidence of considerable impact on emotional, identity and relationship functioning
Level of neglect, educational difficulties and care issues	Limited evidence of impact on health, neglect, educational, development, self-presentation and self-care	Presence of considerable impact on health, neglect, educational difficulties, self-presentation and self-care
History of how needs met in general, previous harm, trauma, neglect, emotional and developmental harm	Reasonable strengths and evidence of needs being met. Limited previous harm, trauma, neglect and/or emotional/developmental harm	Evidence of needs not being met. Extensive history of previous harm, trauma, neglect, emotional and developmental harm.

Step 2: Level of parenting, protection and therapeutic work the child requires

The next stage is putting in place the protection, parenting (often foster parenting) and therapeutic work required to ensure that the child will not be subject to future harm and to help achieve the child's potential. Children who are subject to considerable levels of harm, higher risks and poorest prospects for rehabilitation require the highest level of protection through appropriate legal proceedings. They may also require specialist parenting and the provision of extensive therapeutic help to recover from harm. Those children with moderate or less severe levels of harm may require less extensive therapeutic parenting and support, and lesser levels of protection.

Step 3: Whether parents judged responsible for harm can acknowledge the level of harm or harmful behaviour to the child

The next level is concerned with the level of parental responsibility taken for harmful behaviour, whether parents can acknowledge harm which has occurred, and whether there is contemplation or taking responsibility for abusive action and for harmful effects and an acknowledgement that the child has a need for protection and appropriate therapeutic work. See Table 6.3.

Table 6.2 Step 2: Areas to be considered and prospects for rehabilitation

Areas to be considered	Better prospect for rehabilitation	Poor prospect for rehabilitation
Level of protection required	Do not require high levels of protection, use of conference and core group approaches	The highest level of protection required through appropriate legal proceedings
Level of parenting required	Potential to respond to variety of parenting	Requires specialist parenting for recovery
Level of therapeutic work required	Focused therapeutic help required for specific forms of harm	Extensive therapeutic help required for recovery from harm

Table 6.3 Step 3: Areas to be considered and prospects for rehabilitation

Areas to be considered	Lesser risks, better prospects for rehabilitation	Greater risks, poorer prospects for rehabilitation
Parental acknowledgement of level of harm or harmful behaviour and responses	Acknowledgement of level of harm or harmful behaviour	Failure of parents and/or child to acknowledge level of harm or harmful behaviour
Degree of responsibility taken for abusive action and impact	Appropriate degree of responsibility taken for harm	Denial of responsibility for abusive or neglectful action Alleges falsification by professionals
Acknowledgement of impact of abuse and harmful effects	Acknowledgement of traumatic responses and emotional, relationship and developmental harm	Failure to acknowledge level of traumatic responses, emotional, developmental and relationship harm
Acknowledgement of the need for protection and therapeutic work	Acceptance of need for protection and care arrangement and therapeutic help for child	Failure to acknowledge a need for protection or therapeutic help

Step 4: Level of parenting that has been provided for the child

This section describes the level and quality of parenting which has been provided for the child, and assesses the parents' capacity to provide adequate parenting (see Table 6.4). This includes consideration of basic care, organiza-

tion and safety, the provision of emotional warmth, stimulation and encouragement, guidance and boundaries and behavioural management, and general stability. Serious harm is usually associated with considerable parenting
difficulties.

Table 6.4 Step 4: Areas to be considered and prospects for rehabilitation

Areas to be considered	Lesser risks, better prospects for rehabilitation	Greater risks, poorer prospects for rehabilitation
Level of parenting provided	Reasonable provision of basic care	Extensive difficulties in the provision of basic care
Basic care and organization and safety	Reasonably adequate family organization	Unreliable, fragmented chaotic organization of family functioning
Management of behaviour and safety	Reasonable discipline and acceptable level of safety within the home and environment	Punitive or rejecting, failure to provide adequate safety inside and outside the family
Level of emotional warmth and responsiveness	Adequate emotional warmth and response to emotional needs	Negative emotions, exploiting, disqualification, critical, attacking, coldness
Provision of stimulation and encouragement	Reasonable degree of stimulation, encouragement of development and educational achievement	Critical lack of stimulation, praise, encouragement of educational attendance and achievement
Boundaries and behavioural management	Adequate boundaries, behavioural management	Rigid boundaries, parentification, enmeshment, failure to manage behaviour
Stability of relationships	Reasonable stability and maintenance of network of relationships	Transient, disrupted unstable network

Step 5: Assessing parental capacity to acknowledge the level of parental difficulties present and establishing the motivation to achieve change

The next area is to consider whether there is an acknowledgement of the level
of parenting difficulties – ranging from reasonable parental acknowledgement
and acceptance of the level of parenting difficulties and awareness of resulting
harm and children's needs through to lack of parental awareness or denial of
the level of parenting difficulties and a pattern of blaming the authorities and
family and environmental factors (see Table 6.5). Motivation to achieve
changes range from adequate motivation to limited or little motivation.

Table 6.5 Step 5: Areas to be considered and prospects for rehabilitation

Areas to be considered	Lesser risks, better prospects for rehabilitation	Greater risks, poorer prospects for rehabilitation
Acknowledgement of level of parenting difficulties	Reasonable acknowledgement and acceptance of level of parental difficulties and awareness of resulting harm	Failure to acknowledge level of parenting difficulties, or harm, blames family or environmental factors, agency failures, mutual blame
Motivation to achieve change	Motivation to achieve adequate levels of parenting	Limited or little motivation to contemplate the need for change

Step 6: Assessing parents' potential to respond to the child's needs and to develop their parenting capacity to help children recover from abusive effects and achieve their potential

Professional judgement is required about the potential of parents to develop the capacity to respond to the child's needs within the time framework and willingness to accept assistance and to develop an adequate capacity to care (see Table 6.6). Alternatively, professionals may have to decide whether it would be unlikely that parents could develop adequate skills to provide protection, support and meet children's needs, as a result of the extensiveness of harm and extensiveness of parenting difficulties.

Table 6.6 Step 6: Areas to be considered and prospects for rehabilitation

Areas to be considered	Lesser risks, better prospects for rehabilitation	Greater risks, poorer prospects for rehabilitation
Potential for parenting capacity to respond to child's needs within timeframe, given level of harm and parental level	Potential to achieve level of parenting to meet children's needs Harm is of limited degree, fewer parenting difficulties	Highly unlikely that parents could develop adequate skills to protect, support and meet children's needs, extensive harm, and extensiveness of parenting difficulties
Motivation to accept help required to achieve change	Willingness to accept appropriate assistance, reasonable prospect for response to parenting work, appropriate planning of intervention feasible	Failure to contemplate need or benefit from parenting work, considerable doubt about commencing work

Step 7: Identifying the influence of individual and family factors on parenting and the parents' capacities to meet the child's needs

This section describes factors in relation to individual and family issues, and their influence on parenting capacity (see Table 6.7). This includes factors from the adults' childhood; their individual health and development; their couple relationships; the level of family organization and links with the wider family. There are lower risks and better prospects for rehabilitation when parents have stable adequately protected childhood, disruption and traumatic loss adequately processed with reasonably supportive, confiding relationships, acknowledgement of violence, flexibility of family organization and a general supportive network. There is a poorer prognosis in families where exposure to violence, abuse and rejection in parents' own childhood results in the development of conflictual relationships, serious borderline and antisocial personality disorders, substance abuse, psychotic illness, denial of the impact of violence and ineffective, unsupportive family relationships.

Table 6.7 Step 7: Areas to be considered and prospects for rehabilitation

Area to be considered	Lesser risks, better prospects for rehabilitation	Greater risks, poorer prospects for rehabilitation
Influence of individual and family factors on parenting	Reasonably stable protected childhood, traumatic loss and disruption processed, reasonable coming to terms with experience	Exposure to violence, abuse, rejection, instability continuing, unresolved, unprocessed events
Factors from childhood	Reasonable secure attachment	Disorganized attachments
Individual health and development	Positive functioning physical and mental health	Negative functioning, physical and mental health
	Adequate functioning, acknowledgement, management of mental health difficulties and impairment, antisocial activities, adequate support for learning difficulties and disabilities	Antisocial, sadistic, aggressive, borderline personality disorders, paranoid psychosis, substance abuse, criminal history, severe physical health, learning difficulties, worsened by mental health problems
Current relationships	Reasonably supportive confiding relationships, responsibility acknowledged for violence and adequate management	Isolated unsupportive relationships, violent partner, ignores impact on children

Table 6.7 *cont.*

Area to be considered	Lesser risks, better prospects for rehabilitation	Greater risks, poorer prospects for rehabilitation
Family organization	Flexible family organization to meet changing needs	Rigid, chaotic family organization, failure to respond to changing family needs
Management of conflict, decision-making, communication and emotional support	Adequate conflict management, decision-making, communication, emotional support and identity	Considerable difficulties in conflict management, decision-making, communication, alliances emotional support and identity
Relationships with wider family	Reasonably supportive network in wider family, support and substitute	Intrusive, over-involved, ineffective relationships with wider family

Step 8: Investigating parents' acknowledgement of the role of individual and family factors, and their effect on parenting and a motivation to change

The question then arises as to the acknowledgement of the role of individual and family factors and motivation to change (see Table 6.8).

Table 6.8 Step 8: Areas to be considered and prospects for rehabilitation

Areas to be considered	Lesser risks, better prospects for rehabilitation	Greater risks, poorer prospects for rehabilitation
Acknowledgment of role of individual and family factors	Acknowledgement of role of childhood individual functioning, relationship and family relationships in affecting parenting	Failure to acknowledge role of childhood factors, individual functioning or relationship and family difficulties on capacity to parent
Motivation to change	Motivation to change, willingness to engage in therapeutic work	Low motivation to change, unwillingness to acknowledge or to be involved in therapeutic work

Step 9: Assessing the potential for change in individual and family factors, and improving parenting to meet the child's needs

The final question is the potential for change in individual and family factors for parenting to meet children's needs, whether there is an acknowledgement of the role of childhood individual functioning, family relationships, a motivation to change, an openness to therapeutic work within the child's timeframe, the availability of therapeutic resources and the potential to respond to a period of work (see Table 6.9).

Table 6.9 Step 9: Areas to be considered and prospects for rehabilitation

Area to be considered	Lesser risks, better prospects for rehabilitation	Greater risks, poorer prospects for rehabilitation
Potential for change in individual and family factors to impact on parenting to meet children's needs	Individual relationship and family factors, modifiable within child's timeframe	Extensiveness of individual family and relationship factors highly unlikely to be changeable within child's framework
Availability of therapeutic work, and prospect of response to therapeutic work	Therapeutic work available and likelihood of change to improve parenting to meet children's needs	Requisite therapeutic work unavailable or potentially ineffective as a result of level of difficulties in child, individual, relationship and parenting difficulties
	Good prospect for trial of intervention	Poor prospect of any trial of therapeutic intervention

Steps 10, 11 and 12: Explaining the role of environmental factors and their impact on parenting, individual and family factors and children's needs

The final section is environmental factors, which are treated in a similar way, looking at the different elements including housing, employment, income, family integration and family resources, whether these environmental factors are recognized, whether there is a potential for change. The nature of family–professional relationships is important whether again there are understandable levels of negative feelings and grievances, extending to negative combative relationships. Table 6.10 illustrates the factors.

Table 6.10 Steps 10, 11 and 12: Areas to be considered and prospects for rehabilitation

Area to be considered	Lesser risks better prospects for rehabilitation	Greater risks, poorer prospects for rehabilitation
Step 10 **Housing**	Stable, reasonably maintained housing and adapted for needs	Unstable, disrupted, poorly maintained housing
Employment	Consistent working patterns support family life, sustained	Unpredictability, inconsistency of employment, failure to support, provide for family life
Income	Adequate income and entitlements claimed	Inadequate income, entitlements not claimed
	Available resources used to support needs	Income used for adult needs
Family integration	Acceptance valuing of diversity	Resources not used, opportunities rejected, climate of threat, discrimination, antisocial influence
Resources in community	Available adequate resources	Absent, inadequate resources, not fitting needs of the family
Step 11 **Recognition of role of environmental factors**	Parental recognition of the role of environmental factors	Failure to acknowledge environmental factors and its impact on individual and family functioning
	Motivated to change, seek support and help to improve and modify where required	Refusal to acknowledge needs for change, refusal to engage with appropriate agencies
Potential for change	Level of environmental difficulties modifiable with positive motivation and work with support agencies	Extensiveness of environmental difficulties considerable
	Achievable within child's timeframe	Unlikely to achieve sufficient change within the child's timeframe
Step 12 **Family–professional relationships**	Relationships between family and professionals, understandable levels of negative feelings and grievances, dependence	Negative combative relationship between family and professionals, endless conflicts, divisive, inconsistent responses
	Resources available in community to meet individual, family and parenting needs as well as the needs of the child	Resources not available within the timescale of the child and family

Assessing the prognosis for change

On the basis of the profile of harm (drawn up using steps 1, 2, 4, 7 and 10) and the prospect of rehabilitation (determined using steps 3, 5, 6, 8, 9, 11 and 12), a view can be taken about whether overall the prognosis is *reasonably hopeful*, i.e. there are sufficient factors to predict that a positive outcome is achievable within the child's timeframe, or alternatively that the factors make it highly unlikely that a safe context can be achieved for the child.

Frequently there is a *degree of doubt*, as it is unclear whether (a) parents are able to take responsibility, (b) the child's state can improve with increased contact with the parent, (c) parenting itself can improve sufficiently to meet the children's needs, and (d) individual factors or environmental contexts can also change. This indicates the requirement for further assessments to determine whether a degree of clarity about prognosis can be achieved.

INTEGRATED INTERDISCIPLINARY ASSESSMENTS

Family centre attendance, participation of parents in drug, alcohol or mental health services, residential assessments, attendance at a parenting course or family or individual therapy may be indicated. Other specialist assessments may be required if the family is involved with Family Court proceedings. Inter-disciplinary consultations and conferences, between professionals, or family group conferences may contribute to the decision-making process. The courts may arbitrate between differing views about the potential for rehabilitation or the need for the child to have alternative long-term care.

The 12-step process for assessing risks of re-abuse, parenting capacity and the prospects for rehabilitation – the Ward family

We return to the Ward family to illustrate the use of the 12 steps to assess the prospect of adequate care and the reversal of harm, the outlook for re-abuse or the likelihood of continuing harm to the children, Michael, aged eight, and Laura, aged 14, as well as the potential for change by their mother, Moira Ward, and her new partner, Ian Ross, and their capacity to protect each of the children from harm. The use of the 12-step process follows the assessment and analysis of both children's developmental needs, parenting capacity and the impact of family and environmental factors, as illustrated for Michael in Chapters 4 and 5.

Case example: The Ward family

This case example uses the 12-step process for assessing the risk of re-abuse to a child, parenting capacity and prospects of rehabilitation.

Step 1: Level of harm

Michael and Laura are children who have been reasonably well cared for in the past, and have had no significant earlier episodes of major harm being sustained, despite Moira Ward's drinking pattern. Over the past six months there has been evidence with Michael of moderate to severe levels of harm: there are signs of significant neglect, his reports of being hit as physical chastisement by Ian Ross, heightened levels of anxiety and poor concentration, educational failure, poor self-presentation and self-care. In terms of both Ian Ross and Moira Ward's parenting of Michael and Laura, there is evidence for moderate levels of punitive responses and their exposure to domestic violence and moderate to severe emotional harm as a result of the very changed parental expectations of both children with negative harmful effects to both – resulting in neglect on Michael's part and oppositional defiance on Laura's part.

Step 2: Level of protection required and the therapeutic work

It is essential that both Laura and Michael have good quality parenting. They have a positive history of care in the past. They need to be protected from the increasing levels of conflict within the family between their mother and Ian Ross and the higher levels of punitiveness and inappropriate demands being made on them as children and young people. There may be a requirement for therapeutic help for both children in addition to good quality parenting and therapeutic support to reverse their current patterns of responses to harmful parenting behaviours. If Moira Ward and Ian Ross cooperate with parenting training and practical support to help them change the patterns of care provided for Michael and Laura at home, and with suggested interventions at school (e.g. Breakfast Club at school for Michael) this would improve the situation somewhat for the children immediately while longer term work is undertaken.

Step 3: Is there parental and children's acknowledgement of harmful situation?

There is a high level of concern, particularly by Laura on behalf of Michael, given her perception and reporting of his increased neglected appearance and withdrawal, and the failure of her own attempts to support and protect him. She has directly brought to the attention of professionals both Ian Ross's abuse of Moira Ward, and Moira Ward's increasing level of drinking. Moira Ward has acknowledged Michael's indications that Ian Ross hits him as physical chastisement. However, there is a minimization on Ian Ross and Moira Ward's part of the traumatic and emotional developmental impact of current family relationships on the children as Ian Ross continues to assert his views of the children's needs, and Moira Ward fits into his views to comply with his expectations. There is limited acceptance of the need for protection, care and therapeutic help for Michael and Laura.

Step 4: Level of parenting

Moira Ward and Ian Ross have moderate to severe difficulties in providing basic care and adapting to Michael and Laura's current needs. There is inadequate stimulation or support for the children's educational needs. Basic care is becoming increasingly inadequate, particularly of Michael, with Moira Ward's increasing alcohol use. Ensuring safety is compromised because of the 'new rules' which Ian has brought in, which mean that Michael is newly expected to get himself to school. Both children have not been protected from witnessing an incidence of domestic violence. Guidance, boundaries and behavioural management are punitive and ineffective, and there is a sense of instability of family life and relationships and parenting. Family organization is marked by high levels of conflict, disagreements, withdrawal and separations and therefore affecting family stability.

Step 5: Acknowledgement of level of parenting difficulties and motivation to achieve change

There is an acceptance and acknowledgement by Moira Ward and Ian Ross of some of the current parenting difficulties of conflict, although harm is minimized. There is an uncertain degree of motivation to achieve change given the complexity of factors which are associated with the need to provide more effective parenting potential.

Step 6: Is there a potential for parenting capacity to respond to child's needs within timeframe in the light of level of harm and parenting difficulties?

There is a potential for Moira Ward to be able to parent the children more effectively, as noted in the earlier history when she cared for the children without Ian Ross. In the current climate of conflict and given Moira Ward's attempts to fit in with Ian Ross's expectations, Moira Ward and Ian Ross have a limited understanding of the negative effect of Ian Ross's parenting style. There is doubt about whether they will be able to respond to the children's needs within their framework of time, given the considerable differences in the parents' ideas about all aspects of parenting and the risk of increasing tension, alcohol use and a repeat of earlier domestic violence.

Step 7: Influence of individual and family factors

Both parents have a history of exposure to violence and the use of violence to control. Moira Ward has attempted to parent in a less punitive way, but has had a number of partnerships where there has been violence. Ian Ross has modelled himself on his own paternal models of violence and control. Moira Ward has used alcohol in the past as a coping mechanism and in the current family situation she is depressed and using alcohol and withdrawal to an increasing degree, which is resulting in increasingly poor care of Michael. Laura's attempts to compensate, increasing conflict and critical responses from Ian Ross are associated with a worsening of her alcohol use. As a result, family organization generally has been undermined with a reduction of support from the wider family.

Individual, family and couple factors are therefore having a considerable influence on current parenting capacity in the Ward family.

Step 8: Is there acknowledgement of the role of individual and factors and a motivation to change?

The most powerful acknowledgement of these factors and motivation to change is from Laura who has attempted to draw professionals' attention to the major factors in the worsening situation within the family of her mother's alcohol misuse and the risk of further violence between Ian Ross and Moira Ward. There is therefore some parental acceptance of other factors, but a mixed motivation to engage in work.

Step 9: Potential for change in individual and family factors to impact on parenting to meet the children's needs

The issue of the potential for change will very much depend on Moira Ward's willingness to involve herself with drug and alcohol services, as the level of her alcohol use has now become far more extensive and is affecting her functioning to a considerable degree. This will require an acknowledge of the problem by both herself and Ian Ross as well as an acknowledgement that their conflicting attitudes concerning expectations of the children, discipline and self-care is having deleterious effects. These need to be confronted, in both couple and family work, and this requires involvement with services if change is to be achieved. With an extensive package of treatment, it may be possible to achieve changes but, given the past history of good care by Moira Ward, this would require considerable motivation to achieve change.

The parents' responses to these issues in case conference and core meetings will impact on whether care proceedings are going to be necessary to protect the children, provide adequate parenting and test the parents' capacity to provide more adequate care.

Step 10: Environmental factors and their impact on parenting

The family housing, employment income and use of resources have been affected in part by the family moving recently, after the couple had got together, and establishing the current family home. Moira Ward has experienced the separation from her previous partner and the breakdown of her previous home, which has contributed to her depression. There is evidence that Moira Ward's reliance on Ian Ross's income is a factor in readiness to comply with his views.

Step 11: Is there a recognition of the role of environmental factors?

This is not a major issue in this family for the most part; however, there is limited recognition of the concern of educational and community agencies about Michael moving to a new area with Ian Ross, which may contribute to difficulty in involvement and recognition of these factors.

Are environmental factors changeable within child's timeframe? The care of the home itself is positive, resources are present to be able to care more adequately for the children providing that a more responsive attitude is taken.

Step 12: Family–professional relationships

There is uncertainty about how the Ward family views their relationships with professionals. There is some evidence of openness and the family has cooperated with the assessment process, but there has also been some conflict. However, there is no evidence of extreme negativeness about professional intervention. Prior to Ian Ross's arrival in the family, the school had found Moira Ward to be cooperative with school and supportive of the children's education.

Potential for change

In the Ward family, there is evidence of current significant harm to each of the children, a limited awareness of the parental and individual contribution, and a degree of doubt whether the family can change and respond to the children's needs within their timeframe. It would seem likely that a period of therapeutic work and engagement with the family would be required to test whether change can be achieved within the children's timeframe, or whether a period of alternative care will be required. The recognition of difficulties by Laura is a key factor in bringing concerns to professional awareness, as well as concerns raised within the educational context itself.

Stage 5: Developing a plan of intervention to include therapeutic work in a context of safety and protection from harm

This next stage of the seven-stage process of assessment where there are safeguarding concerns is formulating a plan of intervention. A view has to be taken as to what is the most appropriate plan for the child and other children in the family on the basis of the level of harm which has occurred, the risks of re-abuse, and the prospects for rehabilitation and taking all these factors into account. This will be described in Chapter 8 as an aspect of approaches to rehabilitation.

For the Ward family, a child protection conference was reconvened. Moira Ward and Ian Ross accepted that Michael's name needed to be put on the Child Protection Register, and they agreed with the child protection plan based on Michael and Laura's needs, their parenting difficulties and the considerable stress on their current family relationships.

In terms of formulating a plan for the family, given their positive motivation for help, their acknowledgement of the difficulties and the fact that problems were relatively recent, it would be reasonable to provide a protection plan where both Michael and Laura continued to live at home while attending a specialist child and adolescent mental health service. An abuse-focused family work approach (Kolko 1996) involving family members individually and conjointly, using cognitive behavioural and systemic approaches would be required to help them manage anger more appropriately and ensure each of the children's needs would be met appropriately.

Family members would be assisted to manage conflict more appropriately, mother and stepfather to develop a unified parenting approach. It would be important to support the strengths which reinforced the family's identity, associated with the mother's previous positive pattern of care, and to recognize where Ian Ross's approach could have value.

Moira Ward and Ian Ross would need help with their relationships as partners as well as parents, which could help Moira Ward avoid problem drinking. In addition, she may need to attend local drug and alcohol services to obtain some additional individual help with her problem drinking. The children, particularly Michael, would need help to cope with the traumatic effects of punitive abusive care, and a trauma-focused approach (Cohen *et al.* 2000) would be likely to be helpful. Ian Ross would need help to acknowledge the harm that he has caused to the children and to Moira Ward, and Moira Ward to acknowledge that her attempts to bridge differences between Ian Ross's views and her own have also caused harm.

It would be important to decide on measures to assess whether change had occurred. The findings from the *Strength and Difficulties Questionnaires* filled in by Michael, by the school, parents and from the *Adolescent Well-Being Scale* completed by Michael, as well as the results from the *Adult Wellbeing Scales, Alcohol Scales* and the *Parenting Daily Hassles Scale* completed by Moira Ward and Ian Ross, all gave useful baseline information in the early stages of the assessment and a combination of them would help to assess whether change has taken place. Changes in the findings from the use of the *HOME Inventory* and *Family Assessment* would reflect whether a more positive environment of care and relationships had been achieved at the end of a programme of intervention. It would also be useful to devise some case-specific measures for assessing the qualitative shifts in key relationships between family members at specific times of day, e.g. between Moira Ward and Michael when he gets home from school, when Ian Ross comes in from work, at family mealtimes or when Michael goes to bed. Such information would be reported to child protection conferences and close links between therapeutic and care agencies would need to be maintained. There needs to be openness about therapeutic process, reflecting the child protection concerns and the need to demonstrate that changes have occurred. When Family Court proceedings have resulted in parental responsibility being shared with a social services department, and therapeutic services are commissioned by the care authorities, then it is appropriate that the therapeutic processes are reported back to both the family and any safeguarding meetings which hold responsibility for planning and making decisions about intervention and monitoring and evaluating the outcomes of the intervention. This is in contrast to the situation where the family requests or commissions help themselves, expecting confidentiality to be maintained.

Stage 6: Rehabilitation of the child to the family when living separately or moving on from a context of protection and support

The therapeutic stages to test the capacity of families to achieve the necessary changes to make rehabilitation possible are described in Chapter 8. If rehabilitation is to be achieved, it is crucial to target interventions in a focused way to achieve change in the identified areas of difficulty in parenting capacity, the family and environmental factors affecting parenting and to meet the needs of the child more directly where necessary. It is essential for the issue of protection to be central.

This can be achieved:

- By providing support for the family through a professional network of support provided in the home.

- By providing contexts outside the home for the family to attend. Facilities can range from family centres to residential contexts which provide levels of supervision indicated by the assessment of the level of harm and potential to harm which indicates the degree of protection required.

- Separation of children from sources of harm, either through care being provided by a non-abusive parent, or children being placed with foster carers, or in contexts which meet their needs, depending on levels of harm and extensiveness of the impact of harm.

Therapeutic work

Therapeutic work needs to be multimodal focused on offending parent(s), children and family contexts. There is a growing body of evidence-based approaches now available to focus on the areas of parenting which results in negative impacts, on the effects on the child, and on the family and environmental factors which have a negative impact on parenting, and on the capacity of families to meet the needs of children (see Chapter 8 for further details).

Stage 7: Placement of children in new family contexts where rehabilitation is not possible

There is now growing evidence about children who have had extensive harmful experiences benefiting from alternative care. Rutter's work with Romanian orphanage children (Rutter 2001; Rutter and ERA Sudy Team 1998) illustrates the positive impact of early placement of severely neglected children. It also illustrates the harmful effects of later placements, and the negative long-term effects which cannot be reversed. Bingley Miller and Bentovim (Department for Children, Schools and Families 2008; Bingley, Miller and Bentovim 2007) have explored in greater detail elsewhere the work required to support adoptive placements.

There is a current emphasis on placing within the family network before considering placements in non-family placements. Kinship placements have the strengths of maintaining the child's sense of identity, and the maintenance of established relationships. However, there may be risks of the child being exposed to significant adversity, depending on the patterns of strength and difficulty of the extended family network, and there may be risks of re-traumatization and undermining of placement security through contact with abusive family members.

There are a number of key issues to be considered in placing children for long-term fostering or adoption. Attachment, grief and loss are often prominent issues for the child who has to face the loss of perhaps the only family he or she may have known. The repetition of attachment responses – clinging, avoidance, ambivalent and disorganized responses – may be confusing, and require intervention to manage without becoming perpetuated through inappropriate responses. There is also the risk of the evocation of unresolved attachment responses for the adoptive parent in a similar way to a birth parent. There is evidence that when such processes are set in train, the child develops a poorer relationship with the carer, and instead of growing security and improving relationships, there is a maintenance of insecurity and poor emotional development (Steele *et al.* 2003).

Loss is a pervasive issue for the adopters, and the adopted child, and can occur at various phases of the adoptive family life cycle (Bingley Miller and Bentovim 2007). At each stage of development the adoptive parent may become aware of discrepancies with the 'lost ideal child' and the adopted child the loss of the 'idealized' parent which may have sustained older children in the face of trauma and family violence.

As a result of early adverse experiences and the later placements of children who have suffered maltreatment, there may be persistent emotional and behavioural difficulties, and the emergence of difficulties, e.g. around later phases of development. It is essential that adoptive parents who take on the care of children who have lived with trauma and family violence are supported through the provision of therapeutic work. A key to successful outcome is the provision of good quality care. The adoptive parent is a key partner in the task of promoting resilience, and the journey to recovery, but their care needs to be enhanced through specific approaches to meet the considerable needs of the children placed in their care. These are described in Chapter 7 and apply to parents, foster carers and adoptive parents alike.

Chapter Seven

Therapeutic Intervention with Children Living with Trauma and Family Violence

Arnon Bentovim

Introduction

The ultimate goal of intervening in the life of children living with trauma and family violence, subject to a cumulative set of traumatic and stressful experiences is to prevent further harm and transform their lives to recover and fulfil their potential.

In this chapter

- The different levels of prevention that guide the delivery of services are described.

- The roles and responsibilities of the Local Safeguarding Children Board are examined.

- The range of services which may need to come into play when intervening in families are explored.

- Specific treatment approaches and the evidence for their effectiveness is reviewed.

- Key themes of the therapeutic work involved are explored in some depth.

- Core elements of evidence-based practice for parents and children living with trauma and family violence are considered with reference to the domains and dimensions of the *Assessment Framework*.

Levels of intervention

In looking at the services and treatment approaches which can be considered when working with children and families, it is useful to look at the different levels of prevention and interventions which are conventionally used. To understand the process it is helpful to use the language of *primary, secondary and tertiary intervention.*

Primary prevention

Primary prevention is concerned with the provision of services to prevent children living with trauma and family violence. This includes:

- the provision of universal services for all children and families which will support and prevent trauma and family violence

- services targeted on those families and individuals who may be at particular risk perpetrating violence.

Secondary prevention

Secondary prevention is concerned with the recognition and intervention with children and families where there is evidence of children being subject to trauma and family violence, to ensure adequate protection from further harm and to assess children's and families' needs. It involves the provision of interventions aimed at supporting strengths and addressing difficulties for children and families so that children's needs can be met.

Tertiary prevention

Tertiary prevention is concerned with interventions for children and parents and families to ensure that the cycle of intergenerational re-enactment and recreations of context of trauma and violence is interrupted and positive pathways to resilience and fulfilling lives are promoted.

Roles and responsibilities of Local Safeguarding Children Boards in intervention

In the UK there has been a long history of development in terms of agencies 'Working Together' to safeguard and promote the welfare of children in their areas. A sequence of publications in the 'Working Together' series (Department of Health, Home Office and Department for Education and Employment 1999; HM Government 2006) have promoted the work of professionals in reporting, and intervening with children who are subject to trauma and family violence. A key approach is the establishment of Local Safeguarding Children

Boards whose role is to intervene effectively to safeguard and promote the welfare of children. The responsibilities of Local Safeguarding Children Boards include primary, secondary and tertiary prevention.

PRIMARY PREVENTION

Level One: *To prevent maltreatment,* or impairment of health or development, and ensure children grow up in circumstances consistent with safe and effective care, ensuring the children know who they can contact when they have concerns about their own or other's safety and welfare.

Level Two: *Proactive work* which aims to target particular groups, for example, to safeguard and promote the welfare of groups of children who are potentially more vulnerable than the general population. These include children living away from home, children with a disability, or children of parents with mental illness, drug and alcohol abuse or domestic violence who are particularly prone to suffer trauma and family violence.

SECONDARY PREVENTION

Level Three: *Reactive work* to protect children who are suffering, or at risk of suffering maltreatment, for example, children abused and neglected within their families. Recovery and developmental work is required to ensure that children achieve their full potential and have optimum life chances.

TERTIARY PREVENTION

Level Four: *Developmental work* with the aim of ensuring the children achieve their developmental potential and have the optimum life chances.

Levels of services required to achieve the goals of prevention

To achieve these goals requires a number of levels of services in primary, secondary and tertiary services.

PRIMARY PREVENTION: PREVENTION AND PROACTIVE WORK

Level One intervention comprises universal services available for all children and families.

These are provided by professionals, such as health visitors, general practitioners, early years staff, and teachers in educational contexts, community and neighbourhood facilities.

Level Two services are targeted services for vulnerable children, for example:

- children of parents with mental health, drug and alcohol abuse and domestic violence

- children with parents who themselves have suffered maltreatment

- children and families who have suffered significant disruption as a result of social adversity, unemployment, immigration.

SECONDARY PREVENTION: REACTIVE WORK

Level Three interventions comprise specialist services for children at risk of harm.

TERTIARY PREVENTION: DEVELOPMENTAL WORK

Level Four activities are targeted specialist services for children who have suffered abuse and neglect.

The role of different services

This section looks at the role of these services in more depth.

Level One intervention: universal services

HEALTH, EDUCATION AND SOCIAL WORKER PRACTITIONERS

The role of health, education and social worker practitioners delivering universal services for the population of children and parents is to provide an important scaffolding to support families at all stages of development. This support needs to be focused through pregnancy, birth, the early stages of developmental, pre-school and school years through adolescence and into parenting following the cycle of development and family change. Ensuring families with young children have sufficient financial resources to make provision for their growing needs is an important preventative intervention.

Some family life cycle stages are recognized to be particularly significant in terms of offering support. For example, the provision of the services focused on pregnancy in terms of preparation for parenthood, support around the early days following birth is seen as a key focus. There is interest in the approach adopted in the Netherlands where families are provided with support over the first weeks, an example of the provision of universal services at key points to foster the establishment of attachments (Van Zeijl *et al.* 2006).

UNIVERSAL PRE-SCHOOL SERVICES

Provision of universal pre-school services supports the early development of children, involving parents in developing capacities for play, in early education. Bringing together education, health and social work services to provide an integrated approach to the early years (see *Every Child Matters*: Department for Education and Skills 2004b), moving through to adolescence and later years provides support at key phases of development. The role of extensive programmes to address issues of interpersonal and sexual violence as intro-duced in Canadian schools (Wolfe 2006), focus on managing issues of safety, training in contraception, information about safe sex, access to confidential counselling and ensuring that young people have an appropriate degree of authority over their own lives. Providing information and support as young people move towards autonomy is an important element of universal services for all children and families to prevent premature pregnancy, or young people becoming involved with and organized into contexts of extensive abuse and neglect without their awareness. Mentoring in schools and training in peer support help the development of a supportive social network.

Recognition of children and families living in contexts of family violence

A key role for universal services is to provide appropriate levels of education to ensure that children and young people who are living in contexts of family violence are recognized by professionals with whom they come into contact. There needs to be an awareness of patterns of children's presentations of physical and sexual and emotional harm (see Chapter 6). It is essential that there is thorough knowledge, training and awareness of the different patterns of presentation, routes for consultation and for bringing to attention the appro-priate professionals of contexts of concern.

Access channels to services for children and parents

It is vital that there are accessible channels through which children and family members can report that they are living in a context of family violence. These are essential given the context of absolute secrecy and loyalty to the family which characterizes abusive family situations.

ChildLine

ChildLine is an example of a free telephone helpline for children who have not been able to speak in other contexts. ChildLine can take protective steps to seek help for a child, encourage a child to speak to a protective figure, maintain contact with the child and develop experience in supporting children directly living in a context of family violence

Stop It Now!

A recent development has been the application of a public health approach to sexual abuse: the 'Stop It Now!' campaign aims to inform the public about the nature of sexual abuse, and helps family members concerned about sexual abuse to seek assistance, irrespective of whether they are partners or parents, or are themselves the abuser (www.stopitnow.org.uk, accessed 7 December 2008).

NSPCC, Barnardo's and integrated services for children

Publicity campaigns by organizations such as the National Society for Prevention of Cruelty to Children (NSPCC) and Barnardo's as well as educational programmes in school and the community about the nature of abusive behaviour inform children and parents about the nature of harm and ways of seeking safety. While helplines can offer accessible routes to support, they can be effective only if complemented by services in the community able to offer accessible, face-to-face help and support, e.g. drop-in centres, community-based family centres and children's centres, which should be available as aspects of integrated services for children.

Level Two intervention: targeted services for vulnerable children

There are three key areas of particular focus for targeting services for vulnerable children:

- children growing up in contexts of privation and poverty
- work focused with vulnerable parents to promote secure attachments and positive parenting
- parents suffering mental illness, drug, alcohol abuse and domestic violence.

CHILDREN GROWING UP IN A CONTEXT OF POVERTY AND PRIVATION

Sure Start and neighbourhood regeneration programmes

Smith (2006) reviewed the effectiveness of early interventions with young children and their parents. She described the launch of the UK government initiative Sure Start 1999. This is a programme comprising a number of interventions, located in different disadvantaged areas. The central aim is 'to improve the health and well-being of families and children, before and from birth, so children are ready to flourish when they go to school, to improve the health and well-being of families' (Glass 2001 p.18). The aim is to be achieved by helping the development and coordination of services in disadvantaged areas, so they are available for all families with young children in the area, community driven and professionally coordinated, and flexible at the point of delivery.

Evaluation of this approach has been concerned with whether the multi-agency, community-based programme of early intervention makes a difference to school performance, rather than the detailed contribution of each element of the programme (Glass 2001). There is limited information about effectiveness of this approach. Early observations have indicated that children are treated in a warmer and more accepting manner by their parents or caregivers than in comparison areas (Tunstill *et al.* 2005). In a recent controlled study, Melhuish *et al.* (2008) has indicated that three year olds and their families in disadvantaged areas who have attended Sure Start local programmes show better social development and behaviour and greater independence than children in control areas. Families showed less negative parenting, provided a better home learning environment, and used more services to support child and family development.

Jack (2006) has described the development of neighbourhood regeneration programmes, to identify local needs and patterns of social support and with the goal of alleviating the stressful effects of community-level poverty and other inequalities. The aim was to build the capacity of the community through improved training and employment opportunities.

Although not an explicit goal, there was a reduction of child abuse. Eastham (1990) designed a programme to specifically achieve the goal by establishing small teams of community social workers to develop the social and support network of local families. Community development methods were used to establish and support a wide range of community groups, including pre-school playgroups, youth clubs, women's groups and adult education classes.

A five-year evaluation revealed significant reductions in numbers of children placed on the Child Protection Register and children 'looked after' by the local authority or supervised within their own home. Jack (2006) points out that the focus on high profile child abuse cases continued to skew services to identification of children suffering abuse, whereas the Cawson *et al.* (2000) study demonstrates that there are more 'unidentified' children in the community, than children identified. They therefore argued that it would be logical to provide more resources for intervention in the community to balance out the focus than on identified cases.

In this context it is relevant to observe the rise in concerns about the numbers of neglected children reported through child protection procedures (Rose et al.2006), perhaps reflecting the growth of professional awareness of this pervasive difficulty.

SERVICES FOR PARENTS TO PROMOTE A POSITIVE ATTACHMENT AND GOOD QUALITY EARLY CARE

In Chapter 1 attention was drawn to the nature of risk associated with parenting which fails to be attuned to the growing infant's needs. This can result in children having disorganized attachments and failing to develop a capacity to mentalize, as well as being at risk of other harmful elements.

Early interventions with parents and children

There is now extensive information about the impact of early intervention with parents and infants. Hanson, Morrow and Bandstra (2006) describe the scope of early interventions with young children and parents in the USA, complementing Smith's (2006) review in the UK. Marcenko and Staerkel (2006) review the extensive work with parents and infants in the USA following the groundbreaking work of Olds, Sadler and Kitzman (1999, 2007) which developed the *Home Visiting* approach delivered by public health nurses, complementing the health visiting approaches developed in the UK. Examples of community intervention described by Dixon et al. (2005a, 2005b) described in Chapter 1 noted the factors which predisposed to maltreatment for parents who themselves have been abused, defining the risk associated with this group and the impact of intervention.

Gomby (2000) reviews a number of these approaches in the USA. A factor of considerable importance is that, in addition to intensive parenting programmes, general services in the community need to be available to reinforce direct interventions. Barlow (2006) reviews the effectiveness of programmes in the UK involving postnatal support workers and home visiting by health visitors, noting that identification of early evidence of harm and appropriate referral was an important element of this approach.

Specific focus on promoting positive attachments has been described in the *Mellow Parenting Programme* (Mills and Puckering 2001), which employs a group approach delivered in hospital or community-based family centres. Parenting support groups focused on the development of parenting skills are combined with group work and video feedback sessions. The *STEEP* approach (Egeland and Erickson 2004) promotes the welfare of infants and parents through an intensive group-based discussion and video feedback approach. Toth et al. (2002) described the value of a *parent–infant psychotherapy* approach which attempts to work with the experiences of parents in terms of their own abuse and maltreatment, and helps modify the impact on attunement and responsiveness. The elements of evidence-based intervention which are effective in these approaches will be discussed in further detail later in this chapter.

PARENTS SUFFERING MENTAL ILLNESS OR DRUG AND ALCOHOL ABUSE PROBLEMS OR DOMESTIC VIOLENCE

In Chapter 1 attention was drawn to factors which lead to potential risk to children in contexts where parents suffer mental illness, drug or alcohol abuse or domestic violence. Assessment needs to pay attention to the presence of the risk and protective factors described to ensure that protective factors are provided at each stage of development. These protective factors may include good nutrition and antenatal care in the pre-birth period, the provision of a safe residence, the presence of supplementary caring adults, integrated primary health and social services plans, the timely use of family centres and family support, enhanced income, appropriate respite, practical domestic help. Helping parents develop more effective coping strategies is also essential to mitigate the effect of risk factors.

It is crucial that there is a continuing process of active assessment of whether children's and young people's needs are being met adequately, the quality of parenting capacity and the impact of the family and environmental context. Close collaboration between adult mental health, drug and alcohol services, services for domestic violence and childcare professionals need to be maintained to ensure that the balance of risk and protection is kept under close review. The role of children as carers also needs to be closely monitored so that children's needs are not sacrificed for the benefit of parents. Attempts have been made to bring services for child protection and domestic violence services together through developing shared understanding of the risks to children and ensuring appropriate intervention (Browne, Falshaw and Dixon 2002a).

Psycho-educational approaches and child–parent psychotherapy with pre-school children

There is an important role for psycho-educational approaches, for example, family-based interventions for adults with mental health disorders (Leff 2000) which support family members in understanding the nature of mental health disorders, and promote modes of response which can maintain positive mental health.

Child–parent psychotherapy with pre-school children (Lieberman, Van Horn and Ghosh Ippen 2005; Lieberman, Ghosh Ippen and Van Horn 2006) was specifically designed to assist pre-school children exposed to marital violence. Interventions are guided by unfolding child–parent interactions, with appropriate play material to elicit trauma play and foster positive social interaction. The aim is to change maladaptive behaviour, support development and create a joint narrative of traumatic events. Attempts were made to manage inappropriate behaviour, modify punitive critical parenting and support the development of more positive relationships with abusive parents. Evaluation of the approach suggested that children benefited significantly, and mothers' traumatic scores lessened compared to a control population.

Level Three interventions: proactive services for children at risk from harm

In Chapter 6 an account is provided of the seven stages of the assessment process where there are safeguarding concerns about a child:

- Stage 1: The phase of identification of harm and initial safeguarding.

- Stage 2: Making a full assessment of the child's needs, parenting capacity, family and environmental factors and levels of harm.

- Stage 3: Establishing the nature and level of harm and harmful effects.

- Stage 4: Assessing the likelihood of response to professional intervention in the context of the level of the child's needs and the level of parenting capacity and family and environmental difficulties.

- Stage 5: Developing a plan of intervention to include therapeutic work in a context of safety and protection from harm.

- Stage 6: Rehabilitation of the child to the family when living separately or moving on from a context of protection and support.

- Stage 7: Placement of children in new family contexts where rehabilitation is not possible.

The provision of such services is the statutory responsibility of children and young people's departments of social services, who following the guidelines of *Working Together to Safeguard Children* ensures that appropriate planning and investigation of concerns is operationalized. There is a requirement for investigation to be jointly planned with community child health and police services. Local Safeguarding Children Boards are required to ensure that all professionals are aware of their responsibilities to report concerns, and to participate as is appropriate with investigations and assessments using the *Assessment Framework*. This implies that there may be a need for involvement with services for children and families – education, physical and mental health, young offenders, services for adults, physical and mental health, offending, community services and housing. The aim is to use interdisciplinary work focused on the core assessment process to bring information together, make decisions about the use of child protection conferences, court processes, and recommendations about longer planning to meet the needs of children and families.

Following this assessment a plan for intervention is developed which is likely to involve the use of proactive services such as the continuing provision of services available through children and young people's welfare services, community support, fostering and adoption services, specialist voluntary agencies providing therapeutic services, mental health services for children, parents and families, offender treatment services, drug, alcohol and domestic violence services and specialist educational services.

Level Four interventions: specialist services for children who have suffered abuse and neglect and their parents

Services for children who are living in a climate of trauma and family violence, who have suffered abuse or neglect associated with traumatic experiences require a significant range of services. The overall aim of these services is to ensure that lasting harm to the child does not occur, and that the child and other children in the family are effectively protected from further episodes of harm.

To review specialist services for children and parents who have suffered abuse or neglect, and evidence-based approaches to therapeutic work requires a process which:

- examines the robustness and limitations of the evidence available on effective intervention

- looks at how such interventions may be integrated into an appropriate therapeutic approach tailored to the needs of the children and family.

Evidence on the effectiveness of interventions

There is now a growing literature looking at effectiveness of intervention including Bentovim (2006b), Corcoran (2006), De Panfilis (2006), Finkelhor and Berliner (1995), Jones (1998), Jones and Ramchandani (1999), Ramchandani and Jones (2003), Stevenson (1999) and Tanner and Turney (2006). These studies have examined the impact of therapeutic intervention on children and young people who have experienced neglect, emotional, physical or sexual abuse. In looking at the field as a whole, sexual abuse has been studied most extensively, then physical abuse, neglect far less so and sexually offending behaviour to a moderate extent. Stevenson's (1999) review provides a model for categorizing the sort of studies that have been carried out:

- controlled follow-up studies of treated cases

- studies where repeated measures of the impact of intervention were made without control groups

- control groups using other populations to compare the results of those who had been offered specific treatment programmes

- randomized control trials of interventions concerned with the particular forms of abuse being studied.

Those studies which demonstrate most effective interventions are those which compare a structured intervention with a particular focus and consistent training of those providing therapeutic work, compared to 'treatment as usual' in the community. Differences are far less in evidence when comparisons are made between one or more well-designed therapeutic approaches which are consistently delivered by well-trained personnel.

Looking at some specific findings, early studies by Monck *et al.* (1994) assessed the impact of adding group work to systemic family therapy approaches with children and families where sexual abuse had occurred. Clinical assessments indicated the advantage of the combined approach and children and parents valued group experiences reporting that they helped to reduce their sense of isolation and stigma. However, while standardized measures showed general improvement, they did not distinguish between these standardized approaches. It seemed likely that the firm protective context of care for children may well have provided the foundation for children's and parents' positive response to therapeutic work.

Kolko (1996, 2002) noted that functional family therapy and multifamily cognitive behavioural therapy were equally effective in working with families where physical abuse had occurred, and both were more effective than treatment in the community as usual. Trowell *et al.*'s (2002) research comparing individual work with group work with children who had been sexually abused, again showed some advantage as far as traumatic symptoms were concerned with individual work, but overall there were few differences. Therapeutic approaches using cognitive behavioural therapy for children showing traumatic symptoms of sexual abuse (Cohen *et al.* 2000) consistently show improvements compared to unstructured individual play therapy, again demonstrating the response to well-structured approaches.

Integrated multimodal therapeutic interventions

More recently there has been a move towards bringing together a number of evidence-based approaches delivered over time to intervene on the multifaceted aspects of families where abuse of children occurs, given that a number of different forms of abuse may be co-occurring, with a wide range of effects. This is described as 'multimodal, multisystemic, multi-component' interventions.

What follows is a guide to evidenced approaches to intervention, rather than a full account.

PARENT INTERACTION THERAPY

Chaffin et al. (2004) and Timmer et al. (2005) described parent–child interaction therapy, which is a dyadic intervention to alter specific patterns of coercive interaction. The aim is to modify modes of interaction between the parent and child, diminish child behaviour problems and promote positive parenting. The intervention has several phases:

- The first phase aims to enhance parent–child relationships.

- The second phase focuses on improving child compliance.

- Therapeutic approaches include didactic teaching and coaching skills using direct intervention.

- Video feedback is frequently a complement to this.

- There is a focus on the development of communication skills, positive reflections on play and activities, verbalization and engagement of play, use of selective attention, reward for appropriate behaviour and compliance, the use of time-out.

Generally it was found to be an effective approach to improve behaviour, and reduce likelihood of future abusive action compared to a control group.

ABUSE-FOCUSED COGNITIVE BEHAVIOURAL THERAPY

A further example is abuse-focused cognitive behavioural therapy for families involved in physical and coercive abuse devised by Kolko, Herschell and Baumann (2007). They have developed a multimodal approach which has brought together different approaches so that both individual and family elements have been combined.

A number of overlapping stages of work are described:

- *Engagement and psycho-education*: the focus here is to understand clinical concerns, completing an assessment, and engaging the family. It is essential to establish a safety plan, clarify the foundations for a collaborative working relationship, clarify tentative treatment goals and enhance motivation.

- *Psycho-education about treatment and force or abuse*: this includes helping family members to understand the elements of behaviour, emotions and cognitions which contribute to abusive action, to describe causes and consequences of using force, to set up an agreement that less force would be used, and to introduce a weekly report of discipline practices.

- *The focus on learning* was explained and concepts of developing skills and competency and home practice were introduced.

- *Child disclosure*: this includes discussion of upsetting feelings and experiences to promote the disclosure initially within individual work with the child and then to clarify any issues with parents, followed by a clarification session between parents and children.

- *Individual skills building*: this includes teaching cognitive, affective and behavioural skills, working with individuals until the family is ready to work together and learn new skills.

- *Processing and learning coping skills*: this work focuses on helping family members learning how to process and cope with feelings, including anger, to clarify views on physical discipline and abuse, to maintain positivity for caregivers and to assist in regulation of emotion controlling anger and anxiety.

- *Working on social relationships* with young people, promoting positive behaviour management and helping them to apply these skills to family relationships, developing their communication and problem-solving skills and to establish family routines.

WORK WITH FAMILIES WITH CHILDREN WITH SEVERE NON-ORGANIC FAILURE TO THRIVE

Iwaniec *et al.*'s (2002) work with children with severe non-organic failure to thrive includes a number of stages:

- *Feeding* in a structured, directive manner while supporting carers to desist from screaming and shouting, through the use of modelling, reassuring, observing and prompting.

- *Creating positive interactions* and reducing negative interactions through desensitizing anxiety and fears, encouragement to play, smile and develop proximity in order to promote secure attachment behaviours.

- *Deliberate intensification of primary carer–child interactions* involving intensifying relationships between mother and child to improve the affective relationship between them to promote closeness and intimacy.

- *Supporting older children* to develop pro-social behaviour and to counter the common patterns of negative interaction.

- *Structured parenting training* as well as parent self-help groups and work on resolving issues of wider family and family history.

TRAUMA-FOCUSED COGNITIVE BEHAVIOURAL THERAPY

Trauma-focused cognitive behavioural therapy (Cohen *et al.* 2000) is an approach devised to target the specific traumatic symptomatology associated with experiences of abuse, particularly sexual abuse. It has been widely tested and is one of the best supported interventions in the trauma and family violence field.

A number of variations have been developed, including approaches which involve the children alone, children and parents, separate treatments for children and supportive parents. There has been an extension to include a module for children who have been exposed to a significant traumatic loss and where there is a component aimed at promoting grieving responses as well as working with traumatic responses to maltreatment. Further developments have been its use in association with approaches for young people who had begun to substance abuse as a coping strategy (Cohen *et al.* 2003). There can be the addition of other components, e.g. multisystemic family therapy component (Hengeller *et al.* 2002), to meet the complex needs of children and young people in their families caught up in processes of trauma and family violence. To deal with polyvictimization or multiple maltreatment it is necessary to focus on a 'lifespan' of abusive events, and to introduce more extensive psycho-educational approaches to foster understanding, and a variety of different approaches to promote the 'journey to recovery' (Bentovim 2002).

Key principles in trauma-focused cognitive behavioural therapy include a range of elements:

- *A focus on the here-and-now,* acknowledging that the past may impact on current presentation and interactions. The focus is on behaviour and the work is goal directed towards a functional outcome shared between the therapist and the client. Processing of traumatic events is a time-limited focused activity, although there may be multiple foci to deal with multiple events.

- *Understanding the client's perspective* is central to the therapeutic approach which is active, collaborative and often directive, encouraging skills building to regulate emotions and enhance coping strategies. There is an important modelling of hope, working out with the child or young person what they wish to address and reducing problems into manageable pieces.

- *Addressing affective and trauma symptoms* such as fear, sadness, anger, anxiety and disregulated affects is central, as is working with specific behavioural trauma symptoms including avoidance, anger outbursts, maladaptive behaviours, sexualized behaviours, violence, bullying, self-harming, substance abuse, defiance, disobedience and other social difficulties.

- *Functional components* include psycho-education to provide appropriate information and understanding, building skills in emotional regulation, identification and correction of maladaptive beliefs, developing communication and interpersonal skills and problem-solving strategies. Unique to this approach is the theme of gradually revealing the child's experiences of abuse and trauma and working to create a trauma narrative (see below).

- *Parenting work requires the engagement of families in treatment* through emphasizing the primacy of their role in coping with their distress and their centrality as a therapeutic agent for change. In order to work on enhancing enjoyable aspects of child–parent interaction, the therapist forms an alliance with the parents and takes the role of guide, consultant and supporter, providing reassurance concerning positive outcomes and desensitizing the parents' own distress.

- *Teaching relaxation skills* includes a variety of approaches such as deep muscle relaxation, the use of self-hypnotic techniques, finding a safe place in imagination, learning techniques of thought-blocking and centring to confront flashbacks and re-enactments, all of which help to regulate affective states and mood.

- *Constructing a trauma narrative*: here the aim is to be able to remember and talk about traumatic experiences without extreme distress or the need for avoidance. Drawing out an account of the trauma and abuse experienced and creating a trauma narrative helps to desensitize and habituate disturbing memories, to resolve maladaptive avoidant symptoms, to develop a capacity to talk about past traumatic experiences as part of life putting them into perspective in terms of the present, obtaining support and connecting with others.

Trauma narrative notions are introduced, such as the idea of creating a book which has a number of chapters, including chapters before and after abusive experiences. Creating a trauma narrative occurs over multiple sessions, starting with exploring less distressing events and then moving on to more distressing experiences. The work involves developing details of what happened before, during and after traumatic experiences, exploring thoughts and feelings during the events and moves from less distressing to more distressing. This includes the following:

- *Exploring dysfunctional thoughts and beliefs* which underlie emotional and behavioural difficulties and finding alternative explanations. This promotes the development of healthy trauma narrative processes, addressing feelings and maladaptive cognitions, exploring the meaning of the abusive events for the child or young person.

This moves them forward, putting the experience into perspective so that the individual no longer feels a victim, but a survivor. This work involves multiple approaches to help the process including creative therapeutic use of drawing, writing and the computer-assisted interview *In My Shoes*.

- *Developing the lifespan trauma narrative* and including information from the chronology and records and the family as well as from the young person's memory. Relating the lifespan trauma narrative to both past and current events and relationships and future aspirations and plans is important in helping to develop perspective. Systemic solution-focused approaches are also used to develop a sense of hope and recovery and as a vehicle for change.

- *Connecting experiences with appropriate supportive family members* is crucial, including working with family members to clarify and accept responsibility for inappropriate behaviours, offering appropriate apologies and developing wider protective family change through multisystemic family approaches, reinforcing the processing of traumatic experiences, promoting relationships through the development of communication skills, managing boundaries, and forging alliances and identity.

- *Specific additional modules are required*, for example addressing issues of mourning and loss, promoting the grieving processes, managing substance abuse, developing an understanding of the thinking of abusers, developing self-protective skills or healthy sexuality, and managing anger.

THERAPEUTIC WORK WITH YOUNG PEOPLE WHO HAVE BEEN RESPONSIBLE FOR SEXUALLY ABUSIVE BEHAVIOUR

Edwards *et al.* (2007) have described therapeutic work with young people who have been responsible for significant episodes of sexually abusive behaviour. This is a natural extension of trauma-focused work as these young people (see Chapter 1) have lived with extensive trauma and family violence. They have often had a broad range of experiences of abuse and adversity themselves and may have been responsible for abuse against peers or children younger than themselves and against adults outside the family, often with some evidence of indiscriminate abusive behaviour. They are worked with in a residential context (Social Work for Abused and Abusing Youth, SWAAY) and require an integrated approach which is multimodal, involving the use of several different treatment interventions simultaneously, while responding to needs which are most evident and immediate. The approach is multi-component and multimodal, maximizing the range of resources and services available to young people and placing an emphasis on the need for continuity and coordination among services. Residential, educational, group, family and individual work are all therefore made available over a significant period of time. A comprehensive assessment of needs and risks is always undertaken and the general context of close supervision and emotional support provided by a therapeutic community allows for necessary reparenting and the development of healthy attachments, which in turn supports more specific therapeutic programmes. These comprise:

- *A social and emotional competency group work programme* available for all young people, of all ages, whatever the degree of sexually problematic behaviour and behavioural issues. The function of the group is to build attachments, manage emotional issues and gain a sense of self-confidence in relationships. The approach is both psycho-educational and follows cognitive behavioural principles. Multimedia approaches are used to encourage interests and engagement with, board games, role plays, artwork, videos and creative ideas forming the basis of sessions.

- *A modular offence-specific programme* over an 18-month period with a number of elements four or five weeks in duration. The aim is to find the 'Gateway to Success'. More experienced group members support newer members. The focus is on identifying and challenging maladaptive belief systems noted in the process of moving towards abusive acts. This involves learning to understand the cycle of events, feelings and beliefs (which may be rational or irrational) and consequences which result in feeling states and behavioural consequences which result in abusive action.

- *Specific modules include providing extensive sexual education* to correct the distorted notions that young people have about sexuality and relationships. There is an emphasis on recognizing and accepting that all abusive behaviour is preceded by contemplation and a decision to engage in the behaviour, even though such patterns becomes habitual. Confronting the decision-making process of event, thought, feeling and action is an essential component of reconstructing offending patterns of behaviour.

- *Understanding the process of denial* is essential to assisting young people to confront what they describe as habitual, automatic without thought, i.e. 'trauma-organized systems'. Understanding the impact on victims helps young people identify with their own victimization and the process of externalizing experiences onto others deepens the young person's understanding of the cycle of abusive action.

- *The role of anger and the linking of anger and sexuality* described earlier is a focus in exploring thoughts and feelings relating to offending.

Anger and grievance plays a key role in the preconditions, thoughts and feelings which enables them to justify sexual actions and to overcome internal and external barriers.

- *It is essential that young people take responsibility for their offences* by understanding the sequence of events, thoughts and feeling and developing the notion of offending with thoughts and behaviour in an interconnected cycle. They need to understand their behaviour in relation to the wider context of family violence and traumatic experiences to which they have been exposed, and develop an appropriate approach to managing impulses and becoming appropriately assertive.

- *Establishing the trauma narrative* is a core component, with information from professionals and family members being brought together and integrated with the young person, using a variety of approaches. Helping young people understand the experiences in their own lives and the way that they have felt and thought about it, and its role in the cycle of abusive action is an essential integrating task. Taking appropriate responsibility with child and family victims through an apology session supported by the therapeutic team and appropriate family members forms a significant element of the recovery process for all concerned.

- *Connecting the young person to the family* both for them to take the appropriate responsibility for exposing the young person to contexts of trauma and family violence and to help to understand the young person's role. This involves working together to create a transformation such as a move to the family where possible, or to assist the young person towards adult life. This has an associated goal of helping them develop an appropriate relapse plan so they understand how best to protect themselves and others in the future.

The approach has been observed to be effective in reducing the level of risk presented by the young people on the programme and this is backed up by psychometric evidence. The programme also ensures that as well as a focus on reduction of offending, appropriate attention is paid to the young person's broad-based needs in terms of their health, educational or emotional and behavioural needs and developing a positive sense of identity, a capacity to relate in social and family contexts, to present themselves appropriately and to care for themselves through the development of appropriate social skills (Edwards *et al.* 2007). There is a continuum of work with young people and therapeutic work for adult offenders given the current stress on the lifespan pathway to offending behaviour on the long-term effects of attachment disorganization and failure to regulate emotions (Fisher and Beech 2002).

Although the work with young people described here is provided in a residential setting, elements of the work can be provided in community settings. Intensive work can be provided through the multisystemic model which brings together systemic ways of managing antisocial behaviour through therapeutic help available in the community with approaches focused on offending behaviour (Borduin *et al.* 1990; Letourneau, Chapman and Schoenwald 2008).

Mentalization-based treatments

Bateman and Fonagy (2004) have described mentalization-based approaches for individuals with borderline or unstable personality disorders where mentalization (the capacity to see ourselves as others see us and others as they see themselves) is impaired and arousal states control actions. Although their approach is focused on working with adults, there is an application for this approach in working with young people in adolescence, who are in hospital contexts, secure units or placements for their safety or the safety of others, and who require support and therapeutic work to help their recovery, such as the young people described in Chapter 1 who are at risk of developing antisocial or unstable personality disorders. It may also be helpful for the parents of the children who present with disorganized attachments and early evidence of harm. The evidence for treatment success with such adults or young people used to be limited, but more recent developments of mentalization-based approaches, the use of dialectical behaviour therapy, psychodynamic psychotherapies, the use of day hospital contexts, have provided some hope that even with these individuals, who often have a history of extensive exposure to trauma and family violence, that there can be modification (Bateman and Fonagy 2004). There may also be general protective factors and turning points as noted in Chapter 1.

Bateman and Fonagy (2004) describe the following strategies:

- *The process of mentalization needs to be enhanced and supported* by the therapist by questioning continually what internal mental states the client has and what is being evoked in the therapist that can explain the current situations. This involves questioning: why is this being said now? Why is this action taking place now? What is the feeling state? What does the event trigger? What is its meaning? What is being externalized and not acknowledged? There is a need to work to differentiate between what is happening externally and what internally, because even small events may evoke powerful internal feeling states because of their link with past events and result in states of behaviour which may feel intense and overwhelming. The task is to make sense, to clarify and find the language which expresses the complexity of the situation. A therapist becomes a vehicle for the 'alien' part indicated within the self of the patient which has arisen as a result of past failures of care, exposure to violence and experiences of abuse.

- *There has to be an enhancement of reflective processes* so that the individual learns to understand and label emotional states and to create a linking narrative to recent events and to the past. Experiences which are confusing need to be given meaning with interpersonal understanding bridging the gap.

- *There needs to be closeness between therapist and individual.* While being aware of the risk of entanglement, and working to maintain a sense of reality, the therapist helps by becoming a transitional individual who bridges gaps. Relationships have to be real with empathic responses which are accurate. There is a need for responsiveness which is supportive, compassionate, accepting, focused and yet maintaining appropriate boundaries and to be genuinely understanding when there is uncertainty about experiences, attempting to construct events and their impact. Alternative modes of understanding need to be found to free the self to find new modes of being and relating.

- *Techniques include attempts to manage the intense affects* which can lead to irrational behaviour, impulsive actions of self-harm, suicide attempts, intense sexual interactions and the risk of pregnancy. It is essential to clarify and name feelings, understand the precipitant emotional states, understand feelings in the context of previous and present relationships and to find a way of expressing feelings appropriately and constructively. The fear of abandonment is an intense feeling which drives action.

- *A coherent sense of self emerges* and a capacity to form a secure relationship with a therapeutic team which supports reconnecting with supportive family members and assisting self-development through future scripts which are associated with achievement. This promotes finding a new self in comparison to past, often deeply held, negative self views.

This style of working needs to be linked with the specific modules of work described earlier, e.g. work associated with traumatic responses and offending patterns of behaviour, and approaches which creates an effective multimodal approach to meet the often complex needs of children and young people and their families who have lived with trauma and family violence.

Identifying common elements of evidence-based psychosocial treatments

A variety of different approaches have been described, coming from different theoretical stances, including a number of different yet related therapeutic strategies and approaches. The question is how they can be brought together in a coherent meaningful way.

An approach which takes a broad view of evidence-based approaches and brings them together to focus on a specific problem has been described by Garland *et al.* (2008). Rather than use a particular individual treatment as the focus for implementing evidence-based practice, they have suggested a complementary approach, bringing together common elements of multiple individual evidence-based treatment programmes. They describe a method of identifying common elements from a systematic review of interventions for children with disruptive behaviour problems and their parents. Eight individual treatment programmes with established efficacy for children aged 4 to 13 were reviewed, identifying core elements and determining which elements were common to at least half of the programmes. The validity of these common core elements was confirmed through a survey of national experts, using a modified Delphi technique.

This is a group of approaches which have particular relevance to prevention and treatment in the family violence field, since the principles described relate to working with families where there is physical and sexual coercion, with young people responsible for physical and sexual violence, and in the treatment of children and young people who are victims of trauma and family violence and are showing high levels of emotional disorders in association with conduct difficulties. These are characteristic of children growing up in a context of trauma and family violence. These are interventions which can be family-focused, parent-mediated approaches, or used directly with children and young people. It is possible to apply this approach to review the common elements in the evidence-based approaches summarized earlier.

Common elements of intervention with trauma and family violence

In Chapter 1 the impact of living in a climate of trauma and family violence was described demonstrating:

- The impact on biological levels of brain functioning.

- The impact on basic processes of the development of attachments and mentalization.

- The ecosystemic model – the *Assessment Framework* – which looked at children's developmental needs in a context of parenting capacity and family and environmental factors.

- The context of harm and the relationship between extensive forms of harmful parenting and the impact on children's development and functioning, giving rise to various patterns of harm.

- An understanding of factors related to prognosis and outcome, associated with each level of functioning, the level of harm, parenting capacity, family and environmental factors was described, and an approach to developing an intervention plan was described.

Bringing together knowledge about the impact of trauma and family violence and the content and findings on effective treatment approaches, it is possible to identify a number of key themes in successful therapeutic approaches, as described below.

FORMING A THERAPEUTIC ALLIANCE

A key factor in any therapeutic approach is the establishment of an alliance between the worker or therapist and the child or young person, parents and family members. This encourages the formation of an attachment, which allows mentalization to flourish.

The process of working with children individually, working with parents and children, working with the family in various combinations and with groups of children or young people requires the establishment of an 'interactional matrix'. Providing specific therapeutic inputs and attending to the way in which professionals or agencies provide therapeutic work together are complementary tasks. The explicit content of the work is not the total therapeutic ingredient. Professionals need to have a capacity to understand the experience of living in a climate of trauma and family violence. Being able to articulate this in a variety of different ways and sharing this understanding enables children, parents and families to be able to understand and 'mentalize' rather than to enact their experience of trauma in a mindless action system, as described in the notion of trauma-organized systems.

INITIATING SOCIAL ENGAGEMENT

There needs to be social engagement. Without social engagement there can be no psychological therapy. Without being able to mentalize, to be able to think about oneself and others and relationships without being emotionally overwhelmed, there can be no social engagement. Professionals need to initiate a benign process of social engagement, not being discouraged by failures to respond initially and recognizing and responding to disorganized attachment responses.

ACTIVATING ATTACHMENT SYSTEMS

All psychotherapeutic work activates attachment systems and begins to generate secure base experiences. A virtual cycle of synergy develops between security, exploration and the recovery of a capacity to think about feelings, thoughts and actions. Being understood generates a security which in turn facilitates exploration. Feelings needs to be labelled, cognitions explained and beliefs spelt out. This is described as a 'mirroring' process. Non-verbal responses, drawings and artistic productions help to verbalize the unverbalizable. There is shared joint attention and desires and beliefs need to be represented in a coherent form. Together this results in a gradual integration of what is felt as confusing. Instead of internal and external reality, past and present experiences having no distinction, a capacity is supported to establish an appropriate way of thinking about what is current (Bateman and Fonagy 2004). The interpersonal environment becomes more neutral and benign. Instead of 'alien parts' of the self impacting on other family members and professionals through the process of trauma-organized action processes, there begins to be a more appropriate form of interaction, sharing, tolerating, accepting and managing difference which promotes inherent growth and freedom of thought and development.

FOSTERING SECURE ATTACHMENTS

Therapeutic work with children and family members needs to include a conscious attempt to foster attachments of a secure nature. This requires workers to be consistent in their approach, to be present when expected, to emphasize connection, to understand the different attachment styles of children and parents, to accept there may be avoidant or rejecting or controlling styles and to modify or take these responses into account. Approaches need to be focused on dealing with problems and crises which are felt to be pressing before applying specific programmes of work and to consistently look for positives, areas which are hopeful as exceptions to a climate which may be negative and discouraging. The therapeutic team can act as the minds and awareness which family members may not be able to acknowledge. A stance which is accepting, not critical, but maintaining appropriate boundaries, communicating clearly, managing feeling states with calmness, and looking for solutions and problem-solving is required for a successful outcome.

FACILITATING PROFESSIONALS 'WORKING TOGETHER'

How can such work be provided? There is often a striking contrast in attitudes to social work services, who are seen as 'alien' figures, as the source of control and oppression, evoking hostility for 'taking their children away', and health and educational agencies, who are seen as neutral or more benign. Yet much of the work with children and parents living in a climate of trauma and family violence will be provided by social workers. There are ways of managing the process of 'externalizing' onto the 'protection' worker, as described above in mentalization approaches. Another way is by providing family support workers (or their equivalent) who can develop specific therapeutic skills to become engaged with children and family members, or a team of systemic practitioners, each working alongside social workers, to form a collaborative team around the child and family. It is important that the staff involved receive appropriate training to undertake these often complex pieces of work. In addition, the role of the courts in deciding whether it is safe for a child to remain with or return to their families can often form part of the contract for change with the family.

No one agency can provide the complex range of therapeutic work. Child and adolescent mental health services play a key role (Bentovim, et al. 1988) and specialist voluntary or independent agencies such as the NSPCC and Barnardo's may provide focused work with children and young people who have been maltreated or who are behaving abusively in community, or residential contexts. Adult services for offenders, physical, sexual abuse and domestic violence are provided through health, probation and independent providers (e.g. Lucy Faithfull Foundation) for individuals in prison or the community. Integration of therapeutic work, managing boundaries and the nature of confidentiality are all key issues to be addressed. The core concern is to develop a systemic understanding of the needs of the child in the context of parenting capacities and the environmental context. There needs to be a focus on 'child protection' while ensuring the needs of all members of the family are met. There is considerable scope for splitting, 'conflict by proxy' where different professionals or agencies become identified with competing needs of family members. Work between agencies is a key element in therapeutic work in resolving trauma and family violence (Bentovim et al. 1988). Therapeutic work needs to be commissioned by children's services, i.e. the social work protection services, rather than by the family so reporting arrangements are clear, indicating there cannot be the confidentiality sometimes expected in therapeutic contexts.

Core elements of evidence-based practice for parents and children living with trauma and family violence

So what are the core elements of intervention in terms of children's needs and parenting capacity and relevant family and environmental factors for children and families living with trauma and family violence? Each dimension of parenting capacity will be taken in turn to discuss common elements of evidence-based practice based on a review of research on intervention, and the development of multimodal approaches to intervention and practice, using the approach described by Garland et al. (2008).

Parenting capacity domain

BASIC CARE: PROVISION OF ADEQUATE BASIC CARE AND ATTENTION
TO HEALTH

Parenting failure impacts on children's health and development. Changes include a requirement for parents working together in being responsive to care and health needs.

Intervention

A variety of contexts are required to support parents to provide more adequate basic care and attention to health needs:

- *Alternative care* whether on a temporary basis during assessment or longer term can provide the context of more adequate care.

- *A family aide or family support worker going to the home* on a regular basis can work alongside a parent and model appropriate modes of response. They can help a parent organize and develop capacities to provide adequate nutrition, appropriate clothing, and appropriate care of the fabric of the home, i.e. provide children's basic care. This may include developing skills in basic tasks of feeding, changing, bathing, tending to hygiene, managing the regular patterns of care, times of meals, preparation for school, managing bedtimes, and arranging exercise activities within and outside the home. The use of family centres and residential services to foster basic parenting skills can achieve a similar outcome.

- *Psycho-education or didactic approaches for parents* to provide information on the needs of children, the requirements of different ages and stages of development, understanding of the needs of neglected children and managing the avoidant, resistant responses often associated with attempts to provide adequate care.

- *Modelling appropriate care*, providing prompts, video feedback, reviewing goals and progress and ensuring the development of supportive relationships with parents to meet their needs.

- *Reflections on parents' own experiences of care* and the relationship with current responses are an essential ingredient to improving the quality of basic parenting and response to health needs.

- Specific help with *development of parenting skills* to manage challenges such as feeding, sleeping difficulties and resistant behaviour. Modelling, encouraging, reinforcing skills, developing parents' capacities to play and to develop mutually satisfying responses between themselves and children are an essential element of encouraging adequate basic care and attention to health.

ENSURING SAFETY: PROVISION OF PARENTAL RESPONSIVENESS, SAFETY AND PROTECTION

When parenting does not provide responsiveness, safety and protection, children's needs for safety and protection are not met adequately and this can result in children developing insecure, disorganized or indiscriminate attachments. They may also lack an age-appropriate capacity for safe independent care of themselves. There may be evidence of physical or sexual harm sustained at home or in the environment with injuries sustained not consistent with age and developmental stage.

Intervention

In terms of the goals of intervention, the basic principle is that children need to be provided with a safe environment, appropriate discipline and a secure relationship with an attentive caregiver that fits with their age or stage of development. There need to be reasonable parental expectations of children, adequate supervision of activities inside and outside the home and the provision of safe environment and protection from physical hazards and risky individuals.

This may be achieved by placement with a safe family member, such as a parent not involved with or unaware of abusive activities, who is supportive of the child and who accepts that there has been abuse and is prepared to protect from potentially abusive family members.

When there is acknowledgement of abuse, and levels of abuse are not of such severity, *there may be the potential for a child to remain within the family.* In this event, it is essential that an agreement to create a context of family safety be accepted, and plan for close monitoring with consistent opportunities for reporting and sharing information about stress and the level of violence by family members and others.

The provision of safe contexts for communication with children and appropriate rules for contact with abusive family members are essential to ensuring that there is an adequate context of protection alongside feedback observations which can confirm whether appropriate levels of protection are being offered.

There needs to be an *appropriate acknowledgement of the perpetration of abusive behaviour* against the child or young person accompanied by an appropriate taking of responsibility, with acceptance that the child or young person was forced to take inappropriate levels of responsibility. This work should promote consistent support of the child by non-abusive carers and family members who support a child's disclosure and make the appropriate attributions and responsibility to the adult or older person involved.

When parents are working with professionals to provide a context of safety, there needs to be *extensive work to help parents to understand their own experience of trauma and family violence,* the nature of the impact on their own mental health and emotional states, their emotional attachments to partners, and the factors which have been associated with their using their children as objects of sexual or physical abuse or being unable to provide adequate safety or protection for their children.

Children and young people need to be taught appropriate self-care skills, within the family and within the social context. Specific focus on supporting children to find alternatives to inappropriate sexualized or aggressive modes of relating with peers and putting themselves at risk is an important component of creating a context of safety.

When an older child is abusive to a younger child, the older child needs help to be able to take an appropriate degree of responsibility so that the younger child can acknowledge the older child's responsibility and both can develop an understanding of their own and others' responses to them.

The role of psycho-education to facilitate understanding of the factors associated with violence, sexual abuse and its impact, providing appropriate materials, reviewing goals and progress, developing problem-solving skills are important components of maintaining a context of safety.

Involvement in programmes shared with supportive carers helps to address the interconnected elements of experiences of violence and responses which put the self and others at risk.

EMOTIONAL WARMTH: EMOTIONAL WARMTH AND CONTAINMENT

The impact on the child of a failure of emotional warmth and containment means that the child is part of a network of insecure or disorganized attachments with adults who lack the capacity to respond to emotional communications. The child is then likely to be aroused and respond by becoming frozen, showing evidence of a pervasive negative mood, persistent fear, traumatic responses or developing other forms of negative emotional adjustment.

Intervention

Children need to live in a context where they are valued and where there is a satisfactory expression and reception of feelings, warmth, calmness, humour, empathy, understanding, and a protection from traumatic losses and stressful events. Good quality foster care, specialist foster care, special guardianship placements and adoption can provide the emotional context of good care.

When *parents* are working with professionals to provide adequate emotional care for their children, there needs to be *work on factors in their own history.* The focus is the nature of emotional relationships in their own families, the impact on their own mental health in terms of emotional regulation and the impact on partner relationships so that they can develop an understanding of their emotional response to their children, and acceptance of interventions to model and improve the nature of emotional relationships.

The emotional processing of traumatic and stressful events is a key factor in emotional recovery, assisting a child to respond more appropriately and to develop basic positive emotional mood and achieve positive emotional adjustment. The processing of traumatic stressful events requires a process of emotional support, and the encouragement of the child and young person to be able to expose their experiences in a context of safety and support, sharing where appropriate with parenting figures who are supportive, with abusive family members being able to take appropriate levels of responsibility, acknowledge harm and make an appropriate apology.

A variety of approaches, including psycho-education, are required *to help children and family members understand and process the nature of traumatic events.* This includes the use of play material, sharing in group contexts, finding solutions, reviewing goals and progress, managing arousal and symptoms associated with poor sleep, re-enactments and anxieties and offering help to deal with traumatic responses.

It is essential that there is *an appropriate level of response* not overstressing or forcing disclosure and going at the child's pace, but at the same time spelling out the necessary process and finding the ways to achieve the goals of intervention.

Creating a trauma narrative which links past, present and future scripts is necessary to transform past negative beliefs, guilt, responsibility and blame to survival, hope and a meaningful future

Specific support for particular emotional symptoms such as depressive disorders, self-harming, anxiety states and high levels of distress may be required using individual and family approaches to intervention.

STIMULATION: STIMULATION AND COMMUNICATION

Family contexts where parents have serious difficulties with providing adequate stimulation and communication can result in the child having significant delays or unevenness in the development of cognitive motor and language skills, poor capacity to communicate, poor educational attendance and difficulties with relationships within pre-school and school contexts. In addition, special needs may be unrecognized.

Intervention

Children need appropriate levels of play, warmth, encouragement, and an enriched environment with clear communication, good listening and responsiveness. They need parents who support learning and cooperate with educational settings to support the child's unfolding of skills so that they make satisfactory progress within educational contexts.

Where there is a reasonable prognosis, interventions need to support parents in developing skills in stimulation and communication to promote children's learning and social development. *Family centres and family therapy* have an important role in promoting communication through the use of methods such as video feedback, direct intervention, prompting, role-playing, behavioural rehearsal, modelling, provision of psycho-education, didactics on education. Involving parents in both *developing parenting skills of communication and stimulation*, as well as the specific skills of reading, is an additional element that can assist in achievement of more appropriate goals for parents in relation to meeting their children's needs (Scott and Sylva 2009).

GUIDANCE AND BOUNDARIES: GUIDANCE AND BOUNDARIES AND MANAGEMENT OF BEHAVIOUR

Parenting difficulties in providing guidance, boundaries and managing children's behaviour can result in the development of oppositional or over-compliant responses in children. Children who have seen parents modelling a failure to maintain boundaries and manage their own behaviour may replicate exploitative, fighting, abusive, bullying and/or rivalrous responses with siblings or in social contexts, or through inappropriate drug and alcohol use for older young people.

Intervention

Children and young people need a context where there is more appropriate management, realistic expectations, appropriate rewards and sanctions, and appropriate management of negative states. This involves parents being tolerant and able to provide flexible boundaries and appropriate rules and structures. They need to ensure there is appropriate differentiation between the roles of adult and child and effective management of conflict and oppositional behaviour along with promoting the development of collaborative responses.

- *Principles of positive reinforcement* include strategic attention, praise, physical, verbal and material reinforcement, shaping and behavioural rewards.

- *Principles of effective limit setting or discipline* include the use of time-out procedures, giving commands and limit setting.

- *Parent–child relationship-building* requires supporting affection, avoiding criticism, positive play, building mutual empathy and addressing attachment issues.

- *Problem-solving* includes methods to generate alternative solutions, evaluate options, consider consequences, provide self-rewards.

- *Anger management* includes teaching methods of managing or modulating anger, learning to take an appropriate perspective, learning to take turns, recognizing triggers of anger, relaxation skills, recognizing patterns of events, thoughts, feelings and actions. 'Externalizing' anger as an 'alien' aspect of the self, forming a team with family members to defeat 'Mr Temper' and allow the 'real caring self' to be in control (White and Epston 1989).

- *Managing sexually aggressive behaviour* requires the developing of empathy, the understanding of the link between experiences of sexual and physical abuse, neglect and rejection and consequent feelings of grievance, the externalization of feelings onto those who are less powerful, the cycle of obsessive sexual interest and overcoming barriers, and finding alternatives to prevent relapse.

- *Managing affects* involves understanding, identifying and labelling emotions, recognizing cues of emotional states and emotional response with associated behavioural responses both against self and other.

STABILITY: STABILITY AND FAMILY RELATIONSHIPS WHERE THERE ARE PARENTING DIFFICULTIES WITH A LACK OF STABILITY

Failure to maintain partnerships and family relationships over time and the disruption of attachments results in children who may be anxious, ambivalent and/or enmeshed, hostile, avoidant or disorganized in their attachments. They may lack appropriate interpersonal and relationship-building skills, develop a destructive relationship with family members, identifying with negative family figures, or fail to connect or to develop a sense of family or have a negative or omnipotence sense of self.

Intervention

Parenting needs to provide a level of stability maintaining appropriate family relationships even when there have been separations, parents need to work together to resolve difficulties in creating appropriate partnerships, or establishing appropriate levels of contact so as to reduce confusion for children.

Family therapy approaches fosters sharing and examining shared histories, reconnects family members where there has been a failure of contact, and helps children and other family members begin to develop a more positive sense of self or assertiveness and appropriate individuation.

The importance of reviewing family history includes working on developing a lifespan narrative, reconnecting family members, understanding processes of disruption, and learning to resolve contexts of blame, rejection and attack, to work appropriately to support children, or to provide children with the opportunity to develop a different sense of identity and support through alternative care.

The new identity provided through long-term fostering and adoptive relationships is an essential requisite where parents are not able to provide appropriate levels of stability.

Family and environmental factors

Working with family history and family functioning requires intervention with those elements which continue to impinge on the parent's capacity to provide adequate care. This may include the processing of traumatic events which continue to impact from the childhood of the parents, their individual functioning as adults, the nature of the couple relationship, including interpersonal or domestic violence, and the organization of family life.

Working with wider family, housing, employment, income and social integration factors requires extensive networking with the appropriate agencies, empowering families to ensure they have access to their entitlements and making sure that protection issues are prioritized. Conflict between families and care agencies need to be addressed so that longstanding grievances can be acknowledged and working relationships established, and a case made for therapeutic or care resources which may not be available in the community, e.g. residential assessments for the family, specialist therapeutic resources for children or family members.

INTERVENTION

Working with family history, family functioning and other family and environmental factors requires working collaboratively with child, adult, and family mental health and therapeutic services, and community agencies and gaining access to a variety of individual, couple and family interventions working with specialist agencies in the drug and alcohol field where appropriate.

A key element is helping parents to create their own trauma narrative which helps to link past experiences with current patterns of interaction and parenting. It is important to help parents confront abusive responses, and to be involved in appropriate anger management or management of sexual abuse or contexts of domestic or interpersonal violence, both inside and outside the family.

Common treatment techniques

As described above, a wide variety of treatment techniques are applied across these various treatment goals in the different parenting capacity and family history and family functioning dimensions. They include the following techniques:

- *Delivering positive reinforcements* with praise, shaping, behavioural rewards and delivering punishment limit setting, ignoring time-out, delivering commands clearly and so on.

- *Using psycho-education,* by teaching through didactic instructions or explanations, using videos, reading and other material relating to different forms of trauma with different treatment approaches and different levels of understanding.

- *Role-playing and behavioural rehearsal*, re-enacting hypothetical situations in sessions, modelling demonstration through live or imagined contexts, or video methods and peer modelling.

- *Using video feedback of parent–child interaction*, reflecting, commenting, promoting positive interaction through direct feedback, relating parents' own experiences evoked during interaction and processing past events through current interactions.

- *Making interventions with sub-groups*, child–parent, couples, whole families and multi-family groups for psycho-educational work, restructuring relationships, tasks, shared activities, working towards behavioural goals, enhancing communication, establishing boundaries, forging alliances, strengthening identity.

- *Tracking the processes* of events, emotional, thinking and behavioural and responses *associated with traumatic experiences*, and abusive action, and the way relationships are influenced and organized with individuals, couples, with family members and professionals, enhancing 'mentalization'.

- *Adopting systemic solution-focused approaches*, focusing on success, recognizing and connoting 'recovery' despite continuing difficulties, exploring the 'not yet emergent' coping mechanism, 'creating healthy futures'.

- *Creating trauma narratives* for children, parents, family members, relating abusive and neglectful parenting to family trauma narratives, understanding responses of individuals, clarification, apology sessions, working to promote addressing painful experiences, and taking responsibility through both individual and joint supported sessions.

- *Reviewing goals and progress*, reviewing previous work themes, progressing towards meeting established goals and assigning and reviewing homework for children, young people and families.

- *Using therapist experiences* to understand the emotional states of individuals and family members, helping to clarify the process of past traumatic events, persistent feeling states, responses to current contexts, evocation of intense emotional states and the risk of self-harm and harm to others.

In Chapter 8 a case example is presented to illustrate some of the key themes of assessment, analysis and planning interventions which are discussed in this and earlier chapters.

Chapter Eight

Principles and Practice in a Safeguarding Context

A Case Example – The Green Family

Arnon Bentovim

In Chapters 6 and 7 a process for the assessment of harm and harmful effects and the prognosis for change in the safeguarding context has been described which builds on the assessment, analysis and planning model introduced in earlier chapters.

The process involves:

- making a full assessment of children's needs, family and environmental factors

- creating a profile of protection and harm

- analysing factors that have led to harmful parenting

- assessing the prognosis for change

- using the prognostic framework in planning for intervention.

In terms of intervention in the safeguarding context, the need to use integrated multimodal therapeutic interventions in families living in a context of trauma and family violence has been emphasized.

In this chapter:

- A number of key principles for practice in the context of safeguarding and protection are introduced.

- A case example – the Green family – is used to illustrate the principles of practice and the process of assessment and planning in the safeguarding context introduced in Chapters 6 and 7.

Practice principles for therapeutic work in the context of safeguarding and protection

Having made an assessment and developed a plan for intervention, there are a number of key practice principles which we suggest should underpin therapeutic work conducted in the context of protection or safeguarding. These include:

1. Planning and taking steps to ensure the victim is protected from abuse while therapeutic work is progressing.

2. Working with perpetrators and protective parents in a context where the child remains protected.

3. Developing and planning of a variety of different interventions to meet the needs of individuals.

4. Considering a rehabilitation phase of therapeutic intervention on the basis of:

   (a) assessing the child's and young person's development

   (b) assessing the parenting capacity

   (c) making modifications in the family and environmental factors and looking at family structures which could provide safe contexts.

5. Providing alternative long-term care when rehabilitation cannot be achieved.

Case example: The Green family

The case example of the Green family is used to illustrate these various stages in assessment, planning interventions and conducting therapeutic work in the context of safeguarding and protection.

The Green family had four children, Charlie aged 13, David aged 10, Sarah aged eight and John aged four. Concerns were first raised when Charlie was five, because of reports of the use of physical smacking, which were resolved with social work intervention.

Subsequently, concerns were expressed because Charlie and David were having very poor school attendance. Despite considerable encouragement by the school staff and authorities, there were few occasions when the boys were at school. It was observed that the children appeared neglected and the health visitor was concerned because the atmosphere of the home seemed most unhappy. Initial investigations by children's services revealed that there was extensive and longstanding conflict between the parents, with father spending increasing time out of the home with his own family. The mother was unable to cope. She could not persuade the boys to go to school; there was an atmosphere of neglect, poor boundaries and a sense of hopelessness as the mother withdrew and left the children to fend for themselves.

A process of social work visits to the home followed the initial assessment to undertake a core assessment, which also involved community child health professionals, prior to calling a child protection conference. Information gathering included information about Sarah from her school and about John. The school observed that Sarah's behaviour was becoming highly sexualized so that she was frequently masturbating and behaving in inappropriate ways with other children. John had poor language development and showed extremely oppositional behaviour towards his mother, who was overwhelmed with the needs of all four children. The father was observed to undermine, criticize and speak for his wife. He was marginally more effective than the mother in controlling the children. However he was absent as a result of the conflict between the parents who seemed unable to put the needs of their children first. Mother withdrew to bed and both parents complained of being depressed.

The process leading to a full assessment of children's needs, family and environmental factors

Practice principles (1): initial intervention

It is not feasible to start intervention with children who are suffering both short-term and long-term effects of living in an abusive environment, or to intervene with parents until decisions are made about appropriate levels of protection and need and there is a thorough knowledge of all factors, which have led to abusive action.

Further social work investigation of the Green family revealed that 13-year-old Charlie was taking parental responsibility for the younger children, and was responsible for Sarah's highly sexualized pattern of behaviour. The result of the parents' conflict and withdrawal left children to their own devices. Charlie unsupervised turned to Sarah and commenced sexual activities with her. Charlie was punished, but sexual behaviour continued as there was a lack of supervision. There had been further punitiveness towards Charlie. There was no evidence of Charlie having been abused sexually himself.

It was felt it was essential to separate Charlie from Sarah to interrupt sexual activities which the parents knew about but had not stopped or informed social or health services about. He went to live with a family member. A specialist assessment was arranged to understand the origins of his abusive behaviour to assess the extent of abuse and the degree of traumatic effect suffered by Sarah.

Father agreed to live separately for a time to assess whether the mother could care more adequately for the three younger children without the negative impact of the father's criticism of her.

It was then revealed that David, Sarah and John were also involved in sexualized activity and David was continuing not to attend school. It was accepted he needed to live in foster care while further assessment of the extensiveness of Charlie's sexualized behaviour was made and its impact on his siblings.

Further knowledge about family and environmental factors which might have played a part in such widespread abusive action was also required and whether there was any possible resolution and potential for the parents working together.

The parents had known about sexual activities for some time but had not intervened effectively or reported Charlie's abusive actions. In addition the children's care was neglected. It was felt that a court order was needed to ensure the social services department shared parental care. An extensive assessment was therefore ordered as part of the court proceedings, which included a specialist assessment of the children's needs and the family context of care, as well as the specialist assessment of Charlie and Sarah. The capacity of the parents to provide more satisfactory parenting and to work together was also assessed. The process of specialist assessment built on the previous initial and core assessment phases.

The following assessments were made during the initial, core and specialist assessments:

- The quality of parenting was assessed using the *HOME Inventory*.

- The family interaction, including an understanding of the families of origin of the parents, as well as the relationship between the parents and the children, was assessed using the *Family Assessment*.

- Each of the children's functioning was assessed using the *Strengths and Difficulties Questionnaires* (SDQ), and where appropriate the school provided assessments of the children from their perspectives, including SDQs for each child completed by their teachers.

- There were individual interviews with each of the children to look at issues of trauma and emotional states, as well as exploring the reasons why each of the children had responded to their questionnaires and the way they had.

- Assessments of possible depression in the children using the *Adolescent Wellbeing Scale* and the level of family togetherness and fostering of age-appropriate independence using the *Family Activities Scale*. Parental mental health problems were explored using the *Adult Wellbeing Scale* and the focus of parenting difficulties for each parent using the *Parenting Daily Hassles Scale*.

As a result of this information-gathering, it was possible to describe the family using the dimensions of the *Assessment Framework*. This information below is organized to assist in assessing the level of protection being provided for a child and the level of harm suffered by the child. The six dimensions of parenting capacity are covered in turn and linked with the impact on the children's functioning in terms of met and unmet needs and harm sustained. This follows the process suggested in Chapter 6 (p.216).

Profile of protection and harm: a systematic analysis of harm and harmful behaviour experienced by the Green children

Table 8.1 Profile of protection and harm: parenting capacity dimensions

	Parental capacities strengths and difficulties – protection versus harmful parenting	*Impact on children's developmental needs, strengths and difficulties, profile of needs met and harm sustained*
Basic care Provision of basic care and attention to health	• Parents' longstanding divisive, highly conflictual relationship leads parents to have little ability to work together, the provision of basic care is inconsistent and poor.	• Charlie presents with poor self-care skills, failure of hygiene, unkempt, no interest in adolescent identity, lack of pride or interest in appearance, focuses on his parenting role and sexualized responses. Physically healthy.
	• Care is disorganized, failure to organize suitable clothing, regular and appropriate mealtimes.	• David's hearing needs not attended to, speech and therapy appointments failed, delayed language development.
	• Failure to attend health appointments, or establish routine for bedtimes or regular family activities.	• John presents with poor social presentation, night wetting continuing, wearing pull-ups, lack of independence and self-care skills.
	• Charlie is expected to take care of the younger siblings, which leads to sexualization.	• Sarah evokes the most appropriate care through her demands of her mother, most competent in terms of self-care skills, level of maturity and competence. Continued night wetting.

Table 8.1 *cont.*

	Parental capacities strengths and difficulties – protection versus harmful parenting	Impact on children's developmental needs, strengths and difficulties, profile of needs met and harm sustained
Basic care *cont.*		• John delayed language development, speech and language therapy appointments not kept, poor presentation, continued night wetting, immaturity, puts himself at risk through moving hot objects from stove in pseudo-parental behaviour.
		• Despite nutritional limitations, growth of all four children satisfactory.
Ensuring safety: Providing responsiveness, safety and protectiveness	• Parental care is unresponsive, unreliable, there is failure to have a consistent presence.	• Needs for safety and protection not met.
		• Sarah described vaginal intercourse, behaviour sexualized at school.
	• Father is absent, at work or with his own family.	• Sarah bullied by Charlie and David as part of sexually aggressive activities triggered by intense hide and seek games.
	• Both father and mother are depressed; she spends significant time withdrawn in bed.	• Sexualized behaviour involves all four children, John and David sexually aggressive, Sarah sexualized responses, John frozen.
	• The expectation of Charlie taking on a parental role, creates a context of risk pattern of sexualized excitement in play initiated by Charlie, with David and the younger children, particularly Sarah.	• Charlie and John describe smacking by father.
	• There is inadequate supervision within the home.	• Sarah most seeking of support outside the family.

	• Charlie is punished when Sarah describes sexual abuse; failure of supervision continues.	• Other children marginalized, insecure attachment responses.
	• Environment is unsafe, unsupervised, disorganized, children not protected from physical hazards, hot stove.	• Unsafe environment in the home as a result of inadequate supervision, exposure to hot objects, stove, dangerous environment of care.
	• Failure of children to attend school maintains secrecy and silence.	
Emotional warmth: emotional warmth and containment	• A general absence of a capacity by parents to respond or to express appropriate warmth and nurturing.	• Charlie marginally attached to his father, excitement, arousal towards Sarah and siblings, Sarah a powerful love object. David intense, insecure, clinging attachment to his mother, highly avoidant to father, sleeping with mother.
	• Absence of appropriate emotional responses.	• Frustration responded to with frozenness, obsessional anxiety, withdrawal and wetting.
	• David given most emotional warmth as his mother's comfort object.	• Sarah despite extensive abuse presents as emotionally responsive, related to earlier closer relationships with mother, most security.
	• John receives emotional warmth from Sarah, absence of warmth and responsiveness from his mother and father.	• Post-traumatic symptoms continue, sadness, distress, unprotected.
	• Family atmosphere is uncomfortable, chaotic, failure to protect from parental conflict separations, maternal depression.	• John avoidant, anxious, unable to cope with frustration, screaming tantrums, nursing and cuddling a doll, rejecting family, distancing from father.
	• Lack of empathic responses for Sarah as a result of sexually abusive activities and failure of early responsiveness relating to maternal depression, father blames her.	
Stimulation: providing stimulation and communication	• Failure of support, impoverished environment, rejection, minimal interchange, children left to organize their own stimulation.	• A significant delay and unevenness in cognitive and language skills for Charlie, David and John.

Table 8.1 cont.

	Parental capacities strengths and difficulties – protection versus harmful parenting	Impact on children's developmental needs, strengths and difficulties, profile of needs met and harm sustained
Stimulation cont.	• Charlie's parental role is supported, Sarah organizes most parental stimulation, John is ignored and isolated.	• John and David delayed language development not supported.
	• David is supported to be mother's comfort.	• Charlie and David oppositional and resistant regarding school.
	• There is failure to support or prepare for educational attendance; parents do not work together to ensure school attendance.	• John received special measures to support, attendance erratic.
	• Charlie and David have consistently poor school attendance.	• David unconfident, socially isolated, fearful of failure and frozen obsessional about work.
	• Sarah attends most satisfactorily.	• Charlie socially isolated, underachieving, marginalized.
	• John inconsistent attendance. Limited opportunity for play activities, lack of involvement of participation.	• Poor relationships between parents and school authorities.
Guidance and boundaries: providing adequate boundaries and managing behaviour	• Parental difficulties in management of behaviour.	• A generally oppositional response.
	• Inappropriate expectations of Charlie taking a parental role.	• Exploitative responses within siblings.
	• Punitive or avoidant responses to children's negative states and frustration.	• Charlie's sexualization of responses to Sarah, involving David and John, bullying, rejecting, limited attempts to control.

	• Boundaries are inappropriate, David in role as maternal comforter, paternal absence, punitive responses, inconsistent discipline or involvement of children.	• Sarah controlled, confused, John's response to frustration screaming tantrums, explosions, David frozen, Charlie angry, controlling, dominating, and stormy in response.
	• Atmosphere chaotic, over-excited, poor management.	
	• Failure to manage boundaries between older and younger children.	
	• Unresolved arguments, intolerance, frustration and anger.	
Stability: providing stable and consistent family relationships	• Parents are in a state of partial separation as a result of conflict, and extensive sense of grievance.	• Children are members of a disrupted, unstable family.
	• Mother left to care without support, leads to a withdrawn, depressed state.	• David enmeshed with his mother.
	• Failure to support individuation and identity of the children.	• Charlie taking a pseudo-adult parental and sexualized role.
	• Charlie given parental authority, pseudo-parental role.	• Sarah shows most positive identity, support from mother results in better social relationships with adults and children outside the family, Charlie, David and John isolated. Poor sense of identity.
	• Charlie and David's exploitative, abusive behaviour unchecked.	
	• Some paternal support for Charlie by occasional fishing trips and contact with father's family.	
	• Sense of social isolation and marginalization maintained.	

Table 8.2 Profile of protection and harm: family and environmental dimensions

Family history and family functioning	• Although there had been no permanent change of household and no separation of the parenting in terms of divorce, there has been partial separation in recent years given the extensive marital difficulties.
	• In the early years, mother's family played a key role in stability of the family, in latter years the father is more involved with his own family.
	• Mother providing care alone, overwhelmed by the needs of the four children without support.
	• This has created a disruptive, unstable family context.
	• The mother described a childhood of being protected but with a good deal of firmness.
	• Her family played a key role supporting mother in the family home, causing considerable grievance and resentment for father. No evidence of exposure to abuse or violence.
	• The father has grown up in a context of privation, loneliness, limited involvement. He reports socially isolated in school, a loner, now closer to his family, maintaining a sense of grievance at mother's involvement with her family at an earlier stage.
Impact of family history	• The key impact seems to be the maintenance of a longstanding set of grievances between the parents, for mother's perceived over-involvement with her family, father remains close to his family in a retaliatory response.
	• Perceived failure to create a marriage to fit into the father's expectation has resulted in him maintaining a sense of grievance, failing to be supportive.
	• Mother left to care for the children without support.
	• An atmosphere of criticism, resentment and grievance results in individual functioning where each is depressed, mother complaining of hopelessness and helplessness, and father a continuing sense of anger, grievance and depression.
Couple relationship	• The couple's relationship is a failure of support, anger, grievance, failure to listen, father interrupting, mother withholding, and an absence of intimacy between them for at least seven years.
	• Mother finds closeness through her relationship with David. Father with Charlie. Sexual responses being enacted by Charlie targeting Sarah.
	• The couple's preoccupation with their marital conflict leads to a failure for the parents to work together, or to respond or be concerned about the children's needs.
	• Although John refers to hitting and smacking, there is little evidence of domestic violence, but considerable atmosphere of criticism, distancing and resentment and lack of support.

Response to significant life events	• Sense of grievance over the role of their families of origin in family life.
	• Their response to significant events, awareness of Charlie's abuse of Sarah has been to ignore, blame Sarah and continue the preoccupation with their own conflict in a self-centred way.
Family organization and family functioning	• Family organization is rigid, not responsive to the growing needs of the children. There is a continuing failure to manage and resolve conflicts and difficulties, to meet the children's changing needs.
	• Failure of parenting, boundaries, encouragement and responsiveness except to a very limited degree where Sarah is concerned.
	• Family functioning shows a striking failure to listen; father's voice is heard over all the family members.
	• A failure to focus, maintain a theme for any length of time.
	• Failure of emotional responsiveness, for parents to communicate, work together, mother's voice is not heard. She relates closely to David. Charlie attempts to act in a parental fashion, Sarah looks outside the family, John screams and tries to escape.
	• There is an atmosphere of chaos and unhappiness punctuated by short periods of working together not sustained.
Wider family	• The maternal wider family is intrusive. The paternal family is unsupportive, instrumental in maintaining distance between father and family, and failing to provide support.
Housing	• The family has lived in the same home for 15 years. Wallpaper remains the same, house is generally dirty apart from the bathroom, uncared for, piles of clothes, failure to create warm, welcoming home.
Employment	• Father has worked consistently and family has always had sufficient income to live at a low level of management. Mother has not worked. Early family functioning more satisfactory when parents worked together; failure of support leads to failure of basic care. Income has been sufficient for the family's needs, not spent on parental needs, emotional issues predominant.
Family social integration	• Family, children and parents are isolated, not integrated.
	• The parental role played by Charlie and the failure of mother to be able to manage to support Charlie and David to attend school and the difficulty in managing the routines concerning the younger children's attendance at school has meant that the family has been isolated.
	• Absence of relationships with children in the neighbourhood. Activities are focused on Charlie's intense play with the younger children.
	• Peer groups and friendship networks are not established as family life focused on the home.

Table 8.2 *cont.*

Community resources	• The family live in an isolated venue, limited neighbourhood facilities, and no facilities for meeting other mothers to provide support.
	• Professional resources have been focused on the family, intense work offered during the phase when the boys were not at school, extensive role of family aid worker and social services with little response until the extensiveness of abusive action was noted and care proceedings.

Analysis of factors that have led to harmful parenting and prognosis for change

Having categorized all the information, it then becomes possible to carry out an analysis of factors which led to harmful parenting and harm sustained by the children, and the prognosis for change.

The approach is outlined in Chapter 7 and includes the following steps:

- *A functional analysis* to look at predisposing, precipitating factors, the profile of harm in maintaining and protective factors.

- *Using the prognostic framework* for the assessment of the parents or caregivers' capacity to respond to intervention in the children's timescale.

Functional analysis: predisposing factors

- Predisposing factors relate to elements in the family and environmental domain.

- There has been a longstanding partial separation between the parents, which has affected the parenting capacity to a significant degree.

- In the early years stability was maintained by mother's family supporting the general family functioning and care; closeness between mother and her family created a sense of grievance on father's part.

- His own history of social isolation, being a loner, has meant that the marriage has been an important social support, his sense of grievance at mother's closeness to her family has led to a degree of conflict in a continuing way, with him spending longer periods with his own family as a form of retaliation. This has led to increasing separateness, triggering depression and a significant failure to maintain family organization.

- The family has always focused on the home, living in an isolated venue with limited facilities and sources of support for the family.

- Professional intervention has helped maintain family organization and supplement the parents lack of meeting early unmet needs, particularly speech and language development, school attendance and general family life, but not utilized effectively by parents.

Functional analysis: precipitating factors

- The increasing parental separateness, increasing failure of parental capacity, parents working together, father's absence, leading to mother being left with the care of the four children, leads to her feeling overwhelmed, taking to her bed complaining of depressive symptoms. The couple relationship deteriorated with high levels of conflict, father controlling mother, an absence of intimacy and social support, criticism with significant family organizational difficulties, failures of parenting, maintenance of boundaries and lack of emotional responsiveness.

- Charlie given increasing parental responsibility for the care of the younger children, their needs are not met adequately as the general care of the home becomes poorer, the degree of conflict, oppositional, stormy responses increase.

- Affection and emotional contact are maintained by the children through Charlie's sexualized excitement involving the younger children and particularly Sarah in intense sexualized behaviour.

- David remains a comforter for the mother.

Functional analysis: profile of harm

- There is evidence of significant sexually abusive behaviour perpetrated against Sarah by Charlie, including evidence of vaginal penetration, and the development of highly sexualized responses on Sarah's part, associated with evidence of persistent traumatic symptoms. Charlie develops intense sexualized response towards Sarah, associated with intense masturbatory activities observed; David is organized to be part of the sexualized responses.

- There is evidence of moderate degrees of privation, neglect and a lack of appropriate maintenance of boundaries and control, continuing privation and a lack of appropriate care, disorganization of family life, children not encouraged to attend school, oppositional responses to attempts to maintain Charlie and David's educational attendance.

- Failure to respond to David and John's needs for appropriate stimulation and support for language. Poor capacities for care and presentation, stormy emotional insecure responses of the children associated.

Functional analysis: maintaining factors

- The continued failure of the parents to work together, their longstanding conflict, sense of grievance and separateness without being separate, lack of intimacy or sharing is a maintaining factor.

- The intensity of Charlie's sexualized responses to Sarah, associated with a degree of sexual obsessional responses maintained by masturbatory responses is a further factor.

- Sarah's sexualized responses, and involvement in eroticized play with Charlie, John and David as well as children and young people in school is a further factor.

- The parental lack of capacity to organize family life, organize satisfactory care, their sense of hopelessness and helplessness are further maintaining factors; failure in management of the children's behaviour and boundaries and need for David to comfort an object.

- Father continues to blame Sarah for initiating sexual activities by Charlie against her.

Functional analysis: protective factors

- Sarah has a significant capacity to evoke positive responses from her mother, and as a result has the most competency and capacity to care for herself, significant interest in education and learning and in making relationships with peers and adults based on positive elements of relationships with her mother. Despite limitations of nutrition and the disorganization of family care. The growth of all four children is satisfactory despite the failures in stimulation associated with language, school attendance and achievements to potential.

- There is a willingness to seek help, and a desire by the mother to provide care to her children while acknowledging her failure to manage the children's behaviour, and therefore for Charlie's abusive behaviour to be triggered and maintained.

- Father has maintained a working profile throughout the children's lives. There have been phases of support by the wider family although intrusive, parents do acknowledge there has been significant failure of care.

Using the 12-step prognostic framework

Step 1: Overall levels of harm, impact on the child and how the child's needs were met

- Presence of severe longstanding sexual abuse involving both attempted and actual genital intercourse over a significant period of time between Charlie and Sarah, failure to protect despite knowledge of abuse within the family over a significant period.

- Moderate degrees of privation, neglect, inconsistent responses to physical and mental health issues.

- Moderate delays and unevenness in development, areas of significant delays and failures of preparation for educational context, failure in school attendance, disruption of attendance, poor achievements.

- Moderate emotional states, clinging, avoidant behaviour, mixture of insecure attachments. Distressed frozen responses, mood difficulties, oppositional behaviour, major sexual behaviour problems.

- Considerable problems of identity, confusion concerning appropriate sexual relationships.

- Family relationships exploitative, fighting, aggression from siblings targeted on Sarah.

- Considerable problems concerning self-presentation, hygiene, neglect.

- Moderate problems in development of self-care skills.

Step 2: Level of parenting, protection and therapeutic work the child requires

- Overall considerable levels of harm, protection required through appropriate legal proceedings, specialist parenting required for Charlie and David, considerable doubts about the capacity of mother to care for the two younger children. Paternal role negative because of perpetuation of severe and marital and negative family responses.

- Therapeutic work required for all four children.

Step 3: Whether parents judged responsible for harm can acknowledge the level of harm or harmful behaviour to the child

- Limited recognition of level of harm and children's needs.

- Continuing evidence of father not accepting Charlie's responsibility for abuse of Sarah, mother doubtful but more acceptance of the reality of Charlie's abusive behaviour and impact on Sarah.

- Reluctance to accept David's level of risk to Sarah and his level of emotional needs.

- Difficulties in recognizing the level of John's level of privation, developmental difficulties and emotional needs.

Step 4: Level of parenting that has been provided for the child

- Considerable difficulties in all areas of parenting, some positive elements on mother's part towards Sarah, capacity to show warmth and responsiveness but considerable difficulties in provision of basic care as a result of parental conflict.

- Failure to provide a safe context for Sarah or to intervene in abuse by Charlie.

- Failure to prevent danger within the home.

- Inconsistency of emotional responses, seeking comfort from children by mother with David, father with Charlie.

- Some limited support for Sarah; John isolated self-care.

- Boundaries, establishment of rules, management of routine and response to children's emotional needs, considerable difficulties.

- Some areas of response between mother and Sarah educationally, considerable failure to ensure children's attendance at school, absence of appropriate stimulation, support and encouragement.

- Considerable difficulties with stability over recent years, father's absence and mother's depression and withdrawal.

- Unstable context where Charlie expected to parent which he does inappropriately and abusively.

Steps 5 and 6: Parental recognition and capacity to respond within the child's timeframe

- Because of the level of children's need, levels of harm and parenting capacities, it is not possible for Charlie and David to be parented within their timeframe adequately.

- Limited recognition of abusive impact because of considerable undermining of mother by father, not possible for them to parent together.

- Considerable doubt whether the mother could parent the younger children within their timeframe.

- Limited responsibility taken for the state of the children and relationship with parenting, mother more accepting and understanding but to a very limited degree, father less so.

Step 7: Influence of individual and family factors on parenting and the parents' capacities to meet the child's needs

- Significant mental health difficulties related to longstanding, unresolved conflict between the parents result in their inability to focus and concern themselves with the parenting of the children. Longstanding grievance, brief phases of working together only.

- Considerable difficulties in all areas of family functioning, the capacity of the parents to organize themselves and meet the changing needs of the children, to manage conflict and to make decisions.

- Considerable failure to encourage, support or to create a context where appropriate boundaries can be developed and managed. Considerable difficulties in all alliances, inappropriate cross-boundary relationships between parents and children, older children and younger children, poor communication, chaotic atmosphere, failure of emotional support, older individuals seeking comfort from David, father from Charlie, Charlie from Sarah, inappropriate sexual activities.

Step 8: Parents' acknowledgement of the role of individual and family factors, and their effect on parenting and a motivation to change

- There is limited awareness of the core issue of the parents' marital failure, but level of grievance and conflict at a level where there is a sense of hopelessness about their capacity to resolve their differences to be able to parent adequately, although there is an attachment and a wish for them to remain in relationship with each other.

Step 9: Potential for change in individual and family factors, and improving parenting to meet the child's needs

- Limited awareness of level of family functioning difficulties, presence of neglect and compulsive abuse, sexual activities and abdication of parenting functioning is assessed as not changeable within children's timeframe, not possible for family to remain together, considerable doubt about mother's capacity to care for younger children.

Step 10: Role of environmental factors and impact on parenting

- The main issue is the housing, neglect, failure to maintain appropriate decorative order, cleanliness, hygiene, to provide a warm, caring context for the children within the children's timeframe, to provide adequate nutrition and care.

Step 11: Parents' awareness of and capacity to change environmental factors

- Not of such severity as to be changeable within children's timeframe if motivation present, but doubt about capacity to respond.

Step 12: Nature of relationships with professionals

- Although there has been the 'ordinary tension' between parents and professionals, reasonable working relationships were established until the stage when it was clear the couple needed to remain separate if any children were to live in the family. Mother continued to maintain good working relationships but father rejected professional contact after separation confirmed.

Using the prognostic framework in planning for intervention

Based on this analysis, it becomes possible to begin to plan an approach which tests the capacity of the family to work within the parameters based on the assessment of risks of re-abuse, and potential for rehabilitation. It was not feasible to consider the two older boys, Charlie and David, to return to the parents' care. Nor was it felt possible for the parents to work together towards rehabilitation, and it was decided that therapeutic work would need to take place for Charlie and David in alternative care. The potential for the younger two children to be placed with their mother was tested through an intensive parenting and therapeutic programme to work with Sarah's traumatic experiences of abuse while Charlie's abusive behaviour was being treated. There needed to be a complex set of arrangements made for contact while a process of work was being completed before a final view could be taken about the longer term needs of the children and for the family.

Practice principles (2): therapeutic work in a context of protection

Planning is required to ensure the victim is protected from abuse, this may include a family attending the family centre, or a victim living with a protective parent or family member or foster carer separately from the perpetrator of abuse.

Planning at this stage needed to include whether the mother could protect Sarah so she could receive some specific help as a result of the abusive action perpetrated by her older brother.

Charlie's therapeutic work needed to be carried out in a context where he did not have access to younger children, given that he involved his two brothers in abusive action.

There was a need for the older boys to get back into full-time education which the foster carer and family member helped David and Charlie achieve.

A programme of therapeutic work was arranged for Charlie, Sarah, David and John with a voluntary specialist agency. Sarah's behaviour became challenging during the process of therapeutic work as the full impact of abusive experiences was revealed.

The process of assessment of protective capacities needs to continue throughout the process.

Practice principles (2): work with perpetrators and protective parents

Planning at this stage needs to ensure that the perpetrator is living separately, and needs to access help for their abusive action. Protective parents need support to ensure that therapeutic work is effective, and parenting capacity in general is developed.

The family member caring for Charlie needed considerable support to help Charlie benefit from his therapeutic work, with careful monitoring and protection of the contact with the younger children who he involved sexually.

The foster carer looking after David needed considerable support to help manage his extreme distress at separation from his family, where he saw himself as a key supporter of his mother.

Mother needed considerable support in helping Sarah and John benefit from their therapeutic programme. There were times when she felt overwhelmed.

Practice principles (3): a variety of different interventions are required

Planning is required to ensure therapeutic work is focused on the child, young person and family member individually, or in groups with the aim of ensuring that work is focused on the specific needs of children and parents in accordance with the assessment of both children's and parents' needs. The requirement is to focus on therapeutic work in a context of safety.

Young people such as Charlie require work individually, in groups and with appropriate family members to take full responsibility and understand the origin of his abusive action and develop a way of being safe in the community. Abuse-focused therapy was required.

Sarah needed trauma-focused work to process abusive experiences and not feel responsible for Charlie's actions and to be safe in the future.

David needed help with his emotional difficulties and to ensure he did not behave abusively.

Mother needed a considerable parenting support programme to help manage John's stormy behaviour and Sarah's sexualized behaviour and to promote their development.

Practice principles (4): rehabilitation phase of therapeutic intervention – assessment of children and young people's development and assessment of parenting capacity

It is essential that parents begin to do the work to ensure that they are appropriately protective, can provide more satisfactory basic care, can achieve stability, more effective boundaries, and can provide more adequate stimulation and better care.

It was observed that the mother's psychological state improved, she benefited from the parenting programme, was less depressed and she achieved more stability for the two younger children using parent–child interaction therapy.

Boundaries were asserted more effectively, protection was more adequate, and both children were thriving. There were however continuing periods when she felt overwhelmed and cared less effectively.

Mother's resources were just adequate to meet the needs of the two younger children, however there remained concerns about whether she could also meet the needs of the older children who continued to do well with their respective carers.

Father played a more and more peripheral role, absenting himself to an increasing degree.

Practice principles (4): rehabilitation phase of therapeutic intervention – modification of family environmental factors

Those family and environmental factors, which have contributed to the origins, the triggering and the process of abuse, need to be addressed, so that the damaging effect on the child can be ameliorated.

Work with the parents revealed more extensive information on the origins of their shared sense of grievance, considerable differences of expectation that each parent had of the other from early in their relationship.

There was also a considerable difference in ideas about boundaries and discipline which meant the children had always been given conflicting messages.

Despite attempts through counselling to help them resolve their considerable differences, they both concluded that their marriage had been at an end for some years and there was no prospect of improvement.

The mother parented more successfully on her own with the younger children. As a result of her history of early privation she had the capacity to provide adequate care for the younger children, but could not provide adequate boundaries and consistency for the older children, who had suffered extensive harm as a result of failures to meet their needs.

Appropriate contact arrangements between the sibling and the parents maintained a sense of identity.

Outcomes following intervention with the Green family

Repeated measures used during the assessment include the *HOME Inventory* and the *Family Assessment*. Individual assessments of each of the children using the *Strengths and Difficulties Questionnaire* (Goodman 1997; Goodman *et al.* 1998) indicated significant improvement in all dimensions. There were positive findings for each of the children in terms of their capacity to reach their potential and for the mother to be able to parent the two younger children successfully and the older children to live in alternative care, but to maintain contact with the parents. The parents' highly conflictual marriage, which had such a destructive effect on relationships between themselves and on their capacity to parent, had resulted in a healthier separation maintaining contact with the children and providing more appropriate support without conflict.

Conclusion

It will be noted that in the work with this family a number of different interventions were used, including:

- restructuring the family to ensure that there was a potential for adequate care for the younger children
- basic modelling of care by a family aide with the mother
- alternate care with therapeutic intervention for the older children
- parent–child interactional work with the younger children
- trauma-focused work with Sarah and David
- abuse-focused work with Charlie
- couple counselling with the parents
- whole family meetings for assessment and clarification purposes.

The result of the work undertaken was complex. Using a combination of interventions including rehabilitation of children with a parent who could provide care, alternative care for older siblings and supporting separation in a destructive marriage. Focused therapeutic work meant that all children were making positive progress and meeting their potential to a much greater extent. The work required a multi-component, multi-agency approach, with an appropriate integration of care, and therapeutic intervention delivered by general child and mental health services, health and specialist voluntary services for children and families when sexual abuse had occurred.

In families living with trauma and family violence, therapeutic work requires significant support from social services agencies providing protection, from voluntary agencies providing therapeutic work, potentially from couple counselling agencies and from child adolescent and adult mental health practitioners.

Considering the complex varied needs of the children and other family members reflected in all dimensions of the *Assessment Framework*, without the provision of multimodal and multi-component interventions and therapeutic network meetings, there would be no prospect of children growing up in a climate of trauma and family violence going on the lengthy journey to resilience and recovery. The risks are that although some of the children may find their own routes to recovery in later life, others may find that their attempts to find solutions in their choice of partners, or in coping through drug alcohol, or in making others bear their pain. These actions maintain the cycle of violence rather than break it.

Appendix

Chart of information gathered by use of Standardized Assessment Tools about the *Assessment Framework* domains and dimensions
NB For references for assessment tools see end of charts. See below for guide about use.

O = information that may be revealed by observation when using assessment tools
R = information that is explored in interview schedules
D = information that may be revealed by discussion of specific items in assessment tools. Discussion focuses on the meaning of particular scores or items to person, and explores how that factor affects, or is affected by, aspects of child's developmental needs, parenting capacity and/or family and environmental factors
** = key tool for assessing dimensions in the domain

Child's developmental needs	Health Physical and mental well-being of child	Education Cognitive development and educational needs	Emotional and behavioural development Feelings and responses of child towards others	Identity Child's sense of self and self-esteem	Family and social relationships Development of relationships and empathy	Social presentation Child's understanding of how to present self in outside world	Self-care skills Child's practical, emotional and communication skills
Assessment tools							
Strengths and Difficulties Questionnaires **	Gives screening information about emotional and behavioural problems and needs in children and young people aged 3–16 and may show how problems are impacting on the child's health D	Gives information about the child's adjustment at school and difficulties in learning. It indicates whether there is a need for a specialist assessment D	For children and young people 3–16 screens for pro-social behaviour, hyperactivity, emotional and conduct (behavioural) problems at home and school D	Looks at some aspects of identity, the child's relationships with peers and friendships and how they perceive themselves and are perceived at home and school D	Looks at the child's relationships with peers, their family and other friendships D	Impact of strengths and difficulties on this aspect of child development D	D

Parenting Daily Hassles Scale			May provide cues to emotional and behavioural difficulties and description of strengths and problems encountered D		Quality of relationships between child and parents and brothers and sisters D		D
Home Conditions Scale							State of child's own room and belongings O
Adult Well-Being Scale			D		D		
Adolescent Well-Being Scale **		Discussion of young person's emotional state on their learning and relationships at school D	Screens for depression. Impact of difficulties encountered by a young person on their friendships, home life and leisure activities D	Discussion of impact on self-esteem and other factors in identity and other CDN dimensions D	Helps identify young person's own perceptions of family and social relationships and impact of adolescent's emotional state D		
Recent Life Events Questionnaire	Illness and recent hospitalization of child and impact on other aspects of health and development D	Change of school or in school, e.g. class, teacher, peers D	Impact of recent life events on child's emotional and behavioural development D	Discussion of impact of recent life events on child's identity D	Impact of recent life events on child's family and social relationships D	Impact of recent life events on child's social presentation D	Impact of recent life events on child's self-care skills D
Family Activity Scale	Impact of illness or disability on family activity D	D	Picks up on involvement in independent activities D		Child's participation in child-centred family activity and child's independent activities D	How child manages self-presentation in independent activities D	

Alcohol Scale	Discussion may reveal neglect, lack of supervision etc. and impact on that is leading to impairment of child's health and development D	D	D	D	D	D	D
Sheridan Charts **	Maps developmental progress of infants and young children and helps indicate need for assessment of child's cognitive development when placed and in tracking their progress during placement D	Maps developmental progress of infants and young children and helps indicate need for assessment of child's cognitive development when placed and in tracking their progress during placement D					
HOME Inventory	Through the exploration of events of the day a picture emerges of the child's physical and mental well-being and their development. Contacts with medical services O + R	Assesses the learning environment provided for the child at home and how they are responding and, with older children, how they are responding at school O + R	Child's responses to caregiving by caregivers and to daily events. Observation of emotional states, how distress is managed and the presence of anxiety, mood difficulties and oppositional/defiance problems O + R	Child's assertiveness and confidence in interactions at home. Allows observation of the environment of encouragement, individuality and a sense of belonging and the child's responses O + R	Gathers information about the nature and quality of parent–child interactions and involvement and the child's contact with other family members and extended family O + R	How child is responding to opportunities for social contact and leisure opportunities available for the child. Observed social skills O + R	Systematically explores range of self-care skills, e.g. washing, dressing, mealtimes, getting to school, and encouragement given to develop self-care skills and adaptation to child's specific needs O + R

Family Assessment	Through observation of a child during a *Family Assessment* a picture emerges of the child's physical and mental well-being and their development O + R	Explores key factors affecting the child's cognitive development and education, including stimulation and encouragement, parent–child relationships and communication in the family O + R	Looks at nature of attachments in family, including pattern of care-seeking behaviour of the child, how emotions are expressed/ responded to and difficulties in child's emotional and behavioural development O + R	*Family Identity* can help assess how child is developing as an individual, their self-assertiveness and autonomy, the degree of emotional involvement and sense of 'togetherness' as an adoptive family O + R	Strengths and difficulties in child's relationships with family, including with parents, brothers and sisters, and extended family and birth and foster families O + R	Helps identify how the child is adapting to the family as he or she settles in and becomes a member of the family and the emergence of self-presentation and the nature of social relationships O + R	Through observation and in the evaluation of parenting a picture of the development of the child's self-care skills emerges O + R
Fahlberg's Observation Checklists			Provides a useful guide to assessing attachment behaviours (and caregivers' responses) for children from infancy to adolescence O				
In My Shoes **	Has a module for talking about and gaining an understanding of children's experiences of pain, including accidents, illness, hospital treatment, abuse and emotional pain O + D	Has a set of school scenes and other tools to help a child talk about their school, including their experience, thoughts and feelings about lessons, teachers, peers, playtime, homework O + D	Allows worker to explore with child their emotional and behavioural responses to different scenes, living and other settings and people and how they understand and experience different aspects of their lives O + D	Is used interactively with a child to build up a picture of them and their world and their emotional responses to things that have happen to them and the people in their lives. Pictures generated from the interview can be printed out O + D	Exploring with a child the relationship between a child's emotions and the places and people in their lives (e.g. family, school, park, previous and future families etc.) O + D	Looking at how a child sees themselves fitting in the contexts in which they live and their understanding of how they present themselves and how others see them O + D	Gathering a picture of child's self-care skills in different settings, assistance to gain self-care skills and their feelings about learning to look after themselves O + D

Parenting capacity	Basic Care Providing for child's physical needs	Ensuring safety Ensuring child protected from harm and danger	Emotional warmth Ensuring child's emotional needs are met	Stimulation Promoting child's learning and intellectual development	Guidance and boundaries Enabling child to regulate their own emotions and behaviour	Stability Providing stable environment for developing attachments
Assessment tools						
Strengths and Difficulties Questionnaires	D	D	D	D	D	D
Parenting Daily Hassles Scale (PDH) **	Discussion of PDH may reveal strengths and difficulties in all areas of parenting including basic care D	Discussion may raise issues regarding ensuring safety D	Strengths and difficulties in relation to emotional warmth may arise from discussion D	Allows for discussion of how to provide learning opportunities for child and encouragement, reassurance and praise D	Looks at current areas of difficulty parents may be facing in managing a child's behaviour D	Discussion of PDH can focus whether parents need support in providing a stable environment for the child D
Home Conditions Scale **	Hygiene relevant to health O	Tour of home may identify dangers or risks to child's safety O				
Adult Well-Being Scale	Discussion of impact parental state on all aspects of parenting D	Impact of parental outwards-directed hostility on ensuring safety D	Impact of parental outwards-directed hostility or depression on emotional warmth D	Parental depression may be relevant due to impact on stimulation D	Parental depression and anxiety may impact on guidance and boundaries D	Impact of parental hostility, anxiety and/or depression on stability D
Adolescent Well-Being Scale		Discussion of parental response to what is reported by young person D	Discussion of parental response to what is reported by young person D			Discussion of parental response to what is reported by young person D

	Discussion of impact on child care D	Discussion of impact on child care D	Discussion of impact on child care D	Discussion of impact on child care D	Discussion of impact on child care D	Changes of partners and house moves D
Recent Life Events Questionnaire						Changes of partners and house moves D
Family Activity Scale		Can explore whether there is adequate supervision D		Identifies child-centred family activities and support for independent activity D	Identifies child-centred family activities and support for independent activity D	
Alcohol Scale	Discussion of impact of alcohol misuse on basic care D	Discussion of impact of alcohol misuse on ensuring safety D	Looking at effect of alcohol misuse on providing emotional warmth D	Exploring if alcohol misuse affects parents' capacity to offer child learning opportunities, praise etc. D	Discussion of impact of alcohol misuse on giving children appropriate guidance and boundaries D	Discussion of impact of alcohol misuse on stability of the home environment and caregiving offered D
Sheridan Charts	Discussion of parental response to what is reported about child's health and development D	Discussion of parental response about child's social behaviour D	Information given by parents about play and social behaviour D	Discussion about parents report on children's physical and social development D	Discussion about how parents manage child's developing social behaviour and play D	Discussion of parents' response to child's relationships with them and other family members D
HOME Inventory **	Gives an opportunity to assess in detail whether a child's basic care needs are being met and to identify any difficulties parents may be having in adapting to a child's extra needs O + R	Looks at issues of safety in the child's home environment O + R	Specifically addresses emotional sensitivity and responsivity of the caregiver towards the child and helps to locate the exact nature of any difficulties parents are experiencing in day-to-day care O + R	Covers adoptive parents' provision of stimulation, support, and opportunities for play and learning that support cognitive development of child. Includes provision of play and learning materials, language, academic stimulation and encouragement of play and learning O + R	Specifically addresses modelling by parents, the use of boundaries in parent–child relationships, how parents set limits for children and discipline them, how they encourage the development of socially responsible and mature behaviour O + R	Provides information about changes in the child's circumstances and relationships; and about parental responsivity and acceptance of child and the emotional climate O + R

Family Assessment **	Parenting component explores the way the family manages basic care tasks and responds to the changing needs of the child O+ R	Parenting compoment helps to highlight strengths and difficulties in ensuring safety, looking at the nature of attachments and the protection, care and management of children O + R	Helps to assess nature of attachments, parent–child and other family relationships, how feelings are expressed and responded to, whether relationships are supportive and appreciative and the level of emotional involvement O + R	Explores how adoptive parents promote a child's development through stimulation, emotional warmth and praise O + R	Looks at strengths and difficulties parents have in providing guidance, boundary setting, protection and their expectations of the children, and associated aspects of family life, including decision-making, problem-solving and the management of conflicts O + R	Explores caregiving and the nature of the attachments and the parent–child relationship and how feelings are expressed and responded to in the family O + R
Fahlberg's Observation Checklists		Gives information about parent's sensitivity to child's needs for ensuring safety O + D	Useful guide to child's attachment behaviours level of responsiveness and sensitivity shown by the caregiver O + D	Provides information about stimulation and parents' responsiveness towards child O + D		Explores level of responsiveness and sensitivity of caregiver, helps identify strengths and areas where support may be useful O + D
In My Shoes	Provides information about basic care provided for a child and child's response O + D	Helps gain picture of how far child is kept safe and how far child understands issues of safety O + D	Gains picture of child's view of emotional warmth provided by carers and child's response to that O + D	Child's report on assistance given by carers with educational tasks and opportunities to develop cognitive and social skills O + D	Explores guidance and boundaries provided by carers from child's perspective, including abusive or neglectful parenting O + D	Gathers picture of carers capacity to help child build attachments with family members and child's view of how secure their place in the family feels O + D

Family and environmental factors	Family history and functioning Significant family history, individual well-being and family functioning	Wider family Role and importance of wider family; including adopted child's birth family	Housing Appropriateness of accommodation to needs of child, family and other resident members	Employment Pattern of employment and impact on child and family members' relationship with child	Income Sufficiency of income to meet family needs and available resources	Family's social integration Integration with neighbourhood and community; peer groups, friendships and social networks	Community resources Availability, accessibility and standard of facilities and services available in community
Assessment tools							
Strengths and Difficulties Questionnaires	Discussion may reveal parental mental health issues or difficulties in family functioning D						
Parenting Daily Hassles Scale	Helpful in identifying aspects of care that may put extra strain on adoptive parents D	Helpful in identifying aspects of contact with wider family that may be difficult D					
Home Conditions Scale **			Addresses standards of cleanliness O	D	D		
Adult Well-Being Scale **	Explores how an adult is feeling in terms of depression, anxiety and irritability and can indicate when professional help may be beneficial D	D	D	D	D	D	D
Adolescent Well-Being Scale	D						

Recent Life Events Questionnaire **	Impact of illness and death on family functioning D	Impact of illness and death, recent moves and other life events on wider family D	Effect of recent house moves; can be a major life event for family members D	Impact of employment difficulties on parents and children D	Effect of financial difficulties on family members D	Support or conflicts with neighbours D	
Family Activity Scale	Social activities of family explored D		Discussion may reveal adverse effects of housing on joint activities families can do together D	May reveal adverse effects of employment problems on joint family activities D	Impact of financial difficulties on joint family activities D	Explores family's child-centred use of community facilities and resources in terms of leisure D	
Alcohol Scale **	Impact on health. Valuable way of exploring any potential difficulties with alcohol use D			Impact on employment D	Impact on income D	Social use of alcohol and family's social integration. Impact of any misuse on relationships with neighbours and friends D	
Sheridan Charts							
HOME Inventory **	Information on parental mental health and family functioning may be observed or reported O + R	Looks at the child's contact and relationship with members of the wider family O + R	Provides information on housing as part of an assessment of the child's home environment. Includes context of home in neighbourhood O + R	A Home Inventory conducted with birth parent or foster carer can help predict levels of care child likely to need and the potential impact on the employment pattern of the future carers O + R		Family's contact with friends and neighbours O + R	Family's use of community resources or need for access to additional resources or facilities may be reported O + R

Family Assessment **							
Looks at crucial everyday interactions with which families may need support, including decision-making, problem-solving, managing conflict, family communication and how feelings are expressed and responded to, family alliances and family identity

Family history systematically explores the meaning and impact of past significant events and relationships and can help identify unresolved issues from the past
O + R | Explores the family's relationships with the wider family. Mapping the Problem helps identify resources and areas of difficulty in wider family, and regarding contact with birth family and significant others
O + R | Observation and discussion of housing needs possible as part of *Family Assessment* carried out in home
O + D | Information may be revealed during discussion in *Family Assessment*
O + D | Information may be revealed during discussion in *Family Assessment*
O + D | Family's relationships with the wider family and community gives picture of strengths and difficulties in family's relationships with the wider family and community, including whether the parents are able to maintain their friendships and support networks
R | Family's use of community resources or need for access to additional resources or facilities may be reported
R |

Fahlberg's Observation Checklists							
In My Shoes (IMS)	Explores child's experience of family relationships and their related thoughts, wishes and feelings O + D	Enables child to communicate about their family and, wider family and their contact with each O + D	IMS can be used to help child to talk about the houses they have lived in, with whom etc. O + D	Discussion of family life using IMS can include employment of parents and impact on child O + D	Issues and concerns about income may be revealed through use of IMS with a child O + D	Exploration of child and family's wider social networks facilitated through IMS including gauging child's related feelings O + D	Child's (and family's) involvement with community resources can be tracked using IMS O + D
Attachment Style Interview	Explores adults' attachment styles and use of support offered by their significantly close people in their lives R + O	Assists in assessing support available to parents in the wider family and their views about other people and using support R + O				Gives information about family's involvement with, and attitude towards immediate and wider family network and others R + O	May give information about family's involvement with community resources and their use and views about using them for support R + O

References for assessment tools

The Family Pack of Questionnaires and Scales. Department of Health, Cox A and Bentovim A (2000) The Stationery Office, London.

The HOME Inventory. Cox A and Walker S, (2002) Child and Family Training, London

The Family Assessment: Assessment of Family Competence, Strengths and Difficulties. Bentovim A and Bingley Miller L (2001) Child and Family Training, London

Chart illustrating the developmental progress of infants and young children. Sheridan M, in Department of Health (2000) *Assessing Children in Need and their Families: Practice Guidance.* The Stationery Office, London.

Observation Checklists: Fahlberg V, in Fahlberg V (1994) *A Child's Journey Through Placement.* BAAF, London

In My Shoes: Calam, RM, Cox, AD, Glasgow, DV, Jimmieson, P and Groth Larsen, S (2000) 'Assessment and therapy with children: can computers help?' *Child Clinical Psychology and Psychiatry* 5, 3, 329–343

Attachment Style Interview: Bifulco A, Moran P, Ball C & Bernazzani O (2002a) 'Adult Attachment Style I: Its relationship to clinical depression.' *Social Psychiatry and Psychiatric Epidemiology,* 37, 50–59. Bifulco A, Moran P, Ball C & Lillie A (2002b) 'Adult Attachment Style II. Its relationship to psychosocial depressive-vulnerability.' *Social Psychiatry and Psychiatric Epidemiology* 37, 60–67.

Bibliography

Adoption and Children Act 2002.

Alessandri, S.M. (1991) 'Play and social behaviour in maltreated preschoolers.' *Development and Psychopathology 3*, 191–206.

Angold, A., Predergast, M., Cox, A., Harrington, R., Simonoff, I. and Rutter, M. (1995) 'The Child and Adolescent Psychiatric Assessment (CAPA).' *Psychological Medicine 25*, 739–753.

Asen, K., George, E., Piper, R. and Stevens, A. (1989) 'A systems approach to child abuse: management and treatment issues.' *Child Abuse and Neglect 13*, 45–58.

Banyard, V.L. and Williams, L.M. (2007) 'Women's voices on recovery: a multi-method study of the complexity of recovery from child sexual abuse.' *Child Abuse and Neglect 31*, 275–290.

Barlow, J. (2006) 'Home Visiting for Parents of Pre-school Children in the UK.' In C. McAuley, P.J. Pecord and W. Rose (eds) *Enhancing the Well-being of Children and Families through Effective Interventions: International Evidence for Practice.* London: Jessica Kingsley Publishers.

Bateman, A.W. and Fonagy, P. (2004) *Psychotherapy for Borderline Personality Disorder: Mentalization-Based Treatment.* Oxford: Oxford University Press.

Beck, J.E. and Shaw, D.S. (2005) 'The influence of perinatal complications and environmental adversity on boys' antisocial behaviour.' *Journal of Child Psychology and Psychiatry 46*, 1, 35–46.

Bentovim, A. (1992) *Trauma Organised Systems: Physical and Sexual Abuse in Families.* London: Karnac.

Bentovim, A. (1995) *Trauma Organised Systems: Physical and Sexual Abuse in Families*, revised edition. London: Karnac.

Bentovim, A. (1998) 'Significant Harm in Context.' In M. Adcock and R. White (eds) *Significant Harm, its Management and Outcome.* Croydon: Significant Publications.

Bentovim, A. (2002) 'Preventing sexually abused young people from becoming abusers, and treating the victimisation experiences of young people who offend sexually.' *Child Abuse and Neglect 26*, 661–678.

Bentovim, A. (2006a) 'Physical and Sexual Abuse.' In C. Gillberg, R. Harrington and H.-C. Steinhausen (eds) *Child and Adolescent Psychiatry.* Cambridge: Cambridge University Press.

Bentovim, A. (2006b) 'Therapeutic Interventions with Children who have Experienced Sexual and Physical Abuse in the UK.' In C. McAuley, P.J. Pecord and W. Rose (eds) *Enhancing the Well-being of Children and Families through Effective Interventions: International Evidence for Practice.* London: Jessica Kingsley Publishers.

Bentovim, A. and Bingley Miller, L. (2001) *The Family Assessment: Assessment of Family Competence, Strengths and Difficulties.* York: Child and Family Traning..

Bentovim, A., Elton, A. and Hildebrand, J. (1988) *Child Sexual Abuse within the Family.* London: Wright Butterworth Press.

Bentovim, A., Elton, A. and Tranter, M. (1987) 'Prognosis for rehabilitation after abuse.' *Adoption and Fostering 11*, 26–31.

Bergner, R.M., Delgado, L.K. and Graybill, D. (1994) 'Finkelhor's risk factor checklist: a cross-validation study.' *Child Abuse and Neglect 18*, 4, 331–340.

Bifulco, A. and Moran, P. (1998) *Wednesday's Child: Research into Women's Experience of Neglect and Abuse in Childhood, and Adult Depression.* London: Routledge.

Bifulco, A., Brown, G.W. and Harris, T.O. (1994) 'Childhood Experience of Care and Abuse (CECA): a retrospective intervention measure.' *Journal of Child Psychology and Psychiatry 35*, 1419–1435.

Bifulco, A., Figueiredo, B., Guedney, N., Gorman, L., et al. (2004) 'Maternal attachment style and depression associated with childbirth: preliminary results from a European/US cross-cultural study.' *British Journal of Psychiatry (Special supplement) 184*, 46, 31–37

Bifulco, A., Moran, P., Ball, C. and Bernazzani, O. (2002a) 'Adult Attachment Style I: its relationship to clinical depression.' *Social Psychiatry and Psychiatric Epidemiology 37*, 50–59.

Bifulco, A., Moran, P., Ball, C. and Lillie, A. (2002b) 'Adult Attachment Style II: its relationship to psychosocial depressive-vulnerability.' *Social Psychiatry and Psychiatric Epidemiology 37*, 60–67.

Bingley Miller, L. and Bentovim, A. (2007) *Assessing the Support Needs of Adopted Children and their Families: Building Secure New Lives.* London: Routledge.

Bion, W.R. (1962a) *Learning from Experience.* London: Heinemann.

Bion, W.R. (1962b) 'A theory of thinking.' *International Journal of Psychoanalysis 43*, 306–310.

Birleson, P. (1980) 'The validity of depressive disorder in childhood and the development of a self-rating scale: a research report.' *Journal of Child Psychology and Psychiatry 22*, 73–88.

Borduin, C., Hengeller, S., Blaske, D.M. and Stein, R.J. (1990) 'Multisystemic treatment of adolescent sexual offenders.' *International Journal of Offender Therapy and Comparative Criminology 34*, 105–113.

Bowlby, J. (1959) 'Separation anxiety.' *International Journal of Psycho-Analysis 41*, 1–25.

Bowlby, J. (1969) *Attachment and Loss, Volume 1: Attachment.* London: Hogarth Press and Institute of Psycho-Analysis.

Boxer, P. and Terranova, A.M. (2008) 'Effects of multiple maltreatment experiences among psychiatrically hospitalised youth.' *Child Abuse and Neglect 32*, 637–647.

Brandon, M., Belderson, P., Warren, C., Howe, D., *et al.* (2008) *Analysing Child Deaths and Serious Injury through Abuse and Neglect: What Can We Learn? A Biennial Analysis of Serious Case Reviews 2003–2005.* London: Department for Children, Schools and Families.

Brown, G.W. (2002) 'Social roles, context and evolution in the origins of depression.' *Journal of Health and Social Behaviour 43*, 33, 255–276.

Browne, K., Falshaw, L. and Dixon, L. (2002a) 'Treating Domestic Violent Offenders.' In K. Browne, H. Hanks, P. Stratton and C. Hamilton (eds) *Early Prediction and Prevention of Child Abuse.* Chichester: Wiley.

Browne, K., Hanks, H., Stratton, P. and Hamilton, C. (eds) (2002b) *Early Prediction and Prevention of Child Abuse.* Chichester: Wiley.

Brugha, T., Bebington, P., Tennant, C. and Jurry, J. (1985) 'The list of threatening experiences: a subset of 12 life events categories with considerable long-term contextual threat.' *Psychological Medicine 15*, 189–194.

Buckley, H., Howarth, J. and Whelan, S. (2006) *Framework for the Assessment of Vulnerable Children and their Families: Assessment Tool and Practice Guidance.* Dublin: Children's Research Centre.

Calam, R., Cox, A., Glasgow, D. Jimmieson, P. and Groth Larsen, S. (2005) *In My Shoes: Handbook and User Guide. York: Child Family and Training.* Available via training course only: contact liza.miller@childandfamilytraining.org.uk

Calam, R.M., Jimmieson, P., Cox, A.D., Glasgow, D.V and Groth Larsen, S. (2000b) 'Can computer-based assessment help us understand children's pain?' *European Journal of Anaesthesiology 17*, 284–288.

Calam, R.M., Cox, A.D., Glasgow, D.V., Jimmieson, P. and Groth Larsen, S. (2000a) 'Assessment and therapy with children: can computers help?' *Child Clinical Psychology and Psychiatry 5*, 3, 329–343.

Caldwell, B.M. and Bradley, R.H. (2001) *Home Observation for Measurement of the Environment: Administration Manual,* 3rd edn. Little Rock, AR: University of Arkansas.

Caldwell, B.M. and Bradley, R.H. (2003) *HOME Inventory: Administration Manual Comprehensive Edition.* Little Rock, AR: University of Arkansas for Medical Sciences.

Carlson, E.A. (1998) 'A prospective longitudinal study of attachment disorganisation/disorientation.' *Child Development 69*, 1107–1129.

Caspi, A., McClay, J., Moffitt, T.E., Mill, J., *et al.* (2002) 'Role of the genotype in the cycle of violence in maltreated children.' *Science 297*, 851–845.

Cawson, P., Wattam, C., Brooker, S. and Kelly, G. (2002) *Child Maltreatment in the United Kingdom.* London: National Society for the Prevention of Cruelty to Children.

Chaffin, M., Silovsky, J., Funderburk, B., Valle, L.A., *et al.* (2004) 'Parent–child interaction therapy with physically abusive parents: efficacy for reducing future abuse reports.' *Journal of Consulting and Clinical Psychology 72*, 491–499.

Child Care Act 1991 [Ireland].

Children Act 1989.

Children Act 2001 [Ireland].

Children (Scotland) Act 1995.

Cicchetti, D. and Carlson (eds) (1989) *Child Maltreatment: Theory and Research on the Causes and Consequences of Child Abuse and Neglect.* Cambridge: Cambridge University Press.

Cicchetti, D. and Toth, S.L. (1995) 'A developmental psychopathology perspective on child abuse and neglect.' *Journal of the American Academy of Child and Adolescent Psychiatry 34*, 541–565.

Cicchetti, D., Rogosch, F.A., Lynch, M. and Holt, K.D. (1993) 'Resilience in maltreated children: processes leading to adaptive outcomes.' *Development and Psychopathology 5*, 629–647.

Cleaver, H. and Walker, S. (2004) 'From policy to practice: the implementation of a new framework for work assessments of children and families.' *Child and Family Social Work 9*, 1, 81–90.

Cleaver, H., Unell, I. and Aldgate, J. (1999) *Children's Needs – Parenting Capacity: The Impact of Parental Illness, Problem Drug and Alcohol Abuse and Domestic Violence on Children's Development.* London: The Stationery Office.

Cohen, J.A. and Mannarino, A.P. (1997) 'A Treatment Outcome study for sexually abused preschool children: Outcome during a one year follow up.' *Journal of the Academy of Child and Adolescent Psychiatry 36*, 1228–35.

Cohen, J.A., Mannarino, A.P., Berliner, L. and Deblinger, E. (2000) 'Trauma-focused cognitive behavioural therapy for children and adolescents: an empirical update.' *Journal of Interpersonal Violence 15*, 1202–1223.

Cohen, J.A., Mannarino, A.P., Zhitova, A.C. and Capone, M.E. (2003) 'Treating child abuse-related posttraumatic stress and comorbid substance abuse in adolescents.' *Child Abuse and Neglect 27*, 12, 1345–1365.

Collishaw, S., Pickles, A., Messer, J., Rutter, M., Shearer, C. and Maughan, B. (2007) 'Resilience to adult psychopathology following childhood maltreatment: evidence from a community sample.' *Child Abuse and Neglect 31*, 211–229.

Cooper, T. (2006) '*In My Shoes:* computer-assisted interview.' *Seen and Heard 16*, 3, 59–60.

Corcoran, J. (2006) 'Therapeutic Interventions with Children who have Experienced Sexual and Physical Abuse in the US.' In C. McAuley, P.J. Pecord and W. Rose (eds) *Enhancing the Well-being of Children and Families through Effective Interventions: International Evidence for Practice.* London: Jessica Kingsley Publishers.

Cousins, J. (2006) '*In My Shoes:* a computer assisted interview for communicating with children and vulnerable adults.' *Adoption and Fostering 30*, 1, 89–90.

Cox, A. (2008) *The HOME Inventory: A Guide for Practitioners – The UK Approach.* York: Child and Family Training.

Cox, A. and Walker, S. (2002a) *The HOME Inventory: A Training Approach for the UK.* York: Child and Family Training.

Cox, A. and Walker, S. (2002b) *The Family Pack of Questionnaires and Scales Training Pack.* London: ACPP.

Crnic, K.A. and Booth, C.L. (1991) 'Mothers' and fathers' perceptions of daily hassles of parenting across early childhood.' *Journal of Marriage and the Family 53*, 1043–1050.

Crnic, K.A. and Greenberg, M.T. (1990) 'Minor parenting stresses with young children.' *Child Development 61*, 1628–1637.

Cuevas, C.A., Finkelhor, D., Turner, H. and Ormrod, R. (2007) 'Juvenile delinquency and victimization: a theoretical typology.' *Journal of Interpersonal Violence 22*, 12, 1581–1602.

Davie, C.E., Hut, S.J., Vincent, E. and Mason, M. (1984) *The Young Child at Home.* Windsor: NFER Nelson.

De Panfilis, D. (2006) 'Therapeutic Interventions with Children who have Experienced Neglect and their Families in the UK.' In C. McAuley, P.J. Pecord and W. Rose (eds) *Enhancing the Well-being of Children and Families through Effective Interventions: International Evidence for Practice.* London: Jessica Kingsley Publishers.

Department for Children, Schools and Families (2008) *Practice Guidance on Assessing the Support Needs of Adoptive Families.* London: DCSF.

Department for Education and Skills (DfES) (2004a) *Common Assessment Framework: Introduction and Practitioners' Guide.* London: DfES. Available at www.dfes.gov.uk/consultations (accessed 28 November 2008).

Department for Education and Skills (2004b) *Every Child Matters: Change for Children in Social Care.* London: The Stationery Office.

Department for Education and Skills (2005) *Working Together to Safeguard Children: Safeguarding Children Board Regulations.* Draft Consultation Document. London: DfES.

Department of Education and Science (2001) *Child Protection Guidelines and Procedures.* London: Department of Education and Science.

Department of Health (2000a) *Assessing Children in Need and their Families: Practice Guidance.* London: The Stationery Office.

Department of Health (2000b) *Integrated Children's System: Working with Children in Need and their Families.* Draft Consultation Document. London: Department of Health.

Department of Health (2002) *Safeguarding Children: A Joint Chief Inspectors' Report on Arrangements to Safeguard Children.* London: Department of Health.

Department of Health and Children (1999) *Children First: National Guidelines for Protection and Welfare of Children.* Dublin: Stationery Office.

Department of Health and Children (2002) *Our Duty to Care: The Principles of Good Practice for the Protection and Welfare of Children and Young People.* Dublin: Department of Health and Children.

Department of Health and Department for Education and Skills (2004) *National Service Framework for Children and Young People and Maternity Services: The Mental Health and Psychological Well-being of Children and Young People.* London: Department of Health.

Department of Health, Cox, A. and Bentovim, A. (2000) *The Family Pack of Questionnaires and Scales.* London: The Stationery Office.

Department of Health, Department for Education and Employment and Home Office (2000) *Framework for the Assessment of Children in Need and their Families.* London. The Stationery Office. Available at www.dh.gov.uk/en/Publicationsandstatistics/Publications/PublicationsPolicyAndGuidance/DH_4 003256 (accessed 28 November 2008).

Department of Health, Home Office, and Department for Education and Employment (1999) *Working Together to Safeguard Children: A Guide to Inter-agency Working to Safeguard and Promote the Welfare of Children.* London: The Stationery Office.

Dixon, L., Browne, K.D. and Hamilton-Giachritsis, C. (2005a) 'Risk factors of parents abused as children: national analysis of the intergenerational continuity of child maltreatment (Part I).' *Journal of Psychology and Psychiatry 46,* 1, 47–57.

Dixon, L., Hamilton-Giachritsis, C. and Browne, K.D. (2005b) 'Risk factors and behavioural measures of abused as children: a meditational analysis of the intergenerational continuity of child maltreatment (Part II).' *Journal of Child Psychology and Psychiatry 46,* 1, 58–68.

DuMont, K.A., Widom, C.S. and Czaja, S.J. (2007) 'Predictors of resilience in abused and neglected children grown-up: the role of individual and neighbourhood characteristics.' *Child Abuse and Neglect 31,* 255–274.

Eastham, D. (1990) 'Plan it or Suck it and See.' In G. Darvill and G. Smale (eds) *Partners in Empowerment, Networks of Innovation in Social Work.* London: National Institute of Social Work.

Edwards, R., Dunn, J. and Bentovim, A. (2007) 'Integrated Group Work for High Risk Adolescents with Diverse Needs.' In M.C. Calder (ed.) *Working with Children and Young People who Sexually Abuse: Taking the Field Forward.* London: Russell House.

Edwards, R. (2005) 'Predicting drop out from a residential programme for Adolescent Sexual Abusers using pre-treatment variables and implications for recidivism.' *Journal of Sexual Aggression 11,* 139–155.

Edwards, V.J., Holden, G.W., Felitti, V.J. and Anda, R.F. (2003) 'Relationship between multiple forms of childhood maltreatment and adult mental health in community respondance: results from the adverse childhood experiences study.' *American Journal of Psychiatry 160,* 1453–1460.

Egeland, B. and Erickson, M. (2004) 'Lessons from STEEP: Linking Theory, Research and Practice on the Wellbeing of Infants and Parents.' In A. Sameroff, S. McDonough and K. Rosenblum (eds) *Treating Parent–Infant Relationship Problems.* New York: Guilford.

Egeland, B., Bosquet, M. and Chung, A.L. (2002a) 'Continuities and Discontinuities in the Intergenerational Transmission of Child Maltreatment: Implications for Breaking the Cycle of Abuse.' In K. Browne, H. Hanks, P. Stratton and C. Hamilton (eds) *Early Prediction and Prevention of Child Abuse.* Chichester: Wiley.

Egeland, B., Carlson, E. and Sroufe, L.A. (1993) 'Resilience as process.' *Development and Psychopathology 5,* 4, 517–528.

Egeland, B., Yates, T., Appleyard, K. and van Dulmen, M. (2002b) 'The long-term consequences of maltreatment in the early years: a developmental pathway model to antisocial behaviour.' *Children's Services: Social Policy, Research and Practice 5,* 249–260.

Fahlberg, V. (1994) 'Observation Checklists.' In V. Fahlberg, *A Child's Journey through Placement.* London: British Agencies for Adoption and Fostering.

Felitti, V.J., Anda, R.F., Nordenberg, D., Williamson, D.F., *et al.* (1998) 'Relationship of childhood abuse and household dysfunction to many of the leading causes of death in adults: the Adverse Childhood Experiences (ACE) study.' *American Journal of Preventative Medicine 14*, 245–258.

Fergusson, D.M. and Lynskey, M.T. (1997) 'Physical punishment/maltreatment during childhood and adjustment in young adulthood.' *Child Abuse and Neglect 21*, 617–630.

Fergusson, D.M. and Mullen, P.E. (1999) *Childhood Sexual Abuse: An Evidence Based Perspective. Developmental Clinical Psychology and Psychiatry, Volume 40.* Thousand Oaks, CA: Sage.

Fergusson, D.M., Boden, J.M. and Horwood, L.J. (2006) 'Examining the intergenerational transmission of violence in New Zealand birth cohort.' *Child Abuse and Neglect 30*, 89–108.

Fergusson, D.M., Boden, J.M. and Horwood, L.J. (2008) 'Exposure to childhood sexual and physical abuse and adjustment in early adulthood.' *Child Abuse and Neglect 32*, 607–619.

Field-Fisher, T.G. (1974) *Report of the Committee of Inquiry into the Care and Supervision Provided in Relation to Maria Colwell.* London: HMSO.

Finkelhor, D. (1980) *Sexually Abused Children.* New York: Free Press.

Finkelhor, D. and Berliner, L. (1995) 'Research on treatment of sexually abused children.' *Journal of the American Academy of Child and Adolescent Psychiatry 34*, 11, 1408–1423.

Finkelhor, D., Hamby, S.L., Ormrod, R. and Turner, H. (2005) 'The Juvenile Victimization Questionnaire: reliability, validity and national norms.' *Child Abuse and Neglect 29*, 383–412.

Finkelhor, D., Ormrod, R. and Turner, H. (2007) 'Poly-victimisation: a neglected comparison in child victimisation trauma.' *Child Abuse and Neglect 31*, 7–26.

Fisher, D. and Beech, A. (2002) 'Treating Adult Sexual Offenders.' In K. Browne, H. Hanks, P. Stratton and C. Hamilton (eds) *Early Prediction and Prevention of Child Abuse.* Chichester: Wiley.

Fonagy, P. (2006) 'The Mentalization-Focused Approach to Social Development.' In J.G. Allen and P. Fonagy, *Handbook of Mentalization Based Treatments.* Chichester: Wiley.

Fonagy, P., Gergely, G., Jurist, E. and Target, M. (2002) *Affect Regulation, Mentalization and the Development of the Self.* New York: Other Press.

Fonagy, P., Gergely, G. and Target, M. (2007) 'The parent–infant dyad and the construction of the subjective self.' *Journal of Child Psychology and Psychiatry 48*, 3–4, 288–328.

Garland, A.F., Hawley, K.M., Brookman-Frazee, L. and Hurlburt, M.S. (2008) 'Identifying common elements of evidence based psychosocial treatments for children's disruptive behaviour problems.' *Journal of the American Academy of Child and Adolescent Psychiatry 47*, 5, 505–514.

Gergely, G. and Watson, J. (1996) 'The social biofeedback model of parental affect-mirroring.' *International Journal of Psychoanalysis 77*, 1181–1212.

Gergely, G. and Watson, J.S. (1999) 'Early Socio-Emotional Development: Contingency Perception and the Social-Biofeedback Model.' In P Rochet (ed.) *Early Social Cognition: Understanding Others in the First Months of Life.* Mahwah, NJ: Lawrence Erlbaum Associates.

Glaser, D. (2000) 'Child abuse and neglect and the brain: a review.' *Journal of Child Psychology and Psychiatry 41*, 8, 1076.

Glasgow, D. (2004) 'Achieving Best Evidence: A Comparison of Three Interview Strategies for Investigative Interviews in a Forensic Sample with Mild Learning Disabilities.' In Dale, C. and Storey, L. (eds) *Learning Disability and Offending.* Chichester: Nursing Praxis International.

Glass, N. (2001) 'What works for children – the political issues.' *Children and Society 15*, 14–20.

Gomby, D.S. (2000) 'Promise and limitations of home visitation.' *Journal of the American Medical Association 284*, 11, 138–1391.

Goodman, R. (1997) 'The Strengths and Difficulties Questionnaire: a research note.' *Journal of Child Psychology and Psychiatry 35*, 5, 581–586.

Goodman, R., Meltzer, H. and Bailey, V. (1998) 'The Strengths and Difficulties Questionnaire: a pilot study on the validity of the self-report version.' *European Child and Adolescent Psychiatry 7*, 125–130.

Gray, J. and Bentovim, A. (1996) 'Illness Induction Syndrome: Paper 1 – a series of 41 children from 37 families identified at the Great Ormond Street Hospital for Children NHS Trust.' *Child Abuse and Neglect 20*, 8, 655–673.

Gray, J., Bentovim, A. and Milla, P. (1995) 'The Treatment of Children and their Families where Induced Illness has been Identified.' In J. Horwath and B. Lawson (eds) *Trust Betrayed? Munchausen Syndrome by Proxy: Interagency Child Protection Work and Partnership with Families.* London. National Children's Bureau.

Hanson, K.L., Morrow, C.E. and Bandstra, E.S. (2006) 'Early Interventions with Young Children and their Parents in the US.' In C. McAuley, P.J. Pecord and W. Rose (eds) *Enhancing the Well-being of*

Children and Families through Effective Interventions: International Evidence for Practice. London: Jessica Kingsley Publishers.

Harris, W.W., Lieberman, A.F. and Marans, S. (2007) 'In the best interests of society.' *Journal of Child Psychology and Psychiatry 48*, 3–4, 392–411.

Healy, K., Kennedy, R. and Sinclair, J. (1991) 'Child physical abuse observed. Comparison of families with and without history of child abuse treated in an in-patient family unit.' *British Journal of Psychiatry 158*, 234–237.

Hengeller, S., Schoenwald, S., Rowland, M. and Cunningham, P. (2002) *Serious Emotional Disturbance in Adolescents: Multisystemic Therapy.* New York: Guildford.

Hengeller *et al.* 2002

Hindley, N., Ramchandari, P. and Jones, D.P.H. (2006) 'Risk factors for recurrence of maltreatment: a systemic review.' *Archives of Disease in Childhood 93*, 744–752.

HM Government (2004) *Every Child Matters: Change for Children.* London: The Stationery Office.

HM Government (2006) *Working Together to Safeguard Children: A Guide to Inter-agency Working to Safeguard and Promote the Welfare of Children.* London: The Stationery Office.

Howes, C. and Espinosa, M.P. (1985) 'The consequences of child abuse for the formation of relationships with peers.' *International Journal of Child Abuse and Neglect 9*, 397–404.

Iwaniec, D., Herbert, M. and Sluckin, A. (2002) 'Helping Emotionally Abused and Neglected Children and Abusive Carers.' In K. Browne, H. Hanks, P. Stratton and C. Hamilton (eds) *Early Prediction and Prevention of Child Abuse.* Chichester: Wiley.

Jack, G. (2006) 'Community Programmes in the UK.' In C. McAuley, P.J. Pecord and W. Rose (eds) *Enhancing the Well-being of Children and Families through Effective Interventions: International Evidence for Practice.* London: Jessica Kingsley Publishers.

Jenkins, J.M. and Smith, M.A. (1990) 'Factors protecting children living in disharmonious homes: maternal reports.' *Journal of the American Academy of Child and Adolescent Psychiatry 29*, 1, 60–69.

Jones, D.P.H. (2008) 'Child Maltreatment.' In M. Rutter (ed.) *Rutter's Child and Adolescent Psychiatry.* Oxford: Blackwell.

Jones, D.P.H. (1998) 'The Effectiveness of Intervention.' In M. Adcock and R. White (eds) *Significant Harm: Its Management and Outcome.* Croydon: Significant Publications.

Jones, D.P.H. and Ramchandani, P. (1999) *Child Sexual Abuse: Informing Practice from Research.* Abingdon: Radcliffe.

Jones, D.P.H., Hindley, N. and Ramchandani, P. (2006) 'Making Plans: Assessment, Intervention and Evaluating Outcomes.' In J. Aldgate, D.P.H. Jones, W. Rose and C. Jeffery (eds) *The Developing World of the Child.* London: Jessica Kingsley Publishers.

Kaufman, J. and Zigler, E. (1989) 'The Intergenerational Transmission of Child Abuse.' In D. Cicchetti and V. Carlson (eds) *Child Maltreatment: Theory and Research on the Causes of Consequences of Child Abuse and Neglect.* Cambridge: Cambridge University Press.

Kelly, L. (1994) 'The Interconnectedness of Domestic Violence and Child Abuse: Challenges for Research Policy and Practice.' In A. Mullender and R. Morley (eds) *Children Living with Domestic Violence: Putting Men's Abuse of Women on the Child Care Agenda.* London: Whiting and Birch.

Kempe, C.H., Silverman, F., Steele, B., Broegemueller, W. and Silver, H. (1962) 'The battered child syndrome.' *Journal of the American Medical Association 181*, 4–11.

Kinston, W., Loader, P. and Miller, L. (1987) 'Quantifying the clinical assessment of family health.' *Journal of Marital and Family Therapy 13*, 1, 49–67.

Kolko, D.J. (1996) 'Individual cognitive behavioural treatment and family therapy for physically abused children and their offending parents: the comparison of clinical outcomes.' *Child Maltreatment 1*, 322–342.

Kolko, D.J. (2002) 'Child Physical Abuse.' In J. Myers, L. Berliner, J. Brierre, C. Hendrix, C. Jenny and T. Reid (eds) *The APSAC Handbook on Child Maltreatment.* London: Sage.

Kolko, D.J., Herschell, A.D. and Baumann, B.L. (2007) *Abuse Focussed Cognitive Behavioural Therapy for Child Physical Abuse: Session Guide,* Version 2.2 (1–01–07). Pittsburgh, PA: University of Pittsburgh School of Medicine.

Laming, W.H. (2003) *The Victoria Climbié Inquiry: Report of an Inquiry by Lord Laming.* Cm 5730. London: The Stationery Office. Available www.victoria-climbie-inquiry.org.uk/finreport/finreport.htm (accessed 7 December 2008).

Land, H. (1999) 'New Labour, New Families.' In H. Dean and R. Woods (eds) *Social Policy Review 11.* Luton: Social Policy Association.

Lask, B., Britten, C., Kroll, L., Maganga, J. and Tranter, M. (1991) 'Children with pervasive refusal.' *Archives of Disease in Childhood 66*, 866–869.

Leff, J. (2000) 'Family work for schizophrenia: practical application.' *Acta Psychiatrica Scandinavica 102*, 78–82.

Letourneau, E., Chapman, J.E. and Schoenwald, S.K. (2008) 'Treatment outcome and criminal offending by youth with sexual behaviour problems.' *Child Maltreatment 13*, 133–144.

Lieberman, A.F., Ghosh Ippen, C. and Van Horn, P. (2006) 'Child–parent psychotherapy: six-month follow up of a randomized control trial.' *Journal of the American Academy of Child and Adolescent Psychiatry 45*, 912–918.

Lieberman, A.F., Van Horn, P. and Ghosh Ippen, C. (2005) 'Toward evidence based treatment: child–parent psychotherapy with preschoolers exposed to domestic violence.' *Journal of the American Academy of Child and Adolescent Psychiatry 44*, 1241–1248..

McAuley, C., Pecord, P.J. and Rose, W. (eds) (2006) *Enhancing the Well-being of Children and Families through Effective Interventions: International Evidence for Practice.* London: Jessica Kingsley Publishers.

McGloin, J.M. and Widom, C.S. (2001) 'Resilience among abused and neglected children growing up.' *Development and Psychopathology 13*, 4, 1021–1038.

Macfie, J., Cicchetti, D. and Toth, S.L. (2001) 'The development of dissociation in maltreated preschool age children.' *Development and Psychopathology 13*, 233–254.

Main, M. and Goldwyn, R. (1984) 'Adult Attachment Scoring and Classification System.' Unpublished manuscript, University of California, Berkeley, CA.

Marcenko, M. and Staerkel, F. (2006) 'Home Visiting for Parents of Pre-School Children in the US.' In C. McAuley, P.J. Pecora and W. Rose (eds) *Enhancing the Well-being of Children and Families through Early Intervention.* London: Jessica Kingsley Publishers.

Maughan, A. and Cicchetti, D. (2002) 'Impact of child maltreatment and interadult violence on children's emotion, regulatory abilities and socioemotional adjustment.' Child Development 73, 1525–1542.

Meluish, E., Belsky, J., Leyland, A. and Barnes, J. (2008) 'Effects of fully-established Sure Start Local Programmes on 3 year old children and their families living in England: a quasi-experimental observational study.' *Lancet 372*, 1641–1647.

Mills, M. and Puckering, C. (2001) *Evaluation of Mellow Parenting.* London: Department of Health.

Moffitt, T.E. and Caspi, A. (1998) 'Implications of violence between intimate partners for child psychologists and psychiatrists.' *Journal of Child Psychology and Psychiatry 39*, 2, 137–144.

Monck, E., Sharland, E., Bentovim, A. and Goodall, G., *et al.* (1996) *Professional Intervention in Child Sexual Health.* London: HMSO.

Monck, E., Sharland, E., Bentovim, A., Goodall, G., Hyde, C. and Lewin, B. (1994) *Child Sexual Abuse: A Descriptive and Treatment Outcome Study.* London: HMSO.

Mullen, P.E., Martin, J.L., Anderson, S.E. and Romans, G.P. (1996) 'The long-term impact of the physical, emotional and sexual abuse of children: a community study.' *Child Abuse and Neglect 20*, 1, 7–21.

Olds, D.L., Henderson, C., Kitzman, H.J., Eckenrode, J.J., Cole, R.E. and Tatelbaum, R.C. (1999) 'Prenatal and infancy home visitation by nurses: recent findings.' *Future of Children 9*, 1, 44–65.

Olds, D.L., Sadler, L. and Kitzman, H. (2007) 'Programs for parents of infants and toddlers: recent evidence from randomized trials.' *Journal of Child Psychology and Psychiatry 48*, 3–4, 355–391.

Piccinelli, M., Tessari, E., Bortolomasi, M., Piasere, O. *et al.* (1997) 'Efficacy of the alcohol use disorders identification test as a screening tool for hazardous alcohol intake and related disorders in primary care: a validity study.' *British Medical Journal 514*, 420–424.

Pizzey, S., Cox, A., Bingley Miller, L. and Walker, S. (2009) *Assessing Parenting and the Family Life of Children Using Standardised Assessment Tools. A Training Manual for the HOME Inventory: A Guide for Practitioners – the UK Approach, the Family Pack of Questionnaires and Scales and a Model of Analysis. Planning Interventions and Measuring Outcomes.* York: Child and Family Training.

Prior, V. and Glaser, D. (2006) *Understanding Attachment and Attachment Disorders.* London: Jessica Kingsley Publishers.

Protection of Children (Scotland) Act 2003.

Protection of Children and Prevention of Sexual Offences (Scotland) Act 2005.

Protection of Vulnerable Groups (Scotland) Act 2007.

Public Law Outline: Guide to Case Management in Public Law Proceedings (2008) London: Ministry of Justice and Judiciary of England and Wales.

Ramchandani, P. and Jones, D.P.H. (2003) 'Treating psychological symptoms in sexually abused children: from research findings to service provision.' *British Journal of Psychiatry 183*, 484–490.

Rose, W. and Barnes, J. (2008) *Improving Safeguarding Practice: Study of Serious Case Reviews 2001–2003.* London: Department for Children, Schools and Families.

Rose, W., Gray, J. and McAuley, C. (2006) 'Child Welfare in the UK: Legislation, Policy and Practice.' In C. McAuley, P.J. Pecord and W. Rose (eds) *Enhancing the Well-being of Children and Families through Effective Interventions: International Evidence for Practice.* London: Jessica Kingsley Publishers.

Rutter, M. (2007) 'Resilience, competence and coping.' *Child Abuse and Neglect 31*, 205–209.

Rutter, M. and ERA Study Team (1998) 'Developmental catch-up and deficit following adoption after marked early privation.' *Journal of Child Psychology and Psychiatry 39*, 4, 465–476.

Rutter, M., Moffitt, T. and Caspi, A. (2006) 'Gene–environment interplay and psychopathology: multiple varieties but real effects.' *Journal of Child Psychology and Psychiatry 47*, 226–261.

Salter, D., McMillan, D., Richards, M., Talbot, T., *et al.* (2003) 'Development of sexually abusive behaviour in sexually victimised males: a longitudinal study.' *Lancet 361*, 471–476.

Scott, S. and Sylva, K. (2009) *The SPOKES Project: Report to the Department of Health.* London: Department of Health.

Scottish Executive (2000) *For Scotland's Children.* Edinburgh: Scottish Executive.

Scottish Executive (2002) *'It's Everyone's Job to Make Sure I'm Alright': Report of the Child Protection Audit and Review.* Edinburgh: Scottish Executive.

Scottish Executive (2004) *Protecting Children and Young People: The Charter.* Edinburgh: Scottish Executive.

Scottish Executive (2007) *United Nations Convention on The Rights of the Child: A Report on Implementation of the UN Convention on the Rights of the Child in Scotland 1999–2007.* Edinburgh: Scottish Executive.

Scottish Government (2008) *A Guide to Getting it Right for Every Child.* Edinburgh: Scottish Government.

Scottish Office (1997) *Children (Scotland) Act 1995 Regulations and Guidance, Volume 1: Support and Protection for Children and their Families.* Edinburgh: Scottish Office.

Scottish Office (1998) *Protecting Children – A Shared Responsibility: Guidance on Interagency Co-operation.* Edinburgh: Scottish Office.

Shaffer, A., Huston, L. and Egeland, B. (2008) 'Identification of child maltreatment using prospective and self-report methodologies: a comparison of maltreatment incidence and relation to later psychopathology.' *Child Abuse and Neglect 32*, 682–692.

Sharp, C. and Fonagy, P. (2008) 'The parent's capacity to treat the child as a psychological agent: constructs, measures and implications for developmental psychopathology.' *Social Development 17*, 3, 737-754.

Sheinberg, M. and True, F. (2008) 'Treating family relational trauma: a recursive process using a decision dialogue.' *Family Process 47*, 2, 173–195.

Sheridan, M. (1997) *From Birth to Five Years*, 3rd edn, revised and updated by A. Sharma and H. Cockerill. London: Routledge.

Sheridan, M. (2000) 'Chart Illustrating the Developmental Progress of Infants and Young Children.' In Department of Health, *Assessing Children in Need and their Families: Practice Guidance.* London: The Stationery Office.

Skuse, D., Bentovim, A., Hodges, J., Stevenson, J., *et al.* (1998) 'Risk factors for development of sexually abusive behaviour in sexually victimised adolescent boys: cross sectional study.' *British Medical Journal 317*, 175–179.

Sluzki, C.E. (2007) 'Interfaces: towards a new generation of systemic models in family research and practice.' *Family Process 46*, 2, 173–184.

Smith, M. (1985) 'The Effects of Low Levels of Lead on Urban Children: The Relevance of Social Factors.' PhD thesis, University of London.

Smith, M. (2006) 'Early Interventions with Young Children and their Parents in the UK.' In C. McAuley, P.J. Pecord and W. Rose (eds) *Enhancing the Well-being of Children and Families through Effective Interventions: International Evidence for Practice.* London: Jessica Kingsley Publishers.

Snaith, R.P., Constantopoulos, A.A., Jardine, M.Y. and McGuffin, P. (1978) 'A clinical scale for the self-assessment of irritability.' *British Journal of Psychiatry 132*, 163–171.

Sroufe, L.A. (1988) 'The Role of Infant–Caregiver Attachment in Development.' In J. Belsky and T. Nesworski (eds) *Clinical Implications of Attachment.* Hillsdale, NJ: Erlbaum.

Stafford, A. and Vincent, S. (2008) *Safeguarding and Protecting Children and Young People.* Edinburgh: Dunedin.

Steele, M., Hodges, J., Kanniuk, J., Hillman, S. and Henderson, K. (2003) 'Attachment representations and adoption: associations between maternal states of mind and emotional narratives in previously maltreated children.' *Journal of Child Psychotherapy 29*,187–205.

Stevenson, J. (1999) 'The treatment of the long-term sequelae of child abuse.' *Journal of Child Psychology and Psychiatry 40*, 89–111.

Straus, M.A. and Gelles, R.J. 'Is violence to children increasing?' In R.J. Gelles (ed.) *Family Violence* (2nd edition). London: SAGE.

Strauss, M.A. and Kantor, G.K. (1987) 'Stress and Child Abuse.' In R.E. Helfer and R.S. Kemp (eds) *The Battered Child*, 4th edn. Chicago, IL: University of Chicago Press.

Sylvester, J., Bentovim, A., Strattor, P. and Hanks, H. (1995) 'Using spoken attributions to classify abusive families.' *Child Abuse and Neglect 26*, 23–37.

Tanner, K. and Turney, D. (2006) 'Therapeutic Interventions with Children who have Experienced Neglect and their Families in the UK.' In C. McAuley, P.J. Pecord and W. Rose (eds) *Enhancing the Well-being of Children and Families through Effective Interventions: International Evidence for Practice.* London: Jessica Kingsley Publishers.

Timmer, S.G., Urguiza, A.J., Zebell, N.M. and McGrath, J.M. (2005) *Parent–Child Interaction Therapy: Application to Maltreating Parent–Child Dyads.* Sacramento, CA: Department of Paediatrics, University of California

Toth, S.L., Maughan, A., Manly, J.T., Spagnola, M. and Cicchetti, D. (2002) 'The relative efficacy of two interventions in altering maltreated preschool children's representational models: implications for attachment theory.' *Development and Psychopathology 14*, 877–908.

Trowell, J., Kolvin, I., Weeramanthri, T., Berelowitz, M., *et al.* (2002) 'Psychotherapy for sexually abused girls: psychopathological outcome findings and patterns of change.' *British Journal of Psychiatry 180*, 234–247.

Tunstill, J., Allnock, D., Akhurst, S. and Garbers, C. (2005) 'Sure Start local programmes: implications of case study data from the National Evaluation of Sure Start.' *Children and Society 19*, 158–171.

UNICEF (2006) *The State of the World's Children 2006.* New York: UNICEF.

Van Zeijl, J., Mesman, J., Van IJzendoorn, M.H., Bakemans-Kranenburg, J.J., *et al.* (2006) 'Attachment based interventions for enhancing sensitive discipline in mothers of 1 to 3 year old children at risk for externalising behaviour problems: a randomized controlled trial.' *Journal of Consulting and Clinical Psychology 74*, 6, 994–1005.

Vizard, E. and Tranter, M. (1988) 'Presentation of Children with Sexual Abuse.' In A. Bentovim, A. Elton, J. Hildebrand, M. Tranter and E. Vizard (eds) *Child Sexual Abuse Within the Family: Assessment and Treatment.* London: Wright.

Vizard, E., Hickey, N. and McCrory, E. (2007) 'Developmental trajectories associated with juvenile sexually abusive behaviour and emerging severe personality disorder in childhood: 3–year study.' *British Journal of Psychiatry 190*, s27–s32.

Vizard, E., Monck, E. and Misch, P. (1995) 'Child and adolescent sex abuse perpetrators: a review of the research literature.' *Journal of Child Psychology and Psychiatry 36*, 731–756.

Vranceanu, A.M., Hobfoll, S.E. and Johnson, R.J. (2007) 'Child multi-type maltreatment and associated depression and PTSD symptoms: the role of social support and stress.' *Child Abuse and Neglect 31*, 71–84.

Vulnerable Witnesses (Scotland) Act 2004.

Watson, S., Calam, R.M. and Jimmieson, P. (2002) 'Can computers help in assessing children's postoperative pain? Initial validation of a computer assisted interview.' *European Journal of Anaesthesiology 19*, 107.

Webster-Stratton, C. (1997) 'From parent training to community building.' *Family in Society 78*, 2, 156–171.

Welsh Assembly (2004) *Children and Young People: Rights to Action.* Cardiff: Welsh Assembly.

White, M. (1989) *The Externalising of the Problem and the Re-authoring of Lives and Relationship.* Dulwich Centre Newsletter. Adelaide: Dulwich Centre Publications.

White, M. and Epston, D. (1989) *Literate Means to Therapeutic Ends.* Adelaide: Dulwich Centre Publications.

Widom, C.S. (1989) 'Does violence beget violence? A critical examination of the literature.' *Psychological Bulletin 106*, 1, 3–28.

Winnicott, D.W. (1956) 'Mirror Role of Mother and Family in Child Development.' In D. Winnicott *Playing and Reality.* London: Tavistock.

Wolfe, D.A. (2006) 'Preventing violence in relationships: psychological science addressing complex social issues.' *Canadian Psychology 47*, 44–50.

World Health Organization (WHO) (2002) *World Report on Violence and Health*. Geneva: WHO.

Wynne, L.C., Tienari, P., Nieminen, P., Sorri, A., *et al.* (2006a) 'I. Genotype–environment interaction in the schizophrenia spectrum: genetic liability and global family ratings in the Finnish Adoption Study.' *Family Process 45*, 419–434.

Wynne, L.C., Tienari, P., Sorri, A., Lahti, I., Moring, J. and Wahlberg, K.E. (2006b) 'II. Genotype environment interaction in the schizophrenia spectrum: qualitative observations.' *Family Process 45*, 435–447.

Subject Index

Adolescent Attachment Interview 32

adolescent development
effect of family violence on 54–8
and unstable personality functioning 55–6

Adolescent Wellbeing Scale (Birleson) 104, 111, 135, 198, 199, 267, 326, 330

Adoption and Children Act (2002) 23, 218

Adult Wellbeing Scale (Snaith et al.) 112, 120, 132, 136, 138, 211, 267, 306, 326, 329, 333

Adverse Childhood Experiences (ACE) 38

Alcohol Scale (Piccinelli et al.) 112, 267, 327, 330, 333

Alcohol Use Questionnaire 136–7, 211

Assessing Parenting and the Family Life of Children Using Standardised Assessment Tools (Pizzey et al.) 107

assessment
aims of 76–7, 124–5
and Assessment Framework (Department of Health, Department for Education and Employment and Home Office) 78–88, 149–215
categorizing and organizing information 78–88, 137–41
and child development 79–83, 88–95
child safety 76–7, 124–5
couple relationship 184
environmental factors 86–7, 140–1, 187–92

family factors 85–6, 87, 140–1, 181–7, 210–12
information-gathering approach 77–8, 125–137
intervention outcomes 99–105, 146–7
intervention planning 97–8, 145–6
not-known information 87–8, 141–2
and parenting 83–5, 95, 149–80
possible outlook for child 96–7, 143
referral 76–7, 124–5
self-care skills 165–6, 203
social presentation 163–5, 202
specialist 217–269
and Standardized Assessment Tools (Department of Health and Department for Children, Schools and Families) 123 see also specialist assessment

Assessment Framework (Department of Health, Department for Education and Employment and Home Office) 12, 18–19, 20, 36, 39, 41, 75, 77, 78–88, 123, 137
children's developmental needs 149–66
family factors 181–7
parenting problems 166–80

attachment development 44–6

Attachment Style Interview (ASI) (Bifulco et al.) 78, 103, 107–8, 115–16

Baby P 18
Barnardo's 275

boys
effects of multiple abuses 35–7
effects of sexual abuse 30–5

CECA (Childhood Experience of Care and Abuse) 224

Child and Family Training 20

child safety, and assessment 76–7

childhood development
and adolescence 54–8
and assessment 79–83, 88–95
and Assessment Framework (Department of Health, Department for Education and Employment and Home Office) 149–66
attachment development 44–6, 156–7
behavioural development 154–6
and domestic violence 58–9, 60–2, 65
effect of family violence on pre-birth and young children 42–51
effect of family violence on older children 51
emotional development 154–6
family and social relationships 160–3, 201–2
identification with abuser 47
identity 158–60
and later capacity to parent 68–9
mentalization 44–5
and parenting 43–4, 61–5, 80
processes on 88–95
reality separation 46–7
re-traumatization 47

Author Index

Aldgate, J. 58
Alessandri, S.M. 45
Angold, A. 93
Asen, K. 225

Bailey, V. 102
Bandstra, E.S. 277
Banyard, V.L. 39
Barlow, J. 277
Barnes, J. 11
Bateman, A.W. 289, 293
Baumann, B.L. 282
Beck, J.E. 35
Beech, A. 288
Bentovim, A. 20, 24, 25, 31, 34, 45, 67, 77, 78, 107, 112, 220, 233, 250, 268, 269, 280, 284, 294
Bergner, R.M. 68
Berliner, J. 280
Bifulco, A. 24, 69, 107–8, 224
Bingley Miller, L. 20, 78, 107, 268, 269
Bion, W.R. 43
Birleson, P. 104, 111
Boden, J.M. 24, 28
Booth, C.L. 112
Borduin, C. 289
Bowlby, J. 44
Boxer, P. 38
Bradley, R.H. 35, 107, 114
Brandon, M. 11–12
Brown, G.W. 24, 224
Browne, K. 40, 69, 278
Buckley, H. 19

Calam, R. 78, 107
Caldwell, B.M. 35, 107, 114
Carlson, E.A. 39, 45
Caspi, A. 65
Cawson, P. 23, 24, 276
Chaffin, M. 282
Chapman, J.E. 289
Chung, A.L. 39

Cicchetti, D. 44, 45
Cleaver, H. 58, 59, 61, 62, 75, 97
Cohen, J.A. 39, 267, 281, 284
Collishaw, S. 68
Cooper, T. 107
Corcoran, J. 280
Cousins, J. 107
Cox, A. 20, 77, 78, 107, 112, 126
Crnic, K.A. 112
Cuevas, K.A. 37
Czaja, S.J. 39

De Panfilis, D. 280
Delgado, L.K. 68
Department for Children, Schools and Families 268
Department for Education and Employment 12, 15, 18, 79, 106, 271
Department of Education and Science 19
Department for Education and Skills 18, 19, 217, 274
Department of Health 12, 15, 18, 19, 20, 77, 79, 106, 107, 112, 271, 335
Department of Health and Children 19
Dixon, L. 69, 277, 278
DuMont, K.A. 39
Dunn, J. 34

Eastham, D. 276
Edwards, R. 34, 243, 286, 288
Egeland, B. 39, 40, 277
Elton, J. 250
Erickson, M. 277
Espinosa, M.P. 45

Falshaw, L. 278
Felitti, V.J. 38

Fergusson, D.M. 24, 27, 28
Field-Fisher, T.G. 18
Finkelhor, D. 17, 36, 37, 68, 280
Fisher, D. 288
Fonagy, P. 43, 45–6, 47, 289

Garland, A.F. 291, 294
Gelles, R.J. 66, 67
Gergely, G. 43, 45
Ghosh Ippen, C. 278
Glaser, D. 26, 42
Glasgow, D.V. 107
Glass, N. 276
Goldwyn, R. 32
Gomby, D.S. 277
Goodman, R. 102, 104, 111, 112, 131
Gray, J. 18, 25, 233
Graybill, D. 68
Greenberg, M.T. 112

Hamilton-Giachritsis, C. 69
Hanson, K.L. 277
Harris, W.W. 16–17, 224
Healy, K. 225
Hengeller, S. 284
Herbert, M. 25
Hickey, N. 34
Hindley, N. 250
HM Government 19, 21, 217, 219, 221, 271
Home Office 12, 15, 18, 79, 106, 271
Horwood, L.J. 24, 28
Howarth, J. 19
Howes, C. 45
Huston, L. 40

Iwaniec, D. 25, 283

Jack, G. 276
Jimmieson, P. 107